More praise for *Aftershock*

'A brisk, vivid and wide-ranging survey of a region in the grip of neoliberalism. As Feffer makes clear, this is hardly just a book about Eastern Europe, as the challenges there now seem to be spreading throughout the world. Feffer's sense of the future evinces both pessimism of the mind and optimism of the will.'

Lawrence Weschler, author of *Vermeer in Bosnia* and *Calamities of Exile*

'A breath-taking whirlwind tour through the transformations of eastern Europe over the past 30 years. With its account of the travails of contemporary capitalism, is also astonishingly relevant for understanding pressing political problems in the United States as well.'

David Ost, author of *The Defeat of Solidarity: Anger and Politics in Post-Communist Europe*

Aftershock

A Journey into Eastern Europe's Broken Dreams

John Feffer

ZED

Aftershock: A Journey into Eastern Europe's Broken Dreams
was first published in 2017 by Zed Books Ltd,
The Foundry, 17 Oval Way, London SE11 5RR, UK.

www.zedbooks.net

Typeset in
Index by J
Cover des
Cover ph

A catalogue record for this book is available from the British Library.

ISBN 978-1-78360-949-9 hb
ISBN 978-1-78360-948-2 pb
ISBN 978-1-78360-950-5 pdf
ISBN 978-1-78360-951-2 epub
ISBN 978-1-78360-952-9 mobi

Printed and bound by CPI Group (UK) Ltd, Croydon, CR0 4YY

Contents

Acknowledgements

This book is dedicated to all the amazing people that sat down with me – in 1990, in 2012/13 and occasionally at points in between – and answered my questions with candor and great intelligence. All of the interviews quoted in the text are available, in full, on my website at: www.johnfeffer.com/full-interview-list

Some of these interviewees have passed away since I spoke with them just a few years ago. It is with great sadness that I record their names here: Aleš Debeljak, Miroslav Durmov, Nicolae Gheorghe and Kurt Pätzold.

This book would not have been possible without the generous support of the Open Society Foundation, which funded my return to eastern Europe as an Open Society Fellow in 2012/13. I'd also like to thank the Institute for Policy Studies for allowing me to take a leave of absence to do this work.

I'd like to thank the following people for reading portions of the manuscript and offering their comments: Mladen Jovanović, Vihar Krastev, Miroslav Krupička, Bogdan Łapiński, Margareta Matache, Mira Oklobdzija, David Ost, Sara Pistotnik, Bartosz Rydliński, Neža Kogovšek Šalamon, Ivan Vejvoda, Maria Yosifova, and Jelka Zorn. My editor at

Zed, Ken Barlow, also provided excellent recommendations throughout the editorial process. Whatever errors escaped this vetting process are mine alone.

I'd also like to thank all the people who helped arrange meetings and provide interpretation: Iskar Enev and Vihra Gancheva (Bulgaria), Hrvoja Heffer (Croatia), Sarah Böhm and Adrian Klocke (Germany), Judit Hatfaludi (Hungary), Ewa Maczynska and Anna Maria Napieralska (Poland), Dan Iepure (Romania), Pavol Kustar and Alena Pániková (Slovakia).

Finally, my wife Karin Lee accompanied me on virtually every step of this project, making it possible for me to return to the region, reviewing the manuscript, and providing astute suggestions along the way. She remains my ideal reader.

Introduction: Exile Off Main Street

It was not easy to find Miroslav Durmov.

There were plenty of references to him on the Internet, but the trail went cold in the mid-1990s. Probably he'd just dropped out of politics and returned to private life. More ominously, he might have died, as had several other people I'd interviewed in eastern Europe in 1990. But I didn't turn up an obituary. I wanted to find Miroslav because I was planning to return to Bulgaria. I hoped to interview him again after nearly twenty-five years to see how his life and his thinking had changed in the interim.

When I first met Miroslav in August 1990, he occupied an unusual and prestigious position. He was one of the top people in the Movement for Rights and Freedoms (MRF), a new political formation that was officially devoted to the human rights of all Bulgarians. In reality, the Movement focused on the rights of ethnic minorities, primarily the ethnic Turks who make up 10 percent of Bulgaria's population. What made Miroslav's position unusual was that he himself wasn't an ethnic Turk. A psychologist and lawyer by training, he'd become acquainted with the ethnic Turkish community through marriage. He was incensed by the indignities the communist government had forced upon its ethnic Turkish citizens, first insisting that they Slavicize their names in 1984 and then kicking more than 300,000 of them out of the country in the spring and summer of 1989. Ethnic Turkish activists had formed the MRF to redress these wrongs.

In 2013, the MRF was still a political force in Bulgaria significant enough to determine the composition of coalition governments. But Miroslav Durmov, who had struck me as one of the rare politicians who could successfully make the transition to the new democracy, was nowhere to be found. In the Internet archive of Bulgarian newspapers, I followed the trajectory of his political career. He was mentioned quite frequently in the early 1990s as a spokesman for the MRF. Then he led the Movement's parliamentary faction. Then he split from the Movement and created his own political party.

And then he disappeared.

In desperation, I turned to everyone's last resort for tracking down former college roommates and old flames. I found 'Miroslav Durmov' on Facebook. But he was in the wrong place and doing the wrong thing. This other Miroslav Durmov was living in Lexington, Kentucky, and working in an Amazon fulfillment center. On a whim, I sent this other Miroslav a note in the hope that he would know something about his namesake back in Bulgaria.

They turned out to be one and the same person.

Miroslav, I discovered, had moved to the United States at the age of fifty. He and his wife had arrived in New York

City with virtually no English, no job prospects, and only one slender hope for the future: the contact information of a cousin. New York was a dazzling, cosmopolitan city with a Bulgarian community large enough at the time to support its own newspaper. It was also a very expensive place to live. Even with the help of this cousin, Miroslav and his wife didn't have enough money to survive in the Big Apple. They heard from a fellow émigré that Kentucky was cheap. So, off they went.

A few blocks from Lexington's Main Street, they found a modest two-story house. Miroslav worked in a succession of poorly paid clerical and factory positions while his wife Maria Yosifova, a lawyer back in Bulgaria, started out as a housekeeper. They just managed to make ends meet even as they studied English and returned to school to get new college degrees.[1] They pinned their hopes on their two teenage sons, who were thriving as transplants. Like many immigrants, Miroslav and his wife were making sacrifices for the next generation.

Miroslav was one in a million. Quite literally. The population of Bulgaria on the eve of the changes that took place in 1989, when eastern Europe went through its year of miracles, was nearly nine million people. That number had dropped to just a little over seven million by 2015. More than a million people left Bulgaria after 1989. Combined with a startling drop in fertility – from nearly two children per woman in 1989 to only one child by 1997[2] – Bulgaria experienced the largest percentage drop in population not attributable to war or famine for a country in the modern era. Every day, the country was losing 164 people: over a thousand a week, over 50,000 a year.[3] In the black humor characteristic of the region, Bulgarians like to ask: what are the only two ways to escape our country's crisis? The answer: Terminal One and Terminal Two. It's not really a joke. The airport in Sofia had emerged as Bulgarians' most popular economic development strategy.

Miroslav Durmov was part of this brain drain. Unlike some of his compatriots, who scored jobs in Silicon Valley or London's financial sector, Miroslav and his family suffered a significant loss of status.

In early 2013, I flew down to Lexington to reestablish contact with Miroslav. Clean-shaven in 1990, he now wore a beard, and there were deep lines under his eyes. He was soft-spoken, but there was an undercurrent of bitterness to his words. Whereas in 1990 he spoke as an insider who was very much part of shaping the new realities of Bulgaria, in 2013 he was a weary spectator watching the action from a great distance. His disappointment with the Movement for Rights and Freedom had metastasized into a disillusionment with Bulgarian politics and then with Bulgaria as a whole.

When we met in 1990, Miroslav and I communicated in our only common language, Russian. In 2013, as I interviewed him in his modest home off Main Street in Lexington, he spoke haltingly in English about his predicament. 'Since 1997 it was clear for me that the so-called transition was not what it appeared to be,' he told me. 'Regretfully, at that time not many people in Bulgaria were eager to listen to what I was saying or writing. The moment came when I could not publish anything in the newspapers due to this political isolation, even though I had a pretty good relationship with people working for those newspapers.'

Unwilling to live in such political isolation in Bulgaria, Miroslav insisted on going abroad. But it was not easy for either Miroslav or Maria to adjust to US realities. 'At the moment, I'm unemployed,' he confessed. 'I think it's impossible for people like me to live here. My wife was a lawyer in Bulgaria. She cannot practice her profession here. Now she works as a library assistant and as an English tutor.' He shook his head sadly and with a touch of embarrassment, adding, 'It's just been a disaster … If you can speak without an accent and without any mistakes, it's a lot easier to be hired. But when employers see my name – many Americans cannot even pronounce it correctly – and how I speak English, it's very difficult.'

Miroslav was not happy with what had happened in Bulgaria since 1989. He viewed the transition from communism, and much that has happened since, as the result of powerful forces manipulating events behind the scenes. Public opinion polls and other indicators suggest that many Bulgarians, and many people throughout the region, feel the same way. Over the last quarter-century, millions have lost jobs, suffered tremendous social dislocation, and watched as the corrupt and the criminal become fabulously wealthy. Millions more have simply left their countries in despair or disgust. Lumped together in the popular press as the 'losers of transition,' they have been blamed for a raft of social ills in eastern Europe, from the surge of racism and xenophobia to the rise of far-right politicians and a general turn away from liberalism, the European Union and 'Enlightenment values.'

This is the glass-half-empty picture of what has happened over the last twenty-five years in eastern Europe. It's only part of the story.

Glass half full

Bogdan Łapiński, like Miroslav Durmov, trained as a psychologist. In 1989, I worked with Bogdan at the Psychology Department of the Polish Academy of Sciences in Warsaw. He was particularly interested in phenomenology, a topic of which I had only a vague understanding. An exemplary academic, he loved research, writing and obscure texts. He made the same pittance as other young Polish academics – the equivalent of $5 a month at black market rates – which required him to supplement his income with summer trips to Germany to do manual labor. He drove a tiny Fiat and lived with his wife and child in a small apartment on Jerusalem Avenue near Warsaw's central train station.

When I next saw Bogdan twenty-four years later, he seemed virtually untouched by the intervening years. He still looked boyish, with dimpled cheeks and a mischievous sparkle in his eyes. Only the streaks of grey in his thick hair indicated the passage of time.

Meanwhile, everything had changed in his life. Dramatically.

I'd expected that Bogdan, given his passion for the life of the mind, would continue working as an academic, albeit on a higher pay scale. On the contrary, he left academia in 1989 to try his hand at a series of odd jobs. He and his wife divorced. He wasn't sure what to do with his life, so on a whim applied for a managerial position listed in the newspaper. He had no business experience. But then, neither did anyone else during Poland's topsy-turvy transition.

'At that time, you opened a newspaper and you saw: financial director for Procter & Gamble, marketing director for Colgate Palmolive,' Bogdan remembers. 'I went to interview at major companies, like Arthur Andersen and Hewlett Packard. All those companies were looking [to fill] top positions ... These were incredible opportunities.'

He eventually took a position with IKEA, the Swedish home-furnishings company. Having sourced its products from Poland for some time, IKEA was setting up its first retail outlets to service the emerging Polish middle class. The phenomenologist Edmund Husserl talked of penetrating through language to 'get back to the things themselves.' Thanks to IKEA, my phenomenologist friend Bogdan had dispensed with theory altogether to get back to the things themselves – and start selling them.

The IKEA job – in charge of hiring new personnel – was no mere entry-level position. 'I immediately jumped to the top of the company,' Bogdan told me with the same air of wonderment he must have felt at the time. 'It was in the 1990s quite common in Poland, and probably in other countries in this region – but it's very unusual in established economies. Through an ad in the newspaper, coming from nowhere, I jumped onto the board of directors of IKEA. It took only one week.'

On his first day at IKEA, Bogdan's new boss told him that he'd have to trade up from his little Fiat. It wouldn't do for a manager to drive such a car. Bogdan moved into a larger apartment, bought the appropriate wardrobe for the job, and set about acquiring the skills of his new profession. After helping to establish IKEA in Poland, he took top positions in other multinationals and built a successful career as a management consultant.

Bogdan's story of reinvention conforms to the other popular narrative of what has happened in eastern Europe since 1989. First came the shock, as the old communist order collapsed and the new capitalist order had not yet coalesced. Then came the adjustment period. And finally came the prosperity. As Bogdan successfully navigated the transition, so did Poland and so did its eastern Europe cohort.

If you compare what has happened in the former Warsaw Pact to the chaos and conflict following the Color Revolutions to the east or the Arab Spring to the south, eastern Europe has indeed been a success story of transition – perhaps *the* success story. All of the countries in the region – from Poland and the Baltic states in the north to the lands of former Yugoslavia in the south – eventually achieved a measure of economic growth and political stability. With a few exceptions like Bosnia and Kosovo, they have all joined the European Union and NATO. They have become what Andrei Shleifer and Daniel Treisman called, in a 2014 *Foreign Affairs* article, 'normal countries.'[4] The Polish economist Marcin Piątkowski has gone even farther. Poland, he declared in 2013, is enjoying a 'golden age' unknown in the country *for 500 years*.[5] Even Yugoslavia, which experienced the worst-case scenario of four wars in less than a decade, has put the horrors of the 1990s behind it, as the successor states have begun negotiating accession to the EU and rebuilding ties among themselves.

The changes that took place in the region in 1989 offered many people an opportunity to reinvent themselves. Those in middle age when the changes occurred, like Miroslav and his wife, found it difficult to change gears. Those too young to have established a firm identity for themselves didn't necessarily have much to change. But for people in their twenties and early thirties like Bogdan, the opportunities for personal transformation were often exhilarating.

Some of the activists, scholars, and politicians I met in 1989/90 went on to fame, fortune, or both. The Czech economist Miloš Zeman became the Czech president in 2013. The representative of the Young Liberal Party in Romania, Dinu Patriciu, invested in the oil industry and became one of the country's richest men. Civil society activist Jan Kavan rose through the political ranks to become the Czech foreign minister and then president of the UN General

Assembly. Like Bogdan, they were presented with once-in-a-lifetime opportunities to become born again: as new people in a new world.

This era of opportunity, however, was also an age of anxiety. 'The stakes were too high, and people panicked,' sociologist Elemér Hankiss observed. 'People realized suddenly that in the coming years it would be decided who would be rich, and who would be poor; who would have power and who would not; who would be marginalized, and who would be at the center. And who would be able to found dynasties and whose children would suffer.'[6]

I observed some of that panic in 1990 on one of my flights from the region back to the United States. I sat next to a young Hungarian returning to his MBA program at Wharton. He was, for some mysterious reason, unhappy.

'But everything is changing so rapidly,' I said to him. 'And you'll be well positioned with a business degree.'

'Yes,' he agreed. 'But my friends back in Hungary are becoming millionaires right now. I'm afraid I'm missing my opportunity!'

The upheavals of 1989 were very much like a lottery. Some people – and some countries – held winning tickets. Initially it looked as though Miroslav Durmov had also picked the right numbers. After decades of rigged elections, the first flush of democracy was extraordinary, and many people like Miroslav formed new political parties. Virtually everyone in the region expected rapid entry into the European Union and a sudden improvement in their own fortunes.

But there was a large gap between expectations and outcomes. Even after nearly twenty-five years, eastern Europe has yet to close that gap.

The same river twice

On 17 March 1990, I set off from Brussels for East Berlin to begin what would be seven months of wandering around eastern Europe. I was twenty-six years old, and there was a method to my meandering. I'd been hired to help the international Quaker organization, the American Friends Service Committee (AFSC), establish an office in this rapidly changing part of the world.

AFSC wanted advice on what niche its regional office could fill, and my job was to ask as many people as possible for their suggestions. The Quakers chose me because I could speak some Polish and Russian. I'd completed a report on Soviet foreign policy for the organization and, though not a Quaker myself, was well versed in Quaker values. Plus I was willing to work for pennies. For my trip to the region in 1990, I carried a week's change of clothes in my college backpack, along with an early version of a laptop, one of the first portable printers, a shortwave radio, a tape recorder, and a copy of *Terra Nostra* by Mexican novelist Carlos Fuentes that lasted all the way through Slovakia.

I didn't have many contacts in the region outside of Poland, where I'd lived in 1989. So, as soon as I hit the ground in a new country, I scrambled to locate interesting people to interview.

There was no Internet, no Facebook, no cell phones. The first priority in a new place was to determine which coins the public telephone used. I came to dread these cold calls. I had no idea whether the person on the other end spoke a language I could understand. They didn't know who I was, and I only had a moment to describe my project in a way to capture their interest. Most people were sufficiently intrigued to stay on the line. In some cases, just being an American was enough to open doors, for this was before the stampede of American backpackers to the region. Where I lacked contacts, I would visit the buildings that housed a cluster of new civil society organizations and buttonhole busy activists on the fly.

Every week, I wrote up a report of my conversations, including many transcribed interviews. I then printed them out on the portable printer and sent the hard copies to the AFSC office in Philadelphia. In this bygone era, when news was not instantaneous, reports that arrived a week or two after the fact could still serve a useful purpose. During that initial seven-month tour of eastern Europe, I interviewed more than two hundred people. My reports helped AFSC set up an office in Budapest that eventually focused on women's issues, Roma rights, and the deteriorating situation in Yugoslavia. Out of the many interviews, I put together a book on the region, *Shock Waves*, that focused on a different country and a different topic per chapter (the Polish economy, Czech foreign policy, and so on).[7]

Over the next few years, I made several more trips to the region that resulted in a number of articles. But in

1998, my wife and I went to Asia, also to work for AFSC. I'd developed something of an expertise on communist systems, and those had all collapsed in Europe. For the next fifteen years, then, I focused on the two Koreas and China. During that time, I observed how very differently the 'end of the Cold War' played out in Asia. I watched from afar the exultations and disappointments of the Color Revolutions and the Arab Spring. Meanwhile, I thought about my own roller-coaster experience in eastern Europe in the early 1990s. I wondered what happened to the people I'd met. I was curious not only about what they'd done in the intervening years but whether they'd had any second thoughts about the path their countries had taken more than two decades before. Perhaps they had some hard-won lessons to share with people going through similar experiences elsewhere.

In 2012/13, thanks to the Open Society Foundation, I had an opportunity to retrace my steps from 1990, to step back into the same river twice, as it were. On this second tour of the region, I interviewed nearly three hundred people. I tracked down my original interviewees in the region as well as in London, Trieste, and Lexington, Kentucky – to see how their lives, their families, and their countries had changed. I recorded, transcribed, and edited the interviews, posting them in full on my website along with explanatory introductions.[8] In this way, the people of the region could speak for themselves rather than only in a limited and truncated way through my writings.

For this second extended trip through eastern Europe, I traveled very differently. I carried a Macbook, and WiFi was never very far away. There was no need for a printer. I took a video camera to record the interviews. And I carried not one book in my backpack but an entire library on my phone, including Tony Judt's massive history of postwar Europe.[9] After fifteen years of studying East Asian affairs, I had to catch up on a lot of reading.

Almost everyone that I interviewed in 1990 responded to my out-of-the-blue emails. They generally didn't remember me – more often they remembered my laptop or my portable printer – but they were willing to sit down and talk just as they'd done twenty-two years before. My list had shrunk. Some, like Bulgarian poet Blaga Dimitrova and East German pastor Wolfgang Ullmann, had passed away. Some had disappeared completely, even from Facebook's reach. But I managed to track down about eighty of the original interviewees. To augment my original list and avoid the trap of talking only to a narrow demographic slice of society, I reached out to a wider variety of interviewees: young people, artists, representatives of new social organizations.

Going into the project in 1990, I didn't know where it would lead. I was open to possibilities, just as the region was, though I was also well aware of the gathering storm clouds and the urgency of the situation. I returned to eastern Europe in 2012/13 with a comparable openness and an even greater sense of urgency. I'd been away from the region, with a few exceptions, for two decades. During that time, I'd been immersed almost exclusively in developments on and around the Korean peninsula, trying to learn Korean and absorb Korean culture. I knew, vaguely, that not all was well with eastern Europe. But I was out of touch. I approached each interview with a willingness to strike off in unexpected directions.

Some of my interview subjects – like Jiřina Šiklová, the legendary Charter 77 dissident and women's movement activist in Prague – took some time to warm to this approach. For someone of such slight stature, Jiřina is an imposing figure. In Czechoslovakia, most of the signatories of Charter 77 were men. Several of those men told me that their wives would have signed but had decided, for the children's sake, not to put both parents at risk of imprisonment. Jiřina had a career *and* children. She signed anyway. As a result, she lost her job at the philosophy faculty. Like many Charter 77 signers, she then had to take whatever job was available. She became a cleaning woman at a hospital while providing statistics assistance on the side to the doctors. She also kept working for the opposition, writing and witnessing and participating in a network based in London to smuggle materials in and out of eastern Europe. Arrested after the authorities caught wind of her activities, she spent a year in prison before international appeals by the leaders of France, Austria, and Britain, among others, led to her release.

When we sat down in her book-filled apartment in Prague in 2013, she asked, 'So, what are the questions.'

I always started with a question about whether the person remembered the fall of the Berlin Wall. 'I'll ask you about the period 1989/90, then some questions about the period before, and then ...'

She interrupted. 'Yes, but what is the *topic*?'

No one had pushed back against my open-ended approach before. 'I'm interested in women's issues and ...'

'Yes, but what time frame?'

'Well, under communism and then ...'

'Under communism goes back to 1945.'

'Well, from 1980 on to ...'

'Why 1980? That's just stupid. You can do 1948 to 1968. And 1968 to 1977. And 1977 to 1989. Why 1980? Why did you choose that?'

I felt like saying that I'd chosen that date only because she'd forced me to. Instead, I said, '1980 is important to me because of Solidarity in Poland.'

'Okay. But I have written many articles. And other people have written many books about women's issues under communism.'

'Yes, but I'm interested in your personal experience and opinions.'

She looked dubious. 'Okay, okay, let's start. What's the first question?'

As a professor, Jiřina Šiklová expected me to question her with some degree of academic rigor. But I'd decided to revisit the region with a certain degree of naïveté. 'The advantage of being a stranger who is stupid and doesn't know anything is that you can sometimes move around in ways that your ignorance enables,' the scholar and activist Ann Snitow, who has long been involved with eastern European civil society, told me. This is the classic tactic of the journalist, who coaxes sometimes exasperated interview subjects into revealing more than they intend. I hoped that my ignorance, which was sometimes quite genuine, would put people at ease and encourage them to speak about their feelings and not just their thoughts.

Because this was eastern Europe, I expected that those feelings would be tinged with more than a little pessimism. In 2012, when I began my trip, four out of the top ten most pessimistic countries in the world were in eastern Europe (the Czech Republic, Slovenia, Hungary, and Poland).[10] This was definitely a glass-half-empty region of the world. Bulgarians once took a measure of perverse pride at being the most pessimistic people in the world – according to a 2009 Gallup poll[11] – and one think tank in Sofia even produced a report on the phenomenon. 'An enduring sense of frustration arises from the considerable difference between economic conditions in Bulgaria and the developed countries,' the report noted. 'As a result, society focuses its attention on the country's lagging behind the developed countries rather than on the relative improvement from earlier, more unfavorable economic periods. Contrasted with those countries, the Bulgarian nation views itself as a systematic loser.'[12] The sentiment was not unique to Bulgaria.

'Basically eastern Europe is divided into two,' political scientist Ivan Krastev told me. 'There were the countries in which people believe in the end that the transition was a success – as in Poland, where the majority of the people, no matter how critical they are, basically don't reject the transition. Then there are places like Hungary and Bulgaria, where the transition is perceived as a total failure. Because of this total failure, people have started to rewrite everything that happened, including in their own personal life. Their story has become one of naïveté and being manipulated. People surrendered their subjectivity in the process. They came up with a conspiracy theory that everything was rigged and predictable. It was not.'

Pessimism and paranoia were especially acute among certain sectors of the population, such as pensioners. I was taken aback to discover that a Green Party activist in Prague who'd been so full of energy during our conversation in 1990 had sunk into depression when I talked with him again in 2013. 'In 1990, we were full of hope,' Jaroslav Hofer remembered. 'Now I am sixty-five and there is no hope any more. Partly that's also a question of age and health conditions. But the problem is that society – here and even in the States – has changed a lot in the last quarter-century. Globalization, the loss of our industry. Yes, there were opportunities. You can try to start any kind of business you want. But probably someone richer and stronger has gotten there before you.' Czech society had become so bleak and dangerous for him that Jaroslav was planning to buy a gun, which was easier to do in his country than practically anywhere else in the EU.[13]

NGO activist Raša Nedeljkov told me about his father, who'd become just a little too old to find employment in Serbia in a new company or start a business of his own. 'My father often says that he's a "loser of the transition,"' Raša said. 'That's a phrase we often use here to describe all the people who couldn't find a place in the new circumstances. They didn't want to work in businesses outside the borders of the law. They didn't want to use the new opportunities just to make some profits. They didn't want to join some political parties just to get jobs ... All of the people who stood by their beliefs, who found it so hard to adapt, they were eaten by the dragon in the end.'

Even those who escaped the dragon's maw placed an asterisk of ambivalence next to their enthusiasim. 'Now it's difficult, and I'm very disappointed,' Romanian businessman Tănase Barde told me. 'But we cannot compare the two situations. Today I am free. I can talk with you. I can say what I think. And I'm not afraid.' Bulgarian journalist Irina Nedeva said, 'Maybe not everything is working perfectly, but I do like democracy more than the previous regime.' And Polish sociologist Ryszard Żółtaniecki admitted that 'of course we complain; we are dissatisfied. But no one at that point could have dreamed that we would reach what we have reached by joining NATO and the EU.'

It is through the lives of these individuals – both ordinary and extraordinary, both optimistic and pessimistic

– that I want to tell the story of what has happened over the last quarter-century. By interviewing people at two points in their lives, I want to illuminate the gap in between, on hopes realized and fears confronted.

But there's also a larger story I want to tell: the sudden rise and ignominious fall of the liberal project.

The rise and fall of liberalism

The first question that I should have asked Jiřina Šiklová – and perhaps the only question I really wanted my interviewees to help me answer – was: what went wrong? Whatever success or failure that individuals met with in their own lives, the story of liberalism in the region so far has not had a happy ending.

In 1990, liberalism was triumphant in eastern Europe, as each country began to consolidate both democratic institutions and a free market economy. The region became practically the poster child for the thesis that history had ended, that all great ideological questions had been settled by the collapse of communism and its replacement by McDonald's and the voting booth. As sociologist Jerzy Szacki wrote in the early 1990s, 'Liberalism seems to offer the most total response to the challenge of the new historical situation that came into being after the fall of real socialism' – and not in small steps but in one 'big leap.'[14] Eastern Europeans were embracing not only classic European liberalism – the promotion of democratically accountable government and an unfettered market – but also a larger liberal project that encompassed the protection of civil liberties, the promotion of social tolerance, and the promulgation of the rule of law. American-style liberalism, in which the state adopts a stronger role in regulating the economy, would come later, if at all, for it had an unfortunate family resemblance to the previous communist system.[15]

By the time I returned in 2012, eastern Europe had veered off in an entirely different direction. Both capitalism and democracy had suffered in reputation. Intolerance was on the rise. The rule of law was frayed. Even the European Union, which the countries had sacrificed so much to join, no longer commanded its earlier respect. I soon discovered that this was not something new. Indeed, the region had gone off the rails almost from the beginning – indeed, even before the beginning.

The story of eastern European liberalism, after all, did not begin in 1989. Many of the communist governments in the region introduced some version of market reforms, beginning in a serious way with Hungary in 1968. There were also elements of liberalism – particularly the emphasis on civil liberties – in the programs of the nascent civil society movements that emerged in the 1970s and 1980s. These movements leveraged their marginal position in society as a form of social power. Because they were largely disconnected from an unjust power structure – and suffered considerably from the repression of that power structure – they commanded what Václav Havel famously called 'the power of the powerless.' In most of eastern Europe, however, the powerlessness of dissidents also stemmed from their relative isolation from the population at large, which conformed with the system out of ideological sympathy or, more commonly, fear of retribution. Very few people were cut out for the life of a dissident. Making a virtue out of necessity, oppositionists learned the 'uses of adversity' in turning repression into a spur for resistance, just as non-violent activists from Gandhi to the civil rights movement had learned over the years.[16]

The Warsaw Pact monolith, which was never quite as monolithic as Moscow would have preferred, experienced what historian Joseph Rothschild described as a 'return to diversity' when the communist regimes collapsed in 1989.[17] Indeed, this 'return to diversity' began before 1989, as some countries began top-down reforms while others attempted clampdowns instead. In the immediate lead-up to 1989, a number of important cracks in the edifice of communist control had begun to appear, such as the emergence of proto-parties in Hungary and a 'Slovenian spring' of more vocal dissent in the northwest corner of Yugoslavia.

The collapse, when it came, was rapid, spectacular, and relatively bloodless, and it happened differently in each country. At the beginning of 1989, the Polish government announced that it would talk with the previously outlawed Solidarity trade union movement in a set of round table talks. These negotiations in turn produced the region's first semi-free elections on 4 June 1989 and, by the following

September, the first non-communist government. Though it was not entirely clear at the time, world history cleaved on that day in June. While Poles deliriously participated in their elections, the Chinese government on the other side of the globe was suppressing the Tiananmen Square protests that had broken out that spring. China, along with North Korea, Cuba, and Laos, suppressed any movements that threatened to propel their countries along the trajectory initiated by Poland. At the same time, these holdouts continued to implement some version of capitalist reform to stimulate the economy and mollify the disgruntled. This 'Chinese solution' to countering the liberalizing efforts from below would later influence other authoritarian regimes that faced popular protests, particularly in Central Asia and the Middle East.

Aside from some initial resistance from the communist government in Romania, however, eastern Europe held the specter of Tiananmen Square at bay. Hungary, for instance, accelerated its own democratization in 1989 and, that May, even began to remove the electrified barbed-wire fence between it and its once-imperial partner, Austria. East Germans rejoiced that they had a new, albeit circuitous, path to the West through Prague or Budapest. Those who stayed behind in the GDR were not idle, beginning with a courageous effort to monitor the May elections that revealed that the Party had falsified their announced 98.85 percent victory.[18] In early September, East Germans in Leipzig began gathering in St Nicholas Church every Monday, first a couple of hundred and then a month later several hundred thousand, to demand change, a movement that spread to other cities and ultimately precipitated the fall of the Berlin Wall on 9 November. On that same November weekend, the Bulgarian Communist Party removed its long-serving leader, Todor Zhivkov, prompting changes that would eventually end the party's monopoly on power.

A week later, the Velvet Revolution broke out in Czechoslovakia and dislodged the Communist Party from power in a mere ten days. Finally, in a violent coda to a nonviolent regional movement, the Romanian government attempted but failed to suppress protestors in Timișoara and then Bucharest. Angry crowds chased Nicolae Ceaușescu from power in the waning days of 1989. He, along with his wife, would be executed that Christmas Day.

Democratic elections would take place throughout the region in 1990, including the republics of Yugoslavia. At the end of that year, after a series of student protests, the last communist government in Albania agreed to legalize other political parties, leading to the first free elections the following year. Capping off two years of virtually uninterrupted change, the Soviet Union collapsed in December 1991, and communist power was gone from Europe.

There was considerable debate about what to call the events of 1989. If they were revolutions, they were unusually bloodless. They didn't feature any dramatic, wholesale sweeping away of the *ancien régime*, not even in Romania, where many representatives of the new government that replaced the executed Ceaușescu had been functionaries of the old order. Nor was there a storming of any symbolic Bastille. Even the fall of the Berlin Wall resulted from an East German official mishandling the official government announcement of a relaxation of travel requirements between East and West – the new law would still have required East Germans to apply for permission to visit or emigrate to the West – rather than a premeditated popular mobilization against the hated barrier dividing East from West. Nor, however, could the changes be considered mere reforms, since 1989 did mark the beginning of regime change in the region. No wonder that journalist Timothy Garton Ash coined a new word to describe the events of 1989: refolution.[19] The changes were revolutionary in character but reformist in form.

The speed of these changes left the new political elite ill-equipped to tackle three principal challenges: establishing all the institutions of a democratic state, flipping the communist economy into a capitalist one, and redefining national identity. These were the building blocks of liberalism, and the architects of the post-1989 transformations tended to look at the process as a natural evolution. Other countries – the United States, western Europe – had gone through these stages, sometimes over the course of several generations. To catch up, eastern Europe had to accomplish these tasks at a breakneck pace.

It was clear almost from the beginning that the process was not going to be smooth or even nonviolent. Indeed, after the ecstasies of 1989, the region began to experience – to fuse the two resonant phrases – a *return to adversity*. 'Shock-therapy' reforms sent economies into tailspins. Yugoslavia descended into a series of brutal wars. The new leadership in Prague and Bratislava failed to forge a strong enough Czechoslovak identity and the country split in two. A poisonous cloud of corruption settled on the region.

Outside observers tended to view these developments as temporary (like the economic recessions) or anomalous (like the Yugoslav wars). Even the return to power in one country after another of reformed and renamed communist parties didn't fundamentally alter the trajectory of change, for these parties usually continued the same liberal economic reforms and supported the same preparations for entering the European Union. Still, it was remarkable that the very powers dislodged by popular movements could regain legitimate authority in so short a time – in Poland in 1993 and in Hungary in 1994. In Bulgaria, the Party never really left power since its successor, the Socialist Party, won the first elections in 1990, while in Romania the new National Salvation Front contained many of the same officials from the Ceaușescu era.

Plus ça change, grumbled people on the street. Many even began to wax nostalgic about the communist era. In Hungary in 1991, for instance, a remarkable 40 percent of respondents believed that the old system was better than the new one, a number that rose to 54 percent in 1995.[20] According to a 2014 poll, Romanians feel the same way – 60 percent said that they preferred life under communism to their life in a democratic, EU member nation – and they are comparing life today with the tyranny of Ceaușescu.[21] Even as analysts declared these countries 'normal' and this era a 'golden age,' millions of people in the region were clearly having second thoughts about their countries' trajectories after 1990.

The gathering authoritarianism of Vladimir Mečiar in Slovakia in the mid-1990s did give pause. Here was a prime mover in the Velvet Revolution who not only guided his half of Czechoslovakia to independence but concentrated more and more power in his own hands as his new country's leader. As a result of Mečiar's illiberal, paranoid governance, the EU sent the country to the back of the membership line. A civil movement eventually rose up in response and voted Mečiar from power in 1998. This success of civil society, backed by the EU and US donors, lulled many outside observers into thinking that Mečiar's assault against liberalism was a case of temporary insanity on the part of Slovak society.

In fact, Vladimir Mečiar was a warning sign. A backlash against liberalism was gathering strength in the region. By the mid-2000s, analysts were finally realizing that the end-of-history narrative didn't sit well in eastern Europe. It was becoming obvious that the region was not progressing, even with the usual fits and starts, toward a liberal utopia of democratic capitalism. By 2006, major newspapers were reporting on anti-government riots in Budapest and the rise of populist leaders like the Kaczyński twins in Poland.[22] One of the few spots of hope for liberals during this period, the election of Emil Constantinescu as president in Romania in 1996 and the country's vaunted 'return to normalcy,' gave way to a resurgence of nationalism and extremism in 2000 and Constantinescu's retirement from politics.[23] Even in Slovakia, Mečiar's populism was reappearing in a more mainstream guise, and a neo-Nazi movement was gaining strength. Sixteen years of more or less continuous liberal reforms had produced a kind of counter-reformation that some attributed to 'reform fatigue' and others to a 'hangover' from accession to the European Union.[24] 'The liberal era that began in Central Europe in 1989 has come to an end,' wrote political scientist Ivan Krastev in 2007. 'Populism and illiberalism are tearing the region apart.'[25]

Ten years later, the trends that Ivan Krastev identified have only intensified. Throughout eastern Europe, illiberal populists populate the parliaments, and their brothers-in-arms patrol the streets. Anger has been building at capitalism, at democracy, at the European Union, at urban intellectuals and minorities and foreigners. It's not just eastern Europe's problem. This illiberalism has appeared as well in other parts of the world – Putin's Russia, Erdoğan's Turkey, Duterte's Philippines, and, perhaps most surprisingly, Trump's America.

In epidemiological terms, the outbreak of illiberalism could be a run-of-the-mill flu or a cyclical infection. More ominously, the illiberalism that became more virulent after 2006 could represent a one-of-a-kind avian flu that threatens to become a pandemic. 'It's not cyclical. I don't think it will go away,' anthropologist Rayna Gavrilova told me when presented with these three options. Liberals, and she counted herself among them, 'never cared about what people felt, about our messages, about our choices. That's why we've lost huge constituencies everywhere. If we don't do something serious to engage the minds and the emotions of people, we'll turn into, I don't know, China.'

And thus the paths that diverged on 4 June 1989 threaten to converge once again.

Mind the gap

Many eastern Europeans that I interviewed in 1990 expected that they would be living like Viennese or Londoners within five years, ten years at most. If this was a delusion, it was one fueled by the outside advisors who flooded eastern Europe in 1990. The planners from the US Agency for International Development, for instance, put a five-year window on their assistance package, as anthropologist Janine Wedel points out, 'on the assumption that "transition" would take just five years.'[26]

Two decades later, you could put together an itinerary of the capital cities of eastern Europe that would leave you with the impression that the region had indeed closed the gap with the West. Take the example of Bucharest, which is by no means the star performer of the region. In 1990, I arrived in the dusty Romanian capital at the end of July and wandered practically the entire city in search of something to eat. After the bustle of Budapest, Bucharest seemed deserted, the streets dusty and trash-strewn, and no restaurants in sight. Finally, my traveling companions and I found an old caravansary on the edge of Old Town built several centuries before by an Armenian trader named Manuc. The only item available on the menu was grilled meat, but it was cheap and tasted great with our bottled water. The waiter exchanged out dollars, and we ate our lunch at a balcony table looking down on an empty courtyard where dogs slept around an old pump.

In 2013, I tracked down the same caravansary. Manuc's Inn was now one of many restaurants in the refurbished Old Town. In the courtyard were dozens of tables shaded by colorful umbrellas. A gorgeous old bar occupied one end of the space. Sitting atop a platform where the pump once stood, a performer played Spanish guitar. From two fat menus, one Romanian and the other Lebanese, I ordered the Lebanese appetizer sampler and a Romanian entree of duck with cabbage. Delicious, but not exactly cheap, the meal would have passed muster in Vienna or Amsterdam.

People who visit only the capital cities of eastern Europe and eat at places like Manuc's Inn come away with a distorted view of the economic situation in the region. Warsaw and Bratislava are wealthier than Vienna, and Budapest nearly on a par with it – even though Poland, Slovakia, and Hungary all remain economically far behind Austria (with Bulgaria and Romania languishing even further behind).[27] The gap between the city and the countryside mirrors the gap between Bogdan and Miroslav. As science fiction writer William Gibson once said, 'The future has arrived – it's just not evenly distributed yet.'[28] The capital cities have forged ahead into the future while the countryside stays mired in the past.

This is not a question of perception – of a glass half-full or half-empty – but of stubborn facts. An enormous gap persists between eastern Europe and western Europe. In 1991, according to the World Bank's figures, Hungary's per capita GDP was $3,333 while Austria's was $22,356.[29] By 2015, Hungary's level had risen to $25,581, but Austria's now stood at $47,824. The gap has narrowed considerably. But Hungary and its eastern European cohort – Poland ($26,135), Romania ($21,403), Bulgaria ($17,511)[30] – have only cut the lead in half, at best.

'In 1965, West Germany was already the wealthiest and most productive country in Europe,' Adam Jagusiak, a former peace activist and Polish Foreign Ministry employee, told me in an interview in 2013. 'It took them only twenty years. They produced more than France and Britain. They had their *Wirtschaftswunder*, their economic miracle. What's most disappointing, for most people, not just me, is that after twenty-three years we cannot close the gap ... We closed it to a certain extent, but now it just plateaus. Poland would have to grow ten percent annually to close the gap. That's a neck-breaking pace, like Japan in the 1950s and 1960s or like South Korea in the 1970s. We grow maybe two or three percent. There's no closing the gap in sight.'

A comparison between eastern Europe in 1990 and West Germany in 1945 is revealing. The latter had been broken by the war, many of its factories reduced to rubble, a large portion of its able-bodied population dead. But two decades later, West Germany had not merely caught up with the rest of Europe – it was the continent's most powerful economy, as Adam noted. True, West Germany benefitted from the largesse of the Marshall Plan, the US-sponsored initiative that provided the equivalent of over $100 billion in inflation-adjusted dollars to sixteen European countries after World War II.[31] Also, according to a 1953 agreement, half of Germany's pre-war debt was forgiven, and all payments on the remaining debt were mandated to come out of the country's trade surplus.[32] If the United States had been willing in this way to support its wartime enemies Germany and Italy, surely it would extend as much of a helping hand to the victims of communism.

The expectations of eastern Europeans were fed not only by West Germany's *Wirtschaftswunder*. Earlier expansions of the European Union had come with the implicit promise that new members would eventually rise to the level of their peers. Ireland was at the bottom of the continental heap when it joined the European Community in 1973. Twenty-five years later, and after billions of dollars in Euro-assistance, the Celtic Tiger's economy had surpassed that of its fellow clubmates. Although the bubble later burst, Ireland's GDP today remains comparable to Austria's.

Given the decades of communist mismanagement, perhaps it was foolish to expect to close the economic gap so easily. Still, for all of its defects, the communist era left behind a well-educated population, some decent infrastructure, an organized if inefficient agricultural sector, and an industrial base considerably more advanced than China's on the eve of its economic expansion. Moreover, the dreams of parity were sustained by a new political elite who made grand promises about the future – to get elected, to push through unpopular austerity measures, and to justify regulatory changes to meet EU pre-accession requirements. The sacrifices were worth it, the politicians insisted, as long as everyone kept their eyes on the EU prize. The gap would be bridged.

Of the aid promised to eastern Europe, much of it never materialized, and a good portion of what did make it had to be spent on Western products or consultants.[33] The package was no Marshall Plan.[34] After all, 1990 was not 1948. The West was experiencing a recession in the late 1980s and did not have a large surplus at its disposal.[35] A diminishing Soviet threat, thanks to Mikhail Gorbachev, no longer provided a compelling rationale for the United States to pour money into eastern Europe as a bulwark against communism. And the European Union, under the influence of the new orthodoxy of austerity economics, could no longer finance its commitment to raise its peripheral members, or any members-to-be, to the level of its core founders. Membership in the EU still came with privileges, but economic parity was not one of them.

Liberalism became the new consensus in eastern Europe after 1989, but it was a DIY kind of liberalism that featured shock-therapy structural adjustment and the downsizing of government. Just as the region was not to get a sizable handout from the West, the citizens were not to expect a sizable handout from their own governments. By following this template, the region was supposed to close the development gap with the West largely on the basis of its own resources. Governments could sell off state properties, leverage the relatively cheap labor of workers, and attract foreign investment with access to natural resources and favorable tax deals. But governments could not rely on the kind of innovative financing provided to Germany after World War II.

As a result, this great leap forward promised to the people of eastern Europe dwindled to, at best, a small leap forward – measured by modest economic growth, for instance, or the accountability of political institutions. The failure of eastern Europe to replicate the German and Irish miracles has generated considerable disappointment and a corresponding swerve away from liberalism. It's not simply the glass-half-empty team sparring with the glass-half-full team over their interpretation of what happened over the last twenty-five years. The experiences of *both* sides have contributed to the fall of the liberal project. Every individual or corporate success has kindled a suspicion among the unsuccessful that liberals, despite their claims of evenhandedness, have tilted the playing field in favor of the powerful, the corrupt, and the undeserving.

This is not just an issue for eastern Europe. Greece's rejection of austerity measures reflects a continent-wide dissatisfaction with EU policies of economic management. Euroskepticism, which has contributed to the political success of both the political right in Hungary and the political left in Greece, has gained strength throughout Europe. And the conflict in Ukraine pits a western region that wants to join the EU against an eastern part that leans toward Russia, translating an intellectual debate on liberalism into a bloody confrontation. A new Cold War threatens to scupper what remains of US–Russian cooperation and polarize sentiment even further in the European lands in between.

For the World War II generation in eastern Europe, communism was the 'god that failed.' Many were initially attracted to the Communist Party's appeals to economic justice and social equality. Those who remained in the Party after the thwarted uprisings of 1953 in East Germany, 1956 in Hungary, and 1980 in Poland did so largely for opportunistic reasons.

For the current generation in the region, liberalism is the god that failed. How did this disillusionment happen so quickly, what are the precipitating factors, and what will take its place? And is this trend part of a much larger global backlash against the model of market democracy that Margaret Thatcher famously declared back in the 1980s to have no alternative?

Twenty-two years ago, I chronicled the first stirrings of backlash against liberalism in my book *Shock Waves*. This book is in some ways a sequel. *Aftershock* is the story of the hopes and disappointments of the 1989 generation and the courageous efforts of a new generation to pull the region out of its current slough of despond.

The trauma known as eastern Europe

It should make no sense any more to discuss eastern Europe as a collective entity. More than a quarter-century after the end of the Cold War, the countries of this region deserve to be discussed in their own right or to be grouped with other countries. Poland and the Baltic countries, for instance, have a great deal in common with their Scandinavian neighbors. Hungary, the Czech Republic, and Slovakia are historically more tied to Austria. Bulgaria is a former Ottoman land, just like Greece and Turkey. Area specialists describe an existential crisis in the profession because of the obsolescence of eastern Europe as a category and the consequent reduction of funding and attention.[36]

Still, much unites the region. The Croatian novelist Dubravka Ugrešić refers to the region in one of her books as 'the trauma known as Eastern Europe.'[37] The countries described in this book have indeed experienced a similar set of historical traumas. After the collapse of imperial control in World War I came fitful steps toward nationhood in the interwar period, the horrors of Nazism, and the mixed blessing of Soviet liberation. Then followed Moscow's imposition of communism with the help of national elites.

During the ensuing era of communist fraternity, eastern Europeans all experienced to one degree or another the nationalization of property, the collectivization of agriculture, the creation of a surveillance state, and the application of 'socialist realism' to culture.

True, there were important differences among the countries at every stage. Poland retained private agriculture and a strong Catholic Church. Yugoslavia broke with the Soviet Union. West Germany strongly influenced the culture of East Germany, which never developed much of a separate national identity. Ceaușescu cultivated his unique brand of self-reliant Carpathian nationalism in Romania.

Yet the collective traumas of the twentieth century continue to bind the region together and serve to distinguish eastern Europe from its Western neighbors. The countries all struggle with the economic legacy of communism, the challenge of building democratic institutions virtually from scratch, and the consequences of decades of half-buried nationalist strivings. They all must confront the years of collaboration and surveillance. They all must address the footprint that 'socialist realism' left on their cultures. They all must struggle with their newcomer, second-class status within the European Union.

But it would be a mistake to associate eastern Europe only with trauma. The region is also united by positive experiences: high literacy rates, the greater equity accorded to women, the rebirth of civil society. The reason that the glass is half full in eastern Europe – compared to, say, Egypt after the Arab Spring – owes much to this more positive legacy of communism and even more so to the strengths developed during the resistance to it.

Another important common element that binds the region together is the experience of its intellectuals. As in Russia but not in the United States, the intelligentsia formed a separate class in eastern Europe before and during the Cold War era. As communist parties seized power after World War II and established putative 'dictatorships of the proletariat,' intellectuals were the key architects of the new order as well as some of its first victims. The division between those who collaborated with state power and those who opposed it grew much sharper, particularly after 1968 and the failure of the reform movement in Czechoslovakia that attempted to bridge the gap during the Prague Spring.

In 1979, two Hungarian scholars put forward a daring thesis. Dissident intellectuals and Party politicians, György Konrád and Iván Szelényi argued, belonged to the same dominant class.[38] They imagined that a day would come when these intellectuals would reach across the political divide to collaborate in changing the system from within. Reform-oriented technocrats and dissidents would, in Marxist terms, develop 'class consciousness' and, as a class, take power.

Their analysis was prophetic, for this alliance did in fact bring about change in Poland, Hungary, and then Czechoslovakia. The first major challenge to communist power in Poland came from a workers' movement, Solidarity. But soon enough the intellectuals took over that movement and then, in 1989, negotiated with their intellectual counterparts on the Party side. In the pivotal round table negotiations, for instance, 195 of the 232 participants were intellectuals – from both sides of the divide.[39] In the political section, for instance, medieval historian Bronisław Geremek squared off against psychologist Janusz Rejkowski, both of them sharing more in common politically and intellectually than they did with either the leader of Solidarity (an electrician) or the leader of the government (a general). In the absence of a mass trade union movement elsewhere in the region, the intellectual class played an even more dominant role in the transitions.

It's no surprise, then, that those who orchestrated the changes in 1989 crafted a transition that benefitted their class, whether it was former Party officials who profited from insider privatization or former dissidents who staffed the new government ministries. 'It was a dominant class that needed and received liberation: economic, political, ideological liberation,' human rights activist Dimitrina Petrova told me. 'So from the point of view of social stratification, the limits that held back eastern European elites were broken, and these elites liberated themselves to become free elites.'

These historical similarities, both positive and negative, do not translate into equality. The northern tier – Poland, the Czech Republic, Slovakia, and Hungary – has long enjoyed a higher status than the countries farther south. As historian Lonnie Johnson points out, 'This idea of hierarchy of nations in Central Europe was reinforced during the nineteenth century, when the amalgam of nationalism and Romanticism popularized the idea that the superiority of some nations had been demonstrated by the roles they had played as historical agents in the past, regardless of how remote, and that the passivity or inferiority of others had been documented by the fact that they could not look back on comparable traditions or achievements.'[40] Later, as analysts were attempting to explain the differences in success among the countries of the region, this hierarchy translated into various theories about, for instance, the impact of the Ottoman legacy (negative) versus the Habsburg historical tradition (positive).[41]

The very notion of 'transition' is freighted with such assumptions. The new scholars of transition – the transitologists – assumed that the countries of eastern Europe were on a path from less advanced (oriental, Ottoman, communist) to more advanced (occidental, Habsburg, European). Those in the region itself could be the worst offenders. Ante Trumbić, the former Yugoslav foreign minister, wrote in the aftermath of World War I: 'You are not going to compare, I hope, the Croats, the Slovenes, the Dalmatians whom centuries of artistic, moral and intellectual communion with Austria, Italy and Hungary have made pure occidentals, with these half-civilised Serbs, the Balkan hybrids of Slavs and Turks.'[42] Many years later, novelist Milan Kundera developed the notion of a 'kidnapped' West, of central European countries like Czechoslovakia dragged eastward by the Soviet Union to join countries like Russia and Bulgaria that presumably 'belonged' in that 'backward' part of the world.[43]

After 1989, the West continued to patronize the East, though perhaps in more subtle ways. The writer Péter Esterházy captured these gradations beautifully when he wrote, 'Once I was an Eastern European; then I was promoted to the rank of Central European … then a few months ago, I became a New European. But before I had the chance to get used to this status – even before I could have refused it – I have now become a non-core European.'[44] As this hierarchy suggests, 'Eastern' over the centuries had come to occupy a subordinate position to the West. 'Today, if you say a country is part of the West, it sounds like a mild form of approval,' wrote the playwright Václav Havel. 'On the contrary, if it is part of the East, it sounds like mild condemnation. But all of that is the typical expression of a Western sense of superiority. There is no shame attached to being part of the East, just as being part of the West is not automatically a virtue.'[45]

Like Havel, I don't consider 'Eastern' to be derogatory in any way. I have a fondness for Russian culture, and I lived in the Far East for several years. When I wrote *Shock Waves*, I had no direct experience of China, North Korea, and Laos, or any of the capitalist countries of Asia for that matter. I was thoroughly Eurocentric in my perspective and largely unaware of other paths of economic and political development. East European reformers like Poland's finance minister Leszek Balcerowicz or Czech prime minister

Václav Klaus were confident in 1990 that there was but one path to success. Thanks to my subsequent education on the ground in Asia, I now see that the situation is a great deal more complex.

So, I will use 'eastern Europe' in this book geographically, not normatively, to refer to those countries of the former Warsaw Pact that lie between what was once the European Community and what was once the Soviet Union.

A tale of two eastern Europes

This is a two-part story. In the first half of the book, I will describe the steps backward that the region took in the aftermath of the changes in the early 1990s. This is the story of Miroslav: of economic hardship, political betrayal, disappointment. The second half of the book, meanwhile, will depict the small leaps forward that eastern Europe has also accomplished. This is the story of Bogdan: of opportunity, reinvention, success.

These stories and many others will illustrate what went right and what went wrong in the region over the last twenty-five years. They will explain the mystery of underdevelopment and provide lessons learned for people living through similar disruptions in the Arab world, in Burma, in the former Soviet Union. As we approach the thirtieth anniversary of the fall of the Berlin Wall, these stories from the eastern European transitions have greater relevance today than ever before. What is currently taking place in

Ukraine – a Yugoslav-like war combined with a Polish-style shock therapy – underscores the importance of learning the lessons of eastern Europe.

Disappointed by the half-fulfilled promises of 1989, eastern Europe has moved in a very different direction from the one imagined by those who initiated the transitions away from communism. Can the region muster the energy and resolve to swerve again, but this time in the direction of greater equity, democracy, and inclusion? It's not easy to break away from path dependency – the tendency for a system to persist out of engrained habit even if a better alternative exists – just as it has been difficult to introduce a more efficient keyboard because all typists are accustomed to the old QWERTY design. This QWERTY effect applies across the board: to governments, observers, activists. Inertia is powerful.

But perhaps eastern Europe is in the process of *reculer pour mieux sauter* – stepping backward in order to jump farther ahead – so as to close the development gap with the West. To do so, however, will require a fundamentally different understanding of political, economic, and social change. To do so will require learning how to address the aftershocks of 1989 and build sustainable societies, even as the tremors continue to ripple outward.

Part I
Stepping backward

1
Pyramids of Sacrifice

Jelka Zorn, a petite blonde Slovenian, was conducting ethnographic research on asylum issues for her social work degree. It was 2000. The last war of the Yugoslav succession, over the breakaway region of Kosovo, had recently ended. Yet Slovenia, in the northwest corner of the former multiethnic federation, was still dealing with people who'd fled the conflicts that accompanied the breakdown of Yugoslavia. The detention centers were crowded.

Jelka's interest in immigration was piqued by the experience of a friend from Croatia who wanted to relocate to Slovenia. It had been relatively easy to move between republics in the communist era, but this changed when the country broke apart in the 1990s. 'She had a terrible problem getting papers,' Jelka told me in 2012 over tea in a café in the Slovenian capital of Ljubljana. 'She was not a refugee. She just wanted to move here for personal reasons. I helped her with the papers. This took five or six years!' Jelka made no effort to conceal her frustration. 'Through her, I got to know how it is to come here from ex-Yugoslavia, how people were treated administratively, and what consequences this had for their life.'

Slovenia cultivates an image of itself as the Switzerland of the Balkans. It's small, with an alpine landscape and a relatively prosperous population of 2 million people. Slovenians also tend to think of themselves as tolerant. That tolerance was tested by the waves of ex-Yugoslav refugees that flowed into the country in the 1990s. 'At first, people's reactions were very welcoming toward the refugees,' Jelka explained. 'But after a while this really changed. Politicians gave hostile speeches. Refugees were restricted in their movement around the town. They were kept in those centers, and only their basic needs were met. It's terrible to treat people like this.'

Provoked by her friend's travails and the increasingly intolerant rhetoric of politicians, Jelka decided to visit a Slovenian detention center to learn more about asylum issues. It was not an easy task. For one thing, the head of the institution was not happy to have a graduate student poking around in the center's affairs. It only became more complicated when Jelka spoke with the resident social worker.

'Do you want to talk with our foreigners,' the social worker asked, 'or foreigner foreigners?'

Our foreigners? *Foreigner* foreigners? What could those phrases possibly mean?

With that one visit, Jelka Zorn's life changed completely. She'd stumbled onto a nightmare of a situation that had been going on for nearly ten years. 'Our foreigners' turned out to be a group of 25,000 people who had lost their citizenship from one day to the next. They had been born in many different places, but they had lived in Slovenia for most of their lives. In some cases, they had lived nowhere else. Until 1991, they considered themselves Yugoslav citizens, and that's what it said on their passports.

When Slovenia established its own citizenship law on gaining independence in 1991, the new state promised to grant citizenship to the approximately 200,000 people from other Yugoslav republics living in the country. These prospective citizens just had to demonstrate that they had permanent residency as of 23 December 1990 (when Slovenia passed a successful referendum on independence), prove that their place of residence in Slovenia was real, and apply for citizenship by 31 December 1991. Most of the people in this category – about 170,000 – followed these procedures. Some of the rest left Slovenia.

Everyone else failed to apply for citizenship – 'some of them owing to ignorance and confusion at the time of dissolution of SFR Yugoslavia, some owing to anti-Slovenian propaganda, some because they mixed up citizenship or nationality with ethnicity,' explains Matevž Krivic, an asylum lawyer and former constitutional judge.[1] This group of 25,000 people stayed in Slovenia, but as foreigners: 'our' foreigners. And when the application period for citizenship elapsed in 1992, Slovenia stripped those 25,000 people of their legal status – 'without legal ground and without any administrative decision,' Krivic continued, 'even without any notification to them, simply by erasing them from the register of permanent residents of Slovenia.'[2]

Eight years later, when Jelka encountered them, these stateless persons remained in limbo, many of them living in a permanent state of detention. 'The scene was really terrible at the detention center,' Jelka remembered. 'I had coffee with one man, and I asked him how I could help him. "You can cry with me," he said. This shows a state of resignation, that they had nothing to hope for. They told me, "We worked here for years. We gave our best years here. Now, look where we are? Six beds to one room."'

Perhaps the most startling aspect of what would become the scandal of the Erased was that virtually no one in Slovenia knew about it.

'It's quite remarkable that in a small country like Slovenia something like this could remain hidden for a decade,' Jelka told me sadly. 'When we started to tell students that they had to make interviews with Erased persons, they said, "But we don't know any Erased people!" In the end, though, it turned out that everyone did know someone. This shows the level of oppression. If the Erased weren't so oppressed, they could have gone out and talked about their situation and journalists could have written about it.'[3] As it turned out, not everybody who experienced the Erasure wanted to talk about it. Jelka discovered that some people believed that talking about their situation would make it worse.

The first step for those caught in administrative purgatory was to come up with a name for themselves. Bureaucrats in the municipal offices used the term 'erased' – or *izbrisani* in Slovenian. 'The Erased took it for themselves and changed the meaning of the word completely. It became a term of resistance and courage,' Jelka said admiringly. 'To identify yourself as Erased, it means that you want to reveal the conditions of the Erasure, racism, and xenophobia. So, saying that you're Erased became a very powerful statement in 2002 and 2003. People were really brave to publicly identify as the Erased.'

One of those brave souls was Irfan Beširević.

Born in Bosnia, Irfan came to Slovenia when he was only a year old. Since then, Slovenia has been the only home he has known. At the end of 1990, a terrible car accident put Irfan in a coma. The recovery was long and painful. While he was recuperating, Slovenia declared its independence. After his extended convalescence, Irfan went to register as a citizen of the new Slovenian state only to be told, inaccurately, that he'd missed the deadline. He returned later to clear up the problem. That's when an unfriendly neighborhood bureaucrat declared his documents expired.

'When they made a hole in my identity card, I didn't know what that meant,' Irfan told me through a translator. He spoke slowly, pausing every so often to take a drag on a cigarette. 'They told me that I was erased from the registry of permanent residents, and I had to arrange my status as a foreigner. I didn't know what the extent of the consequences would be, not until I had health issues and I couldn't go to the doctor because they wouldn't treat me, not until my domestic situation worsened and I had an argument with my wife because I wasn't earning any money and I couldn't be an equal part of the community. Only then did I realize what the consequences would be. Without documents I couldn't go to the doctor. Without papers, I couldn't get a job. I went to the Red Cross, and they said they couldn't help me because I wasn't a refugee, I wasn't anything, I wasn't entitled to any help. And then all my problems started.'

Some people in Irfan's situation, those who'd been erased from the official records, left Slovenia. The government forcibly deported others, sending quite a few directly into war zones. But many, like Irfan, stayed. They stayed with families and friends. They stayed because they knew no other home. Irfan went underground. He sometimes slept at the apartments of friends, sometimes in the park. He worked as a waiter in exchange for food and shelter. He suffered from the after-effects of the car accident as well as new ailments like thrombosis. He no longer had health insurance to pay the bills. He also constantly faced the threat of police detention. In 2002, the police finally picked him up. He came very close to being deported to Bosnia, a country he barely knew. After considerable efforts, he finally acquired Slovenian citizenship in 2004, along with health insurance and the possibility of a proper job.

When I first met Irfan in 2008, his financial situation was perilous – he'd suffered more health problems after a stint in the construction industry. At that point, the Slovenian government was resisting any effort to compensate the victims of the erasure. By the time I caught up with him again in 2012, his situation had improved considerably. He'd become the president of the Association of Self-Organized Erased. He gave interviews. He appeared on television. He was committed to building a broader movement. 'If you don't fight for your rights, if you stay at home and don't fight, nothing will happen,' he concluded. 'It's a really important part of this movement that it's been inclusive. We weren't just struggling for the Erased. We were fighting also for the rights of Roma and the LGBT community.'

The Erased received assistance from social workers and activists like Jelka Zorn. Several lawyers also helped them take their case all the way to the European Court of Human Rights. The plaintiffs insisted that the Slovenian government not only acknowledge the human rights violation but also pay damages.

One of those lawyers was Neža Kogovšek Šalamon. Trained in human rights law in the United States, Neža began working on non-discrimination cases when she returned to Slovenia at the end of 2004. But she didn't find the work sufficiently challenging – until she became involved with the Erased.

'It was actually a case that started with eleven applicants,' Neža told me in her office at the Peace Institute in Ljubljana, where she'd recently become the executive director. 'Nothing was happening at the time. The politicians were ignoring the issue, unless they used the issue against the Erased to gather political points. So, it was a very desperate situation for the victims and for civil society. A group of activists decided that something had to be done, and the only thing that hadn't been explored yet was the European Court of Human Rights.'

It was an uphill struggle from the beginning. The activists and the victims, working together, 'looked for an attorney that would take the case pro bono to the European Court of Human Rights, because the people of course had absolutely no money to pay for an attorney,' Neža explained. 'They looked for an attorney in Slovenia, and nobody wanted to take it. Some of the people said that the case had no chance of succeeding. Others said they were scared. Still others said they were not interested or they didn't do pro bono cases. So they were not able to find anybody in Slovenia.' Eventually activists in Italy found an attorney in Rome willing to take the case.

After three years, the European Court ruled in favor of the victims but didn't require any compensation. The Slovenian government, rather than acknowledge wrongdoing, appealed the ruling. That turned out to be a big mistake. In its second judgment, the Court was punitive.

'For the past there has to be compensation – this was the key message of the European Court of Human Rights,' Neža said. 'The six applicants got twenty thousand euros each for non-pecuniary damages. They are still waiting for pecuniary damages to be determined, which means they will probably get something more. Which again, is probably not so much when you think about the twenty years of suffering. But still it is a very high compensation from the European Court of Human Rights when you look at its case law.'

In 2014, in implementing the court decision, the Slovenian government finally established a legal framework to compensate the Erased. One year later, it had granted 20 million euros in nearly five thousand cases – an average payout of about four thousand euros per person.[4]

When Jelka Zorn visited the detention center in 2000, the Erased were not only non-citizens, they were non-entities. They'd been erased from the citizenship rolls but also from the consciousness of Slovenians. Within a decade, through self-organization and the technical assistance of allies, they had regained their voices and their dignity. The Court in Strasbourg had recognized their rights as Europeans. And they were being compensated, albeit modestly, for their involuntary sacrifices.

Slovenia experienced one of the easier transitions in the region. In the 1980s, its communist party was the most committed to changing the system. The ten-day war with Yugoslavia's federal forces in summer 1991 left about seventy-five people dead,[5] but it was not remotely comparable to the catastrophes that subsequently overtook Serbia, Croatia, Bosnia, and Kosovo. The new Slovenian constitution safeguarded human rights for all, declared unconstitutional any hatred or intolerance based on race, religion, or nationality, and accorded special protections to the small Italian and Hungarian minorities.[6] During the independence process, about 170,000 non-ethnic Slovenes received citizenship. In a remarkable gesture of solidarity, the government even abolished university fees for students coming from ex-Yugoslav countries.

Yet even here in Slovenia, a substantial group of people were sacrificed on the altar of transition. Nor was this sacrifice simply the result of a series of clerical errors, for it required the entire machinery of the state to enforce the policy. 'The phenomenon of the Erased demonstrates that no democratic order can be established without the repression of the particular,' poet and literary critic Aleš Debeljak told me. Writer Svetlana Slapšak was even more critical of what she deemed a general lack of accountability in the country. 'Slovenia did not repent for its role in the disintegration of Yugoslavia. It did not take responsibility for the Erased. It did not take responsibility for outbursts of nationalism,' she told me. 'The nationalism is everywhere. You can't even define it anymore as nationalism because everything is imbued with it.' In establishing their first ever state, Slovenians created a narrative of themselves as the oppressed, never the oppressors. They placed their country in peaceful Europe, not the violent Balkans. To make this narrative work, however, they had to ignore all contrary evidence, especially the treatment of the Erased.

Many millions of people suffered during the transitions after 1989. The Erased are unusual because they were ignored for so long and also because they were able to achieve a kind of victory. For the rest, the so-called 'losers of transition,' their sacrifices remain largely unheralded and uncompensated, and together they formed the basis of the backlash against liberalism.

The ideology of sacrifice

Karl Marx, the German theorist of communism, imagined that only industrialized countries could transcend capitalism. It was a great irony of history that two of the world's largest agrarian countries, Russia and China, translated Marxist theories into practice. To do so, however, both countries had to turn peasants into proletarians. Beginning in 1928, the Soviet Union embarked on an unprecedented experiment to boost agricultural production and feed a new class of industrial workers by transforming family farms into state-directed combines. Tens of millions of people in the countryside died as part of the resistance to collectivization as well as the famine that followed.[7]

China experienced even greater losses during its Great Leap Forward when Chinese communists attempted to replicate the Russian example. Between 1958 and 1961, private farmers were expected to work the land as if they were employees of an agricultural corporation rather than, as they had for millennia, as peasant families. To increase the country's production of steel, an essential building block of a new industrial society, even the smallest rural Chinese community set up 'backyard furnaces' to turn random pieces of scrap metal into pig iron for industrial smelters.

Many Chinese were killed for disobeying the government's new directives to turn over virtually the entire harvest to party officials. Many more died during the ensuing famine as village after village was left with no grain to eat, except the seed grain, the disappearance of which doomed future harvests. Communities were reduced to eating ground corncobs, plankton soup, grilled worms, and tree bark. Cannibalism reappeared after a disappearance of many generations.[8] Rather than ushering the country into the modern age, the Great Leap Forward thrust much of the country back into the horrors of the feudal past. At least 45 million people died during this period, according to historian Frank Dikötter.[9]

In the past, Chinese had died in large numbers because of military invasions or large-scale natural disasters. What made the Great Leap Forward different was that an intellectual construct, not a foreign marauder, was responsible for all the deaths. Mao Zedong and his cadre were in thrall to a theory. By the 1950s, the Soviet Union had managed to close the gap, more or less, with the West (though many of it achievements were over-reported). If agricultural collectivization and rapid industrialization had transformed the Russians into a proletariat power, Mao reasoned, surely the same template, with a few adjustments, should work for the Chinese. The peasantry simply had to make the necessary sacrifices.

In his 1974 book *Pyramids of Sacrifice*, sociologist Peter Berger compared social engineering projects like the Great Leap Forward to the ritual sacrifice of the Aztecs. The great pyramids of Mesoamerica stand testament to a society that maintained order by gouging out the hearts of thousands of sacrificial victims. Rather than a bout of collective insanity, the periodic bloodletting was a fundamental cornerstone of Aztec society. 'Sacrifice, and the blood that poured from it, ensured that the Aztec would continue to have access to the necessary elements – sun, water, earth, and air – and all the fruits resulting from these,' writes anthropologist Manuel Aguilar-Moreno.[10]

Berger's comparison was not precise. The Aztecs sacrificed large numbers of people in order to maintain the status quo. The communist elite, in plunging their societies knee-deep in blood, were demanding sacrifice in order to create something new in the future. Nevertheless, both societies justified their sacrifices by appealing to a set of external, inviolable laws – dialectical materialism for Marxists and the cult of Huitzilopochtli (deity of war, sun, and human sacrifice) for the Aztecs. Another overlap was the group responsible for carrying out the mission: 'intellectuals who define reality, the power wielders who shape the world to conform to the definitions.'[11]

What made Berger's arguments even more radical in the 1970s was his willingness to compare communism *and* capitalism to the Aztec ritual. 'Both models are based on the willingness to sacrifice at least one generation for the putative goals of the experiment,' he wrote. 'Both sets of sacrifice are justified by theories.'[12]

The Aztecs made no attempt to conceal their human sacrifices. The rituals were embedded in their way of life. Both communists and capitalists, on the other hand, took great pains to conceal the enormous suffering that attended their efforts to modernize. The Chinese government even today refuses to acknowledge the huge number of deaths associated with the Great Leap Forward, ascribing many of the famine deaths that took place to drought and other natural disasters. The sacrifices undertaken under capitalism – during the Industrial Revolution, for instance, or as a result of 'development' programs in the developing world – are similarly obscured by statistics of rapid economic growth. In both the capitalist and communist worlds, an economic leap forward required what Marx called the 'primitive accumulation of capital.' In largely agrarian societies, this primitive accumulation deprived peasants of their harvests and even their lives.[13]

In eastern Europe after 1989, the sacrifices certainly did not reach the level of the Great Leap Forward or the peak years of Aztec bloodletting. However, entire classes of people in the region – pensioners, industrial workers, collective farmers – were simply incapable of accommodating the profound shifts taking place in their society. These 'losers of transition' have often achieved little more than footnote status when observers tot up all the various post-1989 achievements. Even though many of the people on the ground who made the revolutions of 1989 happen were workers and farmers, the intellectual class took charge of the transition process. As Berger predicted, intellectuals defined the new reality. They then shaped the world to conform to their definitions of markets, democracy, and nation.

The Erased are perhaps the archetypal 'losers of transition.' Slovenia was eager to establish a fully sovereign state in 1991. It was the first country to declare its independence from former Yugoslavia and the first to go to war with the federal authorities to secure that independence. Since the war was short lived, and the loss of life minimal, Slovenians congratulated themselves that they were able to become independent at relatively little cost. But the dissolution of Yugoslavia required much greater sacrifices, even in Slovenia itself, as the Erased were to learn.

Throughout the region, success came at the expense of someone. Economic 'losers' came to symbolize the unsuccessful aspects of the previous system, such as the subsidizing of 'unproductive' industries or the redistributing of wealth to 'unproductive' members of society: these 'losers' had to suffer a loss of status if society were to move forward. Ethnic 'losers,' like the Roma, helped to distinguish the 'white, European' majority that was suitable for EU membership from the unassimilable minorities. In this sense, transition was a zero-sum game. The in-groups needed the out-groups to underscore the merit of their success, just as Slovenes needed the Erased to reinforce their privileged status within the area of former Yugoslavia.

As I interviewed the 'losers of transition,' I wondered whether their sacrifices would be limited to only one generation. In South Korea, for instance, many rural families in the 1960s and 1970s scrimped and saved to send their children to university – even killing the family cow to do so

– a collective sacrifice that helped the country jump from the level of a sub-Saharan African country in 1960 to a member of the club of most developed economies by the mid-1980s.[14] But those South Korean families made their sacrifices voluntarily in order to ensure the success of the next generation. Most eastern Europeans had no desire to scale the pyramid of transition to make such a sacrifice, and any assurances that their children would prosper sounded increasingly hollow. They didn't realize that the transition needed its losers – Yugoslavs, Roma, industrial workers, and others – as much as it needed its winners.

From first to last

In the early 1980s, the citizens of Yugoslavia enjoyed a distinct comparative advantage over their counterparts in eastern Europe. Yugoslavia's per capita GDP was the best in the region.[15] True, $3,230 might not sound like a lot of money, but the closest competition in 1982 was Czechoslovakia at $2,980. By comparison, Poland's was only $1,540 and even European Community member Portugal topped out at $2,500.

'We used to go to restaurants with piles of bills in order to pay for the food,' curator Branko Franceschi told me about his experience as a Yugoslav in the 1980s. 'We were young and we were very cocky in comparison to the rest of the Eastern bloc. Everything was cheap for us whenever we would go to Budapest, to Brno. We would, of course, get drunk, insult people, throw money around. Now I'm a bit ashamed of this.'

Money was only one factor in Yugoslavia's privileged position in the region, and perhaps not even the most important one. Yugoslavs could easily travel and not just to eastern Europe. Many guest workers labored at construction sites in western Europe, sending money back to their families and returning periodically to build their own new houses in the countryside. There was relative freedom of expression – emphasis on relative – and Yugoslavia's music, literature, films, and philosophy were the envy of its neighbors. 'Yugoslavia was referred to by some of my Romanian friends as the America of the so-called Eastern bloc,' literary scholar Predrag Dojčinović told me. 'Many people lost their lives trying to swim across the Danube from Romania to try to get into Yugoslavia – to get a feeling of the free world.' At a time when few would think of a week in Warsaw or East Berlin as a prize, tourists from the West did not hesitate to vacation on Yugoslavia's Dalmatian coast.

As an independent communist country that broke with Moscow in 1948, Yugoslavia benefitted from an early influx of US economic assistance. 'Yugoslavia profited from the Cold War as a bridge between the East and West and with the Non-Aligned Movement,' lawyer Mijat Damjanović explained to me. 'The interests were not only political but economic as well.' Mijat, who went to law school with future Serbian leader Slobodan Milošević, had high hopes for Yugoslavia when the Berlin Wall fell, even though the country would lose its crucial position as an East–West bridge. 'I expected that Yugoslavia would be a more prosperous country,' he continued. 'And I predicted that our country, because we were far ahead of Hungary, Romania, Bulgaria, would have a meaningful role in the dissolution of the Cold War during this period. Yugoslavia could have been a leader and done something good for itself and for its neighbors.'

Indeed, given its relative freedoms and material wealth, Yugoslavia was widely considered to be the first in line of all the communist states for membership in the European Community (the precursor to the European Union).[16] Even as late as 1991, on the eve of war, the Yugoslav federal assembly passed a resolution, prepared by the foreign ministry, about Yugoslavia's accession. 'Slovenia was behind it, and Serbia was against it,' former Yugoslav foreign ministry official Sonja Biserko told me. 'The general secretary of the Council of Europe was present at that session. But now it's just forgotten.'

Instead of contributing to European integration, Yugoslavia dissolved into a half-dozen warring entities. The wars of the 1990s resulted in hundreds of thousands of deaths, the destruction of homes and livelihoods, and ultimately the elimination of a multinational identity. The creation of more ethnically homogeneous nation-states required the sacrifice of an entire generation – the Yugo-generation. Portions of the populations of other eastern European countries suffered as a result of the post-1989 transitions. Yugoslavia, meanwhile, disappeared from the map in the most violent way imaginable.

Some writers, projecting the violence of the 1990s back through history, attributed Yugoslavia's fate to its geography. In *Balkan Ghosts*, perhaps the most influential book on the region during that decade, journalist Robert Kaplan speaks of a 'time-capsule world' where 'people raged, spilled blood, experienced visions and ecstasies.'[17] From a narrow perspective, it wasn't difficult to construct a violence-soaked genealogy, from the battles that took place in the Balkans during the Roman and Byzantine eras, through the equally contentious Ottoman period, and into the genocidal twentieth century. But as historian Mark Mazower points out, 'life in the Balkans was no more violent than elsewhere; indeed the Ottoman empire was better able than most to accommodate a variety of languages and religions.'[18] Poland and the Baltic states endured an even more violent twentieth century, but they didn't succumb to 'ancient hatreds' after 1989.[19] In other words, Yugoslavia was not destined by history to fall apart, nor in such a violent way. For much of the Cold War period, the country functioned as more than the sum of its parts.

Still, despite its privileged economic and geopolitical position among the countries of eastern Europe, Yugoslavia faced considerable centrifugal tensions. The communist government barely suppressed a succession of nationalist uprisings in each of the constituent republics during the late 1960s and early 1970s. These tensions resurfaced when

Slobodan Milošević took advantage of Serbian nationalism, at first against ethnic Albanians in the enclave of Kosovo, to solidify his own position within the Serbian Communist Party in the late 1980s. When I visited Belgrade in 1989, this nationalism could be glimpsed in ways both benign (posters and bumper stickers reading 'I [Heart] Serbia') and deplorable (my landlady gave me an earful at that time about 'Nazi Croatians' and 'lazy Albanians').

If the Yugoslav economy had been prospering in the late 1980s, perhaps Milošević's tactics might not have had much impact beyond Serbia itself. By 1990, however, Yugoslavia was struggling with a huge debt to the West, inflation running around 1,500 percent, and an unemployment rate of 15.9 percent that was unheard of for a purportedly communist country.[20] Some parts of the country, such as Slovenia, were doing okay; other parts, such as Kosovo, were essentially bankrupt. The economic reform efforts of Yugoslav prime minister Ante Marković, if successful, could have eventually strengthened the overall federal project, but they encountered resistance from the increasingly nationalist leadership in Serbia and Croatia.[21] Also, since they associated economic reform at a national level with austerity, the Marković reforms only accelerated the country's disintegration. The party of the early 1980s was over, and the country was dealing with a major hangover.

In addition to rising nationalism and a struggling economy, Yugoslavia was subject to the various conditions imposed by the international institutions that provided it with assistance.

Unlike its neighbors in the region, Yugoslavia experienced political upheaval in 1989 at a regional, not a national, level. The elections that took place in 1990, one of the democratization requirements of the minimal aid package that Europe extended to the country, didn't take place at the federal level.[22] These republic-level elections favored the parties that could prepare in time and tap diaspora communities for funds, namely the nationalists, who also benefitted from the loosened regulations on free speech and party organizing.[23] 'We wanted to reconstitute Yugoslavia in terms of democratic pluralism,' philosopher and activist Žarko Puhovski told me. 'But what we achieved was to help nationalists in the different republics of Yugoslavia.' The movement for a democratic Yugoslavia that Žarko and others organized failed miserably at the polls in 1990. Thereafter, newly empowered nationalists accelerated the disintegration of the country.

European authorities were confounded by what was going on in Yugoslavia. Focused on the prospect of enlarging the boundaries of what was then the European Community to encompass the newly independent countries of eastern Europe, they were not prepared to handle the first armed conflict to take place on the continent since World War II. Europeans didn't completely ignore the situation. The European Community imposed an arms embargo in July 1991 (which largely disadvantaged the weakest army, the Bosnians, when war spread to that part of the country). Several months later, in November 1991, Brussels followed up with trade sanctions, ostensibly to pressure all the parties to come to the negotiation table.[24] However, Europeans were divided on how to address the violence escalating on their periphery. In December 1991, confident that it was doing the right thing, Germany unilaterally recognized independent Slovenia and Croatia.

For its part, the United States was desperate in the early 1990s to maintain the territorial integrity of Yugoslavia. 'The US administration at the time saw Yugoslavia as a precedent for what would happen in the Soviet Union,' political scientist Mitja Žagar told me. 'What they really feared at the time was the uncontrolled disintegration of the Soviet Union and what might happen to the nuclear arsenal. For all the costs, they wanted to preserve Yugoslavia as it was as a lesson for the Soviet Union – and the United States would do everything to achieve this.' He added, 'The federal authorities, particularly the army, considered this as carte blanche to do whatever they needed to do to maintain the territorial integrity of the federal state.'

At the republic level, meanwhile, the leaders of the nationalist movements were equally willing to do whatever was necessary to carve their new states out of what was once Yugoslavia. One of the leaders of the Bosnian Serbs, Biljana Plavšić, was practically apocalyptic in her assessment: 'there are twelve million of us, so if six million die, the remaining six million will live decently.'[25] Nations are thus created, through blood and iron, as Bismarck once remarked.

The staged disappearance of Yugoslavia through four successive wars – over Slovenian independence, between

Croatia and Serbia, in Bosnia, and around the secession of Kosovo – entailed enormous sacrifices in terms of lives and wealth. In the war between Croatia and Serbia, for instance, around 20,000 people lost their lives and 250,000 became displaced.[26] In the Bosnian conflict, at least 100,000 people died, and Sarajevo alone suffered nearly $20 billion of damage during the city's nearly four-year siege.[27] Several thousand people died in the the brief war in and around Kosovo,[28] while the bill for the conflict ran as high as $100–150 billion – including the NATO air war, dealing with the refugees, rebuilding Kosovo, paying for the peacekeepers, and helping the surrounding region recover economically.[29]

The United States and European governments deplored these sacrifices. And yet they blithely ignored the warning signs. I talked with several people in Yugoslavia in 1990 who saw war on the horizon. In 1991/92, European and US diplomats attempted several times to bring the aggrieved parties to the negotiating table, but it was already too late. The Europeans didn't provide critical resources at a time when they could have pressured Yugoslavia to democratize as a federation – rather than as separate entities – and then failed to come up with a unified strategy for ensuring a nonviolent break-up of the country. Neither the United States nor Europe signaled that it wouldn't tolerate military escalation by any party to the dispute. The response to atrocities committed in Croatia and Bosnia was ineffectual. Later, Washington looked the other way during the ethnic cleansing of Serbs in Croatia when Zagreb launched a counter-offensive in August 1995 with US assistance. Nothing confounded the great hopes of the post-Cold War era like the horrors of the Yugoslav break-up. With the United States focused on the Soviet Union and Europe preoccupied with the transitions elsewhere in eastern Europe, Yugoslavia was sacrificed on the altar of geopolitics.

From heroes to victims

The leader of the largest movement to challenge communist rule in eastern Europe was an electrician at the Gdańsk shipyards in Poland. Lech Wałęsa was an entirely new type of dissident. A number of intellectuals stood up to the communist states, like nuclear physicist Andrei Sakharov in the Soviet Union and playwright Václav Havel in Czechoslovakia. But here was a worker in a putative workers' state who, in August 1980, took the proletarian regime at its word and demanded not only better working conditions but also a say in policymaking.

The Solidarity trade union established that August would eventually include one in four Poles. Fully one third of the Polish Communist Party's membership were members. Of the country's 150,000 police, 40,000 were part of the independent union.[30] This was not a handful of dissidents that the Polish state could easily suppress: Solidarity was practically a state within a state. Yet in December

1981, citing the threat of a Soviet intervention, the head of the Polish Communist Party, Wojciech Jaruzelski, declared martial law and ended, temporarily, Solidarity's sixteen months of above-ground existence. The authorities rounded up Solidarity's leaders and threw them in prison. Wałęsa spent nearly a year in detention.

When he emerged, the independent trade union was in disarray. An underground network had survived and even flourished in some areas during martial law, but the divisions within Solidarity over strategy that existed in 1980/81 had only widened. As it angled for influence in the changing political environment of the late 1980s, Solidarity used strikes to strengthen its hand in negotiations with the state. But Solidarity had become more of a political entity than an independent trade union. It saw itself as representing all Poles, not just Polish workers, and its locus of activity was no longer restricted to the workplace.

Wałęsa, the celebrated worker activist, was himself developing a very different outlook. In his autobiography *The Struggle and the Triumph*, Wałęsa revealed his evolving philosophy in a description of renovation work done on his house after his release from prison. Wałęsa originally hired striking Gdańsk shipyard workers to do the work. When they went back to their official jobs, Wałęsa gratefully turned to private workers. 'These private workers, without question, applied themselves more strenuously than their predecessors,' Wałęsa wrote. 'They also talked less. The shipyard workers had spent too long in a state enterprise with a distinct absence of work ethic or motivation.'[31] Wałęsa, the state enterprise electrician, was already putting distance between himself and his former crew.

In September 1989, as Poland formed its first non-communist government, Wałęsa had elevated his changing attitudes about labor to a governing philosophy. 'We will not catch up to Europe if we build a strong trade union,' he declared.[32] Suddenly the very instrument of change in Poland had become, after its victory, the greatest impediment to change. The union continued to function but at a considerably lower profile. Former Solidarity activists who joined the government, meanwhile, imposed economic reforms that ran counter to the interests of workers. The irony was not lost on some. As Solidarity activist Jan Litynski said at the time to those implementing the economic shock therapy: 'We will institute every single one of your reforms, knowing full well that we will spend the rest of our lives fighting their consequences.'[33]

The closure of state enterprises, the privatization and downsizing of factories, and the failure of the new government to provide sufficient resources for job retraining all hit trade union members hard. Unemployment in Poland surged from practically zero to over 16 percent in 1993.[34] Union membership dropped precipitously.[35] People were not just thrown out of jobs, they were plunged into poverty, as the rate increased dramatically from 17.3 percent in 1989 to 31.5 percent one year later, with workers in the state sector suffering the most.[36] Nor was this a temporary hit. 'Poland has the highest level of poverty of any country in Central and Eastern Europe,' analyst Jane Curry concluded in a 2008 study. 'By some government calculations, 58 percent of the population lives below the government-established social minimum.'[37]

The architects of Poland's economic reforms knew that sacrifices were in store but didn't quite comprehend their scale. In an article published in *Foreign Affairs* in June 1990, for instance, economists Jeffrey Sachs and David Lipton expected unemployment in Poland to rise to the level of that in western Europe – between 5 and 10 percent – and perhaps exceed that temporarily.[38] In fact, as late as 2005, Polish unemployment was still hovering around 20 percent (after a modest decline for a couple of years after 1995).

In April 1990, as the reforms began to bite, I trekked out to the Ursus tractor plant on the outskirts of Warsaw. The factory had been a key organizing center for Solidarity in 1980. I was startled when the Solidarity representatives at the factory told me that the economic reforms were necessary precisely because they were draconian. Much sacrifice would be needed to turn the Polish economy into a normal system, they insisted. I asked about the Ursus workers. The Solidarity reps were confident that, even though tractor sales were falling in Poland, the factory would compete favorably in the global market. As it turned out, they were as naive as the economists. Sales dropped from 60,000 in 1986 to below 10,000 in 1991.[39] That year, the company effectively became insolvent.[40]

When I returned to Poland in 1992 to write a follow-up on the country's economic reform, I met with Mariusz Ambroziak, who'd joined the trade union as a worker at the Ursus plant and then risen through the ranks to become the secretary of Solidarity's regional office in Warsaw. I asked him whether he had any doubts about his work now that unemployment was rising and union membership falling. Mariusz's broad, freckled face took on a pained and humble look. 'When Solidarity was registered in 1989, I didn't use an alarm clock to get up and come here to the union headquarters at five a.m.,' he told me. 'Now I need two alarm clocks to get me up in the morning for work.' His voice dropped to a whisper. 'People call here with requests. And I can't give them anything.' The reputation of his beloved Solidarity, the movement he'd joined as a teenager, was taking a beating. 'The union is paying today with its name because under the banner of Solidarity the entire economic reform was undertaken,' he concluded.[41]

Twenty years later, when I caught up with Mariusz in Warsaw, he'd given up on unions altogether and was working in the business sector. 'I have to say that I am satisfied with the way my family and friends accommodated themselves in capitalism,' he told me in 2013. 'The overwhelming majority have their own businesses. Some of them are more successful, some of them less, but the overall result is definitely positive.' As for government, he preferred 'a business-oriented administration that would serve as a helping hand for the business sector.'

'The strikers who brought us freedom – the workers in the mines and the steel industry and in the shipyards and the refineries – were the first victims,' wrote Adam Michnik, a dissident and early Solidarity advisor, in 2011. 'It was not their fault, but they have paid the biggest price. Their work was as good as before, but still they faced the specter of unemployment. We had no idea how to reconcile the pursuit of real economy with care for the people who, through no fault of their own, fell victim to that market. It is not a situation specific to Poland, but nowhere was the position so deeply rooted in big factories as in Solidarity. These people have every right to feel they were betrayed.'[42]

As Michnik points out, Polish workers weren't the only ones to feel betrayed. The economic transition wiped out entire industries and threatened entire social classes throughout the region. Workers in the more successful countries saw their wages drop 10 percent. For those in less successful countries, wages fell between 20 and 25 percent.[43] Even in the supposed success story of East Germany, which got an infusion of funds from West Germany, the country lost nearly three million out of nine million jobs by 1992.[44] According to a survey of non-Baltic eastern Europe, the number of people earning less than four dollars a day quintupled between 1989 and 1996, reaching nearly 20 percent of the population.[45] 'Eastern bloc transition countries are the only nations in the world to have recorded a decline in incomes during the 1990s,' one UN agency concluded.[46]

In Bulgaria, the opposition trade union Podkrepa thought that it could, like Solidarity, lessen the blow of economic reform by participating in the new democratic government. In 1990, I met Oleg Chulev, a child psychologist who was the head of the teachers' union and a top official in Podkrepa. When we touched on bread-and-butter union issues, Oleg tried to chart a position between the government's pro-market stance and what he deemed the 'populist' outlook of the former state-sponsored trade union that was only trying to get the best deal possible for its members. He didn't sound convincing even to himself. When I met him again in 2012, Oleg was still in Podkrepa, but he'd also served in government as the head of the national employment office. 'We made the same mistake as Solidarity,' he confessed. 'I was the head of the national employment service for four years: at the time when the unemployment rate ranged around 18–19 percent. This led to shrinking membership. And the repressions at the enterprise level pushed a lot of people away.' As a result, Podkrepa represented only a small fraction of the workforce, and it failed to protect the interests of even this reduced membership. Anger at the privileges of the communist elite played no small part in the push for regime change in 1989. Yet, as Oleg pointed out, 'The gap between the rich and poor is much higher now in material terms than the gap between the *nomenklatura* and rank-and-file was back then.'

The situation was no better at CITUB, which had once been Bulgaria's official government union. CITUB still owns a skyscraper in the center of Sofia, the fourth-largest building in the country. But whereas many other offices in Bulgaria's capital have been remodeled and modernized, the CITUB building looks much as it did during the communist period, though without the bustle or the security. There was no guard in the booth in the lobby on the day I visited in 2012, so I pushed through the turnstile without having to sign in. I wondered how the union could protect its members' interests if it couldn't even protect its own building. My contact there, Snezhana Dimitrova, was as downbeat as her surroundings. 'Here in Bulgaria,' she told me, 'we say that we are not feeling the crisis because we've always been in crisis.'

The Hungarian trade unions didn't lend their support to the new government elected in 1990, but they were no more successful in forestalling what seemed to be inevitable. Hungary had experimented with market reforms as early as the 1960s, but finance minister Lajos Bokros didn't implement an equivalent package of shock therapy reforms until 1995, after the economy was already in a tailspin. Hungary was struggling with a huge debt burden, and the Bokros reforms cut wages and the standard of living in an effort to rein in government spending, lower interest rates, and service the debt.[47] 'Retrospectively, looking at the measures Mr Bokros instituted twenty years ago, he was right,' union activist Peter Fiedler told me in 2013. 'The Hungarian economy made a U-turn after his measures. On the other hand, a majority of our members lost their jobs during that period. I don't think it really helped them to hear that the next generation would be better off. Every four years, we hear the message that we have to do this now but the next generation will be better off. It's been twenty-five years. Our children are here, and it's not better for them.'

The privatization of state companies rendered around 30 percent of the Hungarian labor force unemployable. 'Roughly thirty percent is just too huge a blow,' economist László Urbán told me. 'In the way the government dealt with the issue, at least one third of that number just left the labor force completely and was probably not employable productively anyway. But we're talking about another two-thirds that we should have found some way to keep in the labor force. Instead, those people were let go into early retirement or given disability pensions, or in some other way they also left the labor force. This was just too large a percentage of taxpaying, employed workers who disappeared from the labor force.' In an effort to save money, the government in fact lost the tax revenues of a huge portion of the populace.

The architects of economic reform in the early 1990s in Poland and throughout the region were unapologetic about the sacrifices that workers in particular would have to make during the transition. Rising unemployment was not a worrisome indicator but, rather, a 'healthy development,' as one observer put it: a sign that the reforms were working.[48] This was, after all, the 'creative destruction' of the market that economist Joseph Schumpeter famously called the 'essential fact about capitalism.'[49] Without destruction, nothing new would be created. According to the 'law' of another economist, Simon Kuznets, market forces must first increase inequality before eventually decreasing it. Along the way, this destruction and inequality also created a nearly permanent underclass.

Perhaps the most chilling example of hopes raised and dashed was the proliferation of pyramid scams in the region in the 1990s. In 1993, when I arrived in Cluj, a city in the Transylvanian region of Romania, I encountered a throng of people at the railway station. They weren't tourists. They'd come to Cluj because of Caritas, a 'bank' that was giving out eight to one on the investment. Dozens of such scams were operating in Romania at the time, but Caritas was the most prominent. News that the payouts had turned several people into millionaires had packed the train station day and night. The stores in town were filled with expensive items – fax machines, stereos, computers – that were sold with greater rapidity than anywhere else in Romania. Ultimately, one in five households in the country was somehow invested in the scam.[50] Speculation at the time was rife: the Romanian nationalists were behind it, the Hungarian minority, the Russian mafia, drug money, even the government. The founder, Ioan Stoica, had been either an accountant, an apparatchik, an embezzler, or all three.[51] Gheorghe Funar, the right-wing mayor of Cluj, lent his support to the operation, providing it with low-rent space in City Hall. Caritas employed 1,500 people at its height and eventually churned through the equivalent of half the Romanian government's annual budget.[52]

The saddest thing about Caritas was that many people knew it was a scam and still invested their money in it. After all, it was one of the few viable operations in Romania at the time, and they thought that they could cash out before it collapsed. When it did collapse, as all pyramid scams eventually do, it plunged Romania into a serious political and economic crisis. Worse was what happened in Albania when a similar set of pyramid scams disintegrated and took the government with them in 1997. A short-lived civil war ensued, turning Albania briefly into a failed state – before the former communists returned to power and restored some measure of order.[53] In both Romania and Albania, a few early investors made off like bandits while many people lost their life savings. The burden fell disproportionately on working people and the unemployed: the transition in a nutshell.

Back in the early 1990s, a casual visitor to Cluj or Tirana would have seen a measure of prosperity or at least a lot of feverish commercial activity. It wasn't readily apparent that a Ponzi scheme lay behind this seeming success. Similarly, a visitor to Warsaw during the same period might visit a thriving Mercedes-Benz outlet or a new expensive restaurant and assume that all was well with the country. 'The economists called me a crazy lefty because I told them that the financial system at the time acted like a pyramid scheme,' Mitja Žagar told me. 'The first people would cash in and benefit, and everybody else would lose.'

At the top of the Aztecs' pyramids, the priests holding their obsidian knives told many of their victims that they would become gods in the afterlife. It's not clear whether anyone believed this story. The industrial workers and laboring peasants in the communist system were also promised a radiant future, if not for them then at least for subsequent generations. Some believed; many did not. After 1989, the new governments made similar claims. Some workers and farmers indeed benefitted from the changes – if they were lucky to have the right skills, possessed the right connections, or were young and enterprising enough to retool for the new economy. But many more took a step backward so that their societies could move forward. This 'lost generation' will never recover.

From the margins to the hinterlands

Aladár Horváth was an elementary school teacher in the Hungarian city of Miskolc in 1989. His students were Roma (also known as Gypsies). 'They lived in a Gypsy ghetto in the center of Miskolc,' Aladár told me. 'It was the same place that I grew up: a working-class Romany ghetto.'

The school was mixed – Roma and non-Roma. But Aladár's class was only Roma. 'The reason I took on this segregated class was that I agreed with the notion that by separating the kids for a few years they'd be able to catch up and then be reintegrated with the rest of the students,' he explained. 'I spoke their language better; I was better friends with the parents because I grew up with them.'

In 1989, Aladár became an activist. The city of Miskolc, located to the north and east of Budapest near the border with Slovakia, came up with a plan to evict the Roma from the center of town and house them in what amounted to barracks several miles from the city. Aladár helped to organize the resistance, and the larger Hungarian opposition movement came out against the plan as well. Within a month, they'd managed to force the city to retract its proposal. It was an early and important victory for the non-communist opposition. Aladár went on to found an independent Roma organization. Later, after the first free elections in Hungary in 1990, he entered parliament on the ticket of the opposition party, the Alliance of Free Democrats.

Aladár had high hopes that the political shift in Hungary would benefit the Roma community. When I first met him in the early 1990s, he was eager to apply the lessons of the American civil rights movement to the struggle for Roma rights in Hungary. Later, in 2013, he told me that he was sorry that he hadn't been more radical in the 1990s. 'I should have been less Martin Luther King and more Malcolm X,' he lamented. After all, events after 1989 did not favor the Roma. 'After the democratic changes and the economy collapsed, hundreds of thousands of Roma lost their jobs,' Aladár said. 'With different methods, they were pushed out of the cities or to the edges of towns. In 1990, we knew of only three villages that were only Roma. Now there are over three hundred.'

The situation in the educational field has been just as distressing. Aladár had experienced the milder form of segregation of classes within the Miskolc schools. In the 1990s, segregation spread until the schools themselves became separate (and decidedly unequal). 'In 1997, there were 128 segregated schools,' he reported. 'Now there are over three hundred. On top of that, there are classes that are segregated within non-segregated schools. This is all connected with the geographic segregation ... There are geographic areas of thirty square kilometers where a child might not meet a non-Roma person.' Aladár concluded bitterly, 'We can clearly say that the school system in Hungary is an apartheid system.' The European Commission has even weighed in, calling on the Hungarian government to end what it considers one of the worst cases of school segregation in the EU.[54]

Under communism, the Roma often experienced discrimination. But the full employment requirements of the regimes at least provided Roma with steady jobs. When communism collapsed, they were the first to be fired. Communities built walls, particularly in eastern Slovakia, to confine Roma to ghettos. Paramilitary organizations comparable to the Ku Klux Klan emerged throughout the region. Skinheads began to assault Roma in Czechoslovakia. A rash of pogroms broke out in Romania, at least twenty of them between 1990 and 1993, in which people killed Roma with pitchforks and shovels and by burning them alive in their houses.[55]

Stereotypes of Roma are pervasive throughout the region.[56] 'We've done research on the type of people who are more likely to be discriminatory,' Roma researcher Maria Metodieva told me. 'The most educated people, in terms of higher education, discriminate the most. This is ridiculous. Once you have a good education, it means that you've been studying in a mixed environment, and you know much more about diversity and cultural pluralism.' But because of the increased segregation of the Roma community, those mixed environments have become few and far between. According to the 'social distance' scale developed by Emory Bogardus in 1925 – which asks people questions about their willingness to intermarry at one end to their eagerness to deport at the other – the majority population generally wants to keep its distance from Roma.[57] True, some Roma are not much interested in marrying non-Roma or living in non-Roma neighborhoods either.[58] But the attempts to bridge social distance generally come from one side. Roma are often expected – and sometimes encouraged – to reach across the social gulf and become integrated into the majority culture. Yet those who do so are often rebuffed.

Many Slovaks 'actually do not want to have Roma as neighbors or have their kids in the same class as Roma kids,' anthropologist Tomáš Hrustič told me in 2013. 'Everywhere anti-Roma sentiments are increasing, not only in Slovakia but also in central Europe. In part, these sentiments increased because of the economic crisis of two or three years ago. It has a lot to do with the fact that it's more difficult for Slovaks in rural areas to find a job and make a living.'

As Aladár's comment about Malcolm X indicates, the situation of Roma parallels that of African Americans in the United States prior to the civil rights movement. But the experiences of the two communities diverge in key respects as well. 'If you're in eastern Europe, even today, Roma are invisible,' US civil rights activist Michael Simmons, who has worked on Roma issues for many years, told me in 2012. 'They don't clean hotel rooms. They don't carry your bags. They don't drive taxis. They aren't the orderlies at the hospital. They don't even have what I call the "colored jobs" in the United States. The result is that they don't have those dysfunctional "positive" relationships with the majority culture that are so common in the United States.'

Roma and non-Roma indeed inhabit separate worlds. Activist Maroš Gabriel told me a story of an exchange program involving eastern Europeans and several Americans, including two African Americans. 'After one week of talking together with those guys, the Americans told us that somehow we completely ignored those black people,' Maroš admitted. 'Nobody talked to them. We are all educated people, and we didn't have anything against them. But somehow, we didn't treat them the same way we did the whites. We are so used to living in the white world. That's why I say this about Roma. We don't have any Roma friends. We play sports and have some contact with people from the Roma community. But no close friends, no one to meet, to go with on holidays. And every tenth person in Slovakia is Roma.'

Roma in Czechoslovakia even experienced the same political disenfranchisement as the Erased. When the country broke up, the Czech Republic required all Slovaks living in Czech territory to apply for citizenship. Since most Roma originally came from Slovakia they suddenly faced a burden of proof even more daunting than Irfan did in Slovenia.[59] Czech Roma not only had to prove long-term residency, they had to demonstrate a clean criminal record for five years – in a country where Roma acquired criminal records for slight or even imaginary infractions. 'Although the law does not specifically refer to Roma, its requirements on residence, ancestry and criminality had a clearly disproportionate impact on Roma, and as such are discriminatory,' Human Rights Watch concluded in 1996. 'In addition, many Roma who met all of the requirements of the law were arbitrarily denied citizenship by local officials.'[60] Tens of thousands of Roma became stateless overnight. Only in 1999 did the Czech parliament finally amend the citizenship law to allow former Czechoslovak citizens who were living in the Czech lands at the end of 1992 to acquire citizenship by declaration. Unlike the Erased, however, the Roma received no compensation for their suffering.[61]

Throughout the region, Roma became the scapegoats for everything that went wrong after 1989. Slovenians eventually felt guilty enough about what happened to the Erased to try to officially right the wrong. Many of the architects of the economic reform packages later confessed that they'd not taken sufficient account of how the changes would adversely affect workers. But with Roma, the racism lies so deep that the public prefers to blame the victims for their predicament rather than understand the reasons for their marginality.

Self-defeating sacrifices

The cruelty of the high priests in sixteenth-century Mexico ultimately proved self-defeating. By tearing out the hearts of so many members of surrounding communities, the Aztecs pushed their adversaries into alliances with the small band of Spanish invaders. Otherwise, the Spanish conquistadors would not have been able to overwhelm the far more numerous Aztecs.

The sacrifices demanded by the communists during the Cold War would also come back to haunt them. Many of the dissidents in eastern Europe and the Soviet Union had direct experience of the injustices perpetuated by the system. They endured prison sentences, blacklisting, surveillance, and other indignities, which only strengthened their determination to overthrow the system. Even in China, where communism nominally still reigns, the reformers of the Deng Xiaoping era drew on their negative experiences under the Great Leap Forward and the Cultural Revolution – Deng himself was exiled to the countryside for 'reeducation' – to move their country in a fundamentally different direction.

The jury is still out on the sacrifices demanded by the liberal reformers of the post-1989 generation. For the Roma, the situation continues to look bleak. Those who lost their jobs in factories in the 1990s and couldn't find regular employment afterwards are a lost generation. The successor states of Yugoslavia have begun the process of reestablishing ties and even economic infrastructure, but those who suffered and survived the wars remain traumatized.

As for the Erased, the resolution of their story is both inspiring and instructive. In 2008, when I first interviewed Neža Kogovšek Šalamon, the human rights lawyer, she was very pessimistic about the prospects for the campaign. 'It will take more than a shift in government,' she told me. 'Generations will have to change. Until all the people who were in power during the Erasure retire and new people come in who can see the situation objectively, there will be very little chance of positive outcome.'

But a mere four years later, the Erased achieved that positive outcome. It serves as a model of resistance and reconciliation. It underscores the importance of transnational institutions – in this case the European Court of Human Rights – in protecting the least powerful members of society. And it proves that it's never too late for a society to acknowledge a mistake and reach out to embrace those who've been forced to make enormous sacrifices.

2
The Journey to Utopia

Vihar Krastev was working as a journalist and editor at *Vek 21* (*Twenty-First Century*) when I dropped by his office in Sofia unannounced one August afternoon in 1990. He explained to me in excellent English that his newspaper represented the views of the Radical Democratic Party, one of several parties that made up the Bulgarian opposition. During that peculiar but exhilarating period of hyperpluralism in 1990, it took only fifty Bulgarian voters to establish a political party.[1] With such a low bar to entry, the political scene exploded with more than forty parties. A party had to be bold to stand out from all the others. The Radical Democrats – established in the 1940s, outlawed by the Communist Party, and reestablished during the democratic awakening at the end of 1989 – tried to be bolder than all the others by taking the most uncompromising positions.

'We stand for radical democracy, for democracy that has no alternative, that makes no compromise,' Vihar explained to me during our rushed conversation in his office. The Radical Democrats was a party of individuals so allergic to anything resembling concentrated power that they envisioned themselves forming a kind of permanent opposition.

Vihar didn't see any future in negotiating with the former communists. He didn't see any future in politics either, at least as it was understood in the West. And he opposed nationalism in its various forms as well.

Finally, Vihar was emphatic about the importance of rapid market reforms. 'It seems to me that the situation as it is depicted at times – with people dying in the streets and mass unemployment – is a portion of the Big Lie,' he said to me at the end of the interview. 'When I am sick, I don't want the cure to be slow. I want it to be quick. If it has to come, why can't it be faster? I think everyone will find his or her best way to cushion the crisis.'

For Vihar in 1990, progress was unidirectional. The sooner Bulgaria could get to the next stage of economic and political development the better, even if the costs were high. Indeed, crisis was, for many oppositionists in those days, part of the cure for communism. The deeper the crisis, the faster the recovery. The Radical Democrats entered the elections in June 1990 confident that the opposition coalition to which it belonged – the Union of Democratic Forces (UDF) – would defeat the former communists, who had renamed themselves the Bulgarian Socialist Party. The Radical Democrats misread the sentiments of their fellow citizens. Bulgarians, particularly those outside the big cities, were not quite ready for the gospel of individualism that Vihar and his colleagues were preaching.[2] Bulgaria bucked the trend in the region in 1990, with the opposition coalition losing to the former communists.

Twenty-two years later, it was not easy to find Vihar. According to the information I found on the Web, he had continued to work as a journalist for several years after 1990. But after a while, as with Miroslav Durmov, Vihar disappeared from view. Thanks to the sleuthing of a Bulgarian colleague, I discovered that Vihar had escaped the country's crisis via Terminal One, like so many of his compatriots. He'd only recently moved back from Canada to the city of Varna on the Black Sea coast. I sent him an email and was surprised that he remembered our conversation from so long ago. He invited me out to Varna for a visit. In September 2012, I rented a car in Sofia and drove the entire length of the country to spend a few hours with him in the lovely house that he and his artist partner own in the hills above the port.

Vihar had journeyed a great distance from that time in the *Vek 21* office, and not just geographically.

'If I have to be more honest, some of us including myself – and I don't know if I said this in my first interview – were in favor of shock therapy,' he told me as we sat at his dining-room table surrounded by the colorful wall hangings that his partner Yasena had created. 'I knew nothing about economy, about shock therapy! I must have been influenced by the Polish experience: what Wałęsa was talking about, the Polish leading experts. I must have been a parrot who heard something and said, "Oh, wow, why not?" That's an example of my own stupidity, ignorance, and incompetence. And that's how the UDF lost their position with society, and that's how people started disliking the opposition.'

Vihar's second thoughts about what happened in the last quarter-century, which reflect the region's evolving ambivalence about the project of 'transition,' are more than just a mature man's reappraisal of his younger self's naïveté. According to the conventional Cold War history of eastern Europe, the communists had taken the region on a grand detour. In the late 1940s, while the rest of Europe established postwar systems anchored in parliamentary democracy and market economics, eastern Europe embarked on an 'experiment' devised in Moscow and based loosely on theories promulgated by a pair of nineteenth-century Germans. After the horrors of World War II, with its contending nationalisms, the internationalist utopia of the communists had a certain appeal. So did the promise of plenty shared equally. Although this 'detour' produced certain successes, such as more widespread literacy and better health indicators, the experiment ultimately failed, leaving the region far behind its Western counterparts. Thanks to the changes in 1989, eastern Europe took a sudden turn to avoid a dead-end street. If the year 1990 possessed a tagline, it would have been: 'No more experiments!'

When we met in 1990 at the *Vek 21* offices, Vihar and I talked exclusively about political and economic developments in Bulgaria at the time. We talked about ideas. In 2012, instead of focusing on abstractions, I asked Vihar about his life. Our conversation lasted for nearly three hours. He told me many anecdotes from his pre-1990 life that helped explain his later allegiance to the Radical Democrats. For instance, he recalled his first run-in with the secret police, after a high-school outing to Sofia when he and a few friends wandered into the American embassy library on a whim. The police immediately collared the boys afterwards and eventually fingered Vihar as the 'ringleader.' He believes that this was the first of several black marks against him.

More damning was his interest in covering Solidarity when it emerged in Poland in 1980. 'You couldn't talk or write favorably about Solidarity,' he remembered. 'I wouldn't have lived much longer if I kept praising Solidarity – not just Solidarity, but the winds of change, the need for "socialism with a human face," as we called it back then.'

Journalism under such restrictions was not to Vihar's liking. Eventually, through friends at an interpretation bureau, he started working for a traveling exhibit the State Department sent to Bulgaria. When the American organizers were packing up the exhibit in Varna for the move to Sofia, the Bulgarian authorities summoned Vihar to explain that he couldn't continue helping out on the project.

'Actually, I was told that I couldn't work on anything else,' he recalled ruefully. 'I was to be put on a bus and sent to Austria. I refused to do that. The other option was to have my family interned in a very small village on the Turkish–Bulgarian border. I checked: there were fewer than a hundred elderly people living in that place, with no school and no jobs.'

In his early thirties at the time with a wife and a nine-year-old daughter, Vihar pushed back. 'What are we going to do there?' he said to the authorities. 'There's no school there, there's nothing. You're sending me there basically to die.'

They said, 'If you don't like communism, you do whatever you want there.'

'I can't live there,' Vihar replied. 'If you want to kill me, do that, but don't kill my family. Really, isn't there something else I can do here?"

That's when Vihar learned that he would not be allowed to do anything except manual labor. This was a common punishment for disobedient intellectuals in the Eastern bloc. In Czechoslovakia, for instance, Charter 77 activists became hospital janitors like Jiřina Šiklová or stokers like future foreign minister Jiři Dienstbier. Vihar would eventually find a position fixing the brakes on streetcars before working his way up to the position of bus driver. Then, in a nice twist of fate, he led a transit strike in late 1989 that played an important role in forcing change in Bulgaria. As a result of that activism, he was brought into the opposition and resumed his chosen profession of journalism at *Vek 21*. What goes around, comes around.

But the new Bulgaria proved to be as exasperating for Vihar as the old Bulgaria. It wasn't just that the opposition UDF lost the first elections in June 1990, it was the opposition itself that proved disappointing. Not long after I met Vihar, his disillusionment began.

'I remember the first and the second elections, all the people lining up at the headquarters of the UDF who wanted to be included in the UDF party ticket,' Vihar told me.

'Those people were fighting, hitting each other. They stayed there overnight. They wouldn't dare go to the washroom, because then they would lose their position in line. It was horrible. They would kill each other to jump ahead in line to be higher on the ticket.'

Vihar's assumptions about how the market and democracy would function in Bulgaria quickly came up against the realities of power and money. Like Miroslav, he decided that Bulgaria was the problem, and he would take his chances abroad. He did stints with Radio Free Europe in Munich and Prague. But he dreamed of working at a major broadcasting outlet like the BBC or even CBC. He eventually opted for Canada. When he arrived there, CBC told him that his English was quite good. But he would still have to go through a retraining course to upgrade his journalism skills and get rid of his residual accent to do broadcasting.

Sure, no problem, he said. The course, he was told, would cost about $10,000.

'That was a lot of money for me, basically all the money that I'd brought with me,' Vihar told me. 'But I said, okay, if I take this course, then I will be able to get a job as a journalist here in Canada. And they said, no, there was no such guarantee. They would *try* to help me. I thought that I just couldn't take that risk. Same thing with teaching English as a second language in Toronto. One has to spend years to get one's credentials acknowledged.'

Such was the world of capitalism: there were no job guarantees. For a year, Vihar worked as a court-appointed interpreter and as a furniture mover. It was hard to make ends meet, and he wanted something more permanent. 'I really needed to get a job,' he said with a rueful smile. 'And, of course, the other experience I had in Bulgaria was driving a bus, so ...'

Once again, what goes around, comes around. Forced by political necessity to drive a bus under communism, he emigrated to a capitalist country where he was forced by economic necessity to drive a bus as well. Eventually he rose through the ranks with Toronto metropolitan transit and retired at a relatively young age. But it wasn't the future that he'd imagined for himself.

The same could be said for many people in eastern Europe after 1989. After all, the changes in 1989 took place in an atmosphere of great optimism, and the transformations were generally peaceful. The world celebrated with the Germans when they tore down the Berlin Wall. Virtually everyone cheered playwright Václav Havel's rapid ascent from political prisoner to president of Czechoslovakia. The surveillance states had crumbled. Once forbidden music and films and books were suddenly available in the open. New economic opportunities beckoned.

True, some people in eastern Europe mourned the demise of their failed utopias. A small nucleus of true believers, joined by a much larger group of complacent functionaries, had cast their lot with the communist system. Some dissidents and Party members believed the system could be reformed, that 'socialism with a human face' could be dusted off from the 1960s and implemented two decades later. For instance, shortly after the fall of the Berlin Wall, the novelist Christa Wolf and other East German intellectuals distributed an appeal decrying the 'sellout of socialist values' of the opposition.[3] Yet most eastern Europeans were glad to be rid of what was often called 'real existing socialism,' whatever they thought about values of egalitarianism or internationalism.

The disenchantment went beyond socialism and its reformability. Consider the utter political failure of the East German opposition movement, the dissidents who organized the protests that eventually precipitated the fall of the Wall and dethroned the Communist Party. In the first – and only – democratic East German elections in March 1990, the coalition of oppositionists in the Alliance '90 coalition barely got into parliament with 2.9 percent of the vote. On the face of it, this electoral result is astounding. Voters in Poland overwhelmingly backed Solidarity-endorsed candidates in June 1989 – they lost only one of the contested seats – and the former dissidents in Civic Forum and their Slovak counterpart Public Against Violence captured nearly 50 percent of the vote one year later in parliamentary elections in Czechoslovakia. Yet the former dissidents in the GDR, the ones who took the greatest risks in the 1970s and 1980s, received considerably less support from the voters than even the despised former communists, who came in third with a little over 16 percent of the vote.

The majority of German voters didn't want experiments. They wanted to go with 'what works,' and that meant supporting West German Chancellor Helmut Kohl and his Christian Democrats (CDU), who promised faster German reunification. It wasn't such a surprise, economist Rüdiger Frank, who was born in the East, told me. 'Freedom of travel, real money, and all the things you could buy for it – that's what they wanted,' Rüdiger pointed out. 'And Kohl said, "This is what I'm going to give you." He was a man whom many East Germans trusted. All the other politicians, they might have had loftier political goals and more balanced approaches, but that's not what the majority cared about. They had heard enough about dreams and ideals, about justice, equality and a land of plenty that was to come someday in the future. They wanted something real, and they wanted it now. Kohl promised to deliver exactly that.'

Like Kohl, the leaders of the transformations elsewhere in the region were careful, for the most part, to be anti-utopian. They, too, stayed away from promising paradise and focused on the concrete, on the changes that would take place in the here and now. But utopianism still lurked in the background. After all, if people were going to suffer the sacrifices outlined in the previous chapter – the economic austerity, the social dislocation – it had to be in service of a better future. That future could be expressed in a variety of different shorthand expressions: popular democracy, capitalism without adjectives, European integration. Each in its own way had a utopian tint.

It may seem strange that the same people who had rejected the social engineering of communism and eagerly embraced the slogan of 'no more experiments' would succumb to another round of utopian promises. But history primed eastern Europeans to fall for grand visions, even though they prided themselves on being once-bitten-twice-shy pragmatists. As much as they disdained the progressivism of the communist period, certain progressive assumptions were bred in the bone, namely a belief that history moved forward in a purposive direction. Polish philosopher Bronisław Baczko puts it another way: utopians and anti-utopians are not distinct people but two sides of the same person who rejects utopia but wants to have one anyway.[4] After all, liberals, too, believe in an inexorable march of progress through market-led growth or incremental improvements in human rights, which historian Samuel Moyn calls the 'last utopia.' Perhaps utopian thinking is an integral part of political life, as we cycle through hope and disillusionment on a continual basis until death leads us to a final utopia or provides a sudden, final disillusionment.

In 1990, when I interviewed Vihar Krastev, he was vehement in his anti-communism. But he was also confident that a major economic and political leap forward was at hand. He had a form of faith. When I talked with him nearly a quarter-century later, he had lost that faith. Lived experience had turned him into a political atheist. In the 1990s many of his fellow eastern Europeans also 'lost their religion,' much as an earlier generation had done in successive waves during the communist period. The first generation of communist apostates shed their illusions as a result of the show trials, imprisonments, and executions that took place throughout the region in the late 1940s and early 1950s in the aftermath of Tito's break with Stalin and the latter's fear that other satellites would follow Yugoslavia's lead. The next generation of 'true believers' abandoned their faith after Soviet tanks crushed the 1956 uprising in Hungary and the 'Prague Spring' in Czechoslovakia in 1968. A third wave left the Party in 1981 when the Polish government declared martial law and banned Solidarity.

In the 1990s, eastern Europe's liberals went through their own process of disillusionment. It began with the realization that not everyone in their countries held the same views. 'When I realized that the majority of people didn't think like I did, that was a big slap,' anthropologist Rayna Gavrilova told me of her experience after the 1990 election in Bulgaria. 'I truly thought that people would see the promise of real change. But many of them preferred to stick with the past.' Then came successive waves of disillusionment as capitalism, democracy, and European integration, because of their complexity, messiness, and frequently unpleasant side effects, failed to meet the high expectations of eastern Europeans. This journey to utopia, through an often-difficult 'transition,' proved to be as illusory as the aborted trips of the past.

Transitology

Let's imagine the history of eastern Europe after 1989 as a train leaving a station.

At the beginning of its journey, this train is idling at an old, decrepit station where it's difficult to buy any tasty snacks or interesting reading material for the journey. The public address system issues garbled announcements that virtually everyone ignores. The bathrooms are out of order and the help desk is unstaffed, though plenty of station personnel can be seen engaged in activities with no clear purpose.

As the final boarding chimes echo through the station, the passengers pile onto the train. The lucky few occupy first class, a somewhat larger group finds their seats in second class, and everyone else crowds into the unreserved cars. The train begins to move. All the passengers hold tickets to the same ultimate destination: a lovely terminal with well-provisioned stores, clean public restrooms, and a responsive administrative system, a station as well run as the city and country that it services. At least, that's what the passengers have been told or what they've gleaned from pictures. They don't know how long the journey will be. Those in first class, with access to a surprisingly good café and plush sleeping compartments, might be forgiven for believing that they'd already arrived at their destination. Those in the unreserved seats, who are largely left to their own devices when it comes to food and sleep, are fearful that they'll never see the promised land.

This is the train of 'transition.' Even if the length of the journey is unknown, everyone on the train seems convinced that a single track connects the embarkation point of regime change with the disembarkation point of market democracy. Particularly if the trip promises to be onerous, it's no surprise that travelers prefer the express train to the local, even if that means a more uncomfortable ride or the uncoupling of several cars at the rear to increase engine speed. Thus, Vihar told me in 1990 that 'if it has to come, why can't it be faster?' Others at the time informed me that it didn't make sense to jump across a chasm in two leaps or to cut off the tail of a cat with two blows.[5]

The certainty about the destination was so marked that it produced what American political theorist Francis Fukuyama famously called the 'end of history.'[6] All the great ideological struggles were over, in theory if not yet in practice, Fukuyama argued, and history's arrow pointed inexorably toward a particular future. 'Today,' he wrote in 1992, 'we have trouble imagining a world that is radically better than our own, or a future that is not essentially democratic and capitalist.'[7] The end of history meant the end of utopian thinking, the closing off of alternative routes and destinations. All that was left were pragmatic decisions, chewed over by policymakers and implemented by bureaucrats.

If eastern Europeans knew what they'd left behind and were fervent about where they were heading, they knew little about the journey itself. German political scientist

Ralf Dahrendorf tried to provide a few time stamps for this transition: six months to create parties and political institutions, six years to establish the basis of a market economy, and sixty years to build a proper civil society.[8] The precise numbers were less important than their magnitudes. Establishing formal democratic structures would be a comparatively easy task, followed by formal market mechanisms. A functioning civil society, however, would require a couple of generations.

For the new intellectual elite and their foreign advisors, the term 'transition,' with its refreshing vagueness, offered a sense of moving forward even without any definitive prospects.[9] It put the best spin on an awkward situation, just as an unemployed person might say that they are 'between jobs.' However, 'transition' was also a problematic term. First there was the question of when the 'transition' had begun. The region had been playing catch up with the rest of Europe for hundreds of years, before communism was even a glint in Karl Marx's eyes.[10] Eastern Europe had long been considered to be suffering from a 'deficit of civilization' that required assistance from an enlightened West.[11] Even the communists introduced their own kind of transition. Hungary had experimented with market reforms as early as the late 1960s with its New Economic Mechanism. The citizens of Yugoslavia enjoyed many of the benefits of a kind of socialist liberalism well before 1989. More ominously, Romanians began to suspect that the 'transition' had taken place in the weeks or months before Nicolae Ceaușescu gave his final, fateful speech, when members of his inner circle began plotting a coup that would preempt a revolution.[12]

Then there was the question of the differential pace of the transition. Some transitologists came up with propositions about why some countries were succeeding more quickly than others.[13] Perhaps it was because of their geographic location (in the north and west), their imperial background (part of the Austro-Hungarian rather than the Ottoman lineage), or the type of political system chosen (parliamentary rather than presidential).[14] But when Hungary, which should have been at the head of the pack because of its location, history, and political system, started to move backward, it confounded such geo-historical attempts to explain differential success.

Finally, the monorail nature of the transition didn't make much sense either. During its 'transition,' Yugoslavia moved not forward toward the twenty-first century but backwards into the blood politics of the 1940s. Much of eastern Europe suffered from such tremendous economic dislocation that the 'transition' never seemed to end. Because of the corruption that flourished during the 1990s, 'transition' seemed at times to mean simply the transfer of resources from one ruling elite to another, with considerable overlap between the two groups. Most mystifyingly, a number of countries veered off onto a spur of authoritarian populism.

Tibor Várady, an international lawyer and writer, had a first-hand look at the 'transitions' in both Yugoslavia and

Hungary. He does not like the term very much at all, for it reminds him of the circumlocutions of a previous era.

'In no communist country during the communist period did we say that we had communism,' he told me. 'We said that we were "in transition" to communism or "in the process of building" communism. There was a simple reason for this demagoguery. What we had wasn't so great at all. Communism was supposed to be something shiny and wonderful. If communist leaders said, "This is it," we would have said, "This is it? What is so good about it?" But the magic word "transition" suggested that if we had problems, they were not problems with communism. It was just that we hadn't arrived yet.'

And now the term has been repurposed for use in the new era. 'In this part of the world, people don't say that we have a market economy,' he continued. 'They say, "We are in transition to a market economy." In part, that is true. But it is also a way to deflect criticism, a way of not facing the real problems. The market economy has, of course, its own problems. That's why I don't like the word "transition." It's a popular sleeping pill, and everyone is using it. To continue the dissident spirit of intellectuals under communism, we should say, "No, this is a market economy. We have had it for twenty years. We are not in transition. This is it. If this is not good enough, we have to do something about it."'

The 'transition' was not supposed to last indefinitely: a few months to create political structures, a few years to create a market economy. Perhaps the initial train analogy was a poor fit. Perhaps there was more than one set of tracks with several different possible destinations. Track work caused delays and even some unanticipated reversals. Yet the transition framework has proved quite durable.

The diagram

When I lived in Warsaw in 1989, shopping took up a huge chunk of the day. If you had the money, you could skip the state-owned markets and try your luck on the streets. You might find an old woman selling rolls of toilet paper in front of the Centrum shopping center or a black marketeer hawking hard-to-find dictionaries on a side street. South of the city, outside the SKRA stadium, even luxury items like Western shoes and Russian caviar were available, but only at luxury prices.

One year later, I returned to Warsaw to discover that the market had spread everywhere. All over the city a new generation of shopkeepers sold goods from little stands and the back of trucks. You could get everything on the streets, from citrus fruit to American breakfast cereal, for prices lower than in the state cooperatives. The Solidarity paper *Gazeta Wyborcza*, in its section on various commodity prices, even listed such locations as 'trucks at Defilad Square' and 'cars in front of Supersam market.' Gone was Gruba Kaśka, a state-run canteen where I used to get a cheap lunch of stew, potatoes, and a glass of fruit *kompot*. In its place: Kentucky Fried Chicken, which was more expensive and considerably less nutritious.

Capitalism was no longer an abstract issue for Poles in 1990. The communist government, thanks to its minister of industry Mieczysław Wilczek, had made it easier for anyone with a bit of capital and willingness to take a risk to acquire a permit to buy products from a manufacturer and set up a stand on the street to sell these wares. Many consumers seemed perfectly happy with this arrangement. Although prices were much higher than before the removal of subsidies in summer 1989, the lines were shorter and shopping was no longer a day-long profession.

But the dark side of capitalism was already on display. More beggars were on the street of Warsaw and each, according to their carefully penned signs, had a different story: AIDS, drugs, joblessness. Soup kitchens had been set up. Foreign charities were arriving to see how they could help.

These street-level changes were just the beginning. Poland had to figure out how how to tackle the macro issues as well: inflation, currency convertibility, the large state debt, and the disposition of state property. For help on these big-picture issues, it turned to an outsider: a thirty-five-year-old, Harvard-trained economist who'd cut his transitology teeth in Bolivia but didn't have any previous experience in former communist countries.

Jeffrey Sachs has been lauded and vilified for his role in shaping the economic transition in Poland. Although I didn't have a chance to meet him in 1990, I managed to arrange an interview in 2013 at his office at Columbia University. He retains much of the boyish impatience he was famous for as a wunderkind in the late 1980s flying from one country to another – Peru, Poland, Yugoslavia – providing advice on the run. He was alternately charming and imperious, a temperament forged over the years by advising governments and lecturing students.

Jeffrey Sachs is often criticized for his political transformation – from a neoliberal of twenty-five years ago to a progressive internationalist today.[15] But he really hasn't changed much. In a profile of Sachs written by Lawrence Weschler in the *New Yorker* in 1989, the economist described himself as a social democrat.[16] And he stands by the positions he took back then. 'I would not only stand by these ideas, but also stand by the results: Poland actually transformed,' he told me, insisting that the transformations had a strong social democratic element. 'I'm not a free-market libertarian by a million miles. I wanted a cushion for Poland. That was a large part of my aims and a large part of their interest in me, in terms of what I could get for them. And I did this in a number of ways. I believe in supporting people in unemployment and old-age pensions and a public healthcare system. It was never the idea that people should sink or swim.'[17]

As a transitologist, Jeffrey Sachs has always been convinced that the economic crisis facing eastern Europe after 1989 required a straightforward prescription. In his office at Columbia, he pulled out a piece of paper and drew an arrow on it.

'This is the diagram that I always thought about,' he explained. 'On this end you have state socialism. On the other end, you have free market. Sweden is somewhere in the middle with the United States a little farther toward free market. Poland started over here at state socialism. My point was, whether you want to end up here with the United States or with Sweden, you're going in the same direction and making the same changes ... The United States and Sweden both have convertible currencies, central banks, financial policy. Poland had none of those things in 1989. You want to debate the fine points? I don't think so. I think you want to make these changes.'

For Sachs and other economists, the transition was unidirectional and began from, essentially, a clean slate.[18] They paid little attention to what had come before – either the previous efforts to introduce capitalism lite by government reformers like Wilczek or the residual impact of the structures of state planning.[19] In Poland, the government had actually invested a lot in studying capitalism, putting together a committee of experts in the 1980s to look at different economic models for the country. 'We wanted to look at an economy that was capitalist in form but with very broad social welfare institutions that would still take care of all the values cherished by the socialist system,' the head of this group, economist Marcin Święcicki, told me. The prescriptions of Jeffrey Sachs resembled economic reform plans the communist government itself had proposed.[20] As with the round table negotiations, intellectuals on both sides of the Cold War divide were converging.

But not everyone agreed with the image of eastern Europe proceeding along a single track. Economist Tadeusz Kowalik, for instance, believed that Poland had other choices in 1989. The 'overnight capitalism' model created results very different from the egalitarian economic systems of Scandinavia. 'Naturally, Sachs did not realize that there was a glaring contradiction between the prospect of the Swedish system of negotiation and his proposals of the big jump to the market, which meant that a considerable portion of incomes would be shifted from the poor to the rich, that there would suddenly be high unemployment and poverty,' Kowalik concluded in his book *From Solidarity to Sellout*.[21] There were, in other words, economic development paths that not only didn't pass through Sweden but, worse, made it impossible to ever end up in Scandinavia.

Poland nevertheless became the model for 'shock therapy' when finance minister Leszek Balcerowicz turned Jeffrey Sachs's proposals into a full-blown plan in December 1989.[22] Poles expected their situation to change rapidly – and rapid is what they got. Inflation fell dramatically, from around 80 percent in January 1990 to about 24 percent in February 1990 and then to only around 5 percent in March.[23] The government's finances moved from deficit to surplus. The international financial system gave Poland a qualified thumbs-up. Jeffrey Sachs defends his legacy in Poland by saying that you can't argue with success. 'By any standard, Poland did extremely well in the transformation,' he told me. 'It ended up growing rapidly. The economy expanded, foreign investment came in. Compared to the other countries in the region, it soared in terms of new business, exports, and investment. Especially compared to the dire forecasts of 1989, you don't get better than that.' For Jeffrey Sachs and other transitologists, 'shock therapy' was a response to crisis, not a generator of one.[24]

Yet the Balcerowicz plan also had negative effects that exceeded virtually everybody's expectations. 'Had I known that unemployment would rise to 19%, I would have thought hard over the decisions on economic transformation,' then prime minister Tadeusz Mazowiecki said in 2000.[25] A huge number of Polish firms went belly up. Jeffrey Sachs concedes that 'those companies that couldn't make it employed a lot of people, especially older people who had grown up in a given context, which included living in places with a factory that wasn't going to survive. In the end, they got transfers of some sort. But a lot of unemployment for these older people persisted for ten to fifteen years.' With unemployment surging and industrial output cratering, Poland's national income fell by 11 percent in that first year and 18 percent the next.[26]

It wasn't only unemployment. Homelessness became a serious issue, growing steadily in the 1990s until it has reached at least 100,000 people and possibly as many as half a million today.[27] The birthrate plummeted, from around 2.08 in 1989 to 1.33 in 2014.[28] Yet the birthrate among Poles in the UK in 2011 was 2.13.[29] 'That's an indication of how secure you feel,' anthropologist Dorota Szawarska told me. 'If you feel under threat, you don't have children.' Meanwhile, Poland began to look less and less like egalitarian Scandinavia. Inequality indeed increased dramatically as the GINI index surged from 26.9 in 1989 to 32.7 in 1996 and all the way up to 35.9 in 2006.[30] In one year, from 2006 to 2007, the richest 100 Poles increased their wealth from 18.5 percent of the national total to an astonishing 53.7 percent.[31]

Mariusz Ambroziak, the Ursus tractor factory worker who became a Solidarity activist, looks back on that time as a series of missed opportunities. 'There should have been a determination of which parts of the Polish economy could have been preserved and which ones subjected to total competition,' he told me. 'Poland had several sectors of the economy with potential, which could have been nurtured and, over the years, transformed into competitive sectors, not just in Poland but in Europe and in the world.' But Jeffrey Sachs and his colleague David Lipton disagreed. 'Winners and losers cannot be selected a priori from among Poland's 7,800 industrial enterprises in the state sector,' they wrote in *Foreign Affairs* in 1990.[32] Perhaps this was true for Poland, but countries like South Korea had successfully closed the gap with the West with just this kind of industrial policy.

Another lost opportunity, this time by the West, was the failure to help revive the Soviet economy under Mikhail Gorbachev so that it could absorb products from factories that otherwise would have to close throughout eastern Europe. The collapse of the Soviet trade bloc and the end of Soviet-subsidized energy had a devastating impact on the marketizing economies of the region. A plan by Czech foreign minister Jiří Dienstbier would have provided several billion dollars to pump new life into the old Eastern bloc trade network. It never received any support from Washington, which was skeptical of any proposal that didn't rely exclusively on the unregulated market.[33]

What Poland did get, unlike other countries in the region, was debt relief – half of Poland's debt of $45 billion was forgiven. After shepherding through this relief package for Poland, Jeffrey Sachs argued that 'the West should be preparing similar packages of lending and debt-service relief for other East European countries.'[34] He tried to persuade the Hungarian government to lobby for something similar. But the new leaders in Budapest mistakenly believed that such a restructuring would harm the country's credit rating, and the West considered Poland the exception not the rule. When Bulgaria declared a moratorium because it couldn't pay its debt, it was unceremoniously cut off from capital markets.[35]

In the end, however, neither Poland nor any of the other countries in the region received large assistance packages comparable to what the United States provided Europe through the Marshall Plan. 'As early as May 1990, the United States had ruled out a modern-day Marshall Plan for reviving the economies of the former Communist bloc,' writes scholar Janine Wedel.[36] The West was not interested in providing a safety net during the transition or cushioning the pain of 'shock therapy.' A Marshall Plan would have simply drawn out a process best accomplished quickly, or so the thinking went at the time. It was also a philosophical issue. The original Marshall Plan required all recipients to work together as part of economic recovery, which thus laid the groundwork for later integration. By the late 1980s, the United States was more focused on competition than cooperation and on private initiative than public assistance.[37] Foreign direct investment and a fresh round of borrowing brought in capital from outside, but made the countries dependent on financial institutions and often fickle corporations.[38] In the end, as economist Anders Åslund points out, 'Western governments received more in debt service on old communist loans than they gave in both loans and grants to the postcommunist countries in the crucial period from 1993 to 1996.'[39] The Marshall Plan was proof that the West had learned the lessons of World War I, that throwing part of Europe into more debt sowed the seeds of later conflict. The refusal to consider a Marshall Plan after 1989 in favor of a repeat of the ruinous policies of 1918 is a testament to the failure of institutional memory and the victory of theory (or greed) over demonstrable practice.[40]

It's instructive to compare the eastern European experience with China, which hadn't borrowed from the West in the 1970s and therefore didn't have to struggle with any significant debt as it began to experiment with market reforms. China, writes sociologist Ho-fung Hung, 'could maintain its autonomy vis a vis the United States and experiment with market reform gradually rather than undergo the shock therapy that the World Bank and IMF applied to most of their debtors amid the debt crisis.'[41] Indeed, in the 1990s, the country represented the counter-example to eastern Europe. China didn't try to become a capitalist country overnight. It didn't throw millions into unemployment. The state continued to pick economic winners, such as the sustainable energy sector. And China enjoyed double-digit economic growth for much of the 1990s and 2000s. However, bowing to the forces of economic globalization, China also restructured its state-owned enterprises in the 1990s, stripping out many of the social benefits for workers, and engaged in the same kind of 'insider privatization' as eastern Europe, which created a new economic elite.[42] Even if eastern Europe was not likely to follow the model of an Asian communist country after having just thrown off the yoke of European communism, it might have considered other Asian options, such as Japan and South Korea, where the state played a more important role in helping close the gap with the West.

If Eurocentrism demanded a model closer to home, Spain could have served. In Poland, Adam Michnik famously discussed the political path that Spain took as it peacefully exited the fascism of the Franco years and became a democracy.[43] Hungarian politicians also referred to the Moncloa Pact, the Spanish agreement on economic transition between the different political parties and the trade unions, as an exemplar of compromise.[44] But few bothered to look at how Spain managed the transition from a state-run economy to the market. 'During the 1980s and early 1990s, it drastically reduced its state sector and opened up the economy as part of its integration into the broader European economy,' the World Bank observed. 'Spain protected real wage levels and underwent large labor shedding. As a consequence, it experienced double-digit unemployment for almost two decades. At its peak, unemployment reached 20 percent. Surprisingly, poverty and total income inequality declined.'[45] The Spanish economy suffered inevitable shocks, but the government made sure to provide a strong safety net for it citizens.

Another example of the 'one-way track' mindset was the disparagement of 'third ways' between capitalism and communism. As Adam Michnik put it, 'The third way leads directly to the Third World.'[46] Nevertheless, there were quite a few voices in 1989/90 that wanted to find some way to avoid the ills of both communism and capitalism. 'We have to find somehow a third way,' Hungarian environmental minister Zoltán Illés told me in 1990, since both capitalism and communism had done such a poor job of preserving the planet. There were also some calls for worker self-management, what Czech dissident Václav Havel called 'the genuine [i.e. informal] participation of workers in economic decision-making, leading to a feeling of genuine responsibility for their collective work.'[47] Self-management, or *samorząd*, 'struck a powerful chord in Polish society where it was the Solidarity battle cry in 1981,' Polish journalist Konstanty Gebert told me in 1990. 'This is gone, dead, disappeared completely.' He meant that self-management was dead as a policy option even though it remained popular outside the government. According to a general survey of Poles in 1990, 61.8 percent of respondents favored worker self-management, 66.9 percent backed a full employment policy, and 65.9 percent wanted to retain state control of prices.[48] Such numbers were not unusual in the region at the time. In Czechoslovakia in the immediate aftermath of the changes, for instance, only 3 percent of respondents preferred capitalism over socialism or a mixed economy (November 1989), an overwhelming majority opposed privatization (December 1989), and a slim majority favored gradual rather than rapid economic transformation (January 1990).[49] To swing people away from these preferences, a different radiant future had to be constructed.

Despite popular skepticism about overnight capitalism, the Polish model became the gold standard in the region. Even in Bulgaria, where the renamed Communist Party won the first democratic elections in June 1990, a version of shock therapy prevailed. Here, too, the government appealed to outside experts to draw up a blueprint for the transition. Instead of asking someone with a social democratic pedigree like Jeffrey Sachs, however, the Bulgarian government opted for the US Chamber of Commerce, which assembled a team that included Ronald Utt (later of the conservative Heritage Foundation) and Charles Murray, the author of several conservative books on social policy.[50] 'In general, they suggested quick privatization and no role for the state to play in the economy,' economist Rossitsa Chobanova told me. Bulgarian economists 'proposed measures for transforming a command economy into a market economy that respected specific Bulgarian characteristics,' she added, 'such as allowing a variety of forms of ownership dominated by private ones, and the need to renovate in order to be competitive in a globalized world.' The effect on the Bulgarian economy in terms of declining output and unemployment was comparable to what happened in Poland.

Consider what happened to Bulgaria's IT sector. For all its defects, the Bulgarian communist regime had at least invested considerable sums in research and development. Debuting in 1980, the Bulgarian-made Pravetz desktop became a popular Apple clone for an entire generation of computer enthusiasts. At one point, Bulgaria supplied 40 percent of all the computers used in the Soviet bloc, and the IT sector represented 14 percent of the country's GDP between 1985 and 1990.[51] But when the state followed the prescriptions of the outside experts and withdrew from the economy, the Bulgarian IT sector couldn't survive the collapse of the regional market.

Then a strange thing happened. Bulgaria became the center of a new outbreak of computer viruses. 'The production of viruses happened when this sector, employing mainly young people, was sharply affected by the loss of the COMECON market,' Rossitsa told me. The new viruses produced by these disgruntled, unemployed computer nerds spread rapidly around the world. One Bulgarian virus forced all infected computers to play 'Yankee Doodle Dandy' every Friday afternoon. 'Not only do Bulgarians make the most [viruses], they make the best,' one computer specialist said.[52]

The story had a 'happy' end. When the big foreign companies in the sector figured out who created those viruses, they invited the 'inventors' to work for them. 'After that, most of these computer specialists are now working abroad, and are no longer producing viruses,' Rossitsa concluded.

Compared to Poland or Bulgaria, Slovenia adopted a slower pace of transition, and preserved more of a role for the government in the economy. This gradualist approach was marked by a concern that rapid change would destabilize the economy and throw large segments of the population into unemployment and penury. Since many firms still operated under the old Yugoslav self-management system, the workers in some of these enterprises became part-owners. Also, the state didn't immediately privatize banks, insurance companies, and other major elements of the financial infrastructure. And Slovenia initially went with a flexible exchange rate – rather than a fixed exchange rate – in part to ensure that Slovenian exports remained competitive.

There is considerable controversy over whether the gradualist approach was the better strategy. Slovenia 'has achieved one of the highest and least volatile growth rates among the current group of countries in line for EU membership,' the World Bank concluded in a 2004 report.

'Moreover, after the initial stabilization, its stable and reasonably high growth rate was achieved without any major macroeconomic imbalances during the 1990s, and much the same can be said regarding social and political developments.'[53] By 2007, Slovenia's GDP per capita had reached 90 percent of the EU average. A member of the Eurozone, Slovenia was dragged into recession in 2012 by the financial crisis, but it subsequently rebounded and continues to deliver a higher standard of living than Portugal or Greece.

To use a baseball metaphor, however, Slovenia was starting off the transition on second base. 'Slovenia was already a very sophisticated economy before 1990, and it remained so afterwards,' Jeffrey Sachs pointed out. 'Its links to Austria and to Europe are quite important. Geography matters so much.' And indeed, the same World Bank report notes that 'gradualism seems to be a viable alternative only for relatively well-off economies and may not be an option for many other transition economies.'

Moreover, even with its gradualist approach, Slovenia pursued rather conventional economic reforms. Jože Mencinger, an economist and architect of Slovenia's transition, was frustrated that the government ignored his more unorthodox suggestions. When it came to privatization, he told me, 'I preferred that we count on insiders – managers and workers – but most politicians didn't much appreciate this approach. They said we should forget about self-management and the idea of social property, which I nonetheless believe is a just arrangement in society.'

In their efforts to offload their assets, the governments in eastern Europe were so in thrall to the theory of privatization – or the prospects of their own enrichment – that they failed to anticipate the enormous anger their policies would generate.

Property

Soviet bloc countries all invested enormous resources in creating factories, mines, and farms owned and run by the state. The successor states viewed these resources as the family jewels that could be sold at a pinch – and in 1990 all the countries in the region were pinched – to start a new life in a new world. Absent a new Marshall Plan, privatization was a one-time-only bridge loan until the newly democratic countries could join the European Union and access other resources. It was also an enormous undertaking. Privatization in the UK under Margaret Thatcher amounted to a few dozen firms. By contrast, the Czech Republic alone privatized 23,000 small enterprises by auction and 1,650 large enterprises through its voucher system.[54]

Since these were also public enterprises, citizens expected to benefit from the sale as well. When I talked with widely respected dissident Wolfgang Ullmann in 1990, he struggled to articulate an economic vision that corresponded to his understanding of participatory democracy and an engaged civil society. He pulled down a book from his shelf, *Mainstreet Capitalism*, and spoke speculatively of an East Germany where everyone owned shares in the country's enterprises.[55]

This vision of universal stock ownership enjoyed a brief popularity in the region, particularly in Czechoslovakia, which debuted its voucher privatization in 1992. Many economists hailed the program, which included a second wave in 1994 in the Czech Republic, as enormously successful in transferring 80 percent of Czech assets from the state to private hands within five years. 'Its success may very well become a model for all of Eastern Europe,' concluded two economists in 1995.[56]

It did become a model, but not always for the best reasons. The Czech voucher privatization program introduced by Czech prime minister Václav Klaus became synonymous in many circles with outrageous corruption. Czech citizens could use their vouchers to acquire shares in newly privatized companies – or they could deposit their vouchers with funds that would do the investing for them. One young man newly returned from the United States, Viktor Kožený, established the Harvard Capital and Consulting fund to buy up these vouchers and acquire the privatized firms. In a set of moves that earned him the sobriquet 'the pirate of Prague,' Kožený stripped the assets of the firms, declared the enterprises bankrupt, and 'tunneled' the money out of the country. Then, before he could be found out, Kožený skipped town. Despite an international warrant for his arrest, he continued to run scams – including a privatization swindle in Azerbaijan – and moved into a gated community in the Bahamas.[57]

Kožený was not the only buccaneer. 'As part of the privatization of the national property in the 1990s, there are now a lot of business people who are very rich guys,' Robert Basch of the Open Society Foundation Prague told me. 'Klaus's government privatized the Czech insurance company, which is still the largest one here, and it was privatized for almost nothing and in a very strange way.' The guy who bought it, Robert estimated, was worth about a billion dollars. Given such pilfering, it's no surprise that, one decade later, three-quarters of Czechs were unhappy with the results of privatization.[58] Czechs not only lost money directly, write economists Andrew Weiss and Georgiy Nikitin, but also began to associate free market capitalism 'with tolerance for embezzlement and fraud.'[59] Czechoslovakia started the process of transition with an enviable record – virtually no debt and some very valuable state properties. But Václav Klaus, who was in charge of the economic reforms, was more interested in building up a loyal economic elite. 'That was the primary reason why he prevented the creation of a legal framework for privatization,' political scientist Jan Urban told me. 'It was a completely chaotic, often illegal process where the calculated losses are often mind-boggling.'

Corruption, however, was only one by-product of the process. Perhaps the most controversial aspect of privatization was the role that foreigners played. Instead of going to worker-owners or a mass of citizen shareholders, most firms simply went to the highest bidder, which often turned out to be an investor from overseas.

East Germany prided itself on its huge *kombinat*, which had made the country the most advanced industrial nation in the Soviet bloc. After reunification, however, the new German agency responsible for privatization – the Treuhandanstalt (or Treuhand, for short) – ended up having great difficulty finding buyers for most of the enterprises. So, the Treuhand cut its prices. 'East German enterprises were very often sold way below the market price,' economist Rüdiger Frank told me. 'Enterprises were sold to Western competitors who just wanted to make sure that there was no new competition coming up against them. They pretended to be investors, but all they wanted to do was prevent others from taking over that company and producing a competitive product.' Take the case of the Narva lightbulb company. 'Treuhand closed down an enormous factory that had, to that point, successfully produced and sold bulbs for eighty years,' journalist Rüdiger Rossig told me. 'Narva was basically crushed by its West German competitors.' Labor activist Renate Hürtgen provided another such example – a potash mine in the region of Thuringia. 'There was no reason to close it except that the West German potash industry wanted to get rid of a competitor,' she told me. 'They wanted to keep the monopoly.' In 1993, forty miners at the Thomas Munzer mine in Bischofferode went on a hunger strike to protest against the West German conglomerate BASF's decision to close the facility, but to no avail.[60] Today, the only people working in the potash mines in Thuringia are tour guides for groups of curious travelers.[61]

Treuhand engaged in reverse alchemy, turning gold into lead. As a result of the factory closures and workplace reductions, the privatized companies employed only 23 percent of the original number of workers in the enterprises taken over by the Treuhand.[62] Germany was supposed to make money from the sale of these GDR firms, but because of the fire-sale prices, the paying off of debts, and other costs, the Treuhand was left with a *debt* of more than 300 billion Deutschmarks (around $200 billion in 1995 terms).[63]

The sale of firms to foreign buyers fed perceptions that privatization was destroying the very foundation of the new capitalist economies. Economist Tamás Hegedűs estimated that the Hungarian government probably obtained only about 30–40 percent of the value of the firms it sold. 'There were also many times when foreign industries bought up Hungarian companies to close them down and take over their markets,' he told me. 'The most prominent example was that, out of the six sugar companies in Hungary, only one remains, and we are now importing sugar from other countries. According to the ideology at the time, the production of these companies was not necessary. Even the buildings were destroyed. And now we're buying sugar at twice the price that we had produced it earlier.'[64]

As in other countries, Hungarians are now second-guessing some of the privatizations that took place in the 1990s. 'We did have companies that could have survived in the competitive world of international business, like the steelworks on Csepel Island,' union activist Peter Fiedler told me. 'It was a one-time opportunity, and I don't doubt that many international businessmen with what seemed to us unlimited power and money came here and said, "Okay, I'll buy, name the price." Our politicians were probably naive.'

Thanks to Solidarity, privatization proceeded somewhat differently in Poland. For instance, the World Bank sent in a team in the early 1990s to help with the selling off of the cement sector. Aside from the Soviet Union itself, Poland was the largest producer of cement in the region. The new government in 1990 had to decide what to do with the fifteen or so state-owned factories, and on the World Bank's advice closed several and privatized the remaining ones. It was not an easy task to find buyers, and by law the trade unions had to be part of the process. By preventing the former political elite from grabbing choice assets as they did so blatantly in Russia, writes David Ost, Polish unions were the only ones in the region 'to have had an important influence on the privatization process.'[65]

Union participation made a difference. At the enterprise level, the unions presented a list of demands to the potential buyer. 'In some of the factories the workers wanted things like a coal subsidy or the preservation of the kindergarten,' World Bank team member Seung-Hee Nah told me. 'Some investors guaranteed these for eighteen months. In some cases, they offered even more because they'd look at the demands and realize that it wasn't going to cost that much money and by agreeing to it they would gain a lot more goodwill from the workers. In one case the trade union submitted a list of demands that had forty-five items and went on for three pages. It even included things like: make sure the soccer stadium will continue to be there, make sure that the brass band team will get the budget for travel to the national competition, and so on. To outsiders this would seem trivial, and people quite often would start laughing. I don't think it was trivial for the union. For the workers, this was an important part of their lives.' Meanwhile at the government level, Polish trade unions forced the government to make several concessions such as worker representation on the supervisory councils of enterprises.[66] Elsewhere in the region, by contrast, workers were largely powerless to affect the process.

Seung-Hee went on to work with the World Bank in other countries, including China. She's proud of the work she did in Poland. But she wonders whether the Polish government could have handled the process differently. 'The one thing that keeps coming back to me was the question of whether it might've been better for the government to come up with some big plan to keep the factories alive, say for two years, and do a massive training of the government officials, the factory managers, and the trade union representatives about building a future for the factory,' she concluded, even as she acknowledged that the government didn't have the resources for such an ambitious plan.

Slovenia, meanwhile, decided initially not to sell off the crown jewels. 'All the other countries did the opposite: Hungarians, Czechs, they sold their companies, they sold everything,' diplomat Vojko Volk told me. 'We didn't do that. And it went well for us for fifteen years. It was swell even after we entered the European Union. From 2004 to 2008, we had an average growth of more than four percent every year, and sometimes more than five percent. We achieved, can you imagine, ninety-two percent of the GDP average inside the European Union! It was the record for ex-communist states.'

But when the economy turned sour for Slovenia in the wake of the financial crisis of 2008/09, the state was left holding rapidly depreciating assets. 'We missed the chance to sell our telecom company, which is now practically one hundred percent state-owned, and it's bringing us nothing but problems,' Vojko lamented. 'There is always a best time to sell, and we missed it.'

The experience of large-scale unemployment, widening gaps between the rich and poor, and all the negative side effects of privatization helped undermine public faith in the unfettered free market. It also affected perceptions of the West.

The utopia of the West

My interpreter in Bulgaria, Vihra Gancheva, grew up under communism. She was not a dissident. Nor had she been attracted to the Communist Party. 'For me, it was never an option because I hated the meetings,' she told me over lunch in Plovdiv after that day's interviews. 'I'm not a fighter. I was just bored. For me, communism was something to be endured.'

Vihra learned to speak fluent English and, after the changes in 1989, landed a corporate job. She dreamed of Bulgaria becoming completely Westernized. It was a dream that died hard. 'Twenty years ago, I was a victim of Western influence,' she told me. 'I loved everything Western and hated everything Bulgarian. I was so ashamed at how Bulgarians worked and even attitudes toward hygiene … But back then I wanted to embrace everything Western. And now I realize that this shouldn't have happened because we have our own way.'

Millions of eastern Europeans were so entranced by the West that they went there as soon as they had a chance. Many settled there and were happy. Others, like Miroslav Durmov and Vihar Krastev, were somewhat disenchanted by what they found. Those who stayed behind worked to join the West en masse, through integration into the European Union.

The first country to join the EU was the GDR – though it didn't have to go through the normal accession process. As soon as German reunification took place in October 1990, the citizens of the former GDR found themselves in a united Europe as well as a united Germany. Everything changed overnight. They could suddenly travel and work anywhere in the European Community. Prior to this double leap, East Germans may have idealized the West. But in the early days after the fall of the Wall, they weren't necessarily thinking of joining a united Germany, much less the European Community. In mid-December 1989, polls indicated only 16 percent support for reunification.[67]

Whatever their initial hesitations about reunification, East Germans were clear about one thing: bananas. In the monetary union of July 1990, East Germans could trade their marks for West German ones at a one-to-one rate (up to 4,000 marks). What people had saved in the bank and in their pension plans could also be transferred to the West German currency on a similar basis. To be able to buy – to be able to afford – a luxury item like bananas for the first time was an enormous thrill.

'If I had to come up with a symbol of German unification, or of our East German revolution, it would be a yellow banana on a white flag,' economist Rüdiger Frank told me. 'The banana symbolically stands for tropical fruits, traveling around the world, and basically, consumerism. And that's what I'd say eighty percent of the people in East Germany wanted. The other twenty percent, or maybe even less, primarily wanted freedom. Of course, those eighty percent also wouldn't have minded having political freedom. Who wouldn't? But it's nothing that they would really have risked too much for – away from their TVs and cozy lives, which most of them had.'

But reunification – and membership of the European Union – also meant tremendous economic dislocation for former East Germans. Factories closed down, and the unemployment rate in the east between 1995 and 2002 went up to 18 percent, twice that of the western part of the country.[68] Those who continued to work earned wages that were roughly half the West German average (rising to 75 percent fifteen years later).[69] With the fall in industrial production in particular, economic output dropped by nearly half between 1989 and 1991,[70] and by 2000, over four million people had relocated to the west.[71]

Helmut Kohl, the West German chancellor, had promised to underwrite the costs of reunification, though he estimated at the outset that no new taxes would be needed to finance the process. He had to break that promise in 1991 with a 'solidarity' tax surcharge.[72] Ultimately the equivalent of more than two trillion euros flowed from west to east.[73] But much of this money did not go into the pockets of those living in eastern Germany.

'It was used for infrastructure projects, for building up an efficient administration, for the social security network, for investment,' economist Rüdiger Frank explained to me. 'Now, who benefitted from all that investment? It was West German companies who expanded to the east. So that was a subsidy to West German industry. Infrastructure projects, highways, roads, telecommunication networks, who did that? West German companies, because all the East German construction companies were either bankrupt or bought up by West German competitors. It was another subsidy to West German industry.'[74]

Even the transfer payments for social programs in the east were ultimately a huge boon for West German business. 'If you give money to people who are poor, they have a tendency to spend almost all of it,' Rüdiger added. 'And what do they spend it on? On products that they can buy in shops.

And if you went to a supermarket – a West German chain, of course – in the early 1990s in East Germany, you would have had great difficulties finding East German products. Nobody wanted to have East German products.'

So, everything that seemed to privilege East Germany over the rest of eastern Europe – valuable enterprises, a generous West German government, West German parties leading the way to democracy – could not entirely smooth the way into Europe. And what many had assumed would be temporary dislocation proved quite durable. Although wages had narrowed considerably by 2013, overall household income in the eastern Länder was still only 70 percent of that in the western Länder.[75] As of 2014, the unemployment rate in the east remained nearly double that of the west and, even more tellingly, net household assets in the east had still not reached half those of the west.[76]

Eastern German dissatisfaction with this enduring divide can be measured in a number of ways. The former Communist Party remains popular in the east, where Die Linke (The Left) captured nearly one quarter of the votes in the federal elections in 2013 and obtained more than 10 percent of the seats in parliament. A wave of *Ostalgie* – nostalgia for the old East Germany – has led many to take another look at what disappeared after 1989. Some East Germans tried to become uber-Westerners, Hans Misselwitz, a former East German pastor and dissident who works for the Social Democratic Party, told me. 'But this also brought out a certain kind of resistance, making us want to defend the past, or be proud of the past. People here identified with the music or the culture of their youth.' But this tendency to embrace the past also had its less tolerant aspect. Anti-immigrant and Euroskeptical movements – both PEGIDA (Patriotic Europeans Against the Islamicization of the West) and the far-right-wing Alternative für Deutschland – surged in the lands of the former GDR.

If East Germany, which enjoyed so many more advantages than its eastern neighbors, faced difficulties catching up, the challenge has been that much more daunting for the rest of eastern Europe. Membership in the EU for these other countries didn't come until 2004 (for Poland, Hungary, the Czech Republic, and Slovenia), 2007 (for Romania, Bulgaria, and Slovakia), and 2013 (for Croatia). But ambivalence with the EU began to set in even before accession. According to a Eurobarometer poll from 1995, only a minority of the populations in Hungary (32 percent), the Czech Republic (34 percent), and Poland (42 percent) viewed the EU positively.[77] Sentiment in favor of accession in Poland continued to fall from 1994 to 2002, as Poles worried about the potential loss of jobs and the further deterioration of the agricultural sector.[78] The far right was worried about an erosion of 'national values,' and conservative Church movements like Radio Marija talked about 'the spread of abortion, euthanasia and homosexuality.'[79]

With membership, of course, came benefits: access to 175 billion euros' worth of Regional Development Fund, Cohesion Fund, and Social Fund grants between 2007 and

2013.[80] Led by Poland and the Czech Republic, beneficiaries signed contracts amounting to 87 percent of this total.[81] As these funds flowed into infrastructure development, signs with the EU logo began to pop up along highways and in front of refurbished buildings throughout eastern Europe. Social programs expanded as a result of EU largesse. Students could participate in EU-wide student exchanges like the Erasmus program. Farmers could apply for subsidies under the Common Agricultural Policy. Workers relocating within the EU benefitted from equal treatment clauses. Name a constituency and the EU was likely targeting funds in its direction.

And still, East Europeans were not happy. According to an October 2015 poll, 62 percent of Czechs would vote against staying in the EU if given a choice in a referendum.[82] This in a country where 'With Us to Europe' was the slogan of the victorious Civic Forum in 1990. Of course, the timing of the survey is critical. Europe was slowly emerging from a global financial crisis that, with the exception of Poland, exacted a heavy price from the EU's newest members. But even if Euroskepticism grew as economies tanked, it remained and even intensified when economic growth returned. In Hungary, for instance, barely a third of the population considered membership in the EU to be a good thing in 2013, when the Hungarian economy was again registering positive growth.[83] Even in Poland, where the EU remains consistently popular, the level of support declined from 83 percent in the mid-2000s to 72 percent in 2016.[84]

Part of the reason for their disenchantment was that the EU represented not just carrots, but sticks as well. According to the terms of the EU's Stability and Growth Pact, for instance, member states are not supposed to post budget deficits that exceed 3 percent of GDP or maintain public debt higher than 60 percent of GDP. The obligations of Eurozone members – the countries that use the euro as their currency – are even stricter. Consider the case of Slovenia, whose economic performance placed it at the top of the class for so many years. The financial crisis that began in 2008 threw the Slovenian economy into reverse. The government, which practically went into default over its debt, imposed heavy austerity and was forced to begin privatizing its remaining state-held properties to meet EU requirements. Already the government had come under criticism for retaining ownership of the national telecom provider, the country's second-largest bank, Adria Airways, and Mercator, a supermarket chain that was also the country's biggest employer. The financial crisis provided Brussels with the leverage to force the Slovenian government to sell off its shares in these enterprises, and at a significantly lower price than if they were up for sale at a less desperate time.[85]

Not surprisingly, the favorability rating of the EU leadership plummeted in Slovenia from 52 percent to 38 percent from 2010 to 2013.[86] The following year, only 16 percent of Slovenians reported that they were better off in the last five years as a result of EU membership, compared to

47 percent who declared that they were worse off.[87] It didn't mean that they wanted to withdraw their membership (only 23 percent chose that option in the poll). But it did explain why the EU no longer represented a utopian option – even in Slovenia, which had hitherto appeared to hold a winning ticket in the transition sweepstakes.

Rising Euroskepticism has had direct political consequences. Euroskeptical governments took over in Hungary in 2010 and Poland in 2015. In the Czech Republic, where satisfaction with the EU dropped to a mere 25 percent in 2016, politicians compete to be the most anti-Brussels.[88] As economic growth returns, anger over austerity has largely given way to anger over the migration question.[89] But it boils down to roughly the same thing: a feeling that national governments no longer control what counts, whether it's budgets or borders, and Brussels is at fault.

Many eastern Europeans believe that the borderless playing field created by economic globalization tilts in favor of the more powerful players. Consumers in eastern Europe complain about the quality of food imports from the West: the same products eaten in western Europe are made with cheaper and less healthy ingredients in the east.[90] Intellectuals are upset over the market saturation of Hollywood films, American music, Western media conglomerates. The influx of English has raised concerns about language purity.[91] 'The world is moving in the direction of cultural uniformity,' Hungarian writer Katalin Mezey complained to me. 'People talk of multiculturalism, but the reality is that the world is moving toward uniformity – the Hollywoodization of culture.' What had once represented a utopian future – unification in Germany, integration into the European Union, membership in an idealized West – has lost some of its shimmer.

Much of the reason lies with the divergent effects of economic change. But there's a political dimension as well.

Disappointments with democracy

It was hard to gauge the popularity of democracy among eastern Europeans prior to 1989. Solidarity was focused largely on pocketbook issues and creating an independent trade union movement. Activists in Hungary and Bulgaria were organizing around environmental issues. Considerable anger in the GDR and Romania focused on the activities of the secret police. Real democracy, which would have challenged the Communist Party's monopoly on power, was a bridge too far for most dissidents.

Yet in 1989, enthusiasm for democracy, at least as a tool for regime change, was palpable. Polish voters went to the polls to participate in the partially free elections on 4 June 1989 in numbers far greater than the communist government anticipated. Over 96 percent of eligible voters cast their ballots in the first democratic elections in Czechoslovakia in 1990.[92] Meanwhile, over 90 percent voted in the first Bulgarian democratic election in 1990,[93] nearly 85 percent voted in Croatia that year,[94] and nearly 80 percent came out for the first Romanian elections.[95]

This enthusiasm for democracy, however, was quite shallow. As a 1991 *Times Mirror* survey discovered, 'The vast majority of Eastern Europeans approve of multi-party pluralism and like their new found personal freedoms. But with few exceptions, opinions of fledgling political institutions, political leaders and parliamentary bodies tends [sic] to be unfavorable.'[96] Eastern Europeans liked democracy in the abstract. They were less enthusiastic about the system in practice.

Part of the disillusionment stemmed from a suspicion that the elections were hollow exercises. The vote in Bulgaria reinstalled the former communists, and the winner of the Romanian election – the National Salvation Front – included many of the same old bureaucrats. In East Germany, where the turnout for the March 1990 elections was 93 percent,[97] the new parliamentarians were rendered nearly superfluous by the impending dissolution of the country (and its political institutions), and the major parties ignored a new East German constitution produced by a group of dissidents-turned-legislators.[98] 'We idealized the West,' former Charter 77 signatory Daniel Kumermann told me. 'Then we saw that this basic concept of democracy was idealized. It doesn't solve everything. It just puts in a different government every four years (or earlier if there are earlier elections). The people who are elected are very often corrupt and do it for their own interests and don't care about democracy.'

But there was also a deeper suspicion of politics in general. During the communist era, politics involved collaborating with the authorities. With the dimming of ideological allegiance to communism, that collaboration became more a matter of professional advancement. Politics, in other words, was opportunism. For very brief periods, such as the Prague Spring, politics would again come alive. 'Almost in a single moment, public life came into existence and many people, for the first time in their lives, began to view politics as the work of human beings instead of a tedious, infinitely boring, inaccessible and anonymous annoyance coming from somewhere on high,' wrote dissident Milan Šimečka of his experience of the Prague Spring.[99] As Soviet tanks and domestic repression extinguished these last reform projects, dissidents quite naturally developed an antipolitics, which oppositionist György Konrád formalized in his book of the same name.[100] 'In the 1970s the idea emerged that if you cannot change the system you should try to organize your life independently of the system,' philosopher and future politician Pavel Gantar told me in 2012. 'You should develop alternative forms of socialization that express your interests, and you shouldn't care about what happens around you in institutions. The idea of antipolitics of György Konrád had a great impact upon us.'

So, when the 1991 *Times Mirror* survey concluded that 'another indication of the fragile embrace of democracy in Eastern Europe is evidenced by the fact that majorities of the public in most of these nations said that they are losing interest in politics,' it failed to recognize that, except for a brief moment, the public had never really been interested in politics in the first place. The initial elections in 1990, a novelty, capitalized on the same regime-change sentiment that motivated the upheavals of the previous year. Politics, as a game of give-and-take, was a different matter. In former communist countries, 'compromise' and 'collaboration' had equally negative connotations.

A few years later, when democratic institutions were supposed to have matured, according to Ralf Dahrendorf's timeline, disappointment had merely intensified. By 1995, trust in parliament was in the 20 percent range in most countries in the region while trust in political parties was even lower.[101] Jump ahead another fifteen years and matters had still not improved. According to the Pew Global Attitudes Project's 2009 survey, for instance, Hungarian enthusiasm for the shift to multiparty democracy declined from 74 percent in 1991 to 56 percent.[102] 'There is an exhaustion with politics,' Pavel Gantar told me in 2012. 'There is a general non-confidence in politics. There is a general conviction that politics is something dirty, something you cannot rely on.'

Politics not only had the bad associations of the past to overcome. In the early years of transition, voters associated the institutions of democracy with economic austerity. Governments in the region had administered what everyone referred to as 'shock therapy' – no wonder that the populations had an almost Pavlovian recoil from these politicians. 'One had to be very stupid to believe that society would say, "This is fantastic! We lost our savings. We are four times poorer than we were before you came to power. We love you!"' journalist Jacek Żakowski, the spokesman for the Solidarity-affiliated parliamentary faction in Poland in 1990, told me in 2013. 'No, they had to hate us. And we had to pay this price. The revolution must eat its children, and this is universal.'

Anticipating a public backlash, the new governments pursued their own version of antipolitics as the new reformers pushed through a succession of economic programs. Václav Klaus, the proponent of fast-track market reforms in Czechoslovakia, was typical in his emphasis on the need for fast results: 'We did not want to give the opponents of transformation an opportunity to assemble wide political support.'[103] In this way, the new governments were drawing from a rich tradition that ranged from the theories of the French Physiocrats of the eighteenth century, who favored all-powerful rulers implementing an unencumbered market economy, to the practice of the Leninists of the twentieth century, who cared little for 'bourgeois politics.'[104]

Jeffrey Sachs, who understood that shock therapy had to be administered quickly before the adversely affected could mobilize political opposition, believed that a strong executive was essential to the process.[105] Lech Wałęsa styled himself as just such a strong executive, given his impatience with politics and his preference for decrees 'in the cause of democracy.'[106] Just as he came to perceive the agents of change, workers, as an obstacle to progress, Wałęsa began to identify the very mechanism of transition, democracy, as an impediment to the country's movement forward. The prioritizing of top-down economic reform over bottom-up democratic participation even received the imprimatur of political theorists, such as Claus Offe, who argued in 1996 that, to promote a market economy, 'democratic rights must be held back to allow for a healthy dose of original accumulation.'[107] By 'original accumulation,' he meant the efforts to consolidate capital by a range of economic actors from legitimate entrepreneurs and foreign investors to shady operators and unscrupulous government officials.

During the transition, the former dissidents were generally ill versed in economics and deferred to the experts. 'We the dissidents who were involved in the revolution had nothing to do with economics,' Václav Havel observed. Civil society activist Marta Šimečková agreed: 'Probably it was a mistake to give all our competence and all our political capital to the so-called experts, who were economists.' The workers ceded authority to the intellectuals, and the intellectuals concentrated that authority in the economists. Even after deferring to the experts, the workers could have mounted effective resistance, but they didn't. In Poland, for instance, Solidarity not only green-lighted the reforms but effectively bowed out of the political process. 'It would have changed history if at that time a formal agreement had been reached to the effect that we agreed to this policy, but we would meet after a few months to monitor it,' Solidarity advisor Krzysztof Hagemejer told me regretfully.

According to a Balkan proverb, 'It is permitted you in time of grave danger to walk with the devil until you have crossed the bridge.'[108] The reformers of the early 1990s allowed themselves to walk with their own undemocratic devils across the bridge of economic transformation until the grave danger of instability had passed. To cross the bridge, they accepted a large toll in the form of popular backlash. As austerity economics continued to bite, populations began to react to the stories of corruption – and the rumors of even greater corruption – associated with politicians and political institutions. The stories confirmed what voters had long suspected: politics was just another way of creating a wealthy elite.

In a healthy democracy, watchdog organizations keep tabs on politicians who attempt to grab power or covertly accumulate wealth. The antipolitics of the late Cold War period laid the foundation for a new layer of these watchdogs. In the early transition years, these NGOs could represent citizens when politicians wanted to close off policymaking from public scrutiny. 'Common people were simply interested in their everyday life,' the director of the Open Society office in Bratislava, Alena Pániková, told me. 'They wanted somebody to help them if they were threatened. They didn't want to be afraid of losing their jobs. They didn't want to worry about whether their kid could go to school. It was important to develop this NGO sector as an intermediary that could speak and act on behalf of diverse groups and individuals.' NGOs also served a break-in-case-of-emergency function. The sector proved invaluable in Slovakia when politics turned authoritarian under Vladimir

Mečiar in the 1990s and NGOs spearheaded the efforts to nonviolently push him out of office.

On the other hand, NGOs also frequently contributed to the downsizing of government by taking over services – dealing with the homeless, administering foreign assistance – that were previously the responsibility of elected officials or civil servants. This privatization of social welfare might improve services, reduce costs, and eliminate government bureaucracy. But as governments offload these functions to the NGO sector, they can no longer claim credit for these services. Not only does public enthusiasm for government go down but so does the willingness to give up a portion of wages to fund government activities. 'In neoliberal thinking, NGOs are seen as replacing many of the functions of the state,' Polish activist Michał Sutowski told me. 'NGOs should not take over the roles of the welfare state.' But when governments cut huge holes in the social safety net, it's hard to blame NGOs for rushing to the scene with their patch kits.

Civil society once enjoyed an unimpeachable reputation in the region – untainted by collaboration, courageous in its actions, trustworthy in its motives. But over the last twenty-five years, public disenchantment with NGOs has gone hand in hand with the general disappointments with democracy. Much of that has to do with the professionalization of civil society. What were once labors of love and conscience, staffed by volunteers, have become bureaucratic organizations staffed by a new cadre of professionals. NGO activist Mladen Jovanović told me that sometimes NGOs seem to him 'like the moon going around the earth. It looks like they don't participate in the life of ordinary people. It seems as if they are looking down from a great height on everything that is happening. There is very little communication between NGOs and citizens, so the projects are being developed around what NGOs or donors think should be done, and not around the true needs of communities.' With domestic resources scarce, NGOs in the region are forever scrambling to attract funds from outside sources, either foundations or foreign organizations or the European Union. This scramble has decreased both the flexibility and the independence of NGOs. 'This money from the EU corrupted us,' activist Zuzanna Dąbrowska told me.

Given the fragility of their funding, NGOs can't serve as a very effective safety net. Mihai Rosca works in the Romanian city of Cluj to deliver humanitarian services to the most vulnerable. When Romania joined the EU, many international organizations simply pulled out. 'Everyone thought that Romania would take over some of the projects. But the disaster was that this did not happen. One type of funding disappeared, and nothing else came to fill that gap,' he said with anger and sorrow. 'It's a pity for these NGOs, but the big disaster is for the beneficiaries. Many good projects have been interrupted, and no one has taken responsibility for the beneficiaries, such as people with disabilities or children in special-needs kindergartens where they've been helped to communicate, to socialize, to prepare for school. Too many projects have disappeared.' When these services disappear, public anger is directed at all the levels of politics: the EU, the Romanian government, and the NGOs themselves.

Eastern Europe is now experiencing an entirely new antipolitics. Voter participation has declined steadily. The public holds conventional politicians, particularly those at a national level, in contempt. Even the reputation of civil society is not what it once was. The utopia of democracy has been replaced by a desire for a strong leader who can 'get the job done.' Illiberal populists have come to the fore in nearly every country in the region by following one of the essential strategies of the communists that they excoriate at such great lengths: their rule 'must look democratic, but we must be in charge,' as East German communist leader Walter Ulbricht once said.[109]

This new antipolitics seeks answers to the problems of transition in the past and outside the city. 'In the end,' Ralf Dahrendorf warned about the viability of the liberal project, 'Arcadia is as great of a threat as Utopia and the planned state.'[110] So, now let's turn to Arcadia.

3
The Revenge of the Provinces

The spread in front of us was truly impressive. Like most traditional Serbian *kafanas*, this tavern in the Serbian city of Niš specialized in meat, and lots of it. We ate grilled rib meat and skewers of chicken livers wrapped in bacon. Roasted lamb and potatoes perfumed the air, and the accompanying salads provided splashes of color. We sat on the patio, enjoying the crisp October weather, with the wall of an Ottoman-era fortress on one side and a tennis club on the other. This *kafana* brewed its own brandy, and we sipped from little flagons of quince *rakia*. The patio was crowded with people, including the mayor of Niš, who was sitting several tables away conferring with his associates. The thwack of tennis balls provided a rhythmic soundtrack to the conversations.

As we ate and drank, my lunch companion, Mladen Jovanović, explained how I would never understand Serbian politics – the nationalist obsession with Kosovo, the suspicion of Eurocrats in Brussels – if I talked only to liberal intellectuals in Belgrade, nearly 150 miles away to the northwest. The capital was what most foreigners knew of Serbia. The journalistic shorthand of referring to a country by its capital – 'Belgrade and Washington are currently in talks' – reinforces this bias. Mladen, as the president of the National Coalition for Decentralization, was doing all that he could to counter this Belgrade-centrism.

A short and energetic man in his late thirties, Mladen had lived all his life in Niš, the country's third-largest city, and he proudly showed off his hometown to me. Niš is a thriving center of southern Serbia, with a population just shy of 190,000.[1] The enormous Ottoman-era fortress in the middle of town rested on the foundations of a Roman outpost. Inside this well-preserved structure were cafés, an art gallery in a former mosque, and a lapidarium of exquisite Roman fragments. Formerly called Naissus, where the Roman emperor Constantine was born, Niš lies at an historic crossroads. It was in Niš, during the second Crusade in 1189, that Serbian leader Stefan Nemanja had a celebrated meeting with Frederick Barbarossa. Stefan ate with a fork, according to a story dear to all Serbians, while Frederick ate with his hands. Thus did Serbia demonstrate how much more culturally advanced it was than the rest of Europe.

Niš continues to be a crossroads in the twenty-first century. It's a busy bus portal halfway between Belgrade and Skopje, and on the way from Sofia to Sarajevo. The downtown is full of cafés, which are in turn full of people. This gives Niš a festive air. The bustle can be deceptive. Many people have time to sit around drinking coffee because they don't have steady jobs, and café conversation is one of the few cultural activities available. With Belgrade the artistic center of the country, the provinces are starved of culture. For a ten-year period that ended only recently, Niš didn't even have a movie theater.

In Serbia, all roads lead to the capital. According to a study of the news media by Mladen's National Coalition for Decentralization, only *eighteen seconds* of the thirty-minute national TV news report are devoted to events outside of Belgrade. Blink and you could miss what's going on in Niš or Kragujevac or Pirot. The famous *New Yorker* cartoon by Saul Steinberg depicting how a Manhattanite looks at the world – in which Fifth Avenue looms large in the foreground and the rest of America dwindles into insignificance on the horizon – captures how the inhabitants of Belgrade view their world. Unlike New Yorkers, however, the inhabitants of Belgrade have actually set up their country to conform to this distorted perspective.

It was appropriate that Mladen and I were talking about the inordinate power of Belgrade in a *kafana*, for these pubs have come to symbolize the more traditional values of the Serbian countryside. Derived from the Turkish word for coffeehouse, the *kafana* during the communist years carried a connotation of peasant backwardness. But with the revival of Serbian nationalism in the late 1980s and 1990s, the *kafana* became a space of indigenous authenticity, and Serbian turbofolk songs frequently referenced them.[2] With the wars of the 1990s long over and Serbian nationalism on the ebb, the *kafana* has lost some of its louche reputation and now attracts a younger, more diverse audience.[3]

The cafés and *kafanas* of Niš are not enough, however, to keep people from emigrating. The capital city, after all, has plenty of great places to get coffee, beer, and food, as well as the employment opportunities that Niš lacks. Once an industrial powerhouse in the communist era, Niš has been comparatively fortunate since it's one of the few places in Serbia outside Belgrade to have any economic growth at all.[4] Yet people were still leaving in large numbers – as part of a longer-term trend that was emptying out the Serbian provinces. The Pirot district near Niš dropped from 150,000 people after the World War II to only 60,000 today. 'In the most extreme cases, if this trend continues, twenty out of 175 municipalities will disappear by 2020,' Mladen told me. Serbia has calculated that its population will possibly drop by as many as a million people between 2011 and 2041, with Niš alone losing about 15 percent of its population.[5]

It's a dynamic reproduced throughout eastern Europe. In the most extreme cases, the countryside is now a place only for the very old. Maya Mircheva, a young woman who was working at the Open Society Foundation office in Sofia when we talked in 2012, described how, in the 1990s, her grandmother's village in the Bulgarian countryside had shrunk in size and capacity, as if itself entering dotage. 'There was a local cinema, a library, and now everything is closed down,' Maya told me. 'In the village, it's eighty-nine percent old people, more than ninety percent Turkish. All the young people, like my mother, migrated to the cities. When I was younger, when I went to my grandmother's village, I could go to the library and borrow some books. I can no longer do any of that when I go there now. It's just a dead place.' From 1946 to 1993, the share of the Bulgarian population living in the countryside dropped from 75 percent to 31 percent.[6] By 2012, twenty-four Bulgarian towns had simply disappeared.[7]

Throughout the region, in contrast to the famous Yeats poem, the center indeed holds, and perhaps holds too much. Budapest, for instance, dominates Hungary. It is home to 20 percent of the Hungarian population, attracts the lion's share of foreign direct investment, and serves as a transportation hub. 'The second-biggest city is Debrecen with 200,000 or 250,000 people,' trade unionist Peter Fiedler told me. 'Besides Budapest there is rural Hungary.' The Czech Republic is similarly centralized around Prague, which overshadows its nearest urban competitor, Brno. 'Prague is first, then nothing for a while, then Bohemia, and after that Moravia,' former dissident Milan Horáček told me. 'This has a big influence on the development of the society. If you go outside of Prague, you notice that everything is still quite postcommunist and that people even think in a communist way.' The capitals of the region – Sofia, Bucharest, Bratislava – all attract the best and the brightest, who then occupy positions in an elite that monopolizes the political, economic, and cultural life of the country.

The transformations of 1989 did not create this dynamic. Under communism, central planning required centralized administration, and the commissars ensured that all resources flowed to the capital before distribution to the rest of the country. The creation of an urban workforce – factories were often located just outside major cities – pulled many young people off the land.[8] Even before the implementation of Soviet-style reforms, the modernizing reforms of democratic, autocratic, and imperial systems tended to focus on the urban elite as well. With a few exceptions, the countryside has been fighting a losing battle against the city since the Industrial Revolution. It was in 1770, after all, when Oliver Goldsmith penned his immortal lines about children growing up and establishing themselves in the city, leaving behind deserted villages: 'Ill fares the land,' the poet wrote, 'where wealth accumulates, and men decay.'[9]

The countryside has not passively accepted this longstanding discrimination. Peasants in eastern Europe periodically rose up in revolt against their distant rulers. György Dózsa led such a revolt in Hungary in 1514. It failed, and Dózsa suffered an exemplary punishment designed to dissuade any copycats. 'They took György Dózsa's clothes off up to the waist and tied him to a red-hot iron chair,' eyewitness Antal Verancsics reported. 'Then they forced his soldiers to dance the heyduck around his throne. After the completion of every round they had to take a bite out of his flesh.'[10] Nor did these jacqueries end with the modern age. In Romania, peasant revolts broke out in 1888, 1889, 1894, and

1904 before culminating in a huge uprising that left 10,000 dead in 1907.[11] Peasants also resisted during communism, particularly when forced into collective farming. In Poland, farmers proved so resistant to the new Soviet-style system that the government had to back off and leave much of the land in private hands. A dismayed Stalin called the unsuccessful process of bringing Poland to heel 'saddling the cow.'

Despite the rural resistance, the transformations of 1989 were largely an urban phenomenon. Only in Poland, where Rural Solidarity claimed to represent over three million private farmers in 1980, did the countryside participate in large numbers in the opposition. In East Germany and Romania, the 1989 revolutions broke out in the provinces – in Leipzig and Timișoara – but it wasn't until the unrest spread to the capitals that the regimes fell. Elsewhere, city dwellers had to 'go to the people,' like the nineteenth-century Narodniks in Tsarist Russia, to canvass support for their largely urban revolutions. Michaela Novotná was a medical student in Prague when the revolution broke out in November 1989. 'We didn't study,' she told me over coffee in Prague in 2013. 'Not for several months. We didn't go to school. We were helping out: publishing papers, going to the country, visiting friends, trying to influence them.' It was not always easy to bridge the urban–rural gap. 'We went to the countryside to report on the situation there,' radio journalist Miroslav Krupička told me, 'and many people said, "This is about your students and intellectuals in Prague. It has nothing to do with us. We have other problems. We don't believe that the regime has collapsed. We have to go with the old way, there's no other way."'

In Serbia, where the changes came a decade later, the countryside played a critical role in dislodging Slobodan Milošević. The Serbian leader, who delayed his country's transition to democracy and played an outsized role in precipitating the wars that tore Yugoslavia apart, made a fatal mistake by taking the countryside's support for granted.

Mladen was particularly proud that Niš was the first city to respond to Milošević's crackdown on protestors in Belgrade in a famous March 1991 demonstration. 'We were the first city to say, "No, we are not going to allow it!"' he told me. After the elections in 1996 in which Milošević refused to recognize that the opposition had won at the local level, the residents of Niš began what would at one point become the longest peaceful protest in the world. These protests in Niš and elsewhere around the country ultimately forced Milošević to acknowledge the 1996 election results.

But the Serbian leader took his revenge on the countryside. 'He waited for three months after the protest and instituted a law taking all the property away from the local municipalities. Even today all the state property belongs to the state of Serbia – not to the local self-government,' Mladen explained. 'So, can you imagine that all of a sudden you win the elections but you don't have any property? Even the phone on the mayor's table belongs to Milošević again. Actually it was his plan that these local self-governments would fail, and as a result he would win the next election.'

By the time of the next elections in 2000, however, Serbia had had enough of Milošević. The country had been bombed by NATO. The economy was a shambles. Kosovo had secured de facto independence. In the presidential elections in September 2000, the first free direct elections in Serbia since the breakup of Yugoslavia, the opposition candidate, Vojislav Koštunica, won in the first round. Milošević announced a runoff, claiming falsely that Koštunica didn't get enough votes to win outright. It was the last straw. The opposition had been building strength for more than a year through the nonviolent movement Otpor and the coalition of parties that eventually coalesced around Koštunica. In Niš, Otpor activists organized a mock birthday celebration for Milošević, offering such presents as a pair of handcuffs and a one-way airline ticket to The Hague.[12] But it was strikers at the Kolubara coal mines, to the west of Belgrade, that sparked this final uprising against Milošević. Outraged at their plummeting standard of living and the failure of Milošević to follow through on his promises to defend ethnic Serbs in neighboring regions, the miners were determined to shut down Kolubara, the source of nearly half of Serbia's electricity.[13]

The miners soon had support. 'Workers and peasants arrived from the countryside, armed and ready to fight against Milosevic's army and his tanks,' Janine di Giovanni writes in her account of that period, *Madness Visible.* 'But the all-out battle never happened. In the end, it was short and relatively smooth.'[14] In relatively short order, the Serbian democracy movement deposed Milošević, and the new government, putting the birthday presents offered by the Niš activists to good use, delivered him to The Hague to face charges of war crimes and genocide.

The autocrat was gone, but power was still concentrated in the hands of a Belgrade elite. Six years after the fall of Milošević, Mladen Jovanović began to push the issue of democracy one step farther. Decentralization was a controversial demand. Many Serbs associated the concept with the calls by Slovenes and Croats for greater regional autonomy, which coincided with the breakup of Yugoslavia, and they feared that the same forces would tear apart Serbia. Hadn't Kosovo already broken away?

Mladen understands these concerns, even if he doesn't share them. Both Vojvodina in the north, where many ethnic Germans and Hungarians still live, and Sandžak in the south, which has a large Muslim minority, have pushed for greater autonomy within Serbia. Decentralization, Mladen insists, is part of the solution, not part of the problem. 'I think that Vojvodina and Sandžak might become true problems only if, because of nationalism, Serbia doesn't provide them enough autonomy and enough political rights,' Mladen explained. 'With decentralization you give power to the people. You're not taking power away. The state can still keep some control mechanisms, like the army and the police. But it's necessary to give something to the regions.'[15]

In his decade of work on the issue, Mladen has seen considerable progress, at least at the rhetorical level. Even the ruling Progressive Party has begun to say the right things about decentralization. 'When we started to work on the issue of decentralization in 2006, nobody was talking about it,' Mladen told me. 'Today this is one of the most important political topics.' Even the ruling party, which attacked decentralization in the mid-2000s as a tactic to break up the country, has come around to the concept. Still, Mladen admitted, 'Everything that is decided in Belgrade actually brings more centralization, whether in the government or in the headquarters of the political parties, so in reality decentralization isn't happening.'

One major reason for the resistance to centralization is economic. The national government is reluctant to turn over so much wealth to Niš and other municipalities. As Mladen explained, 'An investor comes to Niš and Niš says, "Oh yeah, the state has this land, we can give you free access to water supply. We can help you with it, but everything else about the location you need to negotiate with the state." These are huge investors. The state can get one million euro or two million euro as a small percentage of the total investment in the municipality.'

In this regard, at least, Serbia is changing slowly. At the airport in Belgrade when I arrived in 2012, a number of banners hung from the ceiling in a colorful attempt to entice investors to different Serbian cities. Pirot was represented by a tire and the tagline 'on the right track.' The Loznica banner, featuring a pear surrounded by cherries and berries, promised 'fruitful investment.' And Subotica displayed a rainbow kite and the 'power of innovation.' The banners, NALED's[16] Violeta Jovanović (no relation to Mladen) told me, 'let investors know which locations are business-friendly in Serbia. It's also a way for municipalities to understand how they can be more successful and independent in attracting investments. They largely rely on the central government to bring investors to them. We don't discourage this approach, which has worked for so long. But in addition to being responsive, we also encourage them to be proactive and develop tools to attract investors.' After all, she added, 'investors are rarely looking just for a location.'

The Serbian government has rhetorically embraced decentralization because it's a key EU strategy for promoting economic growth, democratic consolidation, and corruption reduction. In reality, however, political leaders in Belgrade have been consolidating their power, as Mladen informed me in 2017. 'No significant moves have been made in the decentralization of Serbia,' he wrote to me. 'The tendency is rather in the opposite direction. The concentration of power right now is tied to our prime minister, Alexandar Vučić, who is an absolute control freak and who centralizes everything he can. Currently, we are losing the battle.' Despite the efforts of NALED, Mladen pointed to data showing that 75–80 percent of foreign investments in Serbia between 2000 and 2016 ended up in Belgrade and Novi Sad.

Poland has made more than just a rhetorical commitment, as can be seen in the strength of local political institutions and the vibrancy of so many of its cities (Kraków, Gdańsk, Wrocław, Poznań). The Polish government established seventeen investor assistance centers around the country along with thirty-two business parks focused on new technology.[17] 'This reform was very important because thanks to it Warsaw is not the only development center,' former Solidarity activist Jan Lityński told me. 'The fact that Poland is decentralized is a huge success.' In general, the northern tier of eastern Europe has done better than the Balkans on a decentralization index that measures such factors as civic involvement in local politics, fiscal responsibility, and what Europeans like to call subsidiarity (in which matters are handled at the most local level capable of doing so).[18]

The issue of decentralization is not just about the capital versus other cities, like Belgrade and Niš. It is also about the relative power of urban versus rural areas. The countryside has suffered disproportionately from the liberal reforms after 1989. Workers in the factories in the small towns lost their jobs. Farmers on the collective farms, even if they were now able to own their own land, couldn't compete with the sudden influx of cheap imports.

But just as it had done for centuries, the countryside fought back against the reforms that impoverished or threatened to impoverish them. In Sofia, for instance, the opposition was confident that it would win the 1990 elections because it seemed to have overwhelming support in the capital. The countryside threw its support behind the renamed Communist Party, and the opposition lost. In Hungary, the countryside would eventually back a newly conservative Fidesz and consign the Liberals to electoral oblivion. In Poland, the conservative Law and Justice Party would follow the Fidesz strategy and use the support of the countryside to overwhelm the liberal Civic Platform to gain power in 2015.

When I traveled through the region in 1990, I stayed close to the capital cities. These were the places making the headlines, where the oppositions challenged the communist elites and installed their own political leaders. During my extended journey in 2012 and 2013, I ranged more widely, traveling through the Bulgarian countryside, interviewing farmers in Poland and Slovenia, and talking to businessmen in the Romanian port city of Constanța and the Czech spa town of Mariánské Lázně (the fabled Marienbad). At the moment, these places may be on the margins. But as eastern Europe begins to develop within the European Union, the political and economic life outside the capital cities will become increasingly important in determining whether these countries will be able to 'catch up' to their western European counterparts.

Mladen was right. I couldn't understand Serbia if I just stayed in Belgrade. The same rule applied to Warsaw, Prague, Bratislava, Budapest, Bucharest, Sofia, Zagreb, and Ljubljana. To understand the failure of the liberal project, it was essential to travel to Eastern Europe B.

Eastern Europe B

After its postcommunist transition, Poland cleaved into two parts that Poles refer to as 'Poland A' and 'Poland B.'[19] Poland A links together an archipelago of cities and their younger, wealthier inhabitants. Poland B encompasses the poorer, older parts of the population, many clustered in the countryside, particularly in the country's eastern reaches near the former Soviet border.

After 1989 and the implementation of a punishing series of economic reforms, Poland A took off economically. By 2010, Warsaw had become one of the most expensive places to live in Europe, outranking even Brussels and Berlin.[20] New entrepreneurs and corporate managers took advantage of a host of economic opportunities, particularly after Poland joined the European Union in 2004. Warsaw became a popular place for the regional headquarters of multinational corporations.

In the countryside, on the other hand, Poland B fell ever farther behind. Factories couldn't compete with the West. If they weren't attractive enough to lure foreign buyers to sponsor expensive upgrades, they had to close. Many farms couldn't keep going. Jobs disappeared. Several million Poles decamped abroad in search of better economic opportunities, just as they had in the nineteenth century. As the good times rolled in Poland A, Poland B languished.

In the agricultural lands of Poland B, the Balcerowicz reforms certainly made growing food more efficient. The removal of subsidies – for agricultural inputs like fertilizer, for basic foodstuffs in the marketplace – reduced waste and pushed farmers to be more competitive with their counterparts in the West. But the burden fell squarely on the shoulders of small farmers in particular. In 1990, journalist Konstanty Gebert told me that the Balcerowicz program would mean the 'death of the family farm.'[21] That didn't quite happen, but the situation for farmers became quite dire. 'There was a dramatic shift in the purchasing power of farmers in 1990 compared to the artificial situation of 1989,' economist Marcin Święcicki told me in 2013. 'Real income went down by thirty to forty percent. In any case, and even today, the average productivity of the average farm in Poland, in comparison to non-farm workers, is one fourth. Many small farmers are not able to live on farm income. Even today, farms are still subsidized.'[22]

Solidarity advisor Krzysztof Hagemejer lamented the enduring poverty in the rural areas of Poland. 'The highest unemployment is there, and the poverty has been continuous for more than twenty years,' he told me. 'The farms just disappeared from one day to the other with no program for what to do with the people who were working there. Plus, at the same time the heavy industry and construction sectors – where all the "farmer-workers" were working – were also shrinking. About two million people lost their jobs and had to return to the villages. And there were no programs to help those people find new employment, no programs to create new jobs. There was nothing for years.

Now, with EU money, things are happening in many places. But it's too late for many people.' Some farmers have certainly profited from the changes. After all, Poland went from being a net importer of food to a net exporter by 2002 as more sophisticated farming techniques produced greater yields from less land under cultivation.[23] As in the country as a whole, however, rural areas were marked by a starker division between those who benefited from globalization and those who did not.

Until the elections of 2015, liberals dominated the political, economic, and cultural life of Poland. Although they may not exactly be 'liberal' in the American sense of supporting government entitlement programs, Polish liberals are generally less religious, more tolerant of differences, and more open to the world than their conservative counterparts. Polish liberals pushed through several iterations of 'shock therapy' and squared off as well against the denizens of Poland B over such issues as the role of the Catholic Church in public life, the number of immigrants the country should allow in, and how close Poland should be to the EU.

In 2015, the inhabitants of Poland B took their revenge at the polls. They'd missed out on the country's vaunted prosperity and blamed their predicament on the liberal architects of economic reform. They were anti-abortion and pro-religion. They were suspicious of Middle Eastern immigrants, haughty intellectuals, and intrusive international institutions. And they embraced a rather narrow nationalism that promised to make their nation great again. In 2015, they voted in large numbers for the political party of Poland B, the Law and Justice Party (PiS), providing the Polish right wing with both the presidency and the first outright parliamentary majority since the end of communism in 1989.

Łowicz is located about an hour's drive due west from Warsaw, roughly halfway to the next big industrial city of Łódź. It is also, according to the map of parliamentary election results from December 2015, squarely in the middle of Poland B territory. The liberal Civic Platform (PO) party won majorities in three major areas – the northern coast (which includes Gdańsk), the northwestern region near Germany, and the biggest cities including Warsaw and Łódź. Between these two big cities, and pretty much everywhere else, PiS flourished.

Wojciech Waligórski has not always lived in Łowicz. Backpacking through Europe in 1981, he met his wife in France, at a spiritual center that attracts thousands of young people each year to Taizé. When I first met him in 1990, he was working in Warsaw for a newspaper devoted to sobriety. Later that year, he moved to Łowicz, where his wife's family lived. He started publishing an underground newspaper affiliated with the Citizens' Committee of the Solidarity movement. With a population of around 33,000 people at the time, Łowicz didn't have a local paper. When the Citizens' Committee disbanded, Wojciech and his wife continued to publish the newspaper as *Nowy Łowiczanin.*

'I remember talking to my wife in 1986 or so, and we said that we would never try to run our own business,' Wojciech told me when we met again at the offices of *Nowy Łowiczanin* in 2013. 'Never, never: because it was necessary to pay bribes and so on ... We wanted less money but more time for ourselves. Later we were asked to help launch a newspaper, and after that we took on this work alone. Once we started, we could imagine doing this business. And now we advise our children to choose the kind of education that enables them to have their own private business activity.'

Łowicz has suffered the same fate as much of Poland B. Its population has officially dropped to 29,000. 'But unofficially, we're probably about 26,000. Many people have flown away to Britain,' Wojciech told me. 'If people come back, and they rarely come back, they come back only for holidays.' The primary challenge is employment. Łowicz has two major factories: a local dairy cooperative and a fruit-and-vegetable company. A third communist-era firm that produced socks went out of business. Some people find jobs in Warsaw or Łódź, but the commute is long. As a result, Łowicz has lost a fifth of its population since 1989.

Until recently, the political environment in Łowicz was balanced. 'Politically, in the recent parliamentary elections PiS and PO had almost the same number of votes,' Wojciech told me, referring to the 2011 elections. 'It was astonishingly equal. PO got only a few hundred more votes.' By 2015, however, Łowicz had shifted substantially toward PiS, which garnered nearly twice the percentage of votes as the second-place Civic Platform (PO) in the eleven counties in and around the city.[24] Wojciech didn't think that sociocultural issues determined the outcome. 'The most important factor, in my opinion, was the rejection of the ultraliberal way of managing the economy, the lack of care for common good (weak state), and a need of change,' he wrote me after the election.

It's not any easier in the countryside around Łowicz. I visited a family farm in the nearby village of Wyborów where Adam and Anna Janeczek raise pigs. Although I'm quite familiar with dairy farming, my knowledge of raising pigs is limited to Annie Proulx's *That Old Ace in the Hole*, a devastating indictment of industrial livestock production in Oklahoma. What remains in my memory of that novel are the huge holding ponds of pig excrement and the unholy smell.[25] So I was pleasantly surprised to find that the neighborhood where the Janeczeks lived was practically suburban, with neat houses lined up on one side of the street and well-tended fields on the other side. I didn't smell any pigs, and I certainly didn't see any holding ponds. Behind the Janeczeks' house, small enough to be concealed from the road by a few trees, lay their pig operation. We chatted in their scrupulously clean living room.

Unlike the industrial farmers who dominate American agriculture, the Janeczeks keep only about ninety sows and produce about 1,300 piglets a year that they then fatten up and sell. When Poland entered the European Union in 2004, it became much cheaper for Polish pig farmers to simply buy piglets from countries like Denmark and then raise them for sale. Farmers could then dispense with all the buildings and equipment and expertise needed to raise pigs from birth. But the Janeczeks continue to maintain the older traditions that their family farm has practiced for a century. They've survived the transition, but it wasn't easy.

'When the changes took place and firms collapsed, it was precisely the farmers who suffered,' Adam Janeczek told me. 'And later it was obvious who was opening things up here: various city slickers who had capital.'

Membership of the EU came with its own challenges. 'The truth is that the EU is terribly demanding,' Anna Janeczek said, ticking off all the regulations to be followed and the paperwork to prove compliance. 'On entering the EU the financing of particular farmers, of machines and equipment, suddenly it resulted in agricultural debt,' her husband added. They complained about how little they were getting in subsidies from the EU and how it didn't make up for rising costs for fertilizer and fuel. Since other EU countries were getting higher subsidies – Polish farmers receive roughly half what Dutch and Belgian farmers get per hectare – the Janeczeks felt as though they were constantly losing ground.[26]

'Here's what the government should do: protect us from unhealthy competition with the West,' Adam said. 'We don't have here in Poland people responsible for defending us, people who have the power to wave their hand and help farmers.' In 2015, PiS presented themselves as precisely the people who could wave their hands and defend the interests of farmers like the Janeczeks against foreign competition.

Every country in the region has a similar division between those who have benefitted from the economic transformations of the last two decades and those who have not, between Eastern Europe A and Eastern Europe B. Populists of the left and right have promised to represent the countryside against the 'city slickers.' Elsewhere, dissatisfaction with liberal reforms has pushed the countryside in an even more extreme direction. In Slovakia, for instance, a far-right, xenophobic, anti-Roma movement has gathered political momentum in the countryside. Led by neo-Nazi Marian Kotleba, the People's Party – Our Slovakia has begun to draw the mainstream parties rightward toward greater Islamophobia and Euroskepticism.[27]

Eastern Europe B is a subset of Europe B, which also hasn't seen much advantage coming from the more neoliberal economic reforms of the last two decades. These B populations are more nationalist in orientation and worry that large migration of 'outsiders' will destroy their cultures from within. They are suspicious of 'foreign capital' for much the same reason. And they are deeply skeptical of the European Union. Europe B is the motive force behind the 'exits' that now plague the EU – from the Brexit of June 2016 to all that potentially follow. Support for the EU remains strong in the capitals (London, Paris, Stockholm) and the large cities. The map of the results of the Brexit referendum, for instance, shows islands of 'remain' in a sea of 'leave,' where the islands are urban and the seas are rural.[28] Rural opposition to the EU is particularly ironic given that the EU provides huge subsidies to the countryside through its Common Agricultural Program, which absorbs 40 percent of EU expenditures and attracts broad support.[29]

Ultimately, like the liberal project more generally in eastern Europe, the EU can't survive only with the support of cosmopolitan elites. Europe B must somehow be brought back into the equation.

Reforming agriculture

Because of the splendors of Budapest, Hungary often comes across as a very cosmopolitan place. But nearly 30 percent of the population lives in rural areas, a higher percentage than, for instance, Bulgaria at 26 percent.[30] Even though it has played a key role in the Hungarian economy, agriculture has declined steadily as a value-added portion of GDP – from over 15 percent in 1989 to 3.5 in 2010 (though it bounced back to 4.5 percent between 2011 and 2014 under the Fidesz government).[31] Hungary's rural economy has declined for a number of reasons: the market liberalization reforms in the early 1990s, the influx of cheaper agricultural products from the West, membership of the European Union. This decline affects not only farms – which employ only about one in twenty Hungarians – but everyone in the service sector dependent on agriculture.

Other countries in east-central Europe experienced a similar drop in the GDP share of agricultural production. Although some countries didn't have collective farms (Poland) and other countries have yet to join the EU (Serbia, Albania), this pattern of a sharp drop in agricultural production has held true across the region. In the first eighteen years of transition, production dropped by as much as 30 percent and, despite some recovery, had not yet returned to the levels of 1989.[32] Agricultural employment has dipped as well by more than 60 percent in the northern tier.[33] And the decline was particularly sharp in Hungary.

The transformations that took place in 1989 reflected the concerns of the urban intellectuals who led the fight against the communist governments. The new governments in 1990 focused on macroeconomic changes, on reforming the financial sector, on dealing with the major factories. Agriculture was often an afterthought. This miscalculation came with high political costs. In Hungary, as in Poland, the countryside has retaliated at the ballot box for the reversal of its economic fortunes. In the last two elections, rural areas strongly supported both the ruling Fidesz party and the far-right Jobbik party, both of which promised a different kind of economy that reflected more traditional, nationalist values.[34] This conservative swing was a repudiation of the market liberalism embraced by most of the governments that had been in charge of the economy since 1990.

Gábor Harangozó is one of the new, young leaders of the Hungarian Socialist Party. He started out, as many of his generation did, working with Fidesz, which in the early 1990s was a liberal youth party. Gradually, however, Gábor grew disenchanted with market liberalism and moved toward social democracy. That led him to the Socialist Party, for which he served in the European Parliament in 2004. Gábor grew up in the countryside, where his father worked as an agricultural engineer. His experience living in the shadow of a large agricultural cooperative has influenced his views on rural development even today.

'I could see at that time that almost everybody in the village had work,' Gábor told me in an interview in his office at the Hungarian parliament in 2013. 'Many Roma people were living there as well. They had jobs and lived in quite decent conditions. Everything was organized. The basis was agricultural production, but they also created a system of side businesses that produced machines. It was not so important for each business to make profit because the agricultural production could finance the whole system. There were also what we call social work jobs. The main aim was to create jobs for everybody. And this profitable system could finance the local education and healthcare. It created good living conditions for rural people.'

When the government dismantled the system after 1990, the land restitution was initially very popular. Many people could tell stories of the communist state taking away the family farm and forcing the former owners to work as employees on what had been their own properties. 'Emotionally, people wanted to get back their family properties, like their grandparents' fields,' Gábor related. 'I agreed with giving back these properties. But to give everyone a small plot without any cooperation, without any systematic assistance in the form of expertise, market organization, or logistical help? It provides emotional satisfaction but an unsustainable economic system that causes only problems for the families that got back their properties. Many investors bought up the small fields and created larger farming units. They sold the livestock and built industrial plants that make big profits but don't provide jobs.'

The privatization of land in Hungary substituted for a larger vision of agricultural modernization. For instance, Hungary could have established a comparative advantage by investing in organic farming. But as organic food advocate Ferenc Frühwald told me, the country actually moved backward in this regard. In 1992, Ferenc established the first organic store in Budapest. He negotiated a contract with a state apple orchard that decided to go organic. 'They harvested so many apples that I could sell twenty trucks of apples, twenty tons each,' Ferenc told me. 'Just a year later, however, the farm was privatized and split into 180 different orchards. The individual owners decided what to do on their own, and there was no cooperation.' By 2011, Hungary had one of the lowest levels of organic production in the region, with only Romania and Bulgaria doing worse.[35]

Hungary was not alone in breaking up agricultural cooperatives. Romania, too, dissolved the state farms and gave back the land to those who farmed it. 'The Romania solution undoubtedly was the most just, but it also made the least economic sense by creating a series of small and inefficient farms that cannot compete on the European agricultural market,' writes historian Lonnie Johnson.[36] Neither the Czechs nor the Germans broke up their farms in this way. Nor did the Bulgarians – the proposal by the opposition in Bulgaria to return the land of the cooperative farms to the previous owners was a major reason why it lost to the former communists in those first elections in 1990. Romanian President Ion Iliescu, it turned out, didn't even know that these other options existed. 'I was in Germany three years ago,' he told political scientist Vladimir Tismăneanu. 'I talked to the Brandenburg prime minister, who was very much surprised when he heard about the breaking up of the cooperatives in Romania. "Well, why did you do that? Nobody even thought of such a thing here!"'[37]

The German experience was indeed more successful. True, agriculture in East Germany initially followed some of the same trends as the rest of the region. There was, for instance, a sharp drop in farm employment – 80 percent in the first five years after reunification in 1990.[38] And some farmers couldn't compete with the foreign produce flooding the market. 'They don't want to buy any products coming from our country any more,' an East German farmer told political scientist Johannes Becker. 'They prefer cauliflower coming from the greenhouses of Netherlands or the UK because they are absolutely white and they don't have any blemishes. So, I can't sell them!' As he spoke, the farmer was plowing under an entire field of perfectly edible cauliflower.

But there was also a lot more money, from the united German government, to ease this transformation. Although the government encouraged the development of family farms – which predominate in western Germany – the eastern lands focused more on cooperatives.[39] And whereas industrial production in the former East Germany bottomed out, the farming sector remained stable, with output increasing and yields approaching those in the west only five years after reunification.[40]

I visited one of the former collective farms in the former East Germany – in Brodowin, about an hour's drive north-east of Berlin near the Polish border. The farm store in this small community was clean and cheery, like many German retail outlets. It was full of organic produce, much of which the farm itself produced. The Brodowin farm had once focused on livestock, but now it followed Rudolf Steiner's biodynamics, a mix of agricultural and spiritual precepts.

'As a production unit, it was simply coming to an end,' Bill Beittel explained to me about the farm's trajectory after the Berlin Wall fell. Bill and his wife had settled in the town after working for the AFSC to promote East–West dialogue during the Cold War era. 'They didn't know what to do with all the liquid waste from the animals, so they were simply channeling it into the lakes. As a result, some of the lakes were just on the verge of dying. That stopped overnight. The conversion to an organic farm takes time. For that, they needed financing, and they found financing from a real estate agent in Berlin who had a lot of money.' The agent's wife, suffering serious health problems, had been treated successfully in a hospital that also followed Steiner's principles.

The farm went organic, and it basically saved the town. 'Brodowin has an unemployment rate of roughly five percent. Nationwide in Germany, it's eight or nine percent, and in Brandenburg, it is probably on or above the fifteen percent level,' Bill explained. 'We have a kindergarten right across the street here – which is bursting its seams. There are a lot of kids in Brodowin. We know other villages, perhaps a bit smaller, where the young people from about sixteen on are gone. They have just a handful of younger kids, and the population is getting older and older.'

Elsewhere in the region, organic farming has grown exponentially, but sometimes at the expense of locally grown produce. Boris Fras grows olives, grapes, and vegetables along Slovenia's tiny coastline. One plot of grapevines stretches down to the sparkling waters of the Adriatic. Red poppies interspersed among young olive trees brighten another stretch of land. Everything Fras grows and produces is organic, including his wine and his olives. He sells locally and also at the organic market in the Slovenian capital. He was not born to this work but came to it gradually. 'I started farming against the advice of all the people who said I was crazy,' he told me when I first met him in 2004.[41]

These days, Boris is focused on supporting the local food movement. 'It's a huge debate now – not just in Slovenia but also at the EU level – about how local food is better than imported food not just because of freshness but the waste of energy in transportation,' he told me in 2013 over coffee at a local café in the town of Ankaran. 'All Slovenians say, "Yes, bravo!" But they are still buying cheap imported fruits and vegetables. When they do a public opinion poll, they all say, "Yes, we are for local food." But then you go to the markets and you see that they are buying the opposite.'[42]

One way for the Slovenian government to boost local organic agriculture would be to facilitate institutional purchases by schools and hospitals. Italy adopted this approach and grew its organic sector rapidly up to nearly 10 percent of its agriculture. Slovenia has yet to follow this path.[43] 'Sodexho from France offers food to Slovenian schools for practically nothing,' Boris complains. 'And I'm competing against this huge thing? It's impossible! You break the law if you speak directly with the school. It's crazy.'

In taking on another 50 percent more farmland through the accession of eastern European countries, the EU was also taking on a large number of additional farmers eligible for EU subsidies. This was a plus for eastern European farmers. On other hand, membership also brought in a huge influx of imported food because the more efficient agriculture in western Europe produced cheaper products. In 1991, Hungary imported 32 percent more food from the EU while its exports declined by half during the initial transition period.[44] In 1990, nearly all the food sold in Czechoslovakia was grown or produced in the country, but twenty years later the equation had practically reversed: 90 percent of Czech food was imported in 2009.[45]

Farmers didn't take this transformation without protest. Polish farmers, already angry that they were receiving smaller EU payments than they expected because of budget shortfalls in Warsaw,[46] protested against low prices, the spread of GMO crops, and the sale of land to foreigners.[47] Bulgarian vegetable growers, angry over cheaper tomatoes coming from their northern neighbor, threatened to blockade a bridge over the Danube into Romania.[48] Hungarian dairy farmers brought their cows to Budapest to protest about cheap imported milk.

For Hungary, joining the EU brought a great deal of investment, but the money didn't necessarily trickle down to the village level. 'Instead of reducing the differences between the regions with this EU money,' Gábor explained, 'we increased the differences. Those cities and areas where investment conditions were good – where they could create good projects and the financing was in place – they could use the EU money, make good investments, and create jobs. The economy started to grow there. Miskolc, for instance, grew a lot with EU subsidies. But in the territories surrounding Miskolc there is fifty percent unemployment. It's totally hopeless, with no investments.'

It's especially ironic that the EU has contributed to increasing rather than decreasing the rural–urban divide. In the 1970s and 1980s, the EU worked hard to reduce economic differences within and between European countries. Agricultural subsidies were a key mechanism to reduce disparities. By the 1990s and into the twenty-first century, however, the EU was largely helping Europe A. It's no surprise, then, that Europe B has grown increasingly Euroskeptical. It's borne a greater share of the costs of economic globalization.

So, when someone comes along who criticizes that globalization, who condemns the local politicians who facilitated that globalization, who speaks for all those who did not make the promised great leap forward, Europe B wakes up. And that's what has helped fuel the rise of illiberal reformers.

4
The Faces of Illiberalism

Tamás Hegedűs is a mystery. He is soft-spoken and urbane. He wears an impeccably tailored three-piece suit and sports a neatly trimmed goatee. He looks like a college professor or a hedge-fund manager, which is appropriate since he has a degree in economics and his résumé is about as mainstream as you can get in Hungary. From 1989 to 1994, he was a member of the main liberal political party, the Alliance of Free Democrats. He worked as a manager in the corporate sector. He seems the epitome of a European liberal: worldly and pro-business.

Tamás Hegedűs is a mystery because, despite these middle-of-the-road credentials, he is a member of one of the most successful far-right political parties in Europe. Jobbik, or the Movement for a Better Hungary, was founded by a group of university students in 2002. It has acquired considerable notoriety for the anti-Semitic and anti-Roma remarks of its members. In 2011, for instance, a Jobbik lawmaker said, 'Just as there was a time in the United States for the Ku Klux Klan, the time has come for the emergence of a Hungarian Ku Klux Klan.'[1] In 2012, a Jobbik representative in parliament attempted to commemorate the anniversary of the 1882 'blood libel' against Hungarian Jews.[2] The party has also maintained a relationship with the Hungarian Guards, a paramilitary organization that has conducted an anti-Roma campaign at a local level throughout the country.

The mystery of Tamás Hegedűs is also the mystery of Hungary. For decades the most liberal of eastern European countries under communism and for years the most liberal of postcommunist countries, Hungary has swung all the way to the right. Jobbik attracts the support of one out of every five Hungarian voters. More importantly, it has pulled the ruling Fidesz party in its direction.

By all rights, because of the extremism of his party, I shouldn't have gotten along with Tamas. But I found him an intelligent interlocutor. We also agreed on many things, including the failures of liberalism in Hungary. Although their social politics are firmly on the extreme right, Tamás Hegedűs and his fellow Jobbik members sound like left-wingers when they talk about the economy. They criticize financial elites, decry growing economic inequality, and support government intervention to help the disadvantaged.

Tamas had very little good to say about the initial economic reforms that Hungary implemented in the early 1990s. 'According to the "shock therapy" ideology, if we went through this process very quickly, there might be a sudden economic drop, but then eventually we would have great long-term development,' he told me in a 2013 interview in his office in parliament in Budapest. We used an interpreter though his English was actually quite good. 'The first part happened, but the second part didn't. In three years, the GDP dropped thirty percent. The unemployment rate went from zero to a million people. Inflation went up to thirty percent. The country debt constantly increased. And most of the country's national property just disappeared.'

Having worked in the corporate sector, Tamas was well positioned to evaluate how the liberalization of the Hungarian economy had benefitted multinational corporations at the expense of Hungarian companies. His statistics were more or less accurate (the GDP drop was more like 20 percent; unemployment rose from zero to about 800,000; inflation peaked at 30 percent in 1995). As befitted a member of a Euroskeptical party, Tamas reserved some of his harshest criticism for the European Union, as a bearer of globalization.

'We don't think it would be a tragedy to step out of the EU,' Tamas told me. 'We wouldn't do this irresponsibly, without consideration. But when we were preparing to enter the EU, there wasn't an all-around analysis of the positive and negative sides of EU membership.' Those who supported membership argued that the benefits far exceeded the costs. Tamas's critique of the EU, on the other hand, dovetailed in interesting ways with Rüdiger Frank's analysis of how western Germany benefitted from reunification. A lot of the money that the EU supplies to Hungary 'goes to administration and consultants,' Tamas pointed out. 'And a lot of that money goes to the Western companies doing the consulting and administration. Finally, a lot of the support goes back to the donor countries.'

Skeptical of Brussels, Tamas thought that his country should cultivate economic opportunities in the East. 'Hungary must be open to Eastern markets,' he explained. 'Previously Hungary had really good relations in this region. They need to be either reestablished or newly established. The countries I'm thinking of are China, Russia, and Turkey as well as the Central Asian countries.'

Turkey? Perhaps I didn't hear him correctly. Turkey generally enjoys a very low reputation in Hungary because of the deadly rivalry between the Ottoman Empire and the Habsburgs. And the European right was united in its rejection of Turkey's application to the European Union.

But no, Tamas turned out to be an adherent of the little-known philosophy of Turanism, which links Hungary to a pan-Turkic culture rather than to the Finno-Ugric roots that conventional linguists favor. Among its many peculiarities, Turanism had been influential among Hungarian fascists in the Arrow Cross movement in the inter-war period.[3] This Turanism has prompted Tamas and Jobbik to break with the radical right parties in western Europe on this key element of foreign policy. 'The Austrian Freedom Party wanted to initiate an EU referendum against the accession of Turkey,' Tamas told me. 'If there are one million signatures then it becomes a compulsory referendum for all of Europe. They asked Jobbik to join this, and we refused.'

Aside from this one quirk in its foreign policy, Jobbik fits comfortably in the camp of Europe's radical right, especially on social issues. Tamas didn't mind the term 'radical.' However, 'extremist' bothered him.

'It's true that within Jobbik, or around Jobbik, there are manifestations of extremism,' he confessed. 'These are mostly verbal outbursts. I'm not happy about them. But this is not the mainstream of Jobbik. We are definitely not more extreme than the National Front in France or the Freedom Party in Austria.' Moreover, he denied that the Hungarian Guard, which had once been a kind of 'satellite organization' of Jobbik, was an extremist organization. 'There has not been a violent action that these members were party to,' he told me. 'One thing is true: people might find the marches that they are organizing threatening. But they are unarmed. They never had and never will have arms. Wherever the Guard was formed and wherever it was strong, it was in villages where the locals felt that it was not safe and the state was not protecting them.'

Not protecting them from what? From Roma.

'It's unfortunately true that in some part of the Roma community, violence has become a cult,' Tamas continued. 'Of course this is not true for all Roma Hungarians. But where a lot of Roma live, there are two or three big families where this surely happens, and this is enough to pose a threat to a village. In many parts of the country, the inhabitants feel that the state is not protecting them and preventing the crime.' He admitted that stereotyping of Roma and racism exists in Hungary. 'But it's not more than in any other country,' he insisted. 'There's ten to fifteen percent of the population open to the racism and xenophobia. This is the same rate in any other developed country.'

Unlike in his discourse on the economy, Tamas wasn't entirely accurate about the Hungarian Guard, racism in the country, or the controversial issue of 'Gypsy criminality.'

In 2008, the Hungarian Supreme Court outlawed the Hungarian Guard, ruling that 'the ethnicity- and race-based opinions expressed at the demonstrations and events organized by the Hungarian Guard against "gypsy crime" have in fact breached the basic principle of the right to human dignity.'[4] The European Court of Human Rights upheld the ban. Reappearing the next year under the slightly modified name of the Hungarian New Guard, the organization has repeatedly held paramilitary exercises and preached anti-Roma and anti-Semitic ideology. But, like Jobbik itself, the Guard has been careful not to leave any direct fingerprints on the violence and killings that swept through Hungary and left nine Roma dead and many more injured between 2008 and 2012.[5]

Tamas claimed that Hungary is no more racist than other countries in Europe. True, in a Eurobarometer survey from 2008, 19 percent of respondents in Hungary said that they felt personally discriminated against in the previous twelve months, a figure roughly comparable to other countries – and attitudes toward Roma were approximately as negative as those in other European countries.[6] But Tamas's assertion that only 10–15 percent of the population was open to the racism and xenophobia doesn't hold up. A 2011 poll found that a majority of Hungarians believed that criminality is an inherent part of the nature of Roma, and 40 percent believed it's okay to bar Roma from bars and clubs (roughly the same number of Hungarians held these views in 1994 as well).[7] And in an Anti-Defamation League poll in 2012, Hungarian belief in popular anti-Semitic stereotypes was considerably higher than in other European countries – for instance, 73 percent of Hungarians polled thought that Jews have 'too much power in the business world' (compared to only 30 percent of Austrians). Moreover, the embrace of anti-Semitic stereotypes had increased markedly since the previous poll in 2008.[8]

As for Roma 'criminality,' Hungary doesn't categorize its crime statistics by ethnicity, so it is difficult to make substantive claims on either side of the argument. However, it's also true that Roma in Hungary suffer from endemic unemployment and poverty, and large portions of the population are locked out of legitimate ways of making a living. Even Tamas acknowledged that Roma had been the victims of the economic transition. 'The first companies to go bankrupt were ones that employed Gypsies, like state-owned construction companies,' he told me. 'The unemployment rate among Gypsies is eighty to ninety percent. It wasn't their fault that their jobs disappeared.'

Racism and xenophobia are certainly not new in Hungary. In the 1990s, legislator István Csurka famously spoke of a 'dwarf minority which is controlling mass media and Hungarian political life.' Csurka's party, the Democratic Forum, which won the most votes in the 1990 elections, played on latent anti-Semitism in the Hungarian electorate to discredit the Alliance of Free Democrats, whose membership included a number of prominent Jewish politicians. So many Hungarian Jews went to Israel in the 1990s during Csurka's tenure, expat musicologist Bob Cohen told me, that 'they used to call the El Al flights from here the Csurka flights!' Csurka was an extremist, but he was not organizationally adept. Jobbik, on the other hand, figured out how to turn sentiments into political power.[9]

And indeed, with his three-piece suit and soft-spoken approach, Tamás Hegedűs can be very persuasive. Listening to him, I could understand how Jobbik has acquired cross-over appeal, attracting a hard core of angry and intolerant voters but also reaching out to people who consider themselves centrists and even moderates. In the 2010 parliamentary elections, Jobbik received nearly 17 percent of the vote, and came in third behind the new ruling party, Fidesz, and its chief opposition, the Hungarian Socialist Party. In 2014, Jobbik's share of the overall vote rose to over 20 percent, only a few points behind the Socialist Party. Its influence over the ruling party Fidesz, despite political and rhetorical differences, has been tremendous. As historian Eva Balogh points out, the Hungarian government fulfilled eight of the ten action items Jobbik published in 2010. 'The history of Fidesz and the Orbán government in the last six years has demonstrated that these two parties see eye to eye on almost everything – from history to the European Union to foreign capital,' she concludes.[10] Indeed, having been so successful in pushing Fidesz to the right, Jobbik has recently moved more to the center to better position itself for the 2018 elections, with party leader Gábor Vona denouncing anti-Semitism and promising to appeal more directly to voters on the left.[11]

Most surprising perhaps has been the popularity of Jobbik among youth. Like Fidesz, it started out as an initiative of students, and it styles itself as the more radical upstart to the now stodgy ruling party. Jobbik has an active presence on social media, particularly Facebook.[12] 'If you check out the biographies of Jobbik leaders, you will find there people who studied abroad, who speak several languages, who are handsome (or pretty in the case of the girls), who know how to behave and what to wear,' Hungary expert Dariusz Kałan told me. 'If you think of nationalism, you think of these bald guys wearing these black T-shirts. In Hungary, this is quite different. The faces of nationalism are attractive. There are successful people in Jobbik: lawyers, journalists. These new leaders are attractive to the younger generation.'

Nationalist organizations throughout the region, like Jobbik, have grown in popularity in part because they channel the frustration experienced by the 'losers of transition.' Their politics have been called 'populist,' and they have prospered because of the absence of a strong political left and the grave disappointments attached to the promises of the liberal center. Indeed, these new nationalists manage to attack liberalism from both sides of the political spectrum, just as Jobbik can sound either left-wing (on economic issues) or right-wing (on social issues). And they are usually not as soft-spoken as Tamás Hegedűs.

But the most important impact of the rise of groups like Jobbik has been their disruption of the conventional narrative of eastern Europe proceeding smoothly in one direction toward some steady state of market liberalism.

The nationalist turn

Communism, in theory, was the opposite of nationalism. It imagined a society led by workers that transcended all national boundaries. In practice, however, communism and nationalism were intimately connected.

The early communist years in eastern Europe, for instance, were dominated by a competition between those leaders who leaned closer to Moscow and those who preferred their communism with a more nationalist orientation. Those tensions came to a head when Tito broke with Stalin in 1948 over Soviet interference in what the Yugoslav leader deemed to be sovereign affairs. Stalin and his supporters struck back. Show trials conducted throughout eastern Europe aimed to eliminate what the prosecutors in the infamous Slánský trial in Czechoslovakia called 'Trotskyist-Zionist-Titoist-bourgeois-nationalis traitors' – which was essentially Stalin's attempt to rid Soviet satellites of anyone, even devout Stalinists, who showed any independent spirit.[13] Subsequent reform communists such as Imre Nagy in Hungary in 1956 and Alexander Dubček in Czechoslovakia in 1968 would again attempt to create space between their countries and Moscow, but without Tito's success.

As the legitimacy of their regimes began to wane, some communist leaders began to turn more and more to nationalism to regain popular support.[14] Facing anti-government protests in 1968, for instance, Polish communists used anti-Semitism to appeal to the public in an effort to 'discredit' the protestors, some of whom had Jewish backgrounds. In the 1980s, to boost their sagging legitimacy, the Bulgarian communists targeted the ethnic Turkish population. In Romania, the Ceaușescu government attempted to forcibly assimilate ethnic Hungarians in the countryside by destroying their villages and creating new 'socialist' housing complexes. By the mid-1980s, the waning of Soviet support was pushing communist leaders to find other sources of popular appeal. 'Communism minus Soviet Power equals Nationalism,' writer Miklós Haraszti quipped, updating the Leninist slogan that communism equals Soviet power plus electrification.[15] The trend was so pronounced that dissident Mihai Botez predicted in 1987 that all regimes in the region would converge on what he called the 'ethno-communist state.'[16]

But nationalism was a two-edged sword that could equally be used *against* communists, both the subservience to Moscow and the presumed internationalism. Having deployed nationalism against Stalin, Tito in turn had to put down nationalist uprisings in each of the republics of Yugoslavia in the late 1960s and early 1970s. Explicitly nationalist organizations like the Confederation for an Independent Poland vied with Solidarity for the hearts and minds of anti-government activists in the 1980s. In East Germany, where the state ruthlessly suppressed any vestiges of right-wing extremism, neo-Nazism began to reappear in the 1980s, even among children of loyal Party officials.[17] 'In 1987 alone,' Molly Laster and Sabrina Ramet write, 'the State Security Service had to deal with some 38 functioning rightwing extremist groups.'[18] After the Wall fell, right-wing extremism proved more popular in the former East Germany than in the west.[19]

The revolutions in 1989 drew on certain nationalist themes. Protestors wanted to assert their right of self-determination in leaving the sphere of Soviet influence. Establishing a democratic, market system was a mark of sovereign control over territory, a key element of 'liberal nationalism.'[20] The fusion of nationalism and liberalism was not universally successful, however. Nationalist strivings tore apart Yugoslavia (violently) and Czechoslovakia (nonviolently). And nationalism informed the policies of a number of autocrats who either resisted the first wave of democratization (Slobodan Milošević in Serbia) or consolidated power by way of the polls (Sali Berisha in Albania, Franjo Tuđman in Croatia, Vladimir Mečiar in Slovakia).

Slovakia was perhaps the most interesting example of this nationalist trend. As citizens of communist Czechoslovakia,

Slovaks labored in the shadows of their more prosperous Czech cousins. In an effort to even out development, the communist regime built up the mining and manufacturing capabilities of Slovakia, which made the region both more polluted and more dependent on precisely the heavy industry that suffered the most after the changes in 1989. Politically, however, Slovakia came into its own during the country's Velvet Revolution. The dissident movement had two nuclei, former Slovak foreign minister Pavol Demeš told me. 'One was in Prague and the second was in Bratislava. The Civic Forum was created in the Czech Republic with several main faces: Václav Havel, Jiří Dienstbier, and others. Here in Bratislava, Public Against Violence emerged with figures like Jan Budaj, Milan Kňažko, and many others. Dialogue between the two then eventually led to the collapse of the Communist Party and change.'

After 1989, tensions between the Czech and Slovak parts of the country resurfaced. The combination of economic reforms and Havel's desire to stop exporting arms hit Slovak manufacturing with particular force. Liberalism, in Slovakia, began to be associated with unemployment and a certain favoritism on the part of federal authorities toward the Czech lands. Still, there was very little support for the dissolution of Czechoslovakia prior to 1993. Even after the authorities made the announcement in July 1992, public opinion polls showed that a majority of citizens wanted to keep the country together.[21] And it wasn't Slovaks who precipitated the divorce. 'This was a fifty-fifty political deal,' Pavol Demeš continued. 'There was no referendum. Politicians in the federal parliament came to a conclusion to end the disputes, which could eventually lead to all kinds of turbulences, through a peaceful division of the state. In our case – unlike Yugoslavia or the Soviet Union where ethnic hatred and memories of the past were painful and bloody – we never shed a single drop of blood or had any hostilities or ethnic rivalries.' But there was also a lingering suspicion that the Czechs were happy to uncouple the Slovak caboose – along with its crashing economy and rising nationalism – to make it easier to join Europe.[22]

As the 1990s progressed, Slovak politics grew more and more authoritarian. This had less to do with Slovak culture than with the personality and ambitions of one man: Vladimir Mečiar.

In his youth, Mečiar had been a member of the Communist Party but, like so many other reform-minded communists, was expelled from the Party after 1968. In 1989, after a career in law, he joined Public Against Violence and then entered the new Czechoslovak government as a minister of interior and environment. With Václav Klaus on the Czech side, he presided over the dissolution of Czechoslovakia and became the first Slovak prime minister in 1993.

Mečiar was the quintessential populist. An ex-boxer, he would insert grammatical mistakes into his campaign posters to demonstrate his proximity to 'the people.'[23] He supported a go-slow approach to economic reform. He openly discriminated against the ethnic Hungarian population,[24] at one point in 1997 even proposing a mass population exchange with Hungary to 'solve' the minority issue.[25] He pushed through a campaign to 'Slovakicize' culture – for instance, by mandating that 30 percent of all music on the radio be from Slovak composers –and appointed his own people to regulate the media to make sure it echoed his party's line. He used materials from the files of the intelligence services to advance his own career and, once in power, made sure to cover up his own earlier complicity with the secret police (even to the point, possibly, of pushing for the dissolution of Czechoslovakia to conceal his past).[26] To make matters worse, he then hired former secret police agents who helped him consolidate his undemocratic rule.[27] He was also incorrigibly corrupt, arranging for his cronies to acquire cheap properties through the privatization process, which they later sold for vast profits.[28] Even Mečiar's chauffeur managed to get on the gravy train, acquiring a meatpacking plant at 5 percent of its real value.[29]

'The first years of Mečiar's government were almost worse than under communism,' writer Martin Šimečka told me. 'The regime was not so strong as under communism, but it was uglier with these fascistic tendencies and this nationalism. For me, personally, those were pretty bad years. Psychologically, it was very difficult to see the gap get bigger between the Czech Republic and Slovakia, with the Czechs going west and we Slovaks going east or going nowhere at all.'

By 1998, Slovaks had had enough of their illiberal detour. 'In the first years of the Mečiar government, it really became clear to everyone, not only to the inner circle, that this guy is thinking about a different type of democracy,' Rasto Kuzel of MEMO 98 told me. 'It was good for Slovak NGOs and for the Slovak civil society that we had to again unite and fight for these principles. We had to very actively demonstrate that we didn't want this type of democracy and that we wanted Slovakia to be back on the right track.' A generation too young to participate in the Velvet Revolution came together to combat the new threat. MEMO 98 monitored the media and the government's efforts to control it; Civic Eye monitored the elections to prevent government tampering; Rock Volieb (Rock the Vote) reached out to young people through music to encourage them to vote. 'Thousands of small organizations, initiatives, clubs and volunteer groups have made unique achievements,' Martin Bútora, former Slovak ambassador to the United States, told me. 'Despite a complicated heritage of undemocratic conditions, backwardness and discontinuity, civic actors and volunteers managed to engage and motivate a broader public because they offered understandable, acceptable concepts of freedom, solidarity and activism.'

Foreign organizations, including foundations and political parties, provided substantial assistance to Slovak civil society.[30] Mečiar's undemocratic leanings also cost Slovakia its spot in the first round of accession to the European Union that included the Czech Republic, Hungary, and Poland. In the 1990s, Euroskepticism was negligible in Slovakia, so liberal activists used the widespread fear of losing out on

EU benefits to bolster their case for Mečiar's ousting. 'Over time the EU's leverage strengthened the hand of liberal forces against illiberal ones,' writes political scientist Milada Anna Vachudova. 'Not in a duel where good vanquished evil, but in an iterated electoral game where sooner or later most political actors – especially political parties – saw the benefits of moving their own agenda toward compatibility with the state's bid for EU membership.'[31]

For all their success, the trainings and financial contributions from outside established a divide between illiberal nationalists with indigenous support and cosmopolitan liberals with foreign assistance. This inside–outside partnership effectively addressed the acute crisis (Mečiar) but did nothing to repair the chronic problem (between Slovakia A and Slovakia B). Vladimir Mečiar disappeared into the countryside after his final electoral humiliation in 2006, but his political defeat did not wipe intolerance from Slovak society. Anti-Roma sentiment has continued to build. In regional elections in 2013, Marian Kotleba won the governorship of Banska Bystrica in eastern Slovakia on an anti-Roma, anti-EU, anti-immigrant platform. Kotleba has done little to disguise his neo-Nazi sympathies, which includes an open admiration for the fascist Slovak regime that allied with Hitler in World War II.[32] In its first outing in the 2016 national elections, his party captured 8 percent of the vote and fourteen seats in parliament. Meanwhile, Mečiar's nationalism has resurfaced in the political mainstream as well. Slovak prime minister Robert Fico has been one of the prominent voices in the region decrying the influx of refugees, calling the more liberal EU immigration policy 'ritual suicide.'[33] Fico has labeled critics of his party 'anti-Slovak,' reviving a Mečiar-era tactic, even going so far as to call journalists probing into government procurement irregularities 'dirty anti-Slovak prostitutes.'[34] With Roma, he said, 'the best solution would be to take away all their children and put them into boarding schools.'[35]

Like Tamás Hegedűs and Jobbik, however, Robert Fico has adopted an economic platform that challenges orthodox liberalism. Many Slovaks suffered a great deal as a result of economic globalization – though the country as a whole has also experienced better-than-average growth since the mid-2000s – and Fico has won successive elections by sticking up for those left behind. He has denounced austerity, scrapped a regressive flat tax, and criticized privatization – even as he has engaged in the same kind of corruption as his predecessors.[36] Fico has also sought out a geopolitical middle ground by negotiating energy deals with Moscow and cooperating with Viktor Orbán in Hungary, thus avoiding what might have been costly conflicts.

On social issues, however, it's not clear whether Fico believes in the intolerant positions he has taken or whether he has adopted them in order to steal the fire from challengers on the right wing. Whether he's populist by temperament or by political expediency, Fico has helped make populism a viable political platform in the region. His illiberal trajectory suggests that Vladimir Mečiar's populist tenure in the 1990s was not a political detour. Rather, it was a sign of things to come.

The populist reformation

Europe underwent a profound transformation during the Protestant reformation of the sixteenth century. Martin Luther, John Calvin, and their co-religionists attacked the bureaucracy of the Catholic Church and its corrupt practices. They also advocated a different, more direct relationship between the individual and God. They were aided by the new technology of the printing press, which churned out pamphlets and Bibles, as well as the new ideology of nationalism, which challenged foreign interference, such as that of the Vatican, in the affairs of the state.

The rise of populism in Europe today contains some echoes of this earlier convulsion, though the religious tones have been transposed to a political register. The Rome that so dismayed the Protestants of the past has become Brussels, and today's populists devote considerable energy to decrying the interference of this immense bureaucracy in national prerogatives. They invoke nationalist slogans and symbols not only against the European Union but against immigrants, foreign investors, international economic institutions, and transnational NGOs. The new populists also argue for a more direct relationship between citizens and political power, unmediated by traditional politicians. And they take advantage of the latest technologies (YouTube, social media) to spread their messages.

Insurgent Protestants established their own churches. Insurgent populists have established their own parties and aspire to lead their congregations out from under the rule of Brussels. With some notable exceptions, for instance in the United Kingdom, they haven't yet mobilized sufficient power at a national level to make the break. But the 'miracle' of Brexit is already attracting many converts on the Continent.

Protestants, in addition to their interest in attaining worldly power, had a distinct ideology. Populists, argues Goran Buldioski, the head of the Open Society Think Tank Fund in Budapest, are not interested in arguing the merits of contending proposals. 'The only skill or ability that's important at the moment is the social skill,' he said. 'If you're able to navigate through society by expressing your loyalty upwards and your use of brute power downwards, then you will be successful. If you look at the classic Hirschman view – exit, voice, loyalty – the new status quo will basically be a critical mass of loyalists, a significant number of exits, and very few people who raise their voices.'[37] Populists will tack whichever way the wind blows in order to gain power.

What they lack in specific policy proposals, they make up for in their sophisticated strategies to gain and wield power, as Jan-Werner Müller argues in his book *What Is Populism?* Since they claim to rule on behalf of all people, they dismiss the need for pluralist politics and attempt to suppress civil society.[38] They engage in 'discriminatory legalism' to handicap their adversaries and 'mass clientelism' to enrich their allies.[39] And they continue to build popular support through attacks on 'an elite that does not truly belong and marginal groups that are also distinct from the people.'[40]

Populists romanticize the 'heartland,' which political scientist Paul Taggart identifies as 'a version of the past that celebrates a hypothetical, uncomplicated and non-political territory of the imagination.'[41] It is this tension between the aggressively political competition at the polls and the aggressively non-political rhetoric of the heartland that characterizes the Populist Reformation. What drops out is the middle: the back-and-forth compromises of liberal governance for which populists and their supporters have little patience. The rapid rise of populists, as Goran points out, is directly connected not so much to the defects of the liberal model but to the failure in explaining and building support for that model. Over the last twenty years, liberals have been unable to communicate the reality of trade-offs, which is the essence of politics. The electorate 'didn't understand that we couldn't have everything,' he concluded. 'Then a populist comes and says, "No, no, you *can* have everything."'

The emergence of populism in eastern Europe is connected at a deep level to the antipolitics of the communist period. The dissidents of the communist era, again with the exception of Poland where a mass movement arose under Solidarity, cultivated positions at odds with both the 'masses' romanticized by the Party and the real mass of people who went along to get along. The politicians who emerged in the immediate post-1989 era quickly developed the same ambivalence. At a rhetorical level, 'the people' reigned supreme. Practically, however, voters posed a threat to the interests of the new elite. 'Rather than take this group as a challenge – how to win their votes? – liberals chose to present them simply as a threat,' writes political scientist David Ost. 'They portrayed them as part of what is often called "Poland B" – the other Poland – inhabited by those who don't read books, or as budding fascists, or as incurable "homo sovieticus."'[42] In this way, liberals helped to create populist movements. 'By decrying all opposition as dangerous and populist, and labeling themselves the only voice of reason,' Ost further explains, 'liberals pushed opponents into the illiberal camp, for that became the only space opponents were permitted to inhabit.'[43] As activist Michał Sutowski put it, 'If the Left deserts the masses, then of course the Right fills the vacuum.'

Populism has proved popular in the region in part because the orthodox liberalism that held sway in the region during the 1990s related to people only as individuals. Less attention was paid to the connective tissue of society – the social welfarism of the communist period or the deeper nationalism that persisted despite the communists' rhetorical adherence to socialist internationalism. Some liberals recognized the problem. 'Liberalism must strengthen itself by tapping into national moods and aspirations, just as nationalism needs an infusion of liberal values if it is to be compatible with the emergent democratic framework,' wrote Balkans expert Judy Batt in 1991.[44] By offering only a vision of a government presiding over barely contained chaos – 'anarchy plus a constable,' as Thomas Carlyle memorably called the minimalist state – liberals ceded ground to those who tapped into the national mood by excoriating the economic reforms that failed to benefit the majority. 'Huge sections of the world's population have won the "right of self-determination" on the cruelest possible terms,' wrote political theorist Chantal Mouffe in 1990. 'They have been simply left to fend for themselves.'[45]

In Poland, Andrzej Lepper broke from the 'church' of Solidarity to create one of the first populist movements in the region. As a farmer in the 1980s and early 1990s, Lepper directly experienced the impact of Poland's economic reforms in the countryside. In 1990, he took out a large loan to expand his farm. 'A few weeks later, Balcerowicz introduced his market reform plan,' writes political scientist Ania Krok-Paszkowska, 'and Lepper was faced with huge increases in interest on his loan. Unable to pay off his debts, Lepper joined other farmers in protests.'[46] Lepper soon began leading these protests. It was a natural step to form a new organization, Samoobrona, or Self-Defense. 'Samoobrona's roots are the same as Solidarity's,' Lepper told the Polish newspaper *Gazeta Wyborcza* in 1992. 'The cause of Samoobrona's emergence lies in the arrogance of the power elite.'[47] Lepper gathered around him other indebted farmers, as well as the unemployed and pensioners, to form a bloc nearly half a million strong by 2000. Many of these members had supported *samorząd* – self-management – in the 1980s. When that option disappeared, only the more reactive option was left: self-defense. The workers and farmers that had formed the core of Solidarity were effectively shut out of politics. Self-Defense was one way of getting their voices heard.

If economic transition had been as short as initially imagined, Lepper's political career would have been equally brief. But a decade after the implementation of the Balcerowicz plan, Poland remained mired in unemployment. Economic growth had returned, but it wasn't trickling down fast enough or far enough. In the 2001 parliamentary elections, Samoobrona was the third-largest vote-getter. Voters were not sure where to place the party along the political spectrum. According to one poll at the time, one quarter of respondents viewed Samoobrona as a leftist party, one quarter put the party in the center, and one third considered it right-wing.[48] In part, this speaks to the fluidity of political definitions in eastern Europe, with both right-wing and left-wing parties competing for the votes of the working class. But it also identified a key element of populism. Samoobrona was defined largely by its negative positions: against neoliberalism, against the EU, against ruling elites, against the urban intellectual bias of Polish politics.

Lepper would go on to capture over 15 percent of the vote in the 2005 presidential elections. Transferring his support to the Law and Justice Party (PiS), he became minister of agriculture and deputy prime minister. Scandal chased him from office in 2007 and, amid continuing allegations of sexual abuse, he committed suicide in 2011. Samoobrona is no longer represented in the Polish parliament. It isn't needed any more. As in Slovakia, the political mainstream in Poland awoke to the electoral virtues of populism and created even more popular versions of it.

In Bulgaria, meanwhile, populism emerged as an alternative to the three major political parties: the former communists, the liberal center, and the primarily ethnic Turkish Movement for Rights and Freedoms. GERB, or Citizens for the European Development of Bulgaria, debuted in 2006 with a platform centered around anti-corruption. Its leader, Boyko Borisov, was an unlikely delivery system for this message. A former bodyguard for former communist leader Todor Zhivkov, Borisov ran a private security firm in the 1990s and was allegedly involved in 'money laundering, methamphetamine trafficking, oil deals benefiting the Russian company Lukoil.'[49] Nevertheless, during his two terms as prime minister between 2009 and 2016, Borisov cultivated a reputation for 'law and order' and for such politically incorrect statements as his reference to ethnic Turks, Roma, and pensioners as 'bad human material.'[50]

The disgust with politics-as-usual in the region has even translated into support for a return to the days of kings and queens. In Bulgaria, the only country where the monarch came back to rule, King Simeon II was not a terribly charismatic figure. Years of exile in Spain had weakened his command of Bulgarian, and on the rare occasions when he did speak, it was in vague, roundabout ways.[51] Still, he appealed to the populace by appearing to function above politics. Though he served as prime minister for four years, from 2001 to 2005, he left virtually no institutional imprint on Bulgaria. Elsewhere, royals never even came close to power, whether King Michael in Romania or the elderly Otto van Habsburg, who resisted calls to rule in Hungary.

In the Czech Republic, royalists have been described as 'one of the parties that could fit in an elevator.'[52] But the principle of monarchy has appeal beyond the programs of specific parties. Reinterviewing Václav Havel's sister-in-law, Dagmar Havlová, after two decades, I was surprised to discover that the former spokeswoman for Civic Forum had changed her political views. 'I'm a monarchist,' she told me in 2013. 'I believe that some symbol of morality at a different level is important even if the symbol is just a vision of what we would like to achieve. When you have a king or a queen, who is a human being, you can understand that the symbol and the human being can differ, but you are more attached to the symbol than to the person. So I believe that monarchy is the right system. It continues over generations … Monarchs are responsible to the country, to history somehow.'

In countries where monarchism has only minority appeal, the left has been discredited by its association with communism, and liberals have been irrevocably linked to economic austerity and elitist individualism, populists have managed to thrive in the vacuum of political legitimacy. They provide a veneer of democracy by promising to represent all the people. They capitalize on underlying nationalism and xenophobia. And they offer a whiff of solidarity with economic programs borrowed from the left. It's a powerful combination.

Trumpism in Poland

On a rainy day in April 1990, I journeyed to the outskirts of Warsaw to a functional, communist-era building complex to meet with Antoni Macierewicz. The opposition leader's apartment contrasted sharply with its grim institutional surroundings. It was an aristocratic enclave full of books, antiques, and prints on the wall. Macierewicz himself exuded an Old World charm that Polish intellectuals worked so hard to preserve during difficult times.

A long-time dissident, Macierewicz had been something of a leftist in the 1970s, supporting the Revolutionary Left Movement in Chile and protesting against the US war in Vietnam.[53] He was a key figure, with Jacek Kuroń and Adam Michnik, behind the creation of the Committee for the Defense of Workers (KOR) in 1976 and then Solidarity in 1980. Over the years, however, he'd moved steadily rightward until, by 1990, he was leading a coalition of conservative Christian groups. These groups had cooperated with Solidarity during the 1980s. But now that Poland had moved past the communist era, Macierewicz was staking out a distinct political terrain for his version of clerical anti-communism.

Government policy, he told me that afternoon in 1990, should follow Church teachings, and so should instruction in public schools. The economic reforms that Poland was then undertaking were not, he argued, sufficiently anti-state, for they did not guarantee access to capital and ownership for the largest number of Poles. And the new Polish state, stripped down to its minimal functions, should make a clean break with the past to eliminate any lingering influence from former communist functionaries.

Perhaps naively, I didn't see much of a future for Macierewicz and his Catholic nationalists. The last thing I imagined Poles wanted after 1989 was to swap one variety of political intolerance for another. Poles were overwhelmingly Catholic, of course. But church attendance was far from universal – 53 percent in 1987 – and religious zealotry was a distinctly minority passion.[54] Meanwhile, most Polish voters were gravitating toward the middle of the political spectrum. Solidarity politicians were establishing a set of center-right parties, and the former communists were struggling to rebrand themselves as a center-left party. In the next parliamentary elections in 1991, Macierewicz's forces in Catholic Election Action managed a mere 8.7 percent of the vote for the Sejm (though the coalition captured a bit more, 17.4 percent, for the Senate).

But Macierewicz himself vaulted into the position of minister of internal affairs in 1991. The following year he released what came to be known as the Macierewicz List, which identified sixty-four members of the Polish government and parliament as former secret communist agents. Even more controversially, he also accused then-president Lech Wałęsa of being an informer. These claims produced immediate outrage – from those who believed that the government was unacceptably compromised as well as those who were appalled that such unvetted accusations were made public. A successful no-confidence vote in parliament led to the resignation of the government and the abrupt end of Macierewicz's term in office. A subsequent parliamentary inquiry concluded that only six of the sixty-four had signed any agreements with the secret police. Macierewicz ultimately faced charges of publishing state secrets.[55]

Back on the political fringes, Macierewicz cultivated his passion for conspiracy theories. In the 2000s, he was still convinced that a majority of Polish diplomats were former communist informers, earning him a skeptical appraisal in a US diplomatic cable.[56] He believed that the Russians were behind the 2010 airplane crash in Smolensk that killed then-Polish president Lech Kaczyński and many other prominent Poles on their way to a commemoration of the 1940 Katyn massacre. Holding hearings in parliament that featured 'experts' who relied on Internet photos rather than site visits, Macierewicz rejected the notion that some combination of fog and pilot error caused the Tupolev 154 plane to crash, the conclusion of the official investigations of both Poland and Russia.[57] Russians were not the only villains in his worldview. In an infamous interview with the right-wing Catholic Radio Maryja, Macierewicz put in a good word for the famous anti-Semitic forgery *The Protocols of the Elders of Zion*, adding that 'Polish experience, especially in recent years, shows that there are such groups in Jewish circles who think in a cunning way and act deliberately to the detriment of, for example, Poland.'[58] It wasn't an isolated incident. He published a number of anti-Semitic articles in his right-wing newspaper *Głos*, some of them under his own name.[59]

Macierewicz did not remain on the margins of Polish politics.[60] Neither his past actions nor his inflammatory rhetoric disqualified him from becoming minister of defense in the new Law and Order Party (PiS) government in November 2015. Led behind the scenes by Jarosław Kaczyński, the twin brother of Lech, who died in the Smolensk air disaster, PiS is involved in transforming Poland much as the Trump revolution is attempting in the United States, 'an uncompromising revolution from above that abandons the institutions of liberal democracy and any ethos of compromise in favor of an unchallenged monopoly of power,' as David Ost has written.[61]

PiS moved quickly in February 2016 to reopen an official inquiry into the Smolensk disaster, aggravating the already dicey relations between Moscow and Warsaw. As importantly, the inquiry polarized what is already a deeply divided Polish society. 'Smolensk' has all the hallmarks of the 'birther' movement in which facts count for a lot less than insinuation. Just as one in three Americans believed that former president Obama was a Muslim even after seven years in office, one in three Poles believe that Lech Kaczyński was assassinated.[62] However, the real focus of PiS has not been Russia but the enemy within. If the official Polish inquiry was flawed, the previous government of centrist Donald Tusk and the Civic Platform (PO) – the chief political opposition to PiS – emerge as dangerous co-conspirators.

The goal of PiS is to 'purify' the country of Poles of the 'worst sort,' as Kaczyński has described his opponents. In uglier days, the 'worst sort' of Poles might have been Jews, who were accused of being communists or rapacious capitalists or simply disloyal 'outsiders.' Today, the enemy is a motley collection of liberals, secularists, critical intellectuals, and cosmopolitans. Poland's foreign minister Witold Waszczykowski has warned against 'a new mixing of cultures and races, a world made up of bicyclists and vegetarians, who … fight all forms of religion.'[63] Bicyclists and vegetarians stand in for non-conformists and freethinkers who threaten the integrity of an undivided Polish nation. Even the military has not been above suspicion. Macierewicz undertook a purge of the military as if it were populated by communist-era appointees rather than officials designated by the previous center-right government.[64] The purge included the rector of the National Defense University. The new government even went so far as to conduct a raid to replace the head of the NATO-affiliated Counter-Intelligence Center of Excellence based in Warsaw.[65]

To combat these threats to Polish society, PiS began to ram through legislation in a top-down effort to remake Polish society. It has passed laws giving the government greater surveillance powers as well as the authority to appoint the heads of public media. It has tried to ban abortion – prompting a nationwide women's strike in October 2016 – and restrict *in vitro* fertilization.[66] Lacking a large enough parliamentary majority to easily change the Polish constitution, the government made various changes to the Constitutional Court – such as requiring a two-thirds rather than a simple majority vote for decisions – in order to reduce the court's ability to block government actions as it had done the last time PiS formed a government in 2006. 'The aim of the legislation is to destroy the court, to disintegrate it, to create a kind of private council for our "beloved leader",' the Court's president, Andrzej Rzepliński, said before his term expired in December 2016.[67]

The EU is worried about Poland's apostasy. 'Unlike in the case of Hungary, the European Union has reacted quickly,' wrote Jan-Werner Müller in the *New York Review of Books* in February 2016. 'Leading EU figures declared that fundamental democratic values were threatened by Warsaw. And on January 13, the European Commission was sufficiently concerned to open a "probe" into the workings of the rule of law in Poland, a step that is unprecedented in EU history.'[68] It mattered little, as the Polish government has rejected all European pressure tactics.[69]

The EU is not just worried about Poland's internal politics. The Union has encountered considerable pushback from several central European countries, including Poland, about accepting their fair share of refugees coming from the Middle East. Poland, with a minuscule immigrant population, has also seen a large outflow of population over the last two decades. In other words, there's plenty of room for newcomers. But Kaczyński has made clear that refugees are not welcome. 'There are already signs of emergence of diseases that are highly dangerous and have not been seen in Europe for a long time: cholera on the Greek islands, dysentery in Vienna,' he said during the 2015 election campaign, using rhetoric that echoed Nazi descriptions of Jews as carriers of disease.[70] The more moderate of the anti-refugee politicians in Poland have, like some Republican Party politicians in the United States, argued that only Christians among the asylum-seekers should be allowed in.[71] 'My pet hypothesis: we're an ethnic society that masquerades as a civil society and gets away with it, because those who don't ethnically belong are so few,' journalist Konstanty Gebert told me.

The success of PiS is not simply a function of the failures of the previous center-right government of Donald Tusk, who decamped in late 2014 to become the president of the European Council. Rather, the Kaczyński crowd has benefitted from the collapse of the putative left in Poland. When it was in charge, the former communists embraced a pro-West platform of austerity economic reforms, accession to NATO and the EU, and a (relatively) tolerant set of cultural policies. The support for 'shock therapy' cost the mainstream left its base among those who have not benefitted from economic reforms. This perceived betrayal opened up a vast opportunity for right-wing parties that have fed on the anger and resentment of the 'losers of transition' – farmers, industrial workers, pensioners – by offering, like Trump, vaguely populist economic policies.

With its xenophobia, manipulations of the rule of law, and confrontational attitude toward the EU, PiS is following virtually the same playbook as Viktor Orbán and Fidesz in Hungary. This is no surprise. 'Viktor Orbán gave us an example of how we can win,' Jarosław Kaczyński declared five years prior to PiS taking power. 'The day will come when we will succeed, and we will have Budapest in Warsaw.'[72]

Hungary's illiberal democracy

In 1990, I played soccer with members of the Alliance of Young Democrats, or Fidesz, at their summer camp at Lake Velence, not far from Budapest. I found my fellow soccer players refreshing and exuberant, which corresponded with their liberal, radical, and alternative politics. Even if I didn't agree with everything Fidesz stood for, I definitely appreciated its style. For one thing, it restricted membership to those under the age of thirty-five. It also loved to shake things up. One particularly striking, if heteronormative, campaign poster from that year showed two pictures of a kiss: between two communist dinosaurs, Leonid Brezhnev and Erich Honecker, and between two young Hungarians of the opposite sex. 'Make your choice,' read the inscription. Fidesz captured nearly 9 percent of the vote in the 1990 elections, coming in fifth and sending twenty-one MPs to parliament.

'In 1990, for the first campaign, Fidesz was not a political party,' Attila Ledényi reminded me. In charge of international relations in the organization's early years, he was one of the early shapers of Fidesz. 'We were very easygoing about things. Obviously, there were lawyers and economists who were thinking in bigger terms. But generally speaking, our image and self-image were very youthful. Most of us were between eighteen and twenty-five.' In 1990, the leader of Fidesz was Viktor Orbán, a twenty-seven-year-old lawyer. He, more than perhaps anyone else in the party, was thinking of bigger things. It wasn't long before he transformed Fidesz from a quirky, youth-oriented party into a bastion of illiberal orthodoxy.

In the early 1990s, Hungarian society was divided into three blocs – an old-fashioned conservative group that believed in an authoritarian state, a socialist bloc that believed in a paternalistic state, and a liberal bloc that believed in individual freedom. Each of these blocs attracted the support of a third of the electorate. 'But since 1994,' long-time dissident and journalist Ferenc Kőszeg told me, 'the general conviction became that you had to belong to the right or the left, and there was nothing in the middle, which is very bad.'

In that pivotal year of 1994, Ferenc conducted an interview with Viktor Orbán at a time when Fidesz and the liberal party, the Alliance of Free Democrats (SzDSz), were still very close. 'Orbán said, "If the liberal left and the socialist left come together to make a coalition, then the gap between the right and the left will be like a rift between two mountains, and it will take at least twenty-five years before grass will grow again on the side of this rift,"' Ferenc remembered.

And that's precisely what happened. When the liberals and the socialists formed a ruling coalition after the 1994 elections, Orbán viewed it as both a betrayal of Fidesz principles and an enormous Fidesz opportunity. 'The gap was also very useful for Fidesz,' Ferenc continued. 'The policy of Fidesz was built on this gap. After the coalition happened, Orbán did everything to deepen it and say that Fidesz was good and the socialist-liberals were evil. After that, he pushed Fidesz in the direction of a more radical right-wing politics.'

Charles Gati, a specialist on Hungary who befriended Orbán early on, watched as his friend moved steadily rightward. 'Orbán was a dynamo of a leader, and I understood even then that he had ambitions,' he told me. 'He was a real politician – and I say that in the best sense of the word. Little did I anticipate then, as I guess you didn't either, that he would turn out to be a nationalist demagogue.' In 1998, Orbán became prime minister at the age of thirty-five – after Fidesz had already dropped its under-thirty-five age requirement. Orbán had professionalized what had once been a quirky movement, pushing his party out of the Liberal International and into the camp of the Christian Democrats. Attila Ledényi eventually left the organization, but he doesn't look back in anger. 'I was never disappointed by the way things developed because I thought that these parties had to become institutions and the whole electoral system was changing,' he told me. 'And if Fidesz wanted to have influence in all this, it would have to become a political party. Beyond a certain point, Fidesz was not sexy any more.'

It wasn't sexy, nor was it particularly successful in its first term in office. But Orbán learned from his mistakes. After that one term in office, he spent eight years in the political wilderness, biding his time. In 2010 Fidesz won more than 50 percent of the vote, giving it the power to undo everything that the liberals and socialists had previously accomplished. Orbán's government even had enough votes to change the Hungarian constitution. When the country's Constitutional Court overturned key Fidesz laws, the government simply achieved its goal by changing the constitution. By 2016 it has done so six times – recalling the apocryphal story of the Paris bookseller who, when asked for a copy of the French constitution after World War II, answered that he didn't traffic in periodical literature.[73]

Fidesz also moved proactively to control the media in order to sustain its positive image. The government replaced the heads of Hungarian public radio and television and its news agency with its own yes men. A new media law allowed anyone, even anonymously, to file complaints against a newspaper, website, or TV station, with potentially large fines assessed by a Media Council whose members all come from Fidesz.[74] In October 2016, the government maneuvered behind the scenes to close the country's leading daily newspaper, *Népszabadság*, which just happened to be a mouthpiece for the opposition.[75] 'In the old days – well, five years ago – government advertisements in the press were divided in the following way: approximately seventy percent went to government press, thirty percent to opposition press,' political scientist Charles Gati told me in 2013. 'Today it's one hundred percent government. That gives you an illustration of how harsh this new regime is, how it moved away from the values of pluralism towards authoritarianism.'

'It was completely unexpected what happened in Hungary, where an already consolidated liberal democracy went backwards toward an autocratic or hybrid regime,' sociologist András Bozóki explained to me. 'It never before happened in the EU that a country suddenly made a U-turn back from democracy toward some kind of half-democracy. When Austrians elected the Haider party, there was a huge protest in the EU. There was also a marginalization of Berlusconi. But none of these people had a two-thirds majority in the parliament, so they couldn't change the constitution.'

Fidesz remains popular, retaining a large lead over a variety of opposition parties.[76] To bolster its support, the government plays up Hungarian nationalism. It created a Day of National Unity to commemorate the Treaty of Trianon (which reduced Hungary's territory by two-thirds in 1920 and which 45 percent of Hungarians said in a 2010 poll should never have been accepted).[77] Members of the party have begun to rehabilitate the dictatorial regime of Admiral Horthy – whose signed picture Adolf Hitler kept on his desk as inspiration – by sanctioning new plaques, statues, and street names commemorating the far-right leader.[78] The social agenda of Fidesz veers rightward as well, with its attempt to declare homelessness illegal and redefine marriage as only between a man and a woman.[79]

The flip side of this nationalism is racism and xenophobia. 'A significant part of the Roma are unfit for coexistence,' Fidesz co-founder Zsolt Bayer has written. 'These Roma are animals, and they behave like animals.'[80] Although Orbán has personally declared zero tolerance for anti-Semitism, his Education Ministry made recommendations of anti-Semitic authors to school syllabuses.[81] Europe's refugee crisis has given Fidesz further ammunition for its xenophobia. 'All the terrorists are basically migrants,' Orbán has said. 'The question is when they migrated to the European Union.'[82]

On the economic side, Fidesz has pursued what seemed at first glance to be contradictory policies. It pushed through a labor law that embodied the neoliberal principles of 'greater flexibility' and suspended the trilateral commission that brought together representatives of government, business, and unions. Yet Orbán also lashed out against international finance, instituting a huge levy on the banking sector that international finance institutions consider the most punitive in the world.[83] As the architect of Hungary's economic reforms, Lajos Bokros, has written, Orbán's government 'destroyed private property by nationalizing the mandatory private pension funds; created market-distorting artificial monopolies in tobacco retail trade; undermined agricultural land tenure; rewrote primary and secondary school textbooks; introduced punitive and predatory taxes in banking, retail trade, and public utilities, and engaged in other measures that reversed reform.'[84] Through these often different economic policies, Fidesz is pursuing one essential goal: consolidating state control to facilitate the distribution of resources to its own patronage system – the aforementioned 'mass clientelism.' 'Don't be misled when you hear that some private activities are nationalized,' András Bozóki told me. 'It just means that the larger mafia took over the smaller one.'

What is perhaps most remarkable about the changes in Hungary has been Viktor Orbán's embrace of Russia. On 26 July 2014, in a speech to the party faithful, Orbán confided that he intended a thorough reorganization of the country. The reform model he had in mind, however, had nothing to do with the United States, Britain, or France. Rather, he aspired to create what he bluntly called an 'illiberal state' in the very heart of Europe, one strong on Christian values and light on the libertine ways of the West. More precisely, what he wanted was to turn Hungary into a mini-Russia or mini-China. 'Societies founded upon the principle of the liberal way,' Orbán intoned in the 2014 speech, 'will not be able to sustain their world-competitiveness in the following years, and more likely they will suffer a setback, unless they will be able to substantially reform themselves.'[85] The Hungarian prime minister was also eager to reorient to the east, relying ever less on Brussels and ever more on potentially lucrative markets in and investments from Russia, China, and the Middle East.

Given the disappointing performance of liberal economic reforms and the often burdensome requirements of the EU, it was hardly surprising that Orbán had decided to hedge his bets by distancing himself from liberalism. The Hungarian leader could in this way blame everything that had gone wrong in the country on outsiders, who had 'imposed' a Western model of democracy and free market economy with the help of a coalition of homegrown liberals and socialists. 'Orbán frequently refers in his speeches to the fight between "good" and "evil" as well as to Fidesz's self-proclaimed duty to protect Hungary and Europe from the evil influences of modernity and liberalism,' writes Umut Korkut. 'At the May 2003 Fidesz-MPP congress, Orbán explained that liberalism had fulfilled its historic mission and now has run out of new ideas. Regarding liberalism, Orbán stated that there is no need for further destruction.'[86] Orbán's *democratura* – something in between democracy and dictatorship – appealed to a deeply conservative society that's nostalgic for the generous social welfare policies of the communist period and takes for granted liberal values such as freedom of speech. Orbán's confidence also appeals to many Hungarians. 'Even if Orbán was already hated by a lot of people, by a lot of intellectuals,' Attila Ledényi told me, 'he was someone who could always stand up and look like something and sound like something and have a vision.'

If Orbán's anti-liberal turn made a certain amount of political sense, his embrace of Russia was almost as improbable as Tamás Hegedűs's warm feelings for Turkey. After all, the Soviet Union invaded Hungary in 1956. During the Cold War, students refused to learn the obligatory Russian in school. Orbán's public debut as a young activist was at the reburial of Imre Nagy in 1989 when, at the age of twenty-six, he boldly called for the withdrawal of Soviet troops from the country. His anti-Russian views were so pronounced that Anna Porter, in her 2010 book *The Ghosts of Europe*, remarked that 'Orbán, no matter how high the stakes, would never entertain such a friendly personal gesture to a Russian, even if it was good for business or foreign policy.'[87] For Orbán, however, opportunism trumped ideology. 'It's not that Orbán wants to be a satellite of Russia, far from it,' Charles Gati told me. 'But he thinks he can outwit Putin and get the trade agreements and the economic benefits, so that he will not have to rely on the EU as much.'

The closeness of ties with Moscow and the embrace of illiberal democracy have indeed alienated Orbán from the EU. It's reminiscent of the moment in the 1960s when Albania fled the Soviet bloc and aligned itself with communist China in an act of transcontinental audacity. But Albania was then a marginal player, and China still a poor peasant country. Hungary is an important EU member, and Russia's illiberal model is making inroads in Europe. This, in other words, is no Albanian mouse that roared. A new illiberal axis connecting Budapest to Moscow and even Beijing has far-reaching implications.

After all, the Hungarian prime minister has many European allies in his Euroskeptical project. Far-right parties are climbing in the polls across the continent. In Denmark, the far-right People's Party topped opinion polls for the first time in November 2015. Austria's Freedom Party came within a couple percentage points of putting their leader into the presidential office in 2016. In France, the National Front's Marine Le Pen emerged as a frontrunner in the early polling for the 2017 presidential race. More so even than the Green Party in Germany in the 1980s, groups like Alternative für Deutschland, the Finns Party, the Party for Freedom in the Netherlands, and even Sweden's Democrats are shattering the comfortable conservative-social democratic duopoly that rotated in power throughout Europe during the Cold War and in its aftermath. These various Euroskeptical movements foreground different elements – anti-immigrant sentiment, anger at continent-wide redistributive economic policies, conservative pushback at liberal social policies like gay marriage – but they all focus anger on perceived infringements of sovereignty.

Nor is the swing of Hungary to the right simply the result of a few charismatic individuals. In Hungary, as in eastern Europe more generally, liberalism has essentially dug its own grave. The liberal economic model has produced wealth for some, uncertainty for most, and extreme poverty for an increasing minority. The liberal political model has produced a rotating kleptocracy: each party that comes into power has sought to use the mechanism of the state to enrich its supporters. And the liberal social model has encouraged an individualism that has eaten away at the solidarity of family, neighborhood, and community, all of which traditionally helped people through difficult times.

Going on the attack

Three items in Volen Siderov's office in downtown Sofia reflect his current preoccupations. The religious icons on the wall speak to his embrace of traditional Bulgarian values and to the agreement his party concluded with the Bulgarian Orthodox Church in 2006. The antique sword hanging nearby represents his militancy. And the heavy boxing bag suspended from the ceiling is part of his personal commitment to physical fitness and a willingness to use his fists in public to achieve his goals.

Volen Siderov is the leader of Ataka, the most controversial political party in Bulgaria. Ataka – or Attack – came to prominence in 2005, when it placed fourth in the parliamentary elections. Volen himself came in second in the presidential race the following year. He is an unabashed nationalist. He claims that ethnic Turks don't exist, that they are simply Bulgarians forced to convert to Islam during the

Ottoman period, which was the same line the communist government used when it forced ethnic Turks to Slavicize their names in the 1980s. A rally Volen organized outside Sofia's main mosque devolved into a huge brawl, demonstrating that his party lives up to its name.

Unlike Tamás Hegedűs, Volen Siderov is combative in an interview. Instead of having a conversation, he lectured me, spending an entire hour 'answering' my first question. We might have shared a certain skepticism about laissez-faire economics, but I didn't feel comfortable in his presence. The icon, sword, and punch-bag contributed to my unease, as did the camera crew he'd arranged to film our encounter. But this was part of Volen's pose. A friend of his from the early post-1989 period told me of Volen's deep insecurity, his struggles to fit in, his propensity to equate dissidence with drinking. He'd tried other ways to gain attention: several of his poems appear in a 1991 anthology of young poets from Bulgaria.[88] He edited the opposition daily *Demokratsiya*. But it wasn't until he hosted a TV talk show in the 2000s, also called *Ataka*, that he became famous. The show served as his first political platform.

Despite a propensity to use his fists, Volen Siderov still sounds like the member of the intelligentsia he was as a poet and journalist. 'When I realized that things were going the wrong way, I came to the conclusion that principles of national sovereignty, or nationalism as we define our political party Ataka, were a defensive response to this collapse of the state, the economy, and the social system,' Volen told me. 'I started to realize that the process of globalization might be good for some people but not at all for others.' He cited Joseph Stiglitz. He spoke of the international 'colonization' of Bulgaria as a Marxist might. It wasn't just words. Calling for renationalizing industries acquired by foreign corporations, Ataka successfully made a seamstress strike at a German-owned factory into a national issue.[89]

During our discussion, it didn't take long for Volen's inner pugilist to come out. 'For a period of seven years now, the mass media has presented me as too extreme, as a person who is dangerous, who stirs up hostility against non-Bulgarians, as a very fearful nationalist who would start a civil war,' he told me. 'People are easily scared. They don't want to have clashes or riots.' As the author of several books about Jewish plots to take over the world, Volen seemed to relish the idea of scaring people. Ataka would shake them out of their complacency. He didn't seem concerned about the possibility that it might also inspire more widespread violence.

Illiberalism takes different forms in eastern Europe. In Poland, it tends to be conspiratorial and anti-Russian. In Hungary, it has a strong anti-Roma component. In Romania, it's colored by suspicions of the Hungarian minority.

In Bulgaria, the largest minority is ethnically Turkish and religiously Muslim. It's not surprising, then, that Volen Siderov's intolerance comes with a large dollop of Islamophobia. Ataka views the Movement for Rights and Freedom (MRF), which has represented ethnic Turkish interests since 1990, as 'national traitors.'[90] In a position diametrically opposed to Jobbik, Ataka wants to block Turkish entry into the EU and has insisted that the country pay reparations to Bulgaria for the 'genocide' that the Ottomans inflicted on Bulgarians in 1876. Ataka has benefitted both from an ethnic Bulgarian backlash against the achievements of the MRF and the persistence of a hardline nationalist element within the former Communist Party. It has pushed its agenda into the mainstream through both extremist rhetoric and specific legislation (for instance, a successful effort to ban veils).

'It is very difficult to make a political issue from the rights of the Turkish minority,' observes human rights advocate Krassimir Kanev. 'That was part of the reason why the Union of Democratic Forces could not win a majority in the first elections: because the UDF was perceived (and was made to be perceived) as people who would return the names of the Turks. Within the UDF at that time were people who refrained from taking up the issue of ethnic minorities because they didn't think they could win on this issue.'

Indeed, in the immediate aftermath of 1989, the opposition coalition Union of Democratic Forces (UDF) deliberately marginalized ethnic Turks. 'I still remember the first big public rally,' Yonko Grozev, a lawyer who has represented ethnic Turks in Bulgaria, told me. 'It was the only time when there was a clear dividing line, with people booing when the issue of the rights of Turks came up. It split the audience.' The UDF chose not to bring ethnic Turks on board for the round table negotiations with the communist government. Ethnic Turks saw no other choice than to create their own party. Yonko continued, 'If the UDF had taken a more integrationist policy at the time, things might have developed differently.' And yet many Bulgarians felt at the time that the UDF somehow sided with ethnic Turks.

Despite any number of political challenges and internal splits, the Movement for Rights and Freedoms managed to achieve some concrete results for its constituents. 'The MRF made it possible for the first time for representatives from the ethnic minorities to have a major presence in parliament,' the MRF's Tchetin Kazak said, itemizing the accomplishments of the party for me. It passed bills on the recovery of property and the legal restoration of names. It introduced Turkish-language classes in schools and universities, which required training teachers and publishing the first textbooks. The MRF has also leveraged its kingmaker position to take control of key ministries – such as agriculture – where it has tried to attract EU funds for the underdeveloped areas of Bulgaria where the majority of ethnic Turks live.[91] 'The very fact that ethnic Turks became visible in society reduced a lot of prejudice,' Krassimir Kanev added.

The party's long-serving leader, Ahmed Dogan, was flawed in many ways. But he was also very clear in his allegiance to Bulgaria, not Turkey, and opposed any territorial claims Turkey might have had on disputed lands. 'The good thing is that Ahmed Dogan himself was not an irredentist,' former dissident Deyan Kiuranov pointed out. 'This could have been one of the important factors that saved us from civil war in winter 1989/90.' Many prominent Bulgarian politicians have echoed this sentiment in praising the moderation of the MRF and holding up the 'Bulgarian ethnic model' for the resolution of conflict as a significant success of the transition period.[92]

Still, anti-Turkish and Islamophobic sentiment is pervasive in Bulgaria. Bulgaria is 'a society heavily indoctrinated into nationalism, under communism but also before,' Krassimir Kanev pointed out. 'This nationalism and ethnocentrism is very much part of the Bulgarian national identity. It's how people think: "We are Bulgarians because we were enslaved by the Turks, and we emancipated ourselves from Turkish rule, and therefore these are our basic enemies."' The history that most Bulgarians absorb casts the Ottoman Empire in almost exclusively negative terms. 'State education usually confines to just a few pages the five centuries of Ottoman domination, and then focuses on uprisings and revolts and their extremely bloody subjugation,' relates *A Guide to Ottoman Bulgaria*. 'Little if anything is mentioned about architecture, the arts and sciences and social development under the Ottomans, nor is there any balanced explanation of Ottoman influence in many areas of life in present-day Bulgaria, from cuisine to legislation, and from religion to family matters.'[93] Former journalist Vihar Krastev casts a bemused look at this unbalanced historiography: 'We talk about the five centuries of Ottoman occupation as something that ruined the Bulgarian nation.

Not at all. You know the joke from Monty Python's *Life of Brian*. What have the Romans ever given us? Nothing. Other than the aqueduct and sanitation, and the roads, and irrigation, and medicine, and education, health, public baths, other than government, other than …'

In 1990, when I talked with the head of the international affairs section of the opposition newspaper *Demokratsiya* – the same paper that Volen Siderov was editing at the time – he told me that he seriously believed that Islamic fundamentalism would find its way into Europe through Bulgaria, by which he meant through the ethnic Turkish population. That sentiment has only grown more popular. 'Parents provide their children with the same stereotypes that they themselves have acquired,' Tchetin Kazak said, 'that the Turks are bad, that they are descendants of invaders, that Turkey wants to invade Bulgaria again … that Turks are susceptible to influence from abroad, that Muslims are fruitful soil for the spread of radical Islam.' According to a 2015 Eurobarometer poll, only 27 percent of Bulgarian respondents would be comfortable if their child were in a love relationship with a Muslim (compared to 65 percent of French but only 12 percent of Czechs).[94]

It's not just passive intolerance. The Grand Mufti in Bulgaria once sent a list to the Organization for Security and Cooperation in Europe (OSCE) of more than a hundred incidents of hate crimes against Muslims. 'None of them had been prosecuted,' said Taşkın Tankut Soykan, who worked for the OSCE when I interviewed him in 2013. 'Not even one investigation had been launched. We immediately decided to go to Sofia. We had meetings with civil society organizations from all communities: LGBT, Jewish, Roma, also refugees. All of them were telling us that hate crimes against Muslims were an issue in Bulgaria. But when we started talking to government officials from the Ministry of Justice and the prime minister's office, they told us exactly the opposite, that there was no problem, that Bulgaria was a European Union member state, and that such things could not happen in a European country. They were very angry at the office of the Grand Mufti for sending information to an international organization. They were basically saying that the mufti was lying.'

Taşkın met with the vice minister of interior. 'I showed him pictures of graffiti, the destroyed gates of mosques, the vandalism of graveyards, and I could see that he was turning red,' he continued. 'He said that he'd never seen these incidents before. He'd never been informed. But we knew that the European Court of Human Rights had made a number of decisions indicating that the Bulgarian authorities had violated their obligation to look into the motivation of the crimes when they happened. So, the vice minister of justice must have been aware of the situation.' But out of this effort, the OSCE and Bulgaria agreed to establish training for law enforcement officials on hate crimes. In addition, an OSCE training module for imams in Bulgaria on recognizing and reporting hate crimes has been adapted for use throughout Europe.

Islamophobia has spiked in Europe as a result of the wave of refugees fleeing the civil war in Syria and the atrocities of the Islamic State. The land route out of the Middle East has brought the desperate people through Turkey and into the Balkans. As Germany took in more than a million newcomers, the EU tried to come up with a plan that would more evenly distribute refugees among the member states. The countries of eastern Europe were unified in their rejection of the EU's plan. In Hungary, for instance, the overflow of refugees prompted the Orbán government to erect a new barbed-wire fence along the border with Serbia. Some Hungarians took it upon themselves to put scarecrow heads on the fence to deter refugees. Fidesz politician György Schöpflin, once a respected academic at the University of London, recommended hanging pig heads instead, combining anti-immigrant sentiment and Islamophobia in one sharp image.[95]

Throughout Europe, far-right movements and intellectuals have long predicted an Islamic takeover of the continent.[96] The refugee crisis is giving such arguments new currency. The previously extreme xenophobia of groups like Ataka is going mainstream.

Scratching the surface

Aurel, a lawyer, had volunteered to take me to Gradinari, a small town about an hour outside Bucharest.[97] I'd visited the Romanian orphanage there in 1990 and, like many other visitors that year, was frankly horrified by the conditions: the children in filthy clothes, the overcrowding, the understaffing.[98] Returning to Romania in 2013, I contacted an Irish charity that now worked in Gradinari. I was eager to see how much had changed. Aurel kindly offered to drive me there. But at the last moment I learned that the government, after a scathing BBC report on the conditions in the orphanages, was now requiring pre-authorization to visit the facilities.[99] I didn't have enough time remaining in Bucharest to make those arrangements, so I cancelled the trip.

Aurel met me anyway at a café. He seemed to have time on his hands, and our conversation started out friendly enough. Then he veered into darker territory.

For two hours, Aurel filled me in on why he hated Germany.

Once, on vacation in Greece, he watched two German tourists make fun of the waitress at a bar, comparing her to an ape. So incensed was Aurel that Germans were referring to the Greeks as '*untermenschen*' that he created a shirt with the slogan 'Germany committed genocide and hasn't yet taken responsibility' and began wearing it around Greece. His wife asked him to take it off, but he put it back on when she wasn't looking. Later, when his law firm took on a client suing Germany, Aurel offered to research the case for free. When the firm gave the case to someone else, he did the legal research anyway and sent it to the lawyers on the case. 'Because I want to fuck Germany,' he told me.

I was taken aback. There had been no indication that this white-collar professional harbored such feelings. At the same time, I was overwhelmed with a profound sense of déjà vu. I'd had the same experience twenty-three years ago. A cultural attaché at the American embassy in Bucharest complained off the record of the extraordinary intolerance of the population. I thought she was exaggerating. After all, I'd been taken in by a gracious couple – a taxi driver, Nicolae, and his hairdresser wife Mara – who allowed me and two friends to stay in the apartment they were refurbishing.

Then I got to know my hosts better. 'Mara and Nicolae are extraordinarily warm and generous – if you are their friends,' I wrote in my report back in 1990. 'But there are so many people who, by virtue of ethnic background, would probably never become their friends. They dislike especially Romanian Gypsies. Nico occasionally talks of shooting them (I've come across that sentiment several times here). They have one or two Gypsy friends but these are exceptions. Mara asks me if in America restaurateurs must allow everyone into their establishments. I say yes, although money is often the determining factor. Mara is disappointed: she would have to allow in Gypsies as well as the other peoples she dislikes: Arabs, Hungarians, Russians, Africans.'

Prejudice, racism, xenophobia: these are not feelings peculiar to Romania. The rise of far right-wing movements in every European country testifies to the popularity of the sentiments. Aurel's anti-German screed, however, had a distinctly paranoid element to it. 'I hate Germany,' he kept repeating to me. 'They have to disappear. The people can disperse to different countries. But there should never be a German state. This state is bound to commit genocide again. You're an American, you don't understand. You're over there across the Atlantic. You think everyone is guilty, not just Germans. But you'll see. There will be World War III. But I won't be around for you to say, "Aurel, you were right." I'll be dead, like all Europeans. Because of this war.'

Fear of the larger neighbor – Russia, Germany – has always been a feature of the eastern European worldview. But Aurel perceived more sinister forces at work behind the scenes. Such paranoia takes a particularly virulent form in Romania, where there are conspiracy theories about everything from the CIA covering up evidence of alien skeletons in the Bucegi Mountains to what really happened in December 1989. 'December 1989 was a big set-up,' poet and literary critic Mircea Ţuglea told me over lunch in the Black Sea port of Constanţa. 'That's why nobody is really interested in clearing up the mysteries. This set-up was in fact a *coup d'état* in order to get rid of Ceauşescu and install a new power, a neo-communist one. And that's why nobody can tell, twenty years after, what really happened.'

The Romanian revolution was simultaneously the most violent of the transformations of 1989 and the most opaque. There was no broad-based movement like Solidarity to form a government to replace the Romanian Communist Party. The Group for Social Dialogue, a collection of dissident intellectuals, bore some family resemblance to Czechoslovakia's Civic Forum, but it was a tiny organization of little more than a dozen members when it debuted on 31 December 1989. And it played no significant role in the revolution itself. Romania was, according to some observers, a primary example of how the revolutions of 1989 pitted one faction of the communist elite – the technocrats – against the entrenched, neo-Stalinist bureaucracy.[100] The technocrats got the upper hand by allying themselves with their fellow intellectuals in the opposition, as Konrád and Szelényi had predicted.

The group responsible for dismantling the Ceaușescu regime – and trying and executing Nicolae and Elena Ceaușescu – was the National Salvation Front (NSF). Composed of former insiders like Ion Iliescu, who had once been a member of the Central Committee of the Party, the NSF nevertheless promised a clean break with the past. It banned the Communist Party, put the notorious Securitate under the control of the army, prepared the ground for democratic elections, and, in its 22 December communiqué, outlined an economic program based on 'eliminating the administrative-bureaucratic methods of centralized economic control and promoting *laissez-faire* and competence in running all economic sectors.'[101]

But accusations of a 'revolution hijacked' emerged almost from the beginning. Protests against the Front and its leader Iliescu broke out in Bucharest in January and February 1990. But it was the demonstrations in University Square in May and June that posed the greatest challenge to the new leadership. In the lead-up to the May elections, opposition political parties, students, and fledgling NGOs demanded that the

Front ban former members of the Communist Party and the Securitate from political office for ten years.[102] Given the background of top NSF officials, including Iliescu himself, this was a non-starter. On 20 May, Iliescu won a landslide victory in the presidential race with over 80 percent of the votes, while the NSF captured large majorities in the two houses of parliament. Many protestors in University Square packed up and went home. Others dug in their heels, and the confrontations with the police grew increasingly violent. Ultimately, Iliescu made an appeal to the Romanian public to restore order, and 10,000 pro-government miners descended from the countryside on Bucharest. The clashes left several dead and hundreds injured. Combined with anti-Roma violence and deteriorating relations between ethnic Romanians and Hungarians, the unvelvet revolution was turning into an unvelvet transition.

Even more ominous events were happening in Transylvania, where many of Romania's ethnic Hungarians live. 'There was a short euphoria when the pressure was released, and we were all brothers,' Ágnes Gagyi told me of her experiences as a nine-year-old ethnic Hungarian in the Transylvanian city of Miercurea Ciuc right after the changes in December 1989. 'After a few months, we felt that the pressure was back, but its face had changed and it was ethnic now. The old local Party leaders became the biggest nationalists and Christians.'

The tensions burst into the open in March 1990, and it looked as though Romania would be the first country in the region to descend into communal strife. Ethnic Hungarians and ethnic Romanians squared off in Târgu Mureş, a Transylvanian city that had a rough ethnic balance in the early 1990s. The clashes that took place in the city in March 1990 left several people dead and hundreds injured. 'It was provoked, on the one hand, to send a warning to the Hungarians and give satisfaction to extremist Romanians and align them behind the National Salvation Front,' NGO activist Smaranda Enache told me. It also allowed the government to restart the hated security service, the Securitate, under a new name but with many of the same personnel.

Cluj, a Transylvanian city with an ethnic Romanian majority, followed a somewhat different trajectory. In 1992, Gheorghe Funar became mayor of Cluj, and he immediately set about instituting his own brand of ethnic cleansing. Signs in Hungarian disappeared from the streets. Funar tried to ban the ethnic Hungarian political party. He even denied that there was such a thing as Hungarians in Romania. 'Here there are only Romanian citizens,' he declared.[103] Funar served a dozen years as mayor, and if anything his politics moved farther to the right during that time. He eventually joined the extremist Greater Romania Party (Romania Mare), served in the national parliament, and ran for president in the 2014 elections where he garnered less than .5 percent of the vote.

Funar was a prime example of a 'second-order leader,' sociologist István Horváth told me over lunch at a restaurant that catered to Cluj's Hungarian minority. 'These second-order leaders realized that the Hungarian claims for a new status were a good way of legitimizing themselves as "founders of the nation,"' István observed. Funar began to evoke fears among some Romanians that Hungary intended to reclaim its former realms in Transylvania. He painted ethnic Hungarians as a kind of fifth column helping Budapest in this aim. This nationalist ideology helped Funar whip up the necessary enthusiasm – and fear – to win elections. But it didn't last for ever.

'Eventually the elites around Funar proved to be lazy city administrators,' István continued. 'Their nationalist rhetoric prevented them from taking advantage of some forms of economic capitalist development, including foreign investment. People here started to realize that this kind of rhetoric was just not functional. The "Hungarian danger" was too often invoked in irrelevant situations.' Cluj began to fall behind. 'After 1992, a dangerous stratification started here in Cluj,' István explained. 'Industry fell apart. Nothing was happening economically compared to some other cities like Timișoara and Brașov. And people realized that the "Hungarian danger" had little substance and nothing to do with economic investment.' It took a generation before new leaders would emerge in Cluj who focused on the livability of the city. 'The idea of using competition in Hungarian–Romanian relations as a way of reasserting ethnic hierarchies has simply disappeared,' István concluded. 'Such ideas are considered naive by most Romanians.'

Consider the trajectory of the Romania Mare (Greater Romania) Party that Funar joined. As its name suggests,

Romania Mare has been dedicated to expanding the borders of Romania to encompass Moldova and parts of Ukraine. It has also combined anti-Semitism and anti-Roma sentiment with efforts to combat the political influence of ethnic Hungarians. It joined a ruling coalition in 1993 with one of the spin-offs from the former National Salvation Front. The president at the time, Ion Iliescu, fearing the thunder on the right, brazenly adopted anti-Hungarian rhetoric so similar to that of Romania Mare that its chairman, Corneliu Vadim Tudor, accused Iliescu of plagiarism.[104] In parliamentary elections in 2000, Romania Mare reached the apex of its popularity, coming in second with approximately 20 percent of the vote. Even more surprising perhaps was the performance of Tudor, who captured 28 percent in the presidential election.

With Romania firmly on the path to enter the European Union, however, nationalism ceased to play as visible a political role. Tudor, sensing the shift in the winds, publicly renounced anti-Semitism and even hired an Israeli PR firm to help out in his 2004 election campaign.[105] By 2008, Romania Mare was no longer pulling in enough votes for even a single seat in parliament, and Tudor won a place instead in the European Parliament. His political influence within Romania was negligible, and by 2012 he had returned to denying the Holocaust.[106] He died three years later, a nearly forgotten figure.

Even with the eclipse of Romania Mare and the death of Tudor, veteran journalist Petru Clej doesn't think that

Romania has entered a new era of tolerance. When we met in 1990, he had recently started his new profession at the newspaper *Romania Libera*. I caught up with him in August 2013 in London, where he has lived for more than two decades, first working at the BBC and now serving as an interpreter in the court system. He still follows events in Romania closely, visiting the country several times a year and writing occasional pieces. Not far from the surface of Romanian politics, Petru told me, is a deep strain of intolerance, including pervasive anti-Roma sentiment and anti-Semitism as well. 'It starts with denial of the Holocaust,' he said. 'This is a very sensitive point in Romania's recent history. There was a commission set up by President Iliescu and chaired by Elie Wiesel about Romania's role in the Holocaust. A report was published and endorsed by Iliescu in 2004. The gist of it was that the Antonescu regime was responsible for the deaths of between 280,000 and 380,000 Jews as well as 11,000 Roma.' Ion Antonescu, the dictatorial ruler of Romania between 1940 and 1944, was executed in 1946 for war crimes. Yet he remains a popular figure in the country. In 2006, Romanian Television asked viewers to vote for the hundred greatest Romanians. Antonescu came in sixth (ahead of Nicolae Ceaușescu at number eleven and the original Dracula at number twelve).[107]

'The second aspect of anti-Semitism is international capital – the IMF, the World Bank, the European Union – which they believe is controlled by Jews or the Freemasons,' Petru continued. 'There are also quite a few Israelis of Romanian origin who have come back to Romania. They have recovered their Romanian citizenship, which is more valuable now because of the EU membership, and reclaimed their properties. And this too has created irritation. We don't have parties like Jobbik, so it's not headline news, but it's always very close beneath the surface.'

The identification of scapegoats during a period of economic difficulty is not unusual. Nor is it unusual for populists to exploit fears of the present and nostalgia for the past to vault themselves into office. What makes the extremism in eastern Europe different from that in other countries is that it takes place against the backdrop of the perceived failures of a particular project, namely the establishment of a liberal order, which comes on the heels of the failure of another particular project, the socialist order. The successive bankruptcy of these utopian projects has necessarily produced another strain of utopianism, but one that is suffused with nationalism, racism, xenophobia, and political extremism. This nationalist project has attracted not only those who have adhered to its tenets all along but also renegade liberals, like Viktor Orbán and Volen Siderov – much as certain former liberals flocked to the communist cause in the late 1940s and certain former communists flocked to the liberal cause in the early 1990s.

The xenophobia toward refugees, the attacks on minorities, the Euroskepticism – these are abiding tropes of the new extremism. In its first post-1989 incarnation, this illiberalism proved short lived when it appeared in the guise of

Vladimir Mečiar. It didn't seem to be any more durable when it returned in the mid-2000s, when PiS had its first turn in power in Poland. But today, illiberalism has very nearly attained the status of a reigning orthodoxy in the region. Its staying power and pervasive influence can perhaps be most easily measured in its successful erosion of one of the bedrock values of the post-1989 era: the rule of law.

5
Unexploded Ordnance

It was supposed to be a triumphant and glorious return to the homeland when Pavel Kavan moved back to Czechoslovakia in 1950 with his wife Rosemary and their two small children. Pavel, a student activist in prewar Czechoslovakia, had joined the Communist Party in 1938. In exile during World War II, he became an anti-fascist activist. That's when he met and married Rosemary, an English schoolteacher. After the war, Pavel secured a three-year posting at the Czechoslovak embassy in London. In 1948, the communists took power in Prague. Many Czechs who found themselves abroad at the time decided not to return home. Pavel Kavan, however, chose to do so.

Pavel was, after all, a true believer. Like many ideologues, he was also given to fits of rage. His young wife, even as the recall notice came through, saw 'with chilling clarity' that this marriage of her British understatement and his Czech overstatement 'had been a terrible mistake,' as she wrote in her memoir of the period.[1] But Rosemary agreed nonetheless to follow her husband to Prague, along with their young sons. When everything settled down, she planned to tell Pavel that she wanted a divorce.

It wasn't just the marriage that had been a mistake, though. Czechoslovakia was becoming an increasingly cheerless place as a result of a hardening Party line, and even the returnees were under suspicion. 'Thousands of Czechs and hundreds of English wives had emigrated after February 1948, yet we had returned,' Rosemary Kavan wrote. 'Wasn't that sufficient demonstration of loyalty?'[2]

It wasn't. Soon after the Kavans' return to Prague, the authorities arrested Rudolf Slánský, the general secretary of the Czech Communist Party, and Vlado Clementis, the foreign minister. The Slánský trial would turn out to be the most prominent show trial in eastern Europe in the 1950s. Slánský and ten others were executed. Pavel Kavan, who'd worked with both men, was comparatively lucky. He was arrested on similar charges of treason, but instead of hanging, the court pronounced a sentence of twenty-five years in prison.

Jan Kavan, only five years old at the time, vividly remembers the night the police took away his father.

'From the time I started to attend school, I was branded as the son of a traitor and an imperialist mother, and I somehow had to come to terms with that, to understand it,' Jan Kavan told me in 2013 over breakfast in the dining room of one of the Czech parliamentary office buildings. 'My mother, along with the other wives of the prisoners or of the executed, had to make the difficult decision about what to tell their children. My mother decided it was best to tell me and my brother the truth. "Your father is in prison for something he hasn't done," she told us. "He's totally innocent. He'll be cleared and will come home one day, but we don't know when it will happen."'

Jan's devotion to his father, and his father's innocence, was not easy to maintain at a time of widespread repression and Stalinist paranoia. During the Slánský trial, the son of one of the defendants sent a letter to a newspaper demanding 'that my father receive the highest penalty, the death sentence … and it is my wish that this letter be read to him.' Slánský himself went to the gallows as a true believer in the system and in his own guilt. 'I got what I deserved' were his last words.[3]

Pavel Kavan came home from prison after more than three years of hard labor. 'Unlike my brother, throughout his imprisonment, I was not able to see him,' Jan remembered. 'We were allowed to visit him for only one hour a year, and each time this permission was granted, I was ill in some hospital. So I never went to the prison, never saw him. So when he came out, it took me some time to recognize him as my father.' Several years later, his health compromised by the trial and his time as a prisoner, Pavel Kavan died of a heart attack at the age of forty-six.

'It was the trial that killed him,' Jan burst out at the time of his father's death. 'The execution was only delayed. And we still don't know the names of his murderers.' His mother wrote, 'There and then Jan vowed that he would unravel the truth, even if it took a lifetime.'[4]

As a young man, Jan wanted to study politics. 'My main preoccupation was to find out the truth about the political trials of the 1950s: why they happened, who was responsible for these judicial murders, what in the system enabled them to take place, and why such injustice met with a deafening silence from a majority of the population,' he explained to me. 'I wanted to help to create a system that would forever make such cruel injustice impossible.'

Jan wanted to study politics at university, but the Czechoslovak authorities considered the son of a political prisoner to be a risk and blocked his application. He became a journalist instead. By 1968, he was a leading student activist and critic of the status quo, just as his father had been. It was the time of the Prague Spring, of 'socialism with a human face,' and Jan was able to fulfill his dream of seeing his father's name publicly cleared.[5] It would be a brief reprieve.

When the Soviet troops invaded and crushed the rebellion in August 1968, Jan was overseas, at a US Student Association meeting in Kansas City. He eventually went into exile in London, his birthplace. There he worked with the overseas Czech students' association and later became one of the leading figures in the eastern European dissident movement. His publishing operation, Palach Press, brought out works by Václav Havel, smuggled contraband materials into Czechoslovakia, and created a regional network of oppositionists. If one person could have connected all of the dissidents in eastern Europe, it was Jan Kavan. When East Berlin activists wanted to send something to their fellow dissidents in Prague, for example, they'd first send the message to someone in West Germany. That person, former dissident Gerd Poppe told me, then 'put it into the mailbox in West Berlin and sent it to London addressed to Kavan, who had a secret way of getting it to Prague. The whole thing took some time but it worked.'

When the Velvet Revolution broke out in November 1989, Jan was one of the first émigrés on a plane back to Czechoslovakia. He arrived during the tumultuous period when it was still unclear which side would prevail. At the airport, the secret police saw through Jan's assumed identity and plucked him out of the passport control line for an extended interrogation. When they finally released him, the communist government was on its last legs. Jan teamed up with Civic Forum, the group of dissidents he'd supported for so many years from abroad. Eventually he ran for office on the Civic Forum ticket in June 1990 and won a seat in the new democratic parliament.

That should have been the happy ending to this story. Jan Kavan had seen his father's reputation rehabilitated and the collapse of the regime that had imprisoned him. The dissidents he'd published at great risk had triumphed, and Václav Havel graduated from prison to the presidency by the end of 1989.

Czechoslovakia, however, is the land of Franz Kafka, the author who anticipated the catastrophes of bureaucracy and totalitarianism that would eventually engulf Europe. Kafka's most famous novel, *The Trial*, starts simply and, for the Kavan family, presciently: 'Someone must have traduced Joseph K., for without having done anything wrong he was arrested one fine morning.'[6] What follows in Kafka's tale is absurd, a comedy of errors, except that it is not funny and the ending can't be more tragic. Joseph K. is subjected to a semi-legal nightmare – accusation, interrogation, endless trial, unseen judges, and a sentence executed in the evening on a stone in a quarry. Pavel Kavan, similarly traduced and arrested, would have instantly seen this story as his own.

His son, Jan K., soon descended into a very similar nightmare. Indeed, in a long *New Yorker* article subtitled 'The trials of Jan Kavan,' journalist Lawrence Weschler highlights the uncanny parallels between the story of Jan Kavan and his father Pavel.[7] Both fell foul of the government that they returned to Prague to support. Both underwent lengthy trials to clear their names. Both suffered heart attacks in middle age. And both proved to be enormously divisive individuals. In that initial article, Weschler tried to determine the truth of all the various accusations leveled against Jan Kavan, which led the journalist down a number of rabbit holes without leading to any final conclusions.

My first encounter with Jan Kavan was in spring 1990, when he was heading up the Helsinki Citizens' Assembly, an effort to bring together civil society activists from the eastern and western halves of Europe.[8] He was a driven, prickly, smart, and impatient man. I tried to arrange an interview with him at the time, but he was too busy. He was both intensely political and not at all cut out for politics. In other words, he was very much committed to translating political ideals into practice. But he alienated even his closest friends and colleagues – just as his father had not suffered fools gladly. ('I wouldn't want Pavel for an enemy,' Rosemary Kavan observed at one point in her memoir.[9]) He was a lightning rod for controversy, not just concerning his past but also his personal life after returning to Prague. But Jan was drawn to politics, as if successfully attaining public office would be the ultimate vindication of his father's name. After he won a seat in parliament in June 1990, Jan experienced his first heart attack at his parliamentary swearing in and left the building on a stretcher.[10] Even though he suffered a second heart attack two months later, he persisted.

The political atmosphere in Czechoslovakia in 1990 had shifted away from the joyful, theatrical revolution of the year before. Deep political divisions in the Civic Forum coalition eventually produced a social democratic wing around economist Miloš Zeman and a right-wing, Thatcher-like group around economist Václav Klaus. As president, Václav Havel was temperamentally more inclined toward the left, but he attempted to remain above the fray. Jan Kavan, meanwhile, had been on the left since his student days. This political division played an important role in what happened next.

The story of eastern Europe after 1989 is one of political, economic, and cultural reform. It's also about the creative destruction that took place to clear the ground for all the new growth. Some of that destruction was deliberate, the result of radical economic programs. But some of it was the result of ordnance buried deep in the archives of the intelligence services. All of the new democratic governments in eastern Europe were sitting on this UXO – unexploded ordnance – without any experience of how to defuse it.

During the brief interregnums in 1989 when the communists had lost power but the oppositionists had yet to take the reins of government, the various secret services, from the Stasi in East Germany to the StB in Czechoslovakia, tried to destroy all of their files. They managed to shred only some of the information. The remaining documents contained the names of collaborators who had informed on their colleagues, their friends, even their family. Other collaborators were foreign spies operating in the surrounding capitalist societies – like Günter Guillaume, the trusted aide to West German Chancellor Willy Brandt, who supplied the Stasi with backdoor access to so many of West Germany's secrets.[11] Still others, like Václav Havel, were listed in the records because they'd refused to collaborate. And sometimes it was very difficult to categorize the names as innocent, guilty, or something in between. In the 1990s and even into the 2000s, many of these unexploded bombs went off. The damage was widespread – and not only against individuals. Nowhere was this more evident than Czechoslovakia.

In early 1991, the Czech parliament voted to allow a new commission to use the StB files to vet legislators to see whether any of them had been informers under the previous system. The process was called *lustrace* or lustration, from the Latin verb 'to clean.' The idea was to create a firewall between the impure activities of the past and the pure activities of the future. Lustration would be the functional equivalent of the storming of the Bastille, the kind of cathartic, revolutionary act noticeably absent in eastern Europe in 1989.

'The idea of the lustration law was to check on the past of primarily members of parliament, top civil servants, and government officials to see if they had collaborated with the secret service and to make sure that the secret service would not infiltrate any of the new democratic institutions,' Jan Kavan told me. 'I was then working again very closely with Petr Uhl [a friend and former dissident who was also in parliament representing the Civic Forum]. We both agreed that it was not a perfect piece of legislation, but we agreed that it would be useful to learn who out of our parliamentary colleagues was responsible for sending our friends to prison. And we both believed that the secret service would attempt to infiltrate the new authorities. We both voted for the law, with no hesitation.'

Not everyone was so enthusiastic. Long-time dissident Petr Pithart said that he protested against lists of any kind: 'Today it is Communists who are on the list. It could be wealthy people tomorrow, perhaps macrobiotics the day after, and then certainly the Jews. The logic of lists is implacable.'[12] The population as a whole was divided: only 50 percent of Czechs and Slovaks believed that lustration would be beneficial.[13]

A little over a month after the vote, the vetting commission summoned Jan Kavan to its office. The lustrators informed him that his name had shown up in the files. So had his code name (Kato). The evidence was clear. He had fifteen days to resign.[14] It was an explosive charge: one of the communist regime's most implacable enemies stood accused of collaboration.

Jan refused to resign. 'I perceived this request as absolutely ridiculous, as I did not feel in any way guilty of collaborating with my enemies and thus I had no intention of resigning,' he told me. 'I wanted to confront whatever was in the file, and they agreed. I also got the impression from a relatively short conversation that they were not really aware of the content of the file. I later found out that there were two files for the two years (1969 and 1970), one for each year, and each one contained several hundred pages. The commission hadn't really studied them.'

In 1969 and 1970, Jan had been in London, serving as the head of the overseas Czechoslovak students' association, so he was necessarily in contact with the Czechoslovak embassy. No one disputes that these conversations took place. The issue boiled down to whether Jan knew that his contact at the embassy was in the security service and whether he was knowingly collaborating with this individual. The parliamentary commission itself had a hard time evaluating the events.

'So, strangely, they took a vote,' Jan recalled. 'And I lost by one vote. The vote was clearly divided ideologically, irrespective of the contents of the file. People to the right voted against me, and people slightly to the left voted for me. People with some legal education or at least legal awareness also voted for me because there was clearly no evidence against me in the file. I lost seven to six. Three weeks later, the list was published. There were ten of us, members of parliament, who were discovered to have links with the StB, and we were, therefore, asked to resign. I again firmly refused to do so. I delivered a passionate speech in the parliament. I had a strange feeling of déjà vu. Like my father, I returned home from emigration in England to be accused by my colleagues of collaborating with the enemy.'

Jan took the matter to court, thinking that he could quickly clear his name. The experience of his father should have suggested otherwise. 'The media attacked me every day,' Jan said ruefully. 'Of the ten, I was probably the most well known, the only person clearly linked to the dissident movement. So it was very advantageous for the opponents to suggest that Charter 77 had been infiltrated by the secret service. That some of the others among the ten were members of the Communist Party was taken as natural. I became a sort of cause célèbre. It made my life very difficult indeed: I could not find a job, and it was difficult to communicate with people who only knew me from the media as an StB agent. I was ostracized. Some people were afraid to be seen with me.'

Even his efforts to clear his name implicated him in the eyes of some of his former colleagues in the opposition. Jan Ruml, who had worked closely with Jan in the distribution of underground literature, had become a deputy interior minister in the new democratic government. Ruml categorically rejected his old friend's innocence. 'By taking his case international, the way he's doing, he's undermining the reputation of the country,' Ruml said, 'and that's another reason he deserves to be lustrated.'[15] Jan Kavan's willingness to marshall his international contacts in his own defense damned him for a less savory reason. Jan's father was Jewish, and many of the attacks on both father and son for their international connections had more than a little anti-Semitism behind them.[16]

Confident that he could beat the charges in court, Jan continued to gather testimonials and eyewitnesses. There were several very obvious flaws in the case. First his name was not on the list of StB collaborators that was used in the more widespread lustration process. He had an StB file, but he was not on the StB list, a crucial distinction. Second, the embassy contact in London with whom Jan allegedly collaborated testified that 'I did not at any time recruit Mr. Kavan for any collaboration with the secret police, either verbally or in written form.'[17]

This should have been enough to clear his name. But Jan Kavan had made a lot of enemies over the years. They brought up evidence that he had lied – even if these had been in relatively minor ways – and therefore couldn't be trusted on the central issue of his alleged collaboration. All of this was circumstantial at best: guilt by character flaw. Where others would have folded their cards and walked away from the game, Jan persisted in battling his detractors.

That persistence paid off. After five long years, the court finally cleared Jan Kavan of the charges of collaboration. The interior ministry appealed the verdict, and it went to the appellate court. But after a win there as well, Jan could point to a clean record. The drawn-out campaign, however, had taken a toll on his reputation. The initial *New Yorker* article, various write-ups in books that appeared in the early 1990s: all of these had concluded on ambiguous notes.

'During those five years, the campaign against me frequently hit the headlines, and, especially, the electronic media were full of very unpleasant attacks that many people obviously remember until today,' Jan told me. 'When I was finally cleared, there was only a small notice, tucked away on the bottom of the last pages. So, there are still significant sections of the population, particularly younger people, who didn't know me and my activities, who are prone to believe that maybe there was something: where there was smoke, there could have been fire. This doesn't make my life easy even today, though officially there is no problem since I was cleared of all suspicions. The media still describe me as "controversial."'[18] In the item on his vindication in the 1996 *New Yorker*, Jan reported that he was thinking not only about his father but his children as well – 'so that they wouldn't have to go through the kind of shame I had to endure as a child.'[19]

Here, too, Jan Kavan's story might have ended. Unlike his father, he had cleared his name during his lifetime. He had played a pivotal role in the underground movements that had helped to topple the communist regimes. He served in the first democratic parliament after 1989. He managed to survive the powerful forces of lustration. And yet, those were only the first and second acts of his life.

In 1998, two years after the appellate court cleared his name, Jan Kavan was appointed Czech foreign minister, a position he held for four years. During that time, he helped usher the Czech Republic into NATO and the EU, end the Kosovo conflict, and improve relations with Russia. Still controversy dogged him. In 2002, President Havel himself asked Jan to step down as foreign minister when a scandal broke concerning the general secretary of the Foreign Ministry, Karel Srba, who tried to get an investigative journalist killed. Srba received a prison sentence; Jan maintained that he knew nothing about the affair.[20] From 2002 to 2003, Jan had an even more high-profile job as the president of the UN General Assembly, taking office on the very day that George W. Bush gave a speech on the threat Iraq posed to the international community. Jan ultimately resisted US pressure on the General Assembly to endorse the Iraq invasion, creating a whole new set of enemies.

When I interviewed Jan in Prague in 2013, he was once again on the outskirts of power. He was serving as an advisor to a parliamentarian, but he couldn't get his pass key to work at the door to the dining room. I stood there as he pounded on the door to get someone's attention inside, a rather poignant symbol of his political marginalization. Even though he'd overcome the accusations of collaboration, Jan could not overcome the deep political divisions in his country. He'd been a gadfly during the communist era when all but a few people conformed, during the immediate post-1989 period when people didn't want to be reminded of their past conformity, and in the post-9/11 period when many Czechs just wanted to follow the lead of the United States.

Lustration was, like the show trials of the 1950s, a mechanism by which the revolution devoured itself. As with Jan Kavan, history was repeating itself, not just once but twice. Czechoslovakia had gone through the very same 'cleansing' process after the Prague Spring in 1968. As dissident Milan Šimečka wrote in his account of this experience, the Communist Party went through a screening process to see who 'collaborated' with the reformers, followed by thousands of trials where 'the verdicts were decided at the outset.'[21] Then came the blacklisting and the occupational persecution that deprived more than 100,000 people of their jobs.[22] This 'rectification' campaign undermined whatever remaining faith Šimečka had in law: 'by the beginning of the 1970s, it had become quite possible in my country to send absolutely anyone to jail; anyone taken off the street at random, from a school-child to a trial judge.'[23]

Since 1989 was a nonviolent revolution, the devouring was less hazardous than the show trials of the 1950s or even the post-1968 rectification. Power in the Czech Republic had become vegetarian, as poet Anna Akhmatova once described the Soviet years before Stalin's purges turned deadly.[24] In the 1990s, lustration even gave the appearance of conforming to the rule of law. Yet it was strange, to say the least, that the same people who had emphasized the fallibility of communism would accept the infallibility of documents produced by the regime they'd hated. In fact, the StB officers had quotas to fulfill,[25] had to demonstrate that they were successful in their jobs, had to conjure up threats even when no such threats existed. All of this contributed to error-filled files and erroneous lists.

'I think lustration was one of the worst methods of dealing with the past,' long-time dissident Jan Urban told me in an interview in his office in Prague. 'First, it gave legitimacy to the communist secret police archives. It's kind of funny when you declare the secret police a criminal organization and then you use its archives for the purposes of parliamentary democracy building.' Lustration was a 'clerical operation,' he argued, in which the presumption of guilt substituted for the due process of the rule of law. For scholar Roman David, lustration served an almost sacred function: a 'ritual sacrifice' designed to 'purge the body of politics of the tainted officials in conformity with the new anti-communist religion.'[26] The lustrated thus joined the other sacrificial victims of the period, such as the Roma, the unemployed, and the Erased.

Consider the case of Rabbi Meyer, who served the small Jewish community in Prague. 'He had to make some arrangement with the secret police. Everyone knew that he did,' Daniel Kumermann, a Charter 77 signatory and a member of the community, told me. 'We didn't care. We liked him. He never reported on us. He probably had to report meetings with foreigners and only as much as necessary. We wouldn't tell him anything. When the regime fell, he didn't really change. He was rather simple where politics was concerned. Someone wanted to get a rabbi for a new political party in 1992 and asked him to join. So he was on the election list. Everyone was of course lustrated, so they found out and that was splashed all over the newspapers. Okay, but we knew this! We didn't care … He became the object of a witch-hunt, even though he never really harmed anyone.' Daniel became angrier. 'Not only that: some of those who were after him most probably had major skeletons in their own cupboards.' It was reminiscent of the post-World War II trials in France of Nazi collaborationists in which three out of four judges in the proceedings had themselves collaborated with the Vichy regime.[27]

These unexploded bombs were also weapons to be deployed against political enemies.[28] 'Politicians have an incentive to use lustration against their opposition as a means of discrediting their opponents,' write political scientists Cynthia Horne and Margaret Levi. 'Once this is done, the opposition, when it obtains power, retaliates.'[29] Before the very first Czechoslovak election in 1990, both major parties – Civic Forum and the Christian Democratic Union – used allegations of collaboration to discredit one another. Later, in the lead-up to the 1992 parliamentary elections, Charter 77 signer Petr Cibulka published his list of 160,000 alleged secret service informers. The list included a number of dissidents and even Charter 77 signatories (though not Jan Kavan). For Cibulka, this was no mere reckoning with the past. He believed that Moscow, the communists, and the secret services were still controlling events behind the scenes after 1989.[30]

Cibulka wasn't only interested in the Czech Communist Party, which hadn't changed its name after 1989 and made no secret of its adherence to communist doctrine. After all, post-1989, the party never attracted more than 20 percent of the vote, and because no other party would invite it to form a ruling coalition – at least at the national level – the communists remained in permanent opposition. Rather, Cibulka was intent on rooting out crypto-communists on the left, people like Jan Kavan who were allegedly part of a larger conspiracy. In this, he had a powerful ally – Václav Klaus, the last prime minister of Czechoslovakia and the first prime minister of the independent Czech Republic. Klaus had never been a dissident, had never signed Charter 77, and had a notorious contempt for those who risked their jobs and their very lives to openly protest against the communist regime. He preferred to believe that the masses had brought down communism simply by not doing their jobs efficiently.[31] 'If everybody was an anti-communist, why should former dissidents be celebrated as moral examples?' as political scientist Vladimir Tismăneanu characterized this method of minimizing the achievements of dissidents.[32] Klaus was no conspiracy theorist. But it was enormously convenient for him – and his right-wing party – to have a list that demonstrated that a least some of these left-leaning dissidents had been collaborators all along.

Cibulka's publication indeed helped change the complexion of Czechoslovak politics. In the 1992 elections, Václav Klaus's party came out on top and the former dissidents on the liberal left didn't even manage to exceed the 5 percent threshold to enter parliament. In some ways, it was an even more devastating defeat than the one suffered by East German dissidents in the 1990 elections. The East Germans could at least blame the influx of wealthy, politically savvy parties from the West. The Czechoslovak voters turned their backs on those who'd shown the most courage during the communist era and supported instead a party led by a political opportunist. Lustration had proved a powerful weapon in this political game.

Although Cibulka's concerns about communist infiltration directed by Moscow were absurd, many people intimately involved in the repressive apparatuses of the past did indeed prosper in the new order throughout the region. Employees of the StB and the Stasi found work in private security firms or finance. Top-ranking members of the *nomenklatura* (the communist elite) obtained high government positions in Bulgaria and Romania. And 'red capitalists' throughout the region exploited connections from the communist era to become successful businessmen in the capitalist period, as chronicled in the sobering Romanian documentary *Kapitalism*.[33] Particularly for those who did not benefit under the new order, the success of the former oppressors seemed like an enormous injustice. 'Things were supposed to be right, and they aren't,' journalist Konstanty Gebert told me. 'So, who's the culprit? Well, the bad guys are still around, and they're doing their evil work. Frankly, if somebody had been fired from a company where, before 1989, he was an underground Solidarity activist, and the present owner of the company had been the head of the secret police or the party secretary at the same company, this isn't really a conspiracy theory. You can feel it in your bones!'

Lustration was an attempt to achieve justice. 'In my first studies of post-conflict societies in different parts of the world, I've learned that what people want and expect from revolutions and regime changes is not the immediate rise in living standards but a sense of justice,' Jan Urban told me. 'Here is where we failed terribly. Allowing the communists not to part with their criminal past, allowing them to capture up to twenty percent of the electorate – meaning that more or less democratic parties had to work in coalitions that would embrace a larger portion of the electorate – was a strategic mistake and we have to live with it.'

No country in the region has quite figured out how to handle its communist past. Even a quarter-century later, the secret security files remain a subject of enormous controversy. Hungary has yet to make them fully public.[34] Bulgaria has restricted access to the more sensitive material. Even in Germany, which set the standard for the region with the way it made public its massive Stasi archives, the unexploded ordnance buried in those files continues to explode periodically. The legal mechanisms meant to clearly distinguish old from new have produced a system almost as opaque as the one it replaced. True, lustration will soon fade away. 'In ten to fifteen years, there will be no one like us left,' diplomat Maciej Kozłowski, who was also accused unjustly of collaboration, told me in 2013. 'Biology will solve it.' But the issues raised by lustration will persist.

The liberal systems in eastern Europe were to be established on the basis of the rule of law – new constitutions, new democratic institutions, independent judiciaries. This was the *Rechtsstaat* model pioneered by Germany and taken up by other European countries throughout the nineteenth century. The use of history as a weapon through the lustration process helped to undermine this rule of law even as the architects of liberalism were attempting to establish its foundations. Designed to expiate the sins of communism, lustration turned out instead to be the original sin of the new liberal systems.

The black box

Stanisław Tymiński was an unlikely politician. He'd had a successful career in business, making millions in Canada and creating a commercial empire in Peru. But he'd not had much luck in Canadian politics. His Libertarian Party never got more than 1 percent of the vote. In 1990, he decided to return to his native Poland and try his luck by running for president.[35]

Tymiński was, to say the least, a long shot. The field of presidential candidates in 1990 was impressive. Competing for the job that communist General Wojciech Jaruzelski was vacating were Prime Minister Tadeusz Mazowiecki and former trade union leader Lech Wałęsa. It was supposed to be a battle between the two sides of Solidarity – the somber intellectual Mazowiecki, who was close to the Church, versus the populist Wałęsa, who threatened to use an axe to transform Polish politics. Virtually unknown in Poland, Tymiński seemed to be an afterthought.

All three candidates made promises. Wałęsa, the hero of the 1980s and recipient of a Nobel Peace Prize, announced that he would provide every Pole with $10,000 to invest in new capitalist enterprises. Mazowiecki, the first democratic prime minister in Poland in more than four decades, said that he'd bring the Rolling Stones to perform in Poland.[36] But Tymiński had the strangest pitch of all. He carried around a black suitcase and said that inside was secret information that would blow up Polish politics. A dark horse with virtually no credentials, Tymiński promised to reveal proof that Lech Wałęsa had been an informer with the secret police.

Unexpectedly, Tymiński made it into the second round, garnering strong support from parts of Poland suffering from higher unemployment.[37] Mazowiecki, who was not really cut out for the rough-and-tumble of electoral politics, came in third. The Solidarity government had only been in power for a couple of months and Poles had already become disappointed with the new political elite. Wałęsa, with his solecisms and axe threats, still had the profile of an outsider. Tymiński was even farther out there. He'd self-published a book, *Sacred Dogs*, full of wild proposals, such as Poland acquiring its own nuclear weapons.[38] During the run-off campaign, he ramped up his allegations that Wałęsa was something else altogether: the consummate insider who'd collaborated to survive.

'I have a lot of material, and I have it here, and some of it is very serious and of a personal nature,' Tymiński told Wałęsa in a debate on national television. Wałęsa retaliated by accusing Tymiński of being a front man for former secret police who wanted to return Poland to communist rule.[39] Tymiński parried the charge but admitted that his staff did include former secret policemen.[40] He never opened his briefcase to present his explosive evidence. In the end, Polish voters found Wałęsa the more persuasive politician, electing him president in the second round that December by a margin of 75 to 25 percent.

Tymiński refused to go away. In 1993, he created a political party with a name, Party X, that recalled his 'black box' style of politics. At the press conference launching the new initiative, he finally opened up the infamous briefcase to reveal … a personal computer. It turned out, however, to be a box within a box. He claimed that the computer contained a program that could predict the future of the economy, including the total collapse of the Polish economy in 1994. He also promised to reveal materials compromising the reputation of, not Wałęsa this time, but Tymiński's populist rival at the time, Andrzej Lepper.[41] With his disregard for the facts and penchant for the theatrical, Tymiński was a Trump-style politician *avant la lettre*.

Party X was a stillbirth, and Tymiński eventually returned to Canada, where he continues to spin fanciful conspiracy theories.[42] But rumors of past collaboration continued to dog Wałęsa over the years. In 1992, two years after Tymiński's wild accusations, government minister Antoni Macierewicz released a list of collaborators, and Wałęsa was on it, under the code name 'Bolek.' But the list was widely discredited because of its errors. And in 2000, the Institute of National Remembrance (IPN) cleared Wałęsa of the charges, concluding that the incriminating materials had been forged to disqualify Wałęsa from winning the Nobel Prize.[43] But then the Kaczyński brothers revived the accusations against Wałęsa – to prove that Solidarity under Wałęsa's leadership had been insufficiently anti-communist.

When I revisited Gdańsk in 2013, I bumped into the journalist Krzysztof Wyszkowski, who had also accused Wałęsa in 2005 of being a collaborator with the secret police. Wałęsa took him to court and lost, but chiefly around the issue of freedom of speech. Krzysztof asked me why Americans continued to hold Wałęsa in such high regard. I told him that for most Americans Wałęsa symbolized the anti-communist struggle, that he'd won a Nobel Peace Prize, that he'd served as Poland's first postcommunist president. In the black-and-white mindset of American politics, it was inconceivable that someone could possibly straddle the categories of hero and villain.

By the late 2000s, Wałęsa's collaboration had become common knowledge. In the 1970s, under the code name Bolek, he had told the secret service about anti-communist demonstrations. Worse, when he was president, he'd used his executive privileges to remove his file from the archives and destroy incriminating evidence.[44] But there were other copies of the file that Wałęsa apparently didn't know about. In 2016, IPN released documents found in the home of the widow of a communist general that definitively linked Wałęsa to the collaborator Bolek.[45] Wałęsa continued to assert his innocence, arguing that it was part of his job to talk with the secret service at that time to 'spare courageous people, temper the risk-takers [in Solidarity] and create a team that would eventually destroy the [Communist] party.'[46] Even Wałęsa's critics, like the journalist Krzysztof Wyszkowski, concede that Wałęsa lied to the secret police, and that's why they dropped him.[47] But Wałęsa's attempts to destroy the file only confirmed his duplicity in the eyes of investigators.

The case of Lech Wałęsa, of the files of the secret service more generally, has divided Poles who are determined to come to terms with past collaborators and obtain justice from those who are equally determined to put the past behind them. It's not the first time that Poles have wrestled with this quandary. In the 1794 uprising against Russian rule, Polish insurgents stormed the Russian embassy and found lists of collaborators in the secret archives in the basement. The Jacobin Club, modeled after the Jacobins of the French Revolution, improvised hasty trials and then lynched the collaborators. The leader of the rebellion, the Revolutionary War veteran Tadeusz Kościuszko, who had returned to his homeland to fight the Russian occupiers, was furious about the kangaroo courts. He put 100 of the insurrectionaries on trial for the violence, which resulted in death sentences for seven men.[48]

Perhaps because of this history, Polish intellectuals were less enthusiastic about lustration than their Czech counterparts. Tadeusz Mazowiecki, in a statement that Lech Wałęsa quotes approvingly in his autobiography, declared, 'What has happened in the past must be dropped. What we must deal with now is the state of collapse in Poland today.'[49] This was the famous 'thick line' with which some Poles wanted to separate the crimes of the past from the immediate challenges of the present. Bronisław Geremek, who took charge of Solidarity's parliamentary faction, also believed in the thick line. He refused to sign any document declaring his non-collaboration with the security forces.[50] It was, for him, a matter of principle.

Adam Michnik, a longtime dissident and one of the chief intellectual architects of the bloodless transition in 1989, took an impassioned stance against lustration. The lustrator, he said, 'combines the fanatical zeal of an inquisitor with the cold cynicism of an incisive investigative officer. His philosophy is simple: just give me a man and I will find something to accuse him of. The lustrator knows perfectly well that almost no one, himself included, was exactly a saint in those less-than-saintly times. But it is better to be a lustrator than to be the one who lustrated.'[51] The logic of the witch-hunt would turn Poland into precisely the kind of society Michnik had found so unacceptable under communism. Indeed, he remarked once that his 'blackest dream is that we will take all our communists and send them to Siberia. And then what will we have? Communism without communists.'[52]

Michnik understood that lustration had many political uses. During the round table negotiations, one of the key people on the communist side confided to someone on the Solidarity side: 'Don't mess with those files, let them be – the agents were mostly your own people.'[53] It would turn out to be a prophetic warning. Allegations of collaboration would envelop not only Wałęsa but a number of other top politicians, including Andrzej Olechowski and Zyta Gilowska of the Civic Platform. Three prime ministers – Włodzimierz Cimoszewicz, Józef Oleksy, and Jerzy Buzek – as well as President Aleksander Kwaśniewski, would ultimately face accusations of a compromised past.

Poland had its version of Cibulka's list. In 2005, journalist Bronisław (Bronek) Wildstein copied a list of alleged secret police collaborators at the Institute of National Remembrance and posted it on the Internet.[54] As with the earlier lists, it mixed together collaborators and dissidents that the police hoped to persuade to cooperate. To disprove the charge of collaboration, however, those on the list had to reveal everything in their files. 'Bronek did this in the name of truth and openness. And that's one person less for me to shake hands with!' Konstanty Gebert, a longtime underground Solidarity activist, told me. 'I was of course on the list. I'm not concerned. If anyone would use that to accuse me, I have a biography I can stand behind. I'm a public person. I can fight back. But imagine that this is not downtown Warsaw but a small town in the boondocks and there's a worker named Kowalski whose name is on the list. There's nothing but nothing he can do to clear his name. It's like in the Russian joke. This cat is fleeing Russia because they are executing camels. So, what's his problem? "Hah," the cat says, "try to prove you're not a camel!"'

As in the Czech Republic, many of the witch-hunters in Poland were interested not so much in proving the collaboration of this or that individual. They wanted to discredit a particular approach to politics. Many people in Solidarity were not happy with the compromises of 1989, such as the semi-free elections that guaranteed a bloc of seats for the Communist Party. They were upset that General Wojciech Jaruzelski stayed on as president rather than face a trial and a jail sentence for the crimes of the martial law period. Even the round table negotiations were subject to criticism. Radek Sikorski, who would later become foreign minister in the conservative government of Lech Kaczyński, called the round table the 'original sin of the opposition' that would eventually provide an opportunity for the former communists to return to power – in the person of Alexander

Kwasniewski, who beat Wałęsa in the 1995 presidential elections.[55] Another conservative politician, Wiesław Chrzanowski, went farther: the communists used the round table to actually improve their individual fortunes as they anticipated the collapse of communism.[56]

But this was all simply projecting later attitudes back into the past. In winter 1989, when the Polish government and Solidarity announced the round table negotiations, no one imagined that communism was about to collapse. Some cracks had appeared in Hungary, reform was in the air in tiny Slovenia, and Mikhail Gorbachev was stirring things up in the Soviet Union. But the rest of eastern Europe remained firmly in the grip of conservative communist regimes. Later, when they returned to power in Poland, the former communists would prove as committed as Solidarity, if not more so, to the project of establishing capitalism, guiding the country into NATO and the European Union, and negotiating a modus operandi with the Catholic Church. If individual former communists had improved their fortunes in post-1989 Poland, they had done so by shedding their previous ideology, not adhering to it.

The round table negotiations represented a grand compromise. So, too, did subsequent governments formed by the former communists. For some, like Michnik, these compromises were not simply tactical maneuvers but a new kind of politics. In fact, what drew the most heat from conservatives was not Michnik's imagined collaboration with the secret police in the past – for which there was no evidence

– but his post-1989 collaboration with former communist leaders Wojciech Jaruzelski and General Czesław Kiszczak. Michnik wrote an introduction for Jaruzelski's memoir. He called Kiszczak a 'man of honor' in an interview, an evaluation he subsequently wished he had specified to refer to the general's role in the round table process.[57] It could be said that Michnik was acting in the best tradition of truth and reconciliation. But many Poles argued that he had no right to forgive these two individuals, who had orchestrated martial law in 1981 and the shutdown of Solidarity.

Michnik didn't talk about forgiveness. And he was not simply interested in reconciliation. He wanted to uphold the liberal values of open debate. 'It is impossible today to speak about a political opponent with respect,' he wrote. 'It is impossible to seek a compromise that would lead to the common good; it is even impossible to converse without an internal conviction that our adversary is but a cynical cheat.'[58] Ultimately Michnik was calling for something that has become increasingly old-fashioned: democratic politics.

Perhaps, too, Michnik was thinking of Spain when he made these remarks – for he had referred to Spain's remarkable transition from authoritarianism as a model for Poland in 1989. Spain, too, had drawn a thick line separating the fledgling democracy from the crimes of the fascists. In Spain, 'the whole political spectrum, from the monarchists to the communists, made a deliberate choice not to touch the civil war because it would otherwise explode in their faces. And they managed to do that,' philosopher Ivan Vejvoda told me.

The thick line lasted for a quarter-century. 'It took a whole generation in post-Franco Spain after 1975 to reach the climactic moment of opening mass graves in 2000 and putting the issue on the table,' writes historian Maria Todorova.[59]

Digging up the past in Poland undermined not only the rule of law but trust more generally.[60] Between 1993 and 1998, the number of people in Poland who agreed with the statement 'most people can be trusted' plummeted from an already low 34 percent to 17 percent.[61] Lustration also focused public attention on past injustices instead of current ones, such as the build-up of the government's surveillance capabilities.

Then there was the remarkable arbitrariness of Poland's post-1989 legal system. Citizens, for instance, could be held in pre-trial detention for as many as *seven years* before a trial determined guilt or innocence. I first encountered this strange kink in the Polish legal system when interviewing Lech Jeziorny. In 1990, he was a former Solidarity activist who'd been jailed for eight months for his activities and was then working with a new business association called the Kraków Industrial Society. When I caught up with him twenty-three years later, he'd become an entrepreneur best known for his effort to establish a modern food processing facility in Kraków, Poland's gorgeous medieval city. On the verge of securing an additional outside investor for the project, however, he and his partner were arrested – on suspicion that they'd been engaged in a criminal conspiracy involving money laundering. The tax authority also hit them with a fine of 4 million zlotys. Even worse, they were thrown in jail for nine months without any evidence. During the pre-trial detention, their business went bankrupt.

'We had leased the machinery, and now everything's gone,' Lech told me. 'This was probably the most modern meat processing plant in Poland at the time. Everything was completely new, with the latest technology. And everything was destroyed.'[62] After nine months, he'd been released without being charged – for lack of evidence. Lech was bitter when he talked with me: he'd spent more time in jail in the democratic era than he had under the communists.[63] The courts cleared the two men of the charges and, in 2009, even provided compensation for the injustice. The story seemed so clearly unjust that a Polish film was made of it, casting Lech and his colleagues as victims.[64]

And then, in late 2013 and again in 2016, the appellate court delivered a verdict on a related case, determining that Lech and his partner were both in fact guilty of illegal transfers of funds.[65] They were given suspended sentences and required to pay restitution. Instead of a clear-cut case of prosecutorial error, Lech's story became a much more complicated example of what happens when a flawed legal system intersects with a culture of corruption.

Puppet masters?

Ahmed Dogan has been the most successful minority politician in postcommunist eastern Europe even though he has never served as a president, prime minister, or in any other government position. He was an MP for twenty-three years in the Bulgarian parliament, but he often didn't attend sessions and sometimes had to forgo his salary because of his absences.[66] Nor did the party he create, the Movement for Rights and Freedom (MRF), ever win enough votes to become the ruling party. Yet Dogan transformed a marginalized ethnic minority into an important political force that could both make and break governments in Bulgaria.

The Movement served in several coalition governments in Bulgaria, beginning with the first administration formed by the opposition in 1991. It also formed coalition governments with King Simeon's party and the former communists from 2001 to 2008. Its importance can be measured by the ferocity of the opposition it elicited from parties like Ataka, which argued that MRF was illegal because the Bulgarian constitution forbids parties based on ethnic or religious affiliation. Though it derives most of its support from ethnic Turks and Roma, MRF aspires to represent all Bulgarians, and a number of ethnic Bulgarians are members of the party.

It wasn't only Ataka that expressed concerns about MRF. Some of its original supporters, like Miroslav Durmov, had long ago become disillusioned by the party and its leader. Miroslav had met Ahmed Dogan in 1989. 'Later, it became clear to me that the MRF was created by the Bulgarian intelligence service,' Miroslav told me. 'The Central Committee of the Communist Party ordered the Bulgarian intelligence service to prepare an organization of

Turkish people that would be separate from the Bulgarian opposition and, at the same time, would support the *nomenklatura*. If the Communist Party created the MRF, it was not because it wanted the restoration of communism. The *nomenklatura* simply needed an ally in the transition process, particularly for privatization, and to reduce the level of uncertainty during this period.' In support of Miroslav's contention, the Bulgarian government in April 1990 allowed MRF candidates to run in the first democratic elections even though at least one court decision disqualified the party because it violated the constitutional ban on ethnic parties.[67] The government's decision was clearly intended to split the opposition.

Kasim Dal, one of the thirty-three founders of the party and later a prominent defector, has a slightly different take. 'The ones that were in the secret services of Todor Zhivkov's regime, they took complete control of the political party,' he told me. 'They only got richer and richer by participating in corruption schemes.'

Whether the MRF was compromised from the beginning or only later on, both Miroslav and Kasim agree: Ahmed Dogan was the key player, the one who cultivated the relationship with the secret police. Dogan, a philosophy professor and once-imprisoned leader of the clandestine Turkish National Liberation Movement in Bulgaria, was certainly a known quantity to the Bulgarian intelligence service.[68] After all, he had served as a collaborator for many years. 'Ahmed Dogan was no ordinary agent of the State Security,' writes Toma Bikov of Dogan's intelligence service file. 'He was one of the most valuable, with professional qualities that the totalitarian security services needed. Purposeful, intelligent, loyal, analytical and effective: perhaps these words would be a compliment if used on another occasion. But in the context in which they are used, they are rather ominous.'[69]

Miroslav, because of his own work in the Ministry of Interior, knew about Dogan's past before many others did. 'Former prime minister Andrei Lukhanov told me more about Dogan,' Miroslav remembered. 'Then, there was a general from state security – I don't know why he was so friendly to me, he even pretended that we were relatives (in Bulgaria we are all cousins!) – who gave me the name of Ahmed Dogan's handler and a copy of his file. Later, President Zheliu Zhelev received Dogan's dossier.'

Aside from his compromised background, Dogan engaged in other practices that called his integrity into question. He took $1 million from the government as a consultant for a hydroelectric plant even while he was serving in parliament.[70] He boasted of his party's closeness to oligarchs who provided it with funds.[71] There were even rumors that MRF had supplied money to its archenemy Ataka in order to solidify support in a galvanized ethnic Turkish community (which Ataka leader Volen Siderov vigorously denied).[72] But the shadow cast over the Movement for Rights and Freedoms by Dogan's collaboration with the intelligence services is profound. In a region in which everyone believes that everyone else is being manipulated by hidden puppet masters, it has not helped the cause of minority rights in Bulgaria to be so closely associated with Dogan and his past.

The MRF was not the only compromised institution in Bulgaria. As economist and former deputy prime minister Simeon Djankov writes, 'The former secret police took key positions in banking and actively participated in the initial privatization rounds. The result was a collapse of the banking sector in 1996, a corrupted privatization process that turned the population against market reforms, and the involvement of members of the secret police in an organized crime network that traffics drugs and weapons, among other activities.'[73] Djankov believes that Bulgaria erred in not adopting a lustration law that could have restricted the influence of the secret police.

Ahmed Dogan is now the honorary chairman of the Movement for Rights and Freedoms, which, after the 2014 elections, remains the third-largest party in parliament. Dogan maneuvered his initial replacement out of office by accusing him of being too pro-Turkish. The new leader, Mustafa Karadayi, was born in 1970, too young to have a past compromised by connections to the old security services.

The lives of others

If Bulgaria is a cautionary tale of what happens when the intelligence services play an important role in the transition, East

Germany offers the example of a powerful security institution that was largely absent from the process. Why the Stasi – the Ministry for State Security – didn't fight to preserve the communist system in 1989 is something of a mystery.

The Stasi has acquired an outsized reputation since its dissolution. It maintained 97,000 employees and 173,000 informers out of a population of 17 million people, which means that one out of sixty-three East Germans were somehow affiliated with the institution.[74] It used radioactive tags to track people, cars, and documents.[75] If its activities weren't so sinister, the Stasi's use of the latest technology would seem almost satirical. It maintained a 'library of smells' that consisted of 'a few hundred glass jars containing bits of dissidents' dirty underwear, so trained dogs could sniff and match the smell to an antigovernment pamphlet found on the sidewalk.'[76] And it maintained more than a hundred miles of files on millions of citizens.[77]

When protests broke out throughout East Germany in the fall of 1989, the Stasi also had operatives in the crowds. In one of the largest protests, on 9 October 1989 in Leipzig, 70,000 people crowded the central square of Karl-Marx Platz. Stasi files later revealed that more than half of these protestors were connected to the Stasi as employees or informers. 'They, of course, might have been true protesters as well as Stasi,' writes Tina Rosenberg in *The Haunted Land*. 'But the other thirty thousand must now wonder whether they came to the march of their own free will or in some mysterious way had been sent. They must wonder whether free will existed at all in the perfect Communist society, where no one could possess even his own thoughts.'[78]

With such penetration of society – and even of the protest movements – why didn't the Stasi make a stand in support of the communist order? After all, the Stasi had plans in case of crisis to open sealed envelopes that contained the names of nearly 86,000 people to arrest immediately. The head of the Stasi, Erich Mielke, began to put this plan into effect on 8 October, the day before the huge protest in Leipzig. He sent out 'orders to the local Stasi branches to open their envelopes,' writes Anne Funder in *Stasiland*. 'But things were already too far gone. Instead of incarcerating the people, the Stasi, hiding in their buildings, locked themselves up. In the regional offices they had 60,000 pistols, more than 30,000 machine guns, hand grenades, sharpshooter's rifles, anti-tank guns, and tear gas. Fears of lynching ran high.'[79] They were terrified, not terrifying. The army, given shoot-to-kill instructions by Honecker himself, withdrew in the face of tens of thousands of peaceful demonstrators.[80]

It wasn't just that things had gone too far. The Stasi expected some kind of deal that would have prolonged the life of the East German state with West German cash. It was not an entirely unrealistic expectation. The West German government had paid for all sorts of things in the past, including the exit of East Germans and the dismantling of the automated tripwire at the Berlin Wall.[81] 'I talked to a lot of the Stasi people, and they said that they were told during the period of upheaval, "Stay in your barracks, don't do anything. The Wall's open, we're going to cut a deal, and everything will be okay,"' journalist David Crawford told me. 'If these people had been told, "Stay in your barracks, we're going to have reunification, and when it's over you're going to get 800 DM a month as a pension, and you're going to be unemployed, and you're going to be a pariah to society, and you're not going to be able to work in the public service," there might have been a lot of public resistance.'

Instead of a deal, the Stasi found itself in complete retreat after the fall of the Wall. For the six weeks or so before protestors stormed Stasi headquarters, first in Leipzig in December 1989 and then throughout the country the following month, Stasi officers desperately attempted to destroy those hundred-plus miles of files. But it just couldn't be done at such short notice. In the process, the shredding machines broke down and the officers were reduced to tearing up files by hand. The famously powerful Stasi proved powerless to cover its tracks. As a result, East Germany – and then, after 3 October 1990, a united Germany – had an enormous number of files on its hands: 4 million on East Germans and 2 million on West Germans and foreigners.[82] It also had over 15,000 bags filled with more than 600 million pieces of imperfectly destroyed paper, all of which had to be painstakingly reconstructed.[83] David Crawford contributed to the documentation by publishing three lists – of the real estate held by the Stasi, a list of pensions, and of spies under deep cover.

In contrast to the haphazard and politically motivated process in the rest of eastern Europe, Germany handled all this potentially explosive material dispassionately and methodically. The tradition of the *Rechtsstaat* served Germans well, as did the application of West German laws. East Germans didn't have to create the rule of law on the fly. German punctiliousness also meant that virtually no one went to jail for the Stasi's activities. The head of the Stasi, Erich Mielke, was jailed – but for his complicity in a pair of murders in 1931, not for anything he did during the communist period. Markus Wolf, the spymaster who ran the network of high-level informers inside West Germany, had his sentence of treason reversed in 1995 because, as the Constitutional Court ruled, he'd been doing his job in an internationally recognized sovereign state.[84] Other top officials received suspended sentences.

Nor, for the most part, was lustration used in Germany for political purposes in the same way as in the rest of the region. The files were almost immediately available, which largely eliminated campaigns of rumor and innuendo. But reputations could still be tarnished. East Germany's first and last democratic prime minister, Lothar de Maizière, resigned in December 1990 from his position in the Helmut Kohl government when evidence surfaced of his alleged collaboration with the Stasi. Others quietly went into retirement before they could be publicly outed.

The campaign of de-Stasification also reached beyond the political sphere. Historian Kurt Pätzold, for instance, told me about the campaign against him at the university where he taught. 'There was a small group of young scientists and students who, after the fall of the Wall, made aggressive speeches denouncing the professors,' he said. 'One group called themselves "the independent historians," and they played a role in the process of the laying off the professors.' He continued, 'I wasn't immediately laid off. My dismissal was signed on 31 December 1992. There had to be a justification for this, and the easiest justification was: informal collaborator of the Stasi. As it became clear that there was nothing about me in the archives, I got a certificate of being clean.' Even so he had to write a letter of resignation.

One of the ironies of the process in Germany is that those who collaborated with the Stasi often suffered more – in terms of employment opportunities and social stigma – than those who actually worked for the Stasi. Roland Jahn, head of the Stasi archive, explained this irony to me: 'In general no official Stasi staffer was able to make a public career because their previous position could not be hidden. But there were people who became public figures who kept their unofficial collaboration with the Stasi a secret in the process of German unification. And that became a very outrageous proposition, that people in a new position pretended that nothing happened when they actually had a past with the Stasi.'

Sunlight did not always play a disinfectant role. Take the case of sociologist Irene Runge. She'd done research into the issue of foreigners living in East Germany and was invited to participate in the country's round table in 1990. The Initiative for Peace and Human Rights also asked her to run on their ticket in the elections that March, which she agreed to do on the understanding that she'd be low enough on the list not to have to serve. 'I told them I had had Stasi contacts,' she related to me. 'Someone said, "It's great you are talking about it. It's the past. That's how we see it: we talk about it to solve it." Well, this attitude changed very soon into hate and self-administered justice.' No one wanted to hear the details of her collaboration. 'It didn't even help me when I said that I already had my fights with the Stasi at the end of the 1960s and the 1970s and that I broke with the organization around 1979,' she continued. 'For ten years the Stasi didn't consider me reliable anymore. That's not even taken into consideration.'[85] It probably didn't help that the Initiative for Peace and Human Rights discovered around the same time that half of its founding members had been Stasi agents.[86]

Much of the debate in Germany over the Stasi centers on the truth contained in the files. But little has been done on the other side of the equation: reconciliation. In December 1989, physicist and peace activist Helmut Domke became a member of the civil committee for dissolving the Stasi at the regional level in Potsdam. 'The challenge for the Church is to work for reconciliation in society and not to allow a spirit of revenge,' he told me in 1990. Twenty-three years later, after investing a great deal of effort into just that kind of work, he admitted in a discouraged tone, 'the chance to pay more attention to reconciliation was lost.'

Roland Jahn disagrees. 'Right from the start a lot of people tried to talk with the perpetrators,' he told me. 'But the problem was that the perpetrators were often not willing to join these talks. They were often not willing to admit that injustice had happened. But this is the necessary prerequisite for reconciliation, to admit injustice has happened. You cannot order victims to forgive. You can only ask victims for forgiveness. But this has not happened enough.'

Perhaps it's still too soon for Germany to come to terms with what happened during the communist period. After all, West Germany didn't begin to grapple in a public way with the Holocaust until more than thirty years after the end of World War II and the premiere of the American mini-series *Holocaust* on West German TV in January 1979. Half the adult population of the country watched the show, and suddenly the unspoken subject was on everyone's lips.[87] The 2006 German movie about the Stasi, *The Lives of Others*, might have served a similar function. But as artist Stefan Roloff points out, many people in the former GDR hated the film. 'Imagine we're in 1965, twenty years after the end of World War II and the Holocaust, and a German person makes a movie about the good Gestapo man and shows it in Tel Aviv,' he told me. There hadn't been enough time – or enough detailed examinations of the period – to warrant an even modestly sympathetic portrait of a Stasi agent.

Perhaps that's also because the unexploded ordnance in the files is still going off. Researchers are still piecing together the files that the Stasi tried to destroy as the system crumbled around them. One of those files was for agent V 682/65. In 2012, when the dossier was finally reconstituted, 'unofficial collaborator Thomas' turned out to be Aleksander Radler, an orphan from Poland. He'd been studying theology in Berlin when the Stasi recruited him. After a short stint as a successful informer in Germany, Radler went to Sweden on the Stasi's behalf, where he became a well-connected pastor in the Lutheran Church and a local Christian Democratic politician. He informed for the Stasi for twenty-four years in all. When finally unmasked, he confessed in a public letter, resigned his ministry, and retired from the public eye – more than two decades after the fall of the Berlin Wall.[88]

History commissions

Lustration was only one of the ways that eastern Europe attempted to address the communist period. Most countries established institutes to sift through and assess the past, like the Institute for National Remembrance in Poland. You can also find museums devoted to the crimes of the past, which often focus more on recent crimes at the expense of those from the pre-communist era. The Museum of Totalitarianism in Budapest, for instance, showcases the horrors that took place under communism but devotes little space to the earlier period of 'White Terror' when the extreme right was in power. In Romania, a museum devoted to the victims of communism has been established in the city of Sighetu Marmației, but the country only recently decided to establish one in 2018 on the Holocaust.[89]

Although the Romanian opposition was one of the first to raise the issue of lustration, the government didn't seriously begin considering a lustration law until twenty years later when the lower chamber of parliament adopted a law that banned secret service (Securitate) officials and informants. The law went farther, to ban all communist-era officials, including prosecutors and police chiefs.[90] In 2010 and again in 2012, the Constitutional Court struck down the law as unconstitutional.[91] Several top officials were jailed for the killings in Timișoara in 1989, but for more than twenty-five years no one stood trial for the earlier crimes of the communist era.[92] Finally, in 2015, Alexandru Vișinescu received a twenty-year sentence for his role as a commandant of a prison where inmates were tortured, starved, and killed.[93] A second such prison commander, Ion Ficior, received a similar twenty-year sentence in 2016.[94]

From a criminal justice point of view, Romania faces a narrowing window of opportunity to prosecute those guilty of communist-era human rights abuses. Those prison commanders were both in their late eighties. But from the point of view of more abstract principles of justice, as political scientist Vladimir Tismăneanu points out, it's never too late, and sometimes distance in time can help. 'Only a month ago in Brazil did they create such a commission, three decades after the restoration of democracy,' he told me in April 2013. 'The Dominican Republic only a year ago opened a museum about the Trujillo times.'

Vladimir Tismăneanu knows the challenges of dealing with the past in more than just his capacity as an academic. In 2006, Romanian president Traian Băsescu asked him to head up the Presidential Commission for the Study of the Communist Dictatorship in Romania, known more informally as the Tismăneanu Commission. It was the country's first systematic effort to come to terms with its communist past, and it was not an easy task. 'Initially the archives wouldn't give us anything or hardly anything,' Vladimir recalled. 'Members of the commission were very angry. Then I went to Băsescu. This was in June. "Mr President, I want to be very frank with you. Many of my friends – people that I admire, that you admire – believe that I have been caught in a trap. For you, it's a great achievement. You are the president who created the commission to condemn communism. The issue has been completely defused. For me, I put all my prestige, name, and authority on the line."' As a result of this intercession, Băsescu prevailed upon the interior minister, who in turn called an emergency meeting to demand that his subordinates fully cooperate with the commission.

Another problem had to do with the composition of the commission itself. Vladimir invited Sorin Antohi, an eminent historian who had been a secretary of state at the Ministry of Education, to join the group. Antohi had also been one of the founders of the Group for Social Dialogue, the dissident group that emerged at the very end of the Ceaușescu era. He seemed to be a logical choice.

'He accepted the invitation, which remains the mystery of my life,' Vladimir told me. 'He would still be what he was if he had not accepted.' The day after the appointment, Vladimir received a call from the head of the political prisoners' association with very specific information about Antohi's collaboration with the Securitate. As a result, Antohi withdrew for 'personal reasons.' Then he published a confession. 'His career went spiraling downward, which is a pity since he's a brilliant guy,' Vladimir recounted. 'I had no role in this. On the contrary, I publicly defended him. I said that he remains my friend. I received lots of criticism. People said, "You say that you are very critical, but if it's your friend you change your position. In other cases of informers, you are very tough." Probably they had a point about this double standard.'

The commission eventually produced an 880-page report written by thirty-six people. It produced evidence of considerably more resistance to the communist system than had hitherto been acknowledged, from the late 1940s onward. It helped pave the way for many others to have access to government archives. And it probably generated as much controversy as it resolved. 'I didn't anticipate the level of hatred,' Vladimir concluded. 'The type of letters that I received! But also you have to look at the other side – the tremendous letters that I received in support. Those were signed. The other ones were unsigned.'

Through lustration, court cases, government commissions, museum exhibits, academic investigations, and journalistic exposes, eastern Europeans made many attempts to get at the truth of what happened during the communist period.[95] But there were very few efforts to replicate the kind of 'truth and reconciliation' process that South Africa set up after the end of apartheid and that Helmut Domke wanted to set up in East Germany. 'In postcommunist Central Eastern Europe, only a few saw the reconciliation model as attractive and advocated framing the end of communism as a moment of the coming together of former opponents,' political scientist James Mark writes. He singles out Romanian president Ion Iliescu as an exception – he called for 'national reconciliation' based on 'erasing the problems of the past.'[96] But Romanians were not interested in erasing the problems of the past, and they were deeply suspicious of Iliescu himself given his high rank during the communist period. Iliescu's pledge to erase the problems of the past sounded suspiciously like a pledge to erase his own problems of the past.

Czech president Václav Havel was perhaps the political figure in the region most committed to reconciliation. Unlike Iliescu, he didn't have to contend with a compromised personal history. Even so, he too had great difficulties trying to get people to engage with history rather than simply condemn it. On his first day in office, Havel made an astonishing and dramatic decision. He issued a general amnesty that led to the release of 23,000 out of the country's 31,000 prisoners – all but the serious offenders. 'Suddenly a wave of criticism descended on the new president, with his detractors (many of whom, not surprisingly, belonged to the vanquished *nomenklatura*) painting gleeful populist pictures of an orderly society suddenly invaded by crime, chaos and mayhem,' writes his biographer, Michael Žantovský. 'The threat was grossly exaggerated.'[97] Havel himself was adamant about the importance of providing a fresh start, particularly given how compromised the previous legal system had been (which he knew first-hand as a political prisoner). 'Naturally it would have been easiest to grant pardons to no one,' he wrote in his autobiography. 'I would have been immensely more popular. But I wasn't the president in order to be popular.'[98] Havel's other unpopular gesture in the direction of reconciliation, also in 1989 shortly after taking office, was toward the Sudeten Germans. Havel apologized for their expulsion from the western territory of Czechoslovakia at the end of World War II. Aside from his foreign minister and the Catholic Church, Havel received very little support for the gesture.[99]

Those Czechs who chose to follow Havel's lead were few and far between. An heiress of a prosecutor in one of the first political trials, for instance, gave a portion of her inheritance to the children of former political prisoners.[100] Otherwise, like Jan Kavan, political prisoners and their children were on their own. There was no official compensation, like the package belatedly given to Japanese Americans interned during World War II.

Outside of Yugoslavia, eastern Europe didn't experience a wave of violent revenge. The largely nonviolent 'refolutions' produced largely nonviolent transitions. The lack of reconciliation, however, spoke to the narrow application of liberalism in the region: a focus on the letter of the law rather than on a liberality of spirit. But even this narrower understanding of the rule of law was fatally compromised when the new judicial institutions failed to act impartially. Thoroughly politicized, lustration rarely produced the kind of justice that so many people in the region craved. Few perpetrators went to prison; many managed to profit politically or economically in the new system. As a result, a general cynicism about political and legal institutions infected the population.

The tribunal

I wasn't there to hear horror stories. The refugees that gathered in the living room of the house in a small village outside of Sarajevo in 2008 were participants in a community garden project. In urban plots throughout Bosnia, families from different faiths and backgrounds coaxed vegetables from the ground and rebuilt relationships shattered by war. It was a project established by the AFSC office I'd helped to set up in the region fifteen years earlier, and I'd been rehired as a consultant to visit and evaluate the project.

The refugees I met that day were from Srebrenica. They'd lost husbands and sons and brothers during the terrible bloodletting of 1995. These survivors had escaped through the woods. They were now settled far from home, though 'settled' is really not the right word, since their lives continued to be profoundly unsettled by poverty and discrimination. The vegetables they grew on borrowed land helped to keep them alive.

I asked them questions about their gardens, how much they harvested, the difficulties of getting water for the crops. I studiously avoided questions about the past. To retell a story of tragedy is often to relive that tragedy. I didn't want to make them do that.

But they wanted to talk about the past. For them, it was not really the past. The stories lived with them in place of the relatives they lost. For Selima, the past was particularly close at hand because of the discovery of more of Srebrenica's mass graves that year. 'As we were leaving Srebrenica and my husband said goodbye, he said that maybe we wouldn't see each other again,' Selima recalled. 'When they found his bones, there was no skull. When they found his bones, it was like it was happening all over again.'

Another gardener, Nesib, heard on the radio on that day in July 1995 that the Serb forces would be in Srebrenica by nightfall. His cousin told him not to panic since, after all, the people in Srebrenica were just civilians and had no weapons. Nesib didn't take any chances. He left the city and walked through the woods for six days. His feet were covered with blisters because he didn't have proper shoes. He survived on the fruit and mushrooms he found. He was lucky. Serbian paramilitaries killed twenty people in his extended family, including his optimistic cousin.

Other gardeners in the project – Serbs, Croats – could speak of their own losses. It was wartime. Civilians suffered terribly on all sides. But in Srebrenica, Serb armies killed around seven thousand Muslim men and boys in the worst massacre in Europe since World War II.

It was painful for Nesib to tell his story. But he told it readily and without any prompting. He didn't, however, tell these stories to his children: 'I don't want my kids to hate all the Serbs.'

A number of those who had committed terrible crimes during the wars in Yugoslavia had to face criminal prosecution a thousand miles away at The Hague. The tribunal was unusually successful in helping to re-establish the rule of law in former Yugoslavia and bring an end to the cycle of violence in the region. Although subject to occasional lapses – such as the acquittals of Croatian general Ante Gotovina and Serbian politician Vojislav Šešelj – the tribunal successfully indicted more than 161 individuals, gave 4,000 witnesses an opportunity to testify, established the basis for a common narrative of what happened during wartime, and created precedents that could be used in cases prosecuted in the Yugoslav successor states.

There was a modicum of justice for Selima and Nesib as well. The court brought twenty indictments against individuals for crimes committed in Srebrenica, including genocide, and handed down fourteen convictions by 2015.[101] In March 2016, the court sentenced its most prominent figure – Radovan Karadžić, the former president of Republika Srpska – to forty years in prison for his involvement in genocide in Srebrenica, among other crimes.[102] The court even ruled that Dutch peacekeepers, who handed over 300 men to Serbian forces at Srebrenica in a grotesque example of international fecklessness, had to provide compensation to the victims' families.[103]

In a region plagued by perceptions of injustice, the Hague Tribunal was one of the few institutions that successfully established principles of justice – for both victims and violators alike. Since the tribunal was not located in eastern Europe, the rule of law continues to carry with it the quality of an outside imposition. Sometimes, however, justice requires a measure of distance, which can also confer neutrality. It was, after all, the European Court of Human Rights that ultimately forced the Slovenian government to apologize and provide compensation to the Erased.

For many, the indictments at The Hague were too few and far between. The ones who committed atrocities numbered in the thousands, if not the tens of thousands, not the low hundreds. Who could say that justice had been done when Dragan Jovanović, a Serb from Srebrenica who burned down houses and took away their male inhabitants, could go into business after the war in, unbelievably, home reconstruction. 'If I'd never burnt down those houses, I wouldn't be in business today!' he told an Italian journalist.[104] Even when justice was served, it did not come quickly. 'The tribunal has been a slow and bureaucratic process,' Predrag Dojčinović, who began working at the Office of the Prosecutor at the ICTY in 1998, told me. 'I know it's difficult and complex because I worked there. I don't want to judge anyone in this enterprise. But I think it can be done better and faster.'

For others, of course, the Hague process was too fast. 'I felt that there should be a public debate about the law on extradition,' lawyer Dragoslav Popović told me over dinner in Belgrade. 'At the time we didn't have any such law. There was only a rule that said that no foreign country should judge our citizens. Then we implemented the Hague Tribunal ruling directly on our system and decided to give Milošević away. I personally think that it was done in a rush, more to win some international points than to ensure that everything was done correctly from a legal point of view.' According to this interpretation, the international tribunal was yet another example of a liberal institution undermining the nation-state and its laws.

The tribunal would eventually prompt changes in Serbian laws, but it couldn't completely change Serbian hearts. 'The biggest problem is that the Serbian people never actually faced the past, never faced the role their representatives played during the wars of the 1990s,' NGO activist Raša Nedeljkov told me in 2012. 'If you go out on the streets and ask people about Srebrenica, a significant number of people will denounce it, but a huge number of people will say, "Even if it happened, the number of dead wasn't that high and anyway, what does that matter in 2012?"'

In attempting to establish the rule of law, the Hague Tribunal and other initiatives in eastern Europe were up against a range of obstacles, from the wars in former

Yugoslavia and the legacy of the communist era to the efforts of lustrators so eager to pronounce sentence over collaborators that they disregarded basic rules of due process.

But the problem that proved perhaps most pervasive in undermining public confidence in the rule of law was more mundane, more predictable, and more difficult to address.

The wages of corruption

During the communist era, Bulgaria was a center for organized crime. As Misha Glenny reports in his book *McMafia*, Bulgaria's arms export firm Kintex started smuggling arms to insurgents in Africa in the late 1970s, 'but soon the channels were also being used for illegal people trafficking, for drugs, and even for the smuggling of works of art and antiquities.'[105] The criminality only intensified after 1989. The media tycoon Robert Maxwell, who had close ties to communist dictator Todor Zhivkov, allegedly facilitated a money-laundering operation that spirited $2 billion out of Bulgaria and into Western tax havens.[106] The privatization of national assets was a golden opportunity for established capitalists in the West and red capitalists in the East to join hands in pickpocketing the public.

Iliya Pavlov emerged as one of Bulgaria's key corrupt capitalists. On the surface, he was just a successful businessman, running a large corporation called Multigroup that employed thousands of people. Behind the scenes, however, Pavlov worked closely with Bulgaria's version of the KGB to make huge profits through price-fixing. Before his fall, Pavlov was powerful enough to control Bulgarian politics. As anti-corruption activist Stefan Popov told me, 'Pavlov said, "If the Bulgarian prime minister wants something from me, let's talk at the table." Can you imagine Al Capone saying something like that about the US president? That's unthinkable, unless you're a movie director.' In 2003, a sniper assassinated Pavlov outside his Multigroup headquarters.[107]

As the head of an organization called Risk Monitor, which shines a light on the more shadowy recesses of Bulgaria's illegal economy, Stefan Popov is trying to change the image of Bulgaria as the Wild East frontier of the European Union.[108] Because of Risk Monitor's work, the Bulgarian government has had to face tough questions from journalists, civil society activists, and EU officials about sex trafficking and money-laundering. 'In a country like Bulgaria, it's a senseless distinction between organized crime and white-collar crime,' Stefan told me. 'Right from the beginning, the crime was white collar and had deep roots in the state and the politics of that time. It didn't come from the outside. That makes it very difficult to manage and oppose. These are crimes that imply a close interaction or synthesis between business, politics, and criminal practices at a very high state level.'

Corruption was endemic under communism.[109] Workers stole from their workplaces. Party officials profited from their positions. Bribery greased the wheels of an inefficient economy. During the communist era, corruption helped maintain stability by meeting needs the economic system could not satisfy. Today, corruption contributes to greater volatility in the region, bringing down governments or ejecting ruling parties from power, contributing in the extreme case of pyramid scams to near-economic collapse, and eroding public confidence in the rule of law.

The corruption that accompanied the first years of transition – when enterprising insiders introduced new methods of siphoning off resources such as 'tunneling' in Czechoslovakia and the 'spider trap' in Bulgaria – created a lasting perception that the market favored the unscrupulous.[110] 'If society does not see the new capitalists as legitimate,' wrote Polish sociologist Jadwiga Staniszkis in a prophetic 1991 essay, 'the lack of popular support for the reforms may mean the persistence of political crises.'[111] Indeed, in one survey of Czechs, Slovaks, and Bulgarians in the late 1990s, two out of three people said that 'most' politicians were more corrupt in the democratic era than they were under communism.[112]

'We don't have drug mafias or organized crime as in Bulgaria,' Robert Basch of the Czech office of the Open Society Institute told me. 'They're not mafiosos. The corruption is very often done by smart people doing business with the state, withdrawing state money through business.' The Czech Republic, after all, is famous for its president, Václav Klaus, claiming that there was no such thing as 'dirty money.'[113] Klaus 'was the one that established the current milieu of corruption in the country through his disdain for the rule of law,' former dissident Daniel Kumermann told me. Indeed, in one of his last acts before leaving office in

2013, Klaus issued an amnesty that voided, among others, eighteen high-profile corruption cases.[114]

In Poland, corruption facilitated the transfer of wealth to the political elite. For instance, the Foreign Debt Service Fund operated between 1989 and 1991 to service Polish debt. It received several billion dollars to buy Poland's debt on secondary markets. Instead, as one inspector discovered, the fund 'was siphoning money to military circles, intelligence organizations and clandestine projects.' Investigations into the fund, among other schemes, continued throughout the 1990s. However, only four public officials were convicted of corruption between 1990 and 1996.[115] No surprise, then, that in 2000, 84 percent of Poles believed that 'corruption permeated all walks of life.'[116]

In Croatia, too, corruption coincided with the changeover in the system. 'Croatia and the other countries of the former Yugoslavia have never experienced real free markets,' politician Natasha Srdoč told me. 'They were brought from full state-owned economies or mom-and-pop entrepreneurism to a very criminal capitalism where all of a sudden state-owned companies were being sold. Franjo Tuđman in Croatia, for example, had an idea that he was proudly promoting publicly: having two hundred families own the whole economy. He succeeded in having families, some that were closer to him, get the wealth of the country.' The graft went beyond this small circle. 'There were many opportunities for theft' in Croatia, historian Ivo Banac confirmed, 'if one were connected.'[117]

In Romania, corruption attended the earliest days of the transition. The National Salvation Front, for instance, indiscriminately handed out 'certificates of revolutionists' to anyone who made a 'remarkable contribution' to the overthrow of the Ceaușescus. The certificates entitled their bearers to forgo paying taxes for an indefinite period.[118] 'Blank certificates were circulated,' writes political scientist Liliana Popescu-Bîrlan. 'An awkward situation arose. Certain people who fought against the anti-Ceaușescu demonstrators now possess such certificates. Some of them bought the certificates. Others received them as a reward for their allegiance to some members of the new leadership in Bucharest.'

For all the challenges of dealing with its own history, its lustration process, and its complicated political transition, Romania has nonetheless taken the lead in applying the rule of law to the top leadership. In 2012, for instance, Romania's highest court sentenced former prime minister Adrian Năstase to two years in prison on corruption charges and banned him from public office over the same period. Between 2004 and 2013, prosecutors investigated twenty-one ministers and nineteen secretaries and undersecretaries of state for abusing their political positions.[119] In the Romanian parliament, 15 percent of those elected to office in 2012 were convicted of graft or were under investigation.[120] In contrast to the lustration campaigns, the Romanian prosecutor's office was non-partisan in its investigatory zeal. It was, however, one of the few bright spots in an otherwise dismal landscape of widespread corruption.

It's not just *their* malfeasance, of course. Corruption benefitted Western elites that profited as bankers and middlemen as well as just plain consumers. 'Organized crime is such a rewarding industry in the Balkans because ordinary West Europeans spend an ever-burgeoning amount of their spare time and money sleeping with prostitutes; smoking untaxed cigarettes; snorting coke through fifty-euro notes up their noses; employing illegal untaxed immigrant labor on subsistence wages, stuffing their gullets with caviar; admiring ivory and sitting on teak; and purchasing the liver and kidneys of the desperately poor in the developing world,' Misha Glenny wrote with unconcealed anger.[121]

Corruption is, of course, not unique to eastern Europe. According to a European Parliament study from 2016, corruption costs the EU nearly a trillion dollars a year.[122] Some western European countries are notorious for their culture of corruption: Italy, for instance, routinely scores poorly on Transparency International's Corruption Perceptions Index, ranking below Jordan, Namibia, and South Korea.[123] But in eastern Europe, the problem achieves industrial-strength dimensions. All countries in the region scored above the EU average in their levels of corruption, the European Parliament study concluded, and the three worst performing countries in the EU were Romania, Bulgaria, and Croatia.

In the end, then, eastern Europe faced some of the same challenges to the rule of law as the rest of the continent. But it also had to deal with problems unique to the region, such as the impact of communist-era secret services, the fall-out from the post-1989 economic reforms, and the rise of a new class of oligarchs who became rich on state contracts. This was the problem in a nutshell: eastern Europe took a step backward after 1989 because it suffered from the worst of two worlds, the downsides of both capitalism and communism. As a result, liberalism entered a vicious circle in which resentment, paranoia, and hostility reinforced the natural pessimism of the region.

Interlude: Stepping Backward, Leaping Forward

I was driving one Saturday morning in the late 2000s from Albania to Croatia. The traffic in Tirana, the capital of Albania, had been lawless, vehicles at roundabouts behaving practically like bumper cars at the amusement park. Having survived Albanian roads without a scratch, I was driving through Montenegro when someone in the left lane of a three-lane highway decided to take a right turn directly in front of me. I braked, but not in time, and slammed into the car. I was furious; the other driver was furious. A Montenegrin policeman showed up, took away my passport, and told me to appear in court the following Monday morning.

It was bad enough that I had to spend two days in a nearly empty Montenegrin hotel and miss a rendezvous with friends on the Croatian coast. But then I ate some bad squid and spent the night before my court appointment on my knees in front of the toilet in my ratty hotel room. Tired and queasy the next morning, I tried to argue with the judge about the traffic rules – in a mixture of Russian and a few words of Serbian – only for him to insist, against all evidence, that the accident was my fault. The late-arriving interpreter turned out to be the son of the other driver. Even though he was surprisingly sympathetic to my plight, he couldn't help me convince the judge. It all ended with a minor fine that I would have been happy to pay at the point of impact if I'd only cottoned on more quickly to the local bribe culture. Montenegro wasn't lawless. I just didn't understand how the law operated.

'In western Europe, and there are exceptions of course, generally people follow and obey the rules – the laws, customs, social conventions,' lawyer Viorel Ursu told me. 'In eastern Europe, we think the rules are unfair, and we always tend to negotiate or circumvent those rules. Look at how we cross the street against a red traffic light, or the way we drive, the way we park our cars, the way we bribe our teachers, our doctors, politicians. We all do this in eastern Europe.'

During the transition, the reformers focused first on elections, then on the economy. The judicial system ran a distant third.[124] Leszek Balcerowicz, the architect of Poland's economic reforms, 'would never tell you that he made a mistake,' journalist Ryszard Holzer told me. 'But he knows that the biggest mistake back then was that there was no real reform of the justice system. He didn't know then how important the justice system is for the economy. He knows it now.' It was a mistake repeated in one country after another. The region had a second shot during the accession process to the European Union. But in its eagerness to expand eastward, the EU didn't prioritize rule-of-law reforms.

It was but one of several self-inflicted blows that liberalism has sustained in eastern Europe over the last three decades. Since the political and economic transformations did not spread the pain of adjustment equally over the population, those most adversely affected eventually pushed back. The liberal package also became associated with an urban elite, deepening an already existing divide with the countryside. The further links between the changes and the agendas of various international actors – transnational corporations, specific governments like that of the United States, and institutions like the IMF and the EU – helped to fuel a nationalist backlash as well. Finally, the failure of the rule of law to satisfy the desires for justice and to prevent the blossoming of corruption throughout the region helped undermine public confidence in the overall liberal project.

This book has so far charted the different steps backward that eastern Europe has taken, particularly as illiberal parties, institutions, and individuals have come to the foreground in the region. Proponents of the original liberal model have argued that these are temporary setbacks – the inevitable pendulum swings of politics. According to a more pessimistic scenario, the setbacks could end up becoming further institutionalized if the region follows the Russian model put in place by Vladimir Putin.

Or perhaps eastern Europe has taken these steps backward to make the leap forward all the easier. In the next chapters, I will look at where the energy for this leap forward might come – and what 'forward' might look like.

Part II
Leaping forward

6
Reinvention of Self

When I first met Mira Oklobdzija in Zagreb in September 1990, she was a busy and successful sociologist. She was also active in the feminist and anarchist communities, which put her at the forefront of the liberalizing changes that had swept through Yugoslavia since the 1960s. Croatian and Yugoslav social movements seemed to be thriving in 1990.

'The legislation here in Yugoslavia on women's rights is very good,' Mira told me at the time. 'For example, we have equal rights, in every domain. You can't be paid less for the same job if you're a woman, which in America is quite possible. Also, people who live together after a year have the same rights as married people. And the children born of these couples also have equal rights. It's not just legal recognition, but social acceptance as well. Well, in the countryside it is more patriarchal, but this is at least the case in the cities.'

In 1990, however, these more conservative voices in the countryside were becoming louder. As I traveled through Yugoslavia that summer, people warned me of an upsurge in nationalism, of growing intolerance, and of the inability of the federal structures to handle these challenges.

Yugoslavia had long been the most liberal of the countries in the region, the only communist country with a shot at joining the European Community. And yet a number of movements were emerging that called into question the very integrity of the country. In Croatia, for instance, the conservative Croatian Democratic Community (HDZ) won the republic's first democratic election in April/May 1990 on a platform of turning Yugoslavia into a looser confederation or, if that proved impossible, seceding altogether. It also promoted a more traditional view of Croatian society.

'Ten years ago, feminism was a word that was laughed at. Now, however, it is accepted,' Mira continued. 'But the recent government in Croatia is trying to change things. Because they want to boost the birth rate, there recently was an attempt to make abortion illegal. Until now it was very cheap and very accessible. But women within the Croatian Democratic Community were against it. Other parties, like the Christian parties, would like to put the women back in the family: a strong Croat family and lots of little Croat children.'

In 1990, it was possible to imagine that Yugoslavia would simply continue on its liberal trajectory, becoming more and more like its European neighbors, Austria and Italy. Membership in the larger European community beckoned, which would have required even greater respect for political and social rights. It was also possible to imagine that Mira would continue to teach sociology and champion these more liberal social reforms.

But that didn't happen.

In 1989/90, the course of history changed in eastern Europe. For many people, those changes opened up enormous opportunities. Czech playwright Václav Havel and Hungarian novelist Árpád Göncz, who both had spent time in prison for their political beliefs, vaulted to the very top positions in their country. My friend Bogdan dropped out of academia and reinvented himself as a manager at IKEA in Warsaw. With barriers lifted to acquiring a passport, many people went abroad to create new lives for themselves, as Vihar did when he traveled to Canada or when Miroslav and his family traveled to Kentucky.

Many of the people I interviewed in 1990 had reinvented themselves several times over by the time I caught up with them in 2013. Window washer and dissident Daniel Kumermann had become a journalist and then the Czech ambassador to Israel.[1] Robert Braun was a human rights advocate in Budapest who then became a media entrepreneur, a successful businessman, and an unsuccessful politician. Jacek Czaputowicz was a peace activist and conscientious objector who, after the changes, entered the Polish foreign ministry and later became a university lecturer.

'A totally new public space emerged in 1989,' Bulgarian political scientist Ivan Krastev told me in Vienna in 2013. 'Being young in this period was a major advantage. For me personally and my generation, this was an incredible opportunity. Overnight, what you were saying was perceived as important, and you had the feeling that you were part of making history.'

Stanislav Holec, for instance, was a rock climber and unemployed engineer when the Velvet Revolution broke out in Czechoslovakia. He volunteered with the new opposition group Civic Forum, using his English and French to assist foreign journalists. 'After a few days of that,' Stanislav told me, 'Civic Forum activist Peter Uhl said to me, "You are young, non-communist, independent – you can help me with this independent news agency, the East European Information Agency." I said, "Yes, but I'm not a journalist. I'd like to help you. But I don't know how to write."' Uhl instructed him to buy a grammar book. After two months of study, Stanislav began to write – and spent the next two decades working as a journalist.

In Yugoslavia, as the country lurched toward conflict and then all-out war, very different and very illiberal opportunities presented themselves. Milan Babić was one of those opportunists. In the space of a few months in 1990, he went from practicing dentistry to becoming a local politician in the new democratic sphere to leading a breakaway Serbian republic within Croatia. He next reinvented himself as a war criminal, responsible for helping kill or expel thousands of non-Serbs from his little fiefdom of the 'Serbian Autonomous Oblast Krajina.' Brought up on charges at the Hague Tribunal, he pleaded guilty and eventually committed suicide in his cell in 2006.

Babić and other newly minted nationalists pushed Yugoslavia along a trajectory that many of my interviewees feared most in 1990 – disintegration, war, widespread atrocities. Nikola Koljević, a noted Shakespeare scholar, went into politics as the vice-president of the breakaway Republika Srpska in Bosnia and later ordered the bombing of the national library in Sarajevo. Gojko Šušak started a pizza business in Canada, but returned to Croatia to become the country's defense minister. Peace activist Janez Janša became the minister of defense and then later president in Slovenia (and later still a prison inmate serving time for bribery).

For Mira Oklobdzija, war meant exile. She moved to Amsterdam for personal reasons shortly after I met her in 1990. The war that broke out between Serbia and Croatia in 1991 stranded her in the Netherlands. Initially she decided to return to Zagreb. 'In 1991, I was on my way back in fact and stopped in Italy,' she told me when I interviewed her again in 2013. 'I was speaking with people here and there. The people from Yugoslavia were saying to me that I was crazy: "What can you do here that you cannot also do somewhere else? If we feel that there is something that you can specifically do here, then we'll call you and you can come back."'

She returned to Holland, where she began to raise funds for independent media in former Yugoslavia. From Amsterdam, Mira watched her country of origin fall apart. She wrote an essay titled 'Guilt as destiny,' which she gave to other friends stranded abroad by the war. 'They told me, "Oh yes, I feel the same,"' she recalled. 'It talked about feeling guilty because you are somewhere else. I was feeling worse than people who were getting used to things in Belgrade and Zagreb, before things got worse there.'

This guilt in part motivated her to find work at The Hague, in a new tribunal for addressing war crimes in the region. She had the right skills – knowledge of the languages, familiarity with human rights, training in research methods. She worked there nearly to the end of the tribunal's mandate. A part-time activist in the past, she became a full-time legal crusader and permanent exile because of the war.

'I originally didn't want to work at the tribunal, at the UN, because I knew when I finished working there I would be too old to start an academic career again,' she told me. 'It was also not the money that attracted me, though I have to say that the salary was great. Rather, it was the feeling that we were doing something against the bad guys. I hope that we did at least something, though I often wonder if it was good enough.'

We met in 2013 shortly after several controversial tribunal verdicts exonerated top Serbian and Croatian military leaders. Those decisions had proved so exasperating to one tribunal judge, Frederik Harhoff, that he distributed a letter to friends and associates taking issue with the verdicts.[2] The letter was reproduced widely on the Internet, and Harhoff later left the court when his term was not renewed.[3]

'You really have the feeling again that you are losing your life and time and energy, and for what?' Mira said. 'I had a similar feeling in the 1980s. You were doing things for the common good and what you got was war. Then you work in an institution like the tribunal and something like this starts to happen at the end of the mandate. Again, you have the feeling: did I waste my time trying to do this?' Today, Mira lives in Trieste, near to the Balkans but still part of the Europe that escaped communism and the wars of the 1990s. There she writes essays and is considering picking up the career in sociology that the war interrupted.

The war in Yugoslavia produced a new generation of soldiers, victims, and illiberal leaders like Babić and Koljević. It also produced a new generation of human rights advocates like Mira. What started out in Yugoslavia as a battle over different conceptions of the state devolved into a catastrophic ethnic grudge match in which principles of justice embedded in international law competed with justice determined by force on the ground. The war made liberalism seem like nothing more than a set of paper institutions easily consumed in the fire of human passions.

The tribunal at The Hague was part of the process of delegitimizing the illiberal leaders that brought war to Yugoslavia in the 1990s. It was, however, slow and deliberate, and it encountered numerous obstacles, whether states reluctant to cooperate or defendants who refused to accept the court's mandate. It would leave many unsatisfied with its judgments. But it also contributed to the reinvention of former Yugoslavia as a region of stable, durable liberal institutions.

During the Yugoslav war, the transformation of dutiful citizens into paramilitary leaders was a function of naked power. What undermined popular faith in liberal institutions was a sneaking suspicion that the same forces operated in similar ways beyond the battlefield elsewhere in the region. The envious suspected that those who lived the eastern European equivalent of the American dream – a cadre of ambitious politicians, a handful of new billionaires, a new world of celebrities – succeeded through connections, corruption, or the actions of outside forces. Even the individual stories of successful reinvention in the new liberal order, in other words, could undermine faith in the system as a whole if the transformations appeared to result from anything other than merit.

And yet, stories of individual and collective reinvention speak to the mutative nature of the region. Although such transformations are not particularly unusual in the United States or western Europe, they were virtually unheard of during the glacial communist era. The third necessary sea change in the region after politics and economics – the transformation of mindset – requires just this space for reinvention.

This second half of the book will look at where this reinvention is taking place. Many people schooled in the old system have learned how to reinvent themselves in the post-1989 world, ensuring a smoother transition. A new elite has emerged even among the most marginalized communities. Although the region has taken several steps backwards, another set of dissidents are campaigning against injustices old and new. An up-and-coming generation has begun to challenge the received notions of their elders. And a class of bold artists and activists are creating new worlds on the ground.

These overlapping groups are trying to preserve the best of the changes from the last twenty-five years while at the same time pointing the way toward a different kind of future. It doesn't add up to a coherent paradigm, nothing like the liberal orthodoxy that prevailed in the early 1990s. But the first indications are promising nonetheless.

Creating a new elite

In the 1980s, Smaranda Enache worked in a puppet theater in Târgu Mureș in the Transylvanian region of Romania. She hated the Ceaușescu regime but, like many Romanians, she expressed her opposition privately. When Ceaușescu was still in power and it was still quite dangerous to do so, she penned an Aesopian fable about the Ceaușescu family, all transposed to a fairytale land. She wanted to stage it at the puppet theater. But first the censorship committee of the county's Communist Party had to approve the show.

'Perhaps someone had informed them in advance that the play was a transparent allegory of the Ceaușescu dictatorship,' Smaranda told me. 'Therefore a high-ranking ideological secretary for County Mureș came to see the play.' They pressured her to make changes. And they immediately stopped its public performance. That was in May 1989.

Then, in December, came the changes. Smaranda returned to her play and prepared for its first performance in January 1990. With the Ceaușescus dead, the allegory had lost whatever capacity to move people that it might once have had. Meanwhile, Smaranda received another visit from the authorities. This time, however, the two members of the National Salvation Front (NSF) – the group of former communist officials and dissidents that coalesced in the wake of Nicolae Ceaușescu's fall from power – invited her to join the local council of the organization. Caught up in the revolutionary fervor of the moment, she agreed.

'I was assisting some of the meetings,' she told me. 'I was also watching the transfer of power, because the headquarters used by the NSF was the same county headquarters of the Romanian Communist Party and the same building. All the administrative apparatus of the communist leadership was in place. It was in a way normal, because they were fast typists and good drivers.'

Smaranda was astonished, however, when she saw former communist leaders like the secretary for the economy pass by her in the NSF headquarters. Furthermore, information from the sessions of the council appeared in the pages of what had, until recently, been the *Red Star*, an organ of the Communist Party. 'They were the same communist journalists who had been condemning the revolutionaries as the so-called "enemies of the nation" until the last moment. And then they changed totally,' she recalled. 'I asked, "Why don't you change everybody, the whole apparatus, because this is a new power and the information should be the truth, not distorted by an apparatus still loyal to the *ancien régime*." Everybody was busy with the important priorities. Nobody was interested in these details.'

It was not long before Smaranda was booted out of the NSF – for her vocal criticism of growing interethnic tensions in the country – and then from her job in the theater. The new authorities could be just as vindictive as the old. She then reinvented herself as an NGO activist campaigning for democracy, human rights, and EU membership. Later, after the NSF's successor party fell from power, she became the Romanian ambassador to Finland.

Even if the National Salvation Front had wanted to bring in a completely new crop of leaders and civil servants in 1990, it would have drawn from a small pool of the competent and uncompromised. There had been no major organization of dissidents in Romania. The tiny Group for Social Dialogue came together only after the revolution had begun in Timișoara. Art historian Magda Cârneci was one of the founders. Like Smaranda, she initially joined the National Salvation Front with great hopes – to work on youth affairs. She too discovered that the new government contained many of the old guard.

'The activists of the old political system were still in place,' Magda told me. 'They didn't disappear. They were very afraid at the beginning. During the first months they were very silent and discreet. It looked as though they – the Securitate, everybody – had retired from the scene. Then they realized they could come back because the country needed administrators and managers. And these people were the only ones who knew how to administer, how to manage.'

The new Czechoslovak government, too, had a minuscule dissident class from which to draw in 1990. 'There was a serious shortage of appropriate people for the various posts,' Václav Havel wrote, 'so we had to persuade rock musicians, translators, television hosts, scientists, writers, maybe even our friends from the pub, to accept positions. There were tens of thousands of civil servants, and there were certainly not that many dissidents.'[4] To meet this need for a new, professional bureaucracy, Jan Urban, a dissident and one of Havel's colleagues in the Civic Forum, outlined a plan to train a new generation of public servants. 'Our plan was to have a five-year program to send a thousand selected students abroad to the best Western universities,' he told me. 'There was a hope that within five years we would have a thousand-plus young people to become completely new young bureaucrats with no attachment to the past regime and having connections and contacts with the West. We were trying to create a democratic elite whose loyalty would be to the state and no one else – no political party. We failed.'

A mass movement initiated the transition in Poland, but even there representatives of the 'old guard' took up important positions in politics and economics. To staff the military, the police, the public prosecutor's office, 'there simply is a lack of people involved in the opposition who are both willing and competent,' Piotr Krawczyk, an advisor to one of the ministries in Poland's first democratic government, told me in 1990. 'If we had time, we could wait for a new generation of people. But we simply don't have the time.'[5]

Lustration complicated the process of building this new cadre by winnowing down the already small number of people willing and qualified to serve in government and professions like journalism. Lustration was supposed to keep out the old elite. But nothing symbolized the failure of such strategies like the wholesale return to power of the former communist parties, though controlled now by reformers rather than the former hardliners.

Revolutions promise a clean slate. Even though the taste of victory turns sour if the same corrupt bureaucrats continue to run everything on a local level, some continuity in personnel can ensure a smoother – and nonviolent – transition. Hungary didn't experience a cathartic cleaning of the stables when opposition political parties ousted the renamed Communist Party in the first elections in 1990, but that had certain advantages. 'The major reason why the Hungarian transition is so peaceful – more peaceful than any other country like Czechoslovakia or East Germany since we didn't even need a mass demonstration or a mass strike – was that the beneficiaries of the old regime found some way to survive and build up a new basis for themselves within the structure of the new regime,' economist László Urbán told me in 1990.

Communist revolutionaries executed, imprisoned, or exiled many of the representatives of the old order after they came to power in the region in the aftermath of World War II. These options were generally not available to the architects of the 1989 changes. 'It was not physically possible just to wipe those people out, for many reasons but most of all because when you come in with the idea to return the country to normalcy, your first priority is the rule of law,' economist Krassen Stanchev told me. 'Imposing an institutional arrangement that arbitrarily changes people's economic and social positions would not have been possible.'

Moreover, once the system changed, so did the actions of many of the people who continued to work in the same positions. 'Take a restaurant manager, for example,' diplomat Philip Bokov told me. 'Three years ago, the government started renting these restaurants to people to build a franchise. Many of them started doing much better than when they were government. The same people were doing the job. Which shows that it is not the personalities: it is a matter of the system, of organization, of incentives.' New structures create new roles for the same old people. It's a lesson that occupation authorities failed to learn in Iraq when they purged all the members of Saddam Hussein's Baath Party and sowed the seeds of future conflict in that benighted country.

And yet the very basis for the smooth transition – the option to switch sides and profit in the new order – has proved to be a continuing irritant, particularly for conservative parties like PiS and Fidesz. Even a quarter-century after the changes, they routinely talk of the continued influence of the communist elite on political and economic institutions. Both parties have won votes because the argument has a surface plausibility, even in the more liberal Poland and Hungary. Indeed, one of their more successful arguments has been that liberals facilitated the return of these communists, by allying with them politically or by supporting economic policies that enriched the old elite. 'I was very disappointed when in 1994 the Socialists won,' former Fidesz activist Attila Ledényi told me. 'That was a shock for me. After four years, people seemed to forget everything that happened before 1990. The other shock was when SzDSz [the Alliance of Free Democrats] joined the coalition with the Socialists. Many of those people … decided to go in and go under the Socialists even though SzDSz in that coalition was mathematically unnecessary. They were invited only to be makeup on an otherwise ugly face.'

Romania was an exception to this pattern. The National Salvation Front banned the Romanian Communist Party. However, as Smaranda and Magda discovered, many of the old functionaries carried on. Even when they were not changing labels and remaining in power, elements of the old elite in Romania prospered in the new order. Some of the turnabouts were positively galling. In one of the few Tiananmen Square-like repressions in eastern Europe in 1989, Securitate colonel Filip Teodorescu tried to put down anti-Ceaușescu demonstrations in Timișoara in December 1989, resulting in dozens of deaths. He spent a short time in prison. Then, after his release, he transformed himself into a writer, penning a memoir 'full of surreal stories about foreign plots bound to destroy Romania's sovereignty.'[6]

From the point of view of overall stability, however, it was better that Teodorescu could find his calling as a writer instead of an insurgent against the new order. As Herbert Hoover told Harry Truman after World War II, 'You can have vengeance, or peace, but you can't have both.'[7]

Changing things locally

They are called the *decret* generation. During the communist era in Romania, Nicolae Ceaușescu issued Decret (Decree) 770 in 1967, making abortion and contraception illegal except under certain circumstances. The communist leader wanted to radically increase the population of the country. Those with money or political influence found a way around the regulations. Parents who could not support their new babies often dropped them off at the nearest orphanage.

That was the fate of Vasile Mathe when he was a baby. Now a soft-spoken man, he works as a school mediator in a small town outside of Câmpia Turzii in Transylvania. Of all the people I'd met in the region, he'd overcome the greatest odds in his efforts to reinvent himself.

'Until I was three years old, I was raised by a lady working in the maternity ward,' he told me as we sat with a translator in a café in Cluj. 'She wanted to adopt me. But it was impossible because my mother wouldn't agree to the adoption. We had to wait until I was ten years old. So, I was sent to an orphanage because of this disagreement with my mother. I ended up staying there until I was nineteen years old.'

This experience has made him more philosophical than bitter. He was, of course, lucky enough to come of age just as the Romanian system was changing, so that he could realize his dream of helping children. In addition to working as an educator at an orphanage, he earned a degree in psychology and assisted NGOs devoted to education and Roma rights. He has used his artistic skills to inspire children in hard-luck situations. As a mediator in a school attended largely by Roma, he tries to stand up for the rights of children.

'My goal was to persuade parents to keep their children at school,' Vasile told me. 'Working with Roma children who were already going to school, I managed to convince the others also to send their children because of the good results at school. It didn't happen all the time. But I did manage to bring some of the other children back to school.'

It wasn't easy work because many of the teachers were not on the same page. 'The teachers are not prepared to invest more effort to give Roma children an education,' he continued. 'The children have a lower competence. They feel inferior. So, they already are psychologically ready to quit school.' In many conscious and unconscious ways, teachers were encouraging Roma children to drop out, for instance by threatening to fail them unless they did better. This was, as Vasile pointed out, a form of abuse, which pushed Roma students to drop out. 'The children might not even realize that they are being abused,' he added, 'but they all react in some way.'

The teachers at the school responded to the monitoring program Vasile tried to put in place by effectively kicking him out of his office. He ended up conducting his parent–teacher meetings and after-school programs outside, in the school courtyard. 'But all of these children's activities were supported by the mayor and the local council,' he concluded. 'I told the mayor that all these problems threaten to break out into a social plague. If the town didn't come up with an action plan for the future, the Roma population would start developing increasingly criminal behavior. Finally the mayor agreed and offered to provide support for the actions I wanted to do.'

Vasile had a quiet, dogged persistence. His one-on-one encounters, his commitment to transforming children one at a time, have the potential to erode the terrible intolerance that lurks like a sickness just below the surface in Romanian society. His own reinvention has awakened in him a belief in the potential for transformation in everyone.

Switching sides in Hungary

In 1993, when I met Gáspár Miklós Tamás, a Romanian-born Hungarian, he was perhaps the most significant conservative intellectual in east-central Europe. I was impressed as much by his intelligence as I was by the stacks of books in the living room of his Budapest flat. Each stack corresponded to an article or project he was working on at the time. Seeing those towers was like going behind the counter at a juice bar and ogling the immense amount of fruit that went into a single glass. Here was a man of convictions – and even if I didn't share these convictions, I appreciated the immense erudition that informed them.

Many intellectuals in east-central Europe have traveled considerable ideological distances over the decades. The most common trajectory has been rightward, as former Marxists were born again after 1989 as liberals, neoliberals, neoconservatives, just plain conservatives, and ideologues even farther to the right. János Kis in Hungary, who critiqued Marxism from the left in the 1970s, moved toward the center to become a prominent liberal in Hungary in the 1980s and 1990s. Mihailo Marković, a member of the group of neo-Marxist philosophers in Yugoslavia known as Praxis, became a leading nationalist supporter of Slobodan Milošević in Serbia. Former Polish communist Bolesław Tejkowski swung over to the far right to create a party notorious for its extreme nationalism and anti-Semitism.

Gáspár Miklós Tamás, never one to mimic popular fashions, went the other way.

'I've had this strange trajectory that I once called in an interview a boomerang: from the left to the right and back again,' he told me when I met him again in Budapest in August 2013. 'But I did not land exactly in the same place. I was much more of an anarchist in my youth. And, strangely enough for a east European, I became a Marxist for the first time only in 2000 – perhaps forced by circumstance but also by theoretical considerations.'

What struck me on seeing him again in 2013 was his adherence to what historian Tony Judt describes in a posthumous collection of his essays, *When the Facts Change*, as a willingness to alter one's understanding of reality when that reality evolves.[8] In the 1990s, liberalism became increasingly unpopular in Hungary even as the former communists made a political comeback. 'How is it possible that the regime that my generation of intellectuals so hated and suffered so much at the hands of would be rehabilitated by public opinion and seen unapologetically as the better way by a majority of people, including people on the right?' Gáspár Miklós Tamás asked himself. 'Of course, I don't happen to agree with that opinion. On balance, we are still slightly better off. But I couldn't ignore that view.'

The failure to thrive for so many people in the region was another fact he couldn't ignore. The twenty-five years preceding 1989 had not only produced in Hungary 'the only version of the welfare state that the East had known, but it was perhaps the greatest explosion of east European culture in our history,' he continued. 'Also, it was the only period in which people could count on their lives getting a little better each year in economic and material terms. They also managed to achieve a little more liberty every year. So it was an era of progress. And there was also a feeling of security. And that's something we can't say about our own era.'

Observing the palpable failures of liberalism, Gáspár Miklós Tamás did what many had done: jump ship. He turned to Marxism because it offered an explanation for why the new economic system in the region was not bringing prosperity to the majority and why the working class was getting the worst of it. If former communists hadn't discredited themselves when they returned to power through their continuation of austerity economics and corrupt political practices, the region would have experienced the genuine rebirth of an independent left. Instead, the failures of liberalism pushed most people toward the other political pole.

And that's what happened to Zoltán Illés as well. When I first met Zoltán in 1990, he was twenty-nine years old and in his first month as the youngest state secretary in modern Hungarian history, working in the Ministry of Environment. He granted me quite a long interview and was unusually frank not only about the environmental situation in the country but also about the challenges he faced in his own position. At the end of the interview, he gave himself a 70–80 percent chance of making it through his first year without being fired.

As I learned when I met up with Zoltán again in May 2013, he'd lasted only six months. 'I had a very challenging half a year in 1990,' he told me. 'I did my best for the environment. And finally they fired me. Officially, in written form, the minister wrote that "you are dedicated to the environment." Well, come on, I was sworn in to do that! Then he wrote, "But we have to consider other interests, and you are not capable of doing that. You are for the environment and that is why we are firing you."'

Zoltán had learned an important rule of politics: mavericks rarely achieve significant change within a bureaucratic system, no matter how committed they might be to their issues. After that short tenure in government, Zoltán worked as an advisor to the EU's ambassador in Hungary and taught classes at Duke and the University of North Carolina. He joined Fidesz in the 1990s just as it was shedding its alternative image. In 2010, he returned to government once again as state secretary of rural development, which includes the portfolios for environmental protection, nature conservation, and water management. He was eager to return to government. 'I understood that if I didn't accept the position, then I would destroy my past and what I introduced into the field of environmental protection over the last twenty to thirty years,' he explained. 'I didn't want to miss the opportunity to prove myself not only as an outsider but as an insider in power to make change. For several decades, everyday I went to sleep understanding what I didn't do that day and what was still remaining to do.'

Zoltán certainly learned a thing or two since he first worked in government. 'You have to accept the hierarchy of administration,' he told me. 'If someone doesn't accept hierarchy, they should be, like I was previously, a street fighter – which is an excellent opportunity for high-level performance in the field of environmental protection. And maybe I will return to that after my time as a "general" in this position.'

He lasted only one more year in government. When he left, Zoltán immediately took aim at the government for transferring grasslands from national park control to a fund that could distribute the lands to Fidesz supporters.[9] He pulled no punches in a long interview with the main opposition newspaper *Népszabadság*, declaring that some in Fidesz view environmental protection 'as some kind of leftwing deviation or the eccentric hobby of rich people,' while the majority simply sees it as 'a superfluous obstacle in the path of implementing economic plans.'[10] Zoltán had transformed himself from a maverick into an inside player and then back again. In Hungary's volatile political environment in the early twenty-first century, the 'boomerang' trajectory was a not uncommon response to the decline of liberalism.

Rebranding a country

Over the last twenty-five years, eastern Europe has turned its back on its communist history. All of the political and economic reforms – even those promoted by former communist parties – have repudiated centralized planning in favor of the market, authoritarian control in favor of democracy, and Moscow-centered foreign policy in favor of NATO and the European Union. These changes in the substance of the state matter little, however, if the outside world doesn't also perceive a major change in image. To achieve a 'new and improved look' to go with their transitional institutions, countries enlisted the help of advertising firms.

Kosovo, for instance, is the most recent country to emerge from the wreckage of Yugoslavia. For many outsiders, Kosovo means 'war' and 'organized crime.' To create a new brand, the Kosovo government paid 6 million euros to the Israeli branch of the firm of Saatchi and Saatchi to come up with the slogan: 'Kosovo – the

Young Europeans.' A spokesperson for the firm explained, 'This is probably the very first national slogan which turns the spotlight on the people and the human spirit rather than the country, its natural marvels or history.'[11] Given youth unemployment in Kosovo of nearly 60 percent and the huge numbers of young Kosovars who have joined the stream of emigration from the Balkans, the tagline takes on unintended connotations.[12]

Since the wars of the 1990s barely touched it, Slovenia has had less of an image problem. But it too had difficulties coming up with the right brand. It considered such possibilities as 'a miniature Europe' and 'the green piece of Europe.' One slogan, 'Slovenia: your perfect getaway,' didn't quite work because, translated into Slovene, it became 'Slovenia: a perfect escape from reality.' The government crowd-sourced the problem by enlisting citizens to choose how best to characterize the country in a few words. They chose, ultimately, 'I Feel Slovenia,' with the 'love' highlighted in the middle of the country's name.[13] It didn't capture much about either the people or the country. It also contrasted rather sharply with the experience of the Erased, who didn't necessarily feel a lot of love for the country. But rebranding quite literally airbrushes the past.

The reinvention of nations in the postcommunist era has involved not only references to historical events and invocations of myths of belonging. The countries of eastern Europe must also sell themselves in the global marketplace in order to capture a larger share of tourist dollars and foreign direct investment. The bumper-sticker sentiments of a tagline reflect aspirations rather than reality. If countries fail to close the gap between reality and aspiration, the branding contributes to an erosion of faith in both the state and in the marketplace. In many cases, the fresh coat of paint that the government applies as part of the rebranding can be seen only in certain areas – the nicer parts of the major cities, the mountain resorts, the infrastructure serving lakefront properties. The incoming foreign direct investment and the tourist dollars only serve to sharpen the divide between Eastern Europe A and Eastern Europe B.

Nostalgia for the previous era, then, turns out to be the flipside of the branding process – a longing for an imagined past versus the construction of an imagined present. It's no wonder that those who reject the New Coke in favor of the traditional variety willingly forget that a similarly misleading 'promotion' effort hooked them on the original. This nostalgia can be found in the renewed popularity of certain communist-era products or in the establishment of certain clubs or museums that promise an 'authentic' brush with the communist past. It ranges from voyeurism on the part of outsiders to wistful appreciation on the part of former insiders.

Sometimes the nostalgia has an even simpler explanation. I once asked someone that I was reinterviewing how he would compare his life back in 1988 with his life today. He looked at me as if I were crazy. 'Of course it was better then!' he exclaimed.

'It was better under communism?'

He laughed. 'No, it was better when I was twenty-five years younger!'[14]

Even critics of the socialist system can wax nostalgic. Stephan Stoyanov, a gallery owner in New York, spent the first half of his life in Bulgaria, studying to become an accountant. He was eager to leave the country once the changes took place, and, for the most part, he hasn't looked back. He readily acknowledges all the terrible flaws of the communist system, from censorship to restrictions on movement. But there are other things he remembers with fondness.

'Back then there were some great things – free education, free medical system,' he told me as we sat in his Chinatown gallery. 'And the education was far superior than today. It was also very safe. I could walk through the parks. Now I can't. People had jobs. Yes, our basic needs were barely satisfied. But you don't need much actually. This whole madness of consuming endlessly, it's not good either. It's another extreme. Before, under communism, people were judged by who they are and by their deeds. Now, more and more, particularly in Bulgaria, people are judged by what they own.'

There were few incentives to work under communism, and that too had its charms. 'We were young, energetic, and had plenty of time on our hands, and no motivation to make a career in the official system because there were no rewards, neither at a personal nor a material level,' Dimitrina Petrova told me of her experience in Bulgaria as a dissident intellectual in the 1980s. 'Time was the crucial element: the time to read, to talk, to talk, to talk, and to talk. It was a very oral kind of existence. So that's why it was a happy time.' I had a very similar experience in 1989 when I spent endless hours in tea houses in Warsaw talking with my Polish friends about Solidarity, the future of eastern Europe, and other vital issues. In her book *The Future of Nostalgia*, Svetlana Boym writes, 'The excess of time for conversation and reflection was a perverse outcome of a socialist economy: time was not a precious commodity; the shortage of private space allowed people to make private use of their time.'[15] Not everyone idealizes that time, of course. Nostalgia for the days of schmoozing in cafés, scholar Charles Gati says dismissively, is 'against the imperative of working hard that capitalism imposes on you.'

In former Yugoslavia, nostalgia takes a different form because it isn't just about having more time for stimulating discussion or taking the state-mandated vacation every summer. Yugonostalgia can represent a desire to return to a time before war, before revived ethnic hatreds, before the destruction of an identity. 'The list of things we had been deprived of was long and gruesome,' one of the characters in Croatian novelist Dubravka Ugrešić's *The Ministry of Pain* laments. 'We had been deprived of the country we had been born in and the right to a normal life; we had been deprived of our language; we had experienced humiliation, fear, and helplessness; we had learned what it means to be reduced to a number, a blood group, a pack.'[16]

Yugonostalgia, like everything else in a market economy, is also a commodity. Along the canals in Ljubljana in 2013, for instance, I encountered stalls selling T-shirts emblazoned with Tito's face or with Yugoslavia's coat of arms, its red flame representing brotherhood and unity. 'Slovenians are the most prominent Yugonostalgia suckers,' anthropologist and writer Svetlana Slapšak told me in her apartment in Ljubljana. 'I really hate it. Because it's commercialized, and it buries all the criticism in a deep concrete grave, never to be revealed again … It destroys not only criticism but also freedom of mind, and it makes people non-active, just consumers of silly things. The Internet is full of Yugonostalgia objects. You can buy the old comic books, periodicals, pictures, paraphernalia, all kinds of rubbish: good for research, bad for the spirit.'

In Germany, nostalgia for the former East Germany, or *ostalgie*, is big business. It can be found in movies like *Goodbye Lenin* and the re-release of old GDR TV shows.

One place in Berlin that feeds the *ostalgie*, in this case quite literally, is the GDR Museum. The two parts of the museum, which is devoted to everyday life in the German Democratic Republic, subtly contradict one another. That might not have been the intention of the museum founders, but this tension actually captures the ambiguities of East Germany and the ambivalence that many Germans feel today about the erstwhile communist state.

The experience inside the main part of the museum is interactive. You can put on headphones and watch TV shows from East Germany, walk into an interrogation room and a prison cell, and sit at a high-ranking bureaucrat's desk. You can take a test of your Russian. You can vote in a rigged election. The cabinets and closets lining the wall and dividing up the space provide opportunities to peer at consumer products that have faded into history, such as Wald Gold liquor and Florena Cream. Pull out drawers and open cabinets to reveal even more objects, such as a floor plan of a GDR apartment or a Stasi report. In this way, you feel as though you are uncovering a hidden society, which is appropriate since the society was largely hidden from Western eyes for many years.

The ticket seller told me that most visitors – nearly half a million in 2011 – rated their experience at the museum very highly.

'What about people from the former East Germany?' I asked him. 'What do they think?'

'Eighty to ninety percent of them are very satisfied.'

'And the other ten to twenty percent?'

'Well, they are not happy with … the tone.'

This tone of the museum is most evident in the descriptions. For instance, here is part of the description of GDR tourists: 'GDR citizens were not particularly popular in Eastern bloc states. Waiters in Prague could recognize them easily. Western tourists used paper money: Deutschmarks or dollars. East Germans counted their aluminum play money.' In these exhibits, everyday life in the GDR comes across as quaint, inefficient, boring, and worthy of varying degrees of derision. It's no wonder that some people from the former East Germany have found the experience somewhat upsetting. It's not that they didn't make fun of the system all the time. And they continue to look back at that time with a mixture of humor, horror, and relief that much of that experience is behind them. But the exhibits at the GDR museum are meant for tourists, specifically tourists from the West. The wall texts invite you into a shared joke: how silly/strange/exotic those East Germans were! At Berlin's municipal museum, by comparison, a whole room is devoted to how cool and chic the Kurfürstendamm area of West Berlin was during the 1960s. In general, Berlin museums treat West Germany's past reverentially but East Germany's like an enormous dead end. The proof is obvious: West Germany lives on and East Germany has been absorbed like a heavy, tasteless meal.

Which brings us to the other half of the GDR Museum: the restaurant. Here, in a replica of a restaurant from a fancy East Berlin hotel, you can sample the best of GDR cuisine, washed down with Vita Cola or Rotkäppchen, the Coca-Cola challenger and the sparkling wine that are two of the few GDR products still produced in the united Germany. You can order smoked pork with potatoes and sauerkraut, allegedly Erich Honecker's favorite dish. The food is quite good, at least what I ate, the stuffed cabbage in bacon sauce.[17] It's not prepared in a funny or ironic way. After all, the restaurant is designed to be successful, and no one wants to eat bad food, however representative of a country's cuisine it might be. You can find some mildly amusing descriptions on the menu. But there's nothing amusing about the food.

In other words, the restaurant sends a very different message than the other exhibits. It says there was something good about East German life, something worth praising, saving, and even serving to people today, whether an everyday soft drink or a recipe from East Berlin's most elite restaurant. This is something more than just *ostalgie* for risible Trabants and TV programs. It's an appreciation for the fact that people in East Germany were not simply puppets but active participants in their lives.

Because nostalgia is about an imagined past, some of the East German products served up for today's consumers are not exactly what they once were. Consider Club Cola, the other East German cola. 'In the GDR, it was sometimes made from tap water,' cultural historian Rainer Gries writes, 'but now its main ingredient is always mineral water. And it never ceases to emphasize that it is now "less sweet" and has "more taste." Thus, it indirectly admits to the universally known defects of its GDR past and dedicates itself henceforth to improvement and quality.'[18]

In this way, Germans can have their old GDR soda and drink it, too.

In the immediate aftermath of 1989, liberals offered a future-oriented vision in which individuals could transform themselves and their country. The future was the market, democratic elections, and Europe. When each of those elements of the future proved problematic, and so many individuals found that their own transformations were thwarted, large portions of the population turned instead to the past. Not surprisingly, populists have mobilized support by appealing to an imaginary golden age of plenty.

That conflict was never sharper than in Yugoslavia in 1990. Human rights advocates like Mira Oklobdzija envisioned a democratic country committed to progressive social mores. The nationalists tapped into powerful feelings of nostalgia and ethnic homogeneity. Both sides were offering something different from the stultifying communist status quo. 'So, there was space and time for opportunists, people who were building something new, for better or worse,' Mira concluded.

In the end, the opportunities the liberal order offered for self-transformation applied to a fortunate fifth or perhaps only a talented tenth. It's no surprise, then, that liberalism has failed to thrive.

7
The Talented Tenth

Violeta Draganova made news as she was delivering the news. As the first Roma anchor on Bulgarian national television in the early 2000s, she provided a powerful visual message of ethnic diversity in a society unaccustomed to seeing minorities in positions of power and influence. In addition to being poised and articulate, Violeta possessed that other key attribute necessary for broadcast journalism: good looks. A slim, attractive woman, she has appeared on the covers of various Bulgarian magazines. She couldn't pass for non-Roma, not with her dark skin. Nor would she consider doing so. She proudly defies many of the stereotypes that have accumulated around Roma over the centuries, and she has done so since she was very young.

'I learned to read before the first grade,' she told me as we sat in a café in Sofia. 'On the very first day of school, I was the only one who could already read. From those very early years, I was abused by my classmates, but still they had a kind of respect for me because I knew more than them. So I started to try to be the best, wear the best clothes and so on, to limit as much as possible the different ways they could abuse me. But it was not easy.'

It was not easy because of the enormous discrimination that Roma have experienced in Bulgarian society. It was also not easy because the determination to excel, to prove her ethnic Bulgarian classmates wrong, took its toll over the years. 'All my life I tried to be a perfect person in order to be accepted as an equal,' Violeta continued. 'It's not easy to be a perfect person. After all, no one can say what is perfect. I was the only Roma in the classroom. There was another guy, but he always wore dirty clothes. He came to school from time to time. He is he, I thought, and I am me. I was even kind of angry at him.'

Violeta became a journalist almost by accident. When she was nineteen years old, she happened to be visiting a monastery not far from her home town of Plovdiv, Bulgaria's second-largest city. A TV crew filming at the monastery invited her onto their program. For three years she continued her studies in literature and philology at the university and worked at the TV station. In 2000, she received an offer to work for Bulgarian national TV. Still in her twenties, she became a celebrity by hosting the morning news show and then the evening news.

Despite her accomplishments, Violeta encountered almost non-stop discrimination. 'The first month when I was working for Bulgarian national television I understood that someone was complaining that I shouldn't be there because they could hear my Roma accent,' she told me. 'This was absolutely stupid. I don't speak Roma so I can't have an accent.' When her boss at Bulgarian national TV called her out in front of her colleagues for unspecified failings, she'd had enough. 'My boss and most of my co-workers treat me as "the Roma on TV,"' Violeta wrote in an article about her experience. 'I am looked upon as exotic, like something akin to a talking monkey.'[1]

It wasn't just discrimination in the workplace. One hot day in Sofia, she was walking around with her sister and nephew when they decided to cool off with a dip at a public swimming pool. The woman at the front desk said they couldn't enter because the pool was hosting a private party. But it seemed that other people were going inside without any special invite. Violeta confronted the woman with this information, but they still weren't allowed inside. 'I called the media,' Violeta told me. 'Journalists showed up. It turns out that there was no private party. The woman at the front desk couldn't explain why I couldn't enter. After that, I understood that this is a usual thing for this swimming pool to deny entrance to Roma. It turns out that it doesn't matter how much you struggle, it doesn't matter how much you have succeeded, this woman can make you feel like a nobody. My nephew was crying, asking his mother, "Are we animals or are we people?"'

Giving up her prestigious position in broadcasting, Violeta went to Brussels to work for the European Commission. 'When I worked in Europe as a producer in the information agency, no one ever looked at me like they didn't think I could do the work,' she told me. 'I had a job and I did it and everything was fine. I realized that I had underestimated my skills. If no one believes in you, then you start believing this yourself.'

Violeta is a minority within a minority – a successful professional from a community with a tiny professional class, a community that has been consigned to the very margins of Bulgarian society. Her hometown of Plovdiv, for instance, is infamous for the poor conditions of its Roma neighborhoods. 'The deep squalor of their settlements – urban and rural, indoors as well as out – is indistinguishable from the worst *favelas* of Brazil,' writes Isabel Fonseca about the Plovdiv ghettos.[2] An equally apt comparison would be to the very first ghetto in Europe. Located on an island set aside for a foundry – *getto* in Italian – this Jewish neighborhood in Venice occupied such a small patch of land that the residents had to build higher and higher to accommodate a rising population. One modern commentator called it 'a neighborhood of medieval mini-skyscrapers.'[3] Land is likewise dear for Roma in Plovdiv. 'In the Stolipinovo neighborhood and in other Roma neighborhoods, we are forced to build vertically,' Roma activist Anton Karagiosov told me. 'We will soon explode because of lack of space. There are fifty thousand of us only in the Stolipinovo neighborhood.'[4] Stolipinovo occupies 4.5 square kilometers.[5] That's 11,000 people per square kilometer, a population density greater than in New York City.[6]

Violeta is quite aware of the gap between herself and the Roma crowded into the ghettos of Bulgaria. Particularly after her time in Brussels, however, she sees her country's membership in the European Union as a game changer. 'There are Roma who live in the ghetto who don't know what it means for Bulgaria to be accepted in the EU,' she told me. 'But there are other Roma who want a better education, who are ambitious. For them, this is a good opportunity: to get out of Bulgaria and be part of the EU. Maybe some of them will go to different universities in Europe, and it will be easier for them to come back here and do something. In some way, they will break the glass ceiling by going outside and studying.'

That glass ceiling has already sustained a few cracks. In eastern Europe in 1990, only a handful of Roma managed to serve in parliament or run successful businesses. The notion of a young Roma woman appearing on TV as a news anchor seemed like science fiction back then. Today, a Roma professional elite has emerged. A younger generation, university-educated and fluent in several languages, refuses to accept the limitations that constrained their parents and grandparents. Even so, the ethnic majority continues to marginalize these cases of individual success by declaring them 'exceptional.'

The plight of the small minority of Roma that has broken down barriers and entered mainstream society on nearly equal terms resembles that of African-Americans in the era preceding the civil rights movement of the 1950s and 1960s. To describe these extraordinary African-Americans who succeeded despite pervasive racism, noted intellectual W. E. B. DuBois coined the expression 'talented tenth' in a 1903 essay in his volume *The Negro Problem*. 'The Negro race, like all races, is going to be saved by its exceptional men,' DuBois wrote. 'The problem of education, then, among Negroes must first of all deal with the Talented Tenth; it is the problem of developing the Best of this race that they may guide the Mass away from the contamination and death of the Worst, in their own and other races.'[7] Violeta's childhood encounter with the boy in dirty clothes in her classroom starkly illustrates the divide between the talented tenth and the 'contamination' of the 'Worst.'

Even as the Roma 'talented tenth' moves into mainstream society, the 'Mass' of Roma remains at the bottom of the region's economic and political ladder. It often resembles a zero-sum game. Zeljko Jovanović, who works with the Open Society Foundation on Roma issues, has written critically of what he calls the 'Roma-in-charge,' that is, 'a person of Roma ethnic origin, nominated by government, accorded an advisory role, but denied any decision-making powers. Co-opted, and possessed of a sense of purpose, the Roma-in-charge enters a higher comfort zone in terms of income, status and recognition – a comfort zone at some remove from the quality of life of the average Roma citizen.'[8] Without any substantial power inside the system, these 'Roma-in-charge' don't have the means to help the larger community even if they wanted to do so.

Ultimately, W. E. B. Dubois came to the same conclusion. When he saw how the African-American elite, of which he was a member, had often sought individual advancement at the expense of collective improvement, DuBois repudiated his own 'talented tenth' theory forty-five years after he formulated it. 'When I came out of college into the world of work,' he wrote in 1948, 'I realized that it was quite possible that my plan of training a talented tenth might put in control and power a group of selfish, self-indulgent, well-to-do men, whose basic interest in solving the Negro problem was personal; personal freedom and unhampered enjoyment and use of the world, without any real care, or certainly no arousing care, as to what became of the mass of American Negroes, or of the mass of any people.'[9]

The Roma are on the cusp of their own civil rights movement. In the post-1989 era, their 'talented tenth' have enjoyed an equality of opportunity unprecedented in the community's thousand-year history of exile, slavery, and degradation. As populist reaction to the elites gathers strength in the region, so too have Roma elites faced questions about their privileges. Will this new elite prove Dubois wrong, or is there some other method of ending the most widespread human rights problem in east-central Europe today?

The talented tenth problem applies to the region as a whole. The transformations of 1989 offered tremendous opportunities to a gifted minority who could speak foreign languages or leverage the new technologies of computers and finance. Membership in the European Union provided an additional boost to this same minority, giving them access to a larger set of institutions that value their skills.

The elite of eastern Europe now lives at the level of their western European counterparts. But the problem of underdevelopment in the region stems from the failure of the elite to pull the mass of people into prosperity. The problem of the twenty-first century is the problem of the inequality line.[10]

The setback

Roma represent about 10 percent of the population of Romania. Large numbers also live in the Czech Republic, Slovakia, Hungary, Bulgaria, and former Yugoslavia. They are Europe's largest minority group, with a total population of 10–12 million.[11] But there is little strength in numbers. The Roma are a heterogeneous community divided by nationality, language, customs, and history. They also experience more discrimination than any other European minority.[12]

Originally from India and speaking a language similar to Hindi, the Roma traveled to Persia and Armenia before passing through Byzantium to the Balkans and farther into Europe.[13] Their nomadic lifestyle became their defining characteristic, so much so that other itinerant groups in Europe, like the Travelers in Ireland, are often mistaken for Roma. What they've adopted as a culture, however, may well be a defense mechanism. Although linguistic evidence suggests that they spent considerable time in Persia and Armenia, Roma became nomads as they entered Europe most likely because one settlement after another expelled them.

When they settled in one place, it was often against their will. Roma were rounded up and interned in eighteenth-century Spain. Beginning in the fourteenth century, they became slaves in parts of modern-day Romania, achieving emancipation only in 1856.[14] Even in the more tolerant Austro-Hungarian Empire, Roma suffered. Habsburg Queen Maria Theresa wrested Roma children from their families and gave them to Hungarian peasant households. Violence was an ever-present threat. In 1782, an entire Hungarian Roma community was accused of cannibalism, and the imperial authorities tortured and executed forty-two of their number – only to discover that the original 'victims' were in fact very much alive.[15] One hundred and fifty years later, the Nazis killed several hundred thousand Roma – approximately 25 percent of those living in Europe at the time – in an oft-forgotten chapter of the Holocaust that many Roma call *Porajmos:* the Devouring.[16]

After the horrors of World War II, a measure of multiculturalism prevailed in the West during the Cold War years. 'The Roma have not just contributed to French culture out of proportion to their numbers – the great Manouche guitarist Django Reinhardt, for instance, created one of the few styles of jazz entirely outside America,' writes journalist Adam Gopnik, 'but have even become a sort of exotic ornament of the French state, with a special administrative category all to themselves.'[17] That exoticism extended to cultural stereotypes of Roma as 'free spirits' who sustain a bohemian lifestyle of music, dance, and partying. You can find that exoticism even in the well-regarded and well-written *Bury Me Standing*, the book by Isabel Fonseca that focuses on a 'secret society' of musicians, swindlers, and outcasts. It's a tradition that goes back hundreds of years.[18]

Many Roma find this exoticizing to be insulting. 'If you talk with some Bulgarians, they will say it is wonderful to see a Roma marriage,' Violeta told me. 'Sometimes I don't like this way of thinking about Roma, that Roma is only the fun and the exotic things, because it puts a kind of stamp on Roma. Yes, there are a lot of Roma musicians. It is different and exotic. If I try to be a musician or a belly dancer, they would say that's fine. But if I want to be a lawyer or something else, they don't like it.' In its worst form, this exoticizing can be found in the popular British and US reality TV show *My Big Fat Gypsy Wedding*, with its stereotypes and sensationalism.[19]

The Cold War was in some ways a pause in the hostilities conducted against the Roma in the east as well. In communist eastern Europe, Roma certainly did not live in a workers' paradise. They had to submit to the same social engineering as the rest of communist society, particularly when it came to their caravan lifestyle and their traditional professions. But they did achieve some progress. They had jobs (albeit often unskilled labor), their children went to primary school (albeit often of lesser quality), and there was some social mixing in the new apartment complexes built by the state. It was a harsh social contract: advancement at the price of assimilation as a social class rather than a recognized ethnicity.

With the end of communism, even that modest progress vanished. Unemployment surged to above 90 percent in certain areas. Segregation again became the norm, and many Roma left their countries in search of better lives in western Europe, often to be rounded up and sent back home. The story of the Roma during this period of the early 1990s was oft-overlooked. After all, the entire region was going through economic hardship. But when the economies began to recover from the harrowing shock therapies, the Roma experienced little if any rebound. According to the World Bank, the number of people living in extreme poverty worldwide was cut in half between 1990 and 2010.[20] In eastern Europe, the drop in poverty was roughly comparable to the global average.[21] There is, however, a statistical anomaly in the data for eastern Europe. For the 7–8 million Roma living in the region, the overall economic situation worsened over this period of time. According to a 2016 survey, 93 percent of Roma in Croatia, 87 percent of Roma in Slovakia, and 86 percent of Roma in Bulgaria live below the poverty line.[22]

It wasn't for a lack of resources for poverty reduction. After all, European governments and private institutions marshaled over 25 billion euros during the Decade of Roma Inclusion that began in 2005.[23] The money, however, failed to trickle down to the people who needed it the most. 'The Roma Inclusion Index shows some progress in literacy levels, completion of primary education, and access to health insurance,' Zjelko Jovanović reflected as the Decade of Roma Inclusion came to an end in 2015. 'But all in all, the daily life of Roma remains a struggle no other ethnic group in Europe faces. On average, in the decade countries, only one in ten Roma completes secondary school, almost half of Roma are unemployed, and more than one in three Roma still live in absolute poverty.'[24]

Increased poverty was accompanied by a spike in anti-Roma sentiment, bringing to the surface what had been latent for many years. At a time when walls throughout the region were falling – the Berlin Wall, intra-European borders – a number of communities throughout eastern Europe erected walls to separate Roma and non-Roma parts of town. More serious were the attacks against Roma in the early 1990s. Arson, targeted killings, expulsions: the Roma experienced a frightening wave of hate crimes. Nor did this racism subside when the economies in the region began to improve. In 2008 and 2009, when a group of right-wing extremists went on a killing spree in Hungary, their victims included a five-year-old child. Although three of the culprits received life sentences, the investigation was an embarrassment – the police tried to dissuade the family of two of the victims from reporting the attack and then urinated on crime scene evidence – and it's still unclear whether the state was involved in the killings.[25]

Anti-Roma sentiment is moving from the fringes into the mainstream.[26] Jobbik, for instance, has successfully injected racism into the Hungarian national discourse. 'Mainstream political parties are now trying to have a discourse as popular as Jobbik's,' observes Magda Matache, an instructor at Harvard's FXB Center. 'They are competing to see who is more extreme rather than who is more democratic.'

The apartheid system

Košice is not simply one city. Like any central European metropolis worthy of the name, many urban incarnations coexist cheek by jowl in this charming center of eastern Slovakia. In the Old Town, a medieval church overlooks a beautifully preserved Renaissance palace that abuts an art deco hotel from the 1920s. The city has been known by more than a dozen names over the last 800 years – Kaschau, Kassa, Cassow – as war and politics have reordered the region's geography. The architecture of Košice's many cities now forms one harmonious, unified whole. But Košice contains multiple cities in another, more ominous sense.

Across from Jakab's Palace, a faux-Gothic castle built in 1899, both locals and tourists sit on the patio of a café and drink espresso. There are many such gathering places in Košice. In this democratic, polyglot café society, spirited discussions take place in Slovak, Czech, Hungarian, English, and many other languages.

One major ethnic group, however, is excluded. Outside the palace itself, several Roma are having their own meeting as they lean against the wall of the building or squat on their haunches. Roma constitute about 6.5 percent of the Slovak population: slightly more than 350,000 people.[27] Košice has the largest Roma population in Slovakia, nearly 23,000, which is also nearly 20 percent of the district's population. Although the street that separates the café from the grounds of the palace is very narrow, there is no commerce between the coffee-drinkers and the group of Roma.

Throughout much of eastern Europe, there are two cities: for the Roma and for the non-Roma. These cities rarely intersect. During the communist era, not only did the vast majority of Roma in Slovakia work, as required in a system that espoused full employment, they also interacted with non-Roma at the factories, the farming collectives, the workplace cafeterias, and the bars after work. Today the vast majority of Roma are unemployed. The unemployment for Slovakia as a whole is about 13 percent. In some parts of eastern Slovakia, around Košice, the unemployment rate for Roma rises to about 80 percent.[28]

In his novel *The City and the City*, China Mieville describes two cities, Beszél and Ul Qoma, which occupy the same space in some imaginary corner of eastern Europe. The cities occupy a complex checkerboard in which the inhabitants of Beszél can only walk on the black squares, the residents of Ul Qoma on the white ones. Although they share the same topography, they are legally prohibited from interacting even to the point of 'unseeing' one another if they pass within hailing distance. It would be as if East and West Berlin had existed on top of one another, rather than side by side, with a complex set of rules governing points of contact across the gerrymandered Cold War boundary between them.[29]

This bit of fantasy fiction might sound highly implausible. But in fact this is the reality for Roma and non-Roma throughout eastern Europe. Increasingly, the two communities are acculturated into 'unseeing' each other. Yes, of course there are exceptions. A Roma elite participates in the larger society. And a few non-Roma – anthropologists, social workers, teachers – navigate the world of the Roma. But despite the Decade of Roma Inclusion, eastern Europe has become an apartheid region where Roma and non-Roma inhabit separate and decidedly unequal worlds.

The issue is complicated by the dispersed nature of Roma communities. 'It goes back to the beginning of the twentieth century when different regimes in this part of the world tried somehow to separate the Roma from the mainstream population,' Tomáš Hrustič, an anthropologist who works in Roma communities in Slovakia, told me. 'In the 1940s, for example, the fascist regime here adopted certain laws forcing Roma to move from the centers of the towns. Many villages and settlements in Slovakia today are where they were actually forced to move, where they had to build their houses outside of the cities. So, it's not as though Roma decided to live outside the municipality.'

One of these settlements is Kecerovce, a small village 24 kilometers outside of Košice. Here, more than 90 percent of the residents are Roma. There's not much for the several thousand inhabitants of the town to do, other than walk the streets, visit one of the two humble pubs, or shop at one of three small grocery stores. There's a post office and a municipal building. An agricultural cooperative employs fifteen people, none of them Roma. The Slovak government has had a plan on the books for a couple of decades to build a nuclear power plant near Kecerovce. Otherwise, the prospects for economic development in the area are bleak.

Yet, more Roma are crowding into Kecerovce. In Slovakia, as in other places in the region, gentrification and urban resettlement programs are forcing Roma out of the major cities. They move – or are moved – to places where they have even less chance of getting a job or enrolling their children in integrated schools. The newly uprooted must then compete with the more settled community. In Kecerovce, the newcomers have moved into makeshift accommodation and overcrowded houses. Julius Pecha, the Roma social worker in Kecerovce, lamented to me that the newcomers 'brought their negative habits, such as glue-sniffing, which they taught to the locals. Many of the people here live simple lives. They didn't think about drugs before these people came and introduced this dangerous world. Then we have to make unpopular decisions as social workers to make people safe. For example, we have to call the police to move the people from here back to Košice. As a Roma, I don't feel good about that.'

With unemployment so high, Roma in this countryside village have virtually no opportunities to interact with non-Roma, and that includes the educational system. 'There are three Roma settlements in the village, each at a different social level,' Julius told me. 'Two high schools based in

Košice have remote locations here – one for forest work and the second teaches bricklaying for boys and sewing for girls. All of the students at those two schools are Roma, with ninety-two Roma studying there in total. Seven hundred and twenty pupils are in the elementary school, but only three of them are non-Roma. The elementary school runs on two shifts because there is not enough space there for that many pupils.'

Thanks to a project funded by outside donors, some Roma youth from Kecerovce have met with non-Roma in both Slovakia and Hungary to participate in trainings, conduct formal debates, and just hang out. Inspired by this project and with the help of the municipality, several young Roma created a youth center in Kecerovce with a book-filled library, a computer, and many after-school activities. The center helps Roma from the village connect with the outside world, and it's the envy of young Roma for miles around. 'The main reason behind the club was that young people had no place to meet in this area except for the pubs,' Stano, one of the youth organizers, told me as we sat in the brightly decorated center. 'There are two pubs here in Kecerovce. We didn't like meeting there because of drunk people and smoking … The club serves as an open space for youth to come here to pass the time. But we also run our own activities – some lectures, educational theater plays, and meetings.'

Schools elsewhere in the region are as segregated as in Kecerovce. One of the tactics of school officials is to label

Roma as 'special needs' students who require separate, remedial classes. One 2009 study in Slovakia found that 85 percent of the students enrolled in these special classes were Roma.[30] The figure for the Czech Republic was 75 percent.[31] Some Roma parents of students in the Czech Republic misclassified as 'retarded' took their case all the way to the European Court of Human Rights, which, upon appeal, finally ruled in 2007 that the government had discriminated against the students.[32]

Approximately 15,000 Roma live in Croatia, the majority in Međimurje County. When human right activist Tin Gazivoda visited Međimurje county in the early 2000s, several parents of Roma children appealed to him for help. 'Their children were going to segregated classes,' he told me. 'In one school Roma children were eating lunch on one side of the room and non-Roma kids on the other side. We saw this. The facts were not hidden. The authorities considered this normal at the time.' Tin threatened to bring the school to court. 'I said to the county prefect at that time: "You may win this in the Croatian courts, but eventually in the European Court you will lose,"' he continued. 'We won the case in the European Court in March 2010: barely, it was a very close call.'

The integration of Croatian schools has proceeded fitfully since then. Preschools for Roma are now open year round, with longer hours. The state provides transportation and two meals. An after-school program to help with homework is also now available, though the funding is limited. But there's a lot of catching up to do. 'Of 1,589 Romani pupils attending the county's primary schools, which run from first to eighth grades, only 92 are enrolled in the eighth grade,' wrote Barbara Matejčić in 2013. 'Just 123 Roma are attending high school, according to the county's department for education, culture, and sports. About 20 Roma graduate from high school annually.'[33] Even this modest integration has generated intense pushback from the Croatian majority.

In Bulgaria, Anton Karagiosov runs a program that brings 200 Roma children from the Stolipinovo neighborhood to schools around Plovdiv. Roma children 'should be integrated into the mainstream schools,' he told me. 'With the solid support of the parents, of the grandparents, children will receive better education. Through better education and opportunities, Roma children can change their lives.' An earlier effort to desegregate schools in the Bulgarian city of Vidin through bussing, while successful in many ways, encountered resistance from the parents of non-Roma children and from politicians in Sofia.[34] Without government support, the bussing experiment failed to become standard practice in the country.[35]

Where funding is limited, only a few children can take advantage of better educational opportunities. In Romania, for instance, Maria Koreck of the Project for Ethnic Relations (PER) told me of what happened to the graduates of elementary schools in a Roma ghetto in the Transylvanian city of Târgu Mureș. The children graduate from fourth grade and are supposed to continue on to the integrated school. But either they're not accepted or they fail fifth grade and drop out. Maria and PER stepped in to help. They prepared an after-school program with young Roma volunteers. But, Maria explained, 'these children didn't have support from their families. Half of them are not even going to school much less the after-school program. But those who are coming to the after-school program can now read and write, but they are not up to the fifth grade. Probably five of them will be now put into mixed groups. The others will fail and then they will not come anymore. But those five will go on to the eighth grade. So with them we succeeded.' The talented tenth approach is not, in other words, a deliberate strategy in many places. It's simply making the best out of a bad situation.

The Gandhi school in Pécs, however, is trying a different tactic. It was established in 1994 to provide college prep for educationally disadvantaged and capable Roma students. Funded by a Western foundation and managed through the cooperation of the different Roma communities in Pécs, the school is designed to train a new generation of Roma leaders in Hungary. In 1995, when I visited the school, the president of the board of directors, János Bogdán, spoke of his own experience. Relegated as a child to a special education class presided over by an incompetent teacher, he was taught to read and write by the cleaning lady. Of the thirty-two children in his class, only five continued on to the next grade.[36] More than twenty years later, the Gandhi school remains in operation. It doesn't cater entirely to an elite, however. Rather, it maintains a vocational program, and half the students who graduate don't continue with their education.[37] As such, it falls somewhere between a magnet school for the talented tenth and a program that benefits a larger pool of Roma.

Acknowledging the disappearance of borders within the EU has become second nature to the people in the region. But not all the borders have disappeared. The one that exists between the Roma and the non-Roma may prove far more difficult to erase than even the Berlin Wall.

The NGO strategy

In August 2013, the great Romanian sociologist Nicolae Gheorghe passed away at the age of sixty-six. I first met him in 1990 when he was just embarking on his project of elevating Roma issues to the highest level of European politics. Because he spoke English and had an academic background, he was often the lone Roma representative in European human rights meetings or on TV panel discussions. He worked on Roma issues at the Council of Europe, the EU, the UN, and for many years the Organization for Security and Cooperation in Europe (OSCE). He is the sole representative of the Roma intelligentsia that Fonseca discusses at any length in *Bury Me Standing*.

I saw him again, and for the last time, in Budapest several months before his death. He was very sick, in the late stages of colon cancer, and he moved with great difficulty. Yet he had pushed himself to travel from Italy, where he was staying with his sister, to Hungary to participate in a book launch. The book, *From Victimhood to Citizenship*, is a dialogue among several people knowledgeable about the Roma community, and it provided Nicolae with an opportunity to reflect on his own work and the contrasting views of others.[38] He used his trip to Budapest to speak with a wide variety of people, including Roma students at the Central European University. I managed to interview him in the lobby of his hotel on the morning before he was to return to Italy. His day was scheduled with back-to-back meetings, and even his trip to the airport was an opportunity for conversation. He seemed to know that he did not have much time left, and he was determined to squeeze as many interactions as possible into his day – with old friends, new admirers, and even just passing acquaintances like me.

Having absorbed the credo of cosmopolitanism from his early days in communist circles in Romania, Nicolae was leery of anything that smacked of nationalism. 'His widest ambition for the Roma, who had no land of their own, was that they should be a "transnational" people, a grand pan-European federation of men and women, who, while proper citizens of their own countries, also represented a society broader, freer and more enterprising than that of nation states,' reported *The Economist* in its obituary.[39]

In the 1990s, Nicolae saw a chance to realize this vision at the pan-European level. 'At that time, I shifted my work from the community level to drafting documents and being oriented toward the EU: how to promote change at the commission level, which unlike the Council of Europe or the OSCE didn't at that time have a discourse on Roma issues,' he told me in 2013. 'Now I criticize myself because I somehow deserted the community work to focus at the international level. I thought that operating at a higher level, at the European level, we could accomplish more in the longer term.'

He acknowledged the virtues of this approach – European institutions are engaged on Roma issues in ways unimaginable twenty years ago, and cosmopolitan discourse at this level met with relatively little opposition, at least rhetorically. The real challenge was to work at the local level, where living conditions for Roma have not substantially improved over the last two decades and where the vestiges of earlier cosmopolitanism – from the Ottoman era or even the communist period – have largely disappeared.

'Today I am more skeptical about encouraging talented Roma to seek international posts instead of working at national and particularly at local level,' he concluded, echoing W. E. B. DuBois' repudiation of his own talented tenth thesis. 'This is because I believe the next stage, in the development of the Roma movement and for those involved, is to reconnect with the people we represent.'[40]

That reconnection has not yet happened. Roma activist and Open Society Foundation staffer Zeljko Jovanović, who contributed to the same book launch and seminar in

Budapest, complained to me of how Roma activists have achieved what many have asked for – access to the system – only to be coopted by the same system. 'In too many cases, they can no longer represent the interests of Roma toward authorities but the other way around,' he explains. 'As a result, we have a huge brain drain. Most of the best and brightest Roma activists from ten years ago and those younger ones are today semi-civil-servants or project bureaucrats.'

Critiques of the NGO-ization of the Roma community abound. 'People have Roma trainings, conferences and seminars, just as I was doing because I hadn't known any better,' former AFSC staffperson Michael Simmons told me. 'And then Roma – I don't want to say that they're opportunist, because they don't have any employment options – their goal is to get to some NGO in Budapest, or in Brussels, or now in Poland, the OSCE, Geneva, New York, or to get a scholarship to Cambridge or whatever. But there's no indigenous organizing effort. There is no sense of a democratic community organization. There is no change on the ground.' Larry Olomoofe, a trainer with the OSCE, estimated that each Roma could have received 25–30,000 euros from all the money that went into the Roma community in recent years. 'Even if they squandered it,' he told me, 'at least it would have been them. Whereas the representatives of the Roma have access to these funds, and it has had no impact on their community.'

Some Roma activists blame the national governments. 'The European Commission gives money to the national government on Roma issues and then the national government spends this money in non-transparent ways,' Orhan Tahir, a lawyer and founder of the Roma advocacy group Civil Society in Action, told me. Yet the European bodies continue to fund the national governments, which in turn seem to prefer a stable set of handpicked Roma, however corrupt they might be. 'The better-educated, better-prepared, smarter Roma are considered an even bigger threat to the status quo than the illiterate poor,' Orhan complained. 'They say that it is better to have illiterate poor people, who can be more easily manipulated, than to have a class of well-educated Roma, who could compete for the same resources.'

The Roma issue devolved into 'what I call "project-ism,"' former director of the European Roma Rights Center Dimitrina Petrova told me. 'There are donors, and there are the projects they fund. There is nothing spontaneous, nothing that comes from people's needs, nothing that reminds me even remotely why people wanted to do something when I was young. It is donor-driven, with good intentions, but the whole thing doesn't work.'

NGO activist Roumen Yanovski provided me with an example of such project-ism. Money poured into a project to change the Bulgarian media's terminology from 'Gypsies' to 'Roma.' At a certain level, the project was a success. The term 'Gypsy' largely disappeared from Bulgarian media. However, the media often continued to portray Roma in the same old derogatory way. 'Now it's even worse,' Roumen said. 'There are some people who insist that "Roma" is incorrect, and we should go back to "Gypsy"! And many Roma leaders and rank and file agree. They say, "We are Gypsies." So this is a typical example of a lot of money to achieve a result that did not last. It didn't change the general perception of Roma.'

And yet not all the projects Roumen worked on have been disappointing. One three-year training project partnered aspiring Roma reporters with mainstream journalists. True, when they finished the program, the Roma graduates couldn't get jobs in the media world. 'Instead, they got jobs as Roma health mediators, local community leaders, municipal experts,' Roumen explained. 'All of them have good jobs in the Roma community based on their intensive training in human rights, economics, English, and the practice and theory of journalism. From my point of view this was a good project because we actually helped people jump over this barrier without losing their identity as Roma.'

NGO activist Maria Metodieva set up a similar training program to place young Roma as interns in companies. One of the most promising candidates not only got a job in the same company where she interned but received additional training to join management. 'I believe that her life changed,' Maria told me. 'Actually she's one of the best practices, if we can use that phrase, because she managed to change the stereotypes and the attitudes of her colleagues.' But, Maria continued, this kind of affirmative action program only worked with multinational companies – not Bulgarian companies.

There is certainly a risk of brain drain in the Roma community, of the talented tenth leaving eastern Europe for well-paying jobs, for instance, in the European Union. But the opposite scenario can be even more devastating: the talented tenth not getting any jobs at all because institutional racism shuts them out of the professions. 'If well-educated Roma cannot find jobs, cannot progress, cannot live normally, then how can they be an example for illiterate people?' Orhan Tahir told me. 'They say, "You went to university for five years, and you're staying at home, unemployed? Your parents spend so much money for your education, and you have no job? Look at the salesman at the market, he is doing better!"' Viktória Mohácsi, for instance, represented the liberal SzDSz party in the Hungarian parliament and even served as the EU ombudsman for Roma in Strasbourg. 'When Fidesz came to power, she returned to Hungary,' expat musicologist Bob Cohen told me. 'She couldn't get a job. Nobody would hire her. She couldn't get a job at Central European University [CEU]. She applied for one of the CEU jobs in an area involving Roma education. She was so highly overqualified.' In response to threats she received, she eventually fled Hungary, asking for refugee status in Canada, where she continues to work on Roma issues.

Rita Izsák is precisely the kind of activist that Nicolae Gheorghe had in mind when he imagined a new generation of Roma activists at the highest level of international institutions. Still in law school, she worked as a human rights advocate at the European Roma Rights Center in

Budapest. At one point, Rita decided to move on to other human rights issues, to 'demonstrate that it is possible to protest the intellectual ghetto, the belief and pressure that if you are Roma, you are only able to and are supposed to work on Roma issues,' as she put it. She began working at the UN Office of the High Commissioner for Human Rights in Geneva and eventually became the UN Special Rapporteur for Minority Rights.

But she still wrestles with doubt. 'Sometimes I believe that I would make more change if I established a nice day-care center in northeastern Hungary or somewhere in Africa,' she concluded. 'I've reached a position where I'm in one of the top jobs in the field of human rights (even if it's unpaid). I talk to BBC, Al Jazeera. I have a privilege that I can write down all my thoughts in a report and it will get a UN logo and be distributed to 193 member states without any censorship. But we need to be committed, patient, and persistent to see our work resulting in the actual improvement of people's lives. We need to believe that the seeds we now plant will grow into something in thirty, fifty, a hundred years.'

The business strategy

As the history of segregation in the United State demonstrates, the business community can be thoroughly racist even if refusing to serve minorities hurts the bottom line. Gradually, however, the business community begins to see potential profit in minority consumers. Identity issues, which begin as politics, so often end as product. Hollywood, for instance, realized the potential of African-American audiences in the early 1970s, a trend that later took off with Spike Lee and his successors, and the movie industry is now waking up to the reality of Latino filmgoers.[41] In the early 1990s, writer David Rieff pointed out in a famous *Harper's* essay entitled 'Multiculturalism's silent partner' that corporations were fast off the mark to embrace multiculturalism as a marketing strategy. Music companies, fast food restaurants, clothing designers, political parties: virtually every national brand has targeted the 'minority demographic' as a way to acquire an edge in the marketplace.[42]

When it comes to Roma, eastern Europe is still in its segregation era. The business community hasn't really begun to see Roma as consumers because it's too busy worrying about how an association with Roma adversely affects its image. István Forgács would like to change that. Businesses, he told me, 'don't think of Roma as consumers. I looked at the demographics. If you're a bank and you don't offer services to Roma as clients, then in five years, you'll have to close the bank branch … But, you might say, "Roma don't have money." Do you know that a huge percentage of Roma get payments through the post office? In cash. Why doesn't a bank try to get more Roma clients? This is the future.'

István works with the National Democratic Institute on Roma issues. Before that he served in the Hungarian government and before that he worked with the Open

Society Institute. He has also addressed Roma issues at the European level in Strasbourg. Now he believes in working at a local level, and he has largely abandoned the more confrontational politics he'd once adopted. 'The Roma issue should be an economic issue,' he told me on a car trip from Miskolc to Budapest in May 2013. 'The business community should be thinking about the Roma issue.'

István is a little like Booker T. Washington in his emphasis on work and self-reliance – as well as his discomfort with other leaders of the Roma community. And, in truth, there has always been an accommodationist strain in the Roma community. Many of the Kalderash Romani subgroup, for instance, prospered as blacksmiths and metal workers under communism and then became small-scale businessmen during the transition period. 'This gave them advantages over other Roma groups and, to a certain extent, even over some of the majority population,' Nicolae Gheorghe wrote.[43] István comes from a similarly entrepreneurial background. He grew up in a relatively well-off part of Hungary near Lake Balaton and close to the Austrian border, where he never faced poverty or tensions between Roma and non-Roma. 'Our Roma community was three thousand people,' he told me. 'They had a chance after the changes to start their own businesses and establish relationships with non-Roma. One of my main credos is that economic interest is always the most important. If the economic resources are in the hands of the non-Roma, then you have to establish a relationship with them in order to gain access to some of those resources.'

At the tail-end of communism, István's family started a used-car business. 'At that time, in Hungary, there were no used-car distributors,' he said. 'You had to go to Austria or Germany to buy used cars. During socialism, you only had socialist cars. Then, with the changes, you could buy what you wanted to buy. So, my family had a business where they went to Austria or Germany, bought used cars, imported them into Hungary, and sold them for a higher price. You had to be smart to do this kind of work, but you also had to work really hard.'

István doesn't have much faith in the programs he once worked so diligently to put into place to lift up Roma. 'The majority just doesn't want to give any money to Roma,' he pointed out. 'They don't want to give anything to Roma, because they think the Roma don't deserve it. "I work in a factory," the average Hungarian will say. "I pay my mortgage. I work two, three jobs. Why? Only to provide social benefits to Roma?"'

In recognition of this common attitude, a number of organizations established income-generating programs for Roma in the 1990s – so that they would no longer be at the mercy of the social welfare system. In Hungary, Autonómia used European funds to create workshops for carpenters and roofers. András Bíró, who started Autonómia, told me of the revolving loan fund in Hungary that he adapted from the Grameen microcredit program in Bangladesh. 'The repayment ratio on the loans we gave was extraordinarily high, higher than any banks these days,' he reported.

His partner in Romania, Nicolae Gheorghe, was less satisfied with the results. 'In terms of income-generating activities in Romania, most of the money was wasted,' he confessed. 'Honestly, in some cases it was pure corruption. In other cases, they didn't know how to use the money. They thought that if they put enough money into machines, that was enough. I realized again that it was because I'd been too much influenced by the communist model of economic development and its focus on production. I was not very clear about markets, how to market the products.'

Nicolae had hoped to create a Roma version of the Protestant ethic that sociologist Max Weber identified as a key element in the rise of capitalism. He thought he found this ethos in the Roma notion of *pakiv*, which means trust or respect: 'It's part of the whole group of concepts called *Romanipen*, which is a philosophical outlook toward life stressing solidarity, the sharing of resources, and being self-reliant economically. I thought that if we could connect in the Roma communities I worked with to some of these realities – imagined realities, as it turned out – we could work like a bank.'

It was a noble project. In contrast to the high repayment rate in Hungary, however, Nicolae encountered a different reality with his loans. 'There was no enforcing mechanism,' he said. 'It was just moral. You just gave your word that you would give the money back, and we respected your word, because this is the Roma wisdom. I never received one penny back.'

The political strategy

Unlike the ethnic Turkish movement in Bulgaria or the Hungarians in Romania, the Roma have not created a single influential party in any of the countries where they form a significant minority. Partly that's a function of the diversity of the community, divided as it is by region and language and history. 'People ask the question, "Why, if there are so many Roma here, don't they have a single party and vote for their representatives?"' Tomáš Hrustič told me. 'But that's nonsense, because Roma are a very heterogeneous group with many interests, and they don't have strong representation. They're not like the Hungarian minority in Slovakia, which is a politically more or less homogeneous group, which looks like a community from the outside, and also shares a strong interest with Hungary as a neighbor.'

Roumen Yanovski spent more than a decade monitoring the efforts of the Roma community in Bulgaria to create an effective political party. 'They created fifty to sixty parties, some of which still exist,' he told me. 'But not a single one of these parties managed to develop into a refined political tool for speaking on behalf of a minority. Without such a group speaking on behalf of the minority, a lot of things can't happen. You can't make priorities. You can't do proper decision-making. You lose expertise. Of course, you try to create commissions, state structures, bodies that deal with the Roma community. You try to empower civil society structures in an attempt to do something. But without this general political tool, which is a powerful lever for solving problems, this simply couldn't happen.'

In May 2013, I travelled to the outskirts of Bucharest to meet with Alice Pop Ratyis, who took a break from a training session to talk with me. The National Democratic Institute has been providing training and resources for local Roma politicians in Romania for more than a decade. At a national level in eastern Europe, Roma politicians are few and far between. In Romania there are only three Roma parliamentarians. But Alice estimates that around three hundred Roma have been elected at a local level. Whatever the size of the Roma community in a particular town, Roma 'did not necessarily see the importance of having local representatives in the local council,' Alice explained. 'There was always someone from the Roma party, because they were always competing, but they didn't see the importance of having one more or two more or ten more in the local council. Now I see that everybody's oriented toward trying to maintain the local political representation of the Roma.'

The number of Roma on local councils is not the only indicator of success. And how long the local councilors have served may also not correlate with efficacy. Alice told me about one local Roma councilor who 'was so great in discussing and negotiating that she's done more in her eight months of being a local councilor than others have accomplished in twenty years.'

The main problem with local politics in Romania is not that it's local, but that it's politics. 'Many people are sick and tired of politics,' Alice told me. 'And it doesn't matter if you are running on a Roma Party ticket, a Roma organization ticket, or a mainstream ticket. They just say that if you are a politician, you become one of "them" and they just don't trust you anymore.'

A key question facing Roma politicians is whether to run as candidates with the major political parties or with a Roma-identified initiative. Roma parties have not made much headway, and major parties have been reluctant to embrace Roma issues. Political scientist Martin Kovats writes about a third political choice: identifying a politics of shared interests and articulating how 'identity fits in with the non-ethnic agenda.'[44] This correlates in part with the actual experience of Roma politicians, especially on the local level, where it's often about paving roads or generating jobs or improving schools, issues that can appeal to Roma and non-Roma alike. 'In many municipalities Roma are elected to office and are able to negotiate with their non-Roma colleagues and find good solutions for their people,' anthropologist Tomáš Hrustič told me. 'There are more than twenty-nine Roma mayors in Slovakia, and many of these mayors have been re-elected. Many people, not only Roma voters, are very satisfied with their work.'

In Hungary, the Minorities Act passed in the aftermath of the post-1989 changes created a National Gypsy Minority Self-Government, in essence a separate Roma political structure. 'The minority self-government system allowed minorities to revive patterns of cultural life, such as language and tradition,' writes political scientist Peter Vermeersch, but some Roma critics believe the system simply made it easier for the Hungarian government to manipulate the community by supporting this or that Roma political party. Nor did the self-government structures seem to have much influence on the overall political and economic direction of the country.

Roma have organized several parties in Bulgaria. One of them, the Euroroma movement, is not strictly a party or restricted to Roma. According to the movement's website, 30 percent of the executive body of Euroroma are non-Roma.[45] At different times, it has aligned with the ethnic Turkish party and in a left-wing bloc with the Socialist Party. It has had representatives in the Bulgarian parliament and successfully fielded a number of candidates for local office as well. In cities like the Black Sea town of Kavarna, it has focused on bread-and-butter issues like paving roads and installing sewage systems. In 2005, Euroroma hit the headlines in Bulgaria for running the hugely successful gay Roma pop star Azis and the country's first *Playboy* model, Yuliana Gancheva, as candidates. Despite the publicity, they both lost. In 2009, party candidate Milena Hristova won election as the first Roma woman MP in the country. Still, Euroroma's reputation is mixed. In 2016, the Bulgarian authorities arrested the deputy chairman of the party for running a racketeering and human smuggling operation in a largely Roma neighborhood in Sofia.[46]

Tsvetelin Kanchev, the founder of Euroroma, has represented the movement in the Bulgarian parliament. He is both a successful businessman and a controversial public figure. He has also faced various criminal charges: in 2003 for blackmail and assault, which landed him in jail, and another charge of blackmail in 2010 for which he returned to prison for a couple of months before receiving a pardon. Tsvetelin dismisses these charges as politically motivated. 'I've always avoided commenting on other Roma parties,' he told me over lunch in Sofia. 'But quite a few of them entered politics and established political parties only to get rich. I entered politics rich already. Before I became a politician, I owned a huge factory, two smaller factories, a chain of gas stations, several solid construction companies, and some other businesses. I became a politician because I didn't want to hear Roma children referred to as "dirty Gypsies." This is my dream. Because if they call other Roma children by these names, these will be the names they will use to refer to my children. Three of my children study in Cambridge, but they are also called "dirty Gypsies" in Bulgaria.' To complicate matters further, I've come across several reputable sources claiming that Tsvetelin is actually an ethnic Bulgarian, and had only been 'adopted' into the community of Roma Kardarasha.[47]

The challenges of the 'talented tenth' strategy are by no means limited to the Roma. Other minorities face this same question of individual success and community empowerment. In Bulgaria, however, the ethnic Turkish community has mobilized politically behind one party, the Movement for Rights and Freedom, and pushed for an agenda of collective rights, such as the right to learn Turkish in schools. This political mobilization compensates for the disadvantages from which ethnic Turks suffer, such as their concentration in poorer, more rural areas of the country. Ethnic Turks can also count on the support of another country: Turkey. The same can be said for ethnic Hungarians in Romania, ethnic Ukrainians in Poland, or ethnic Croats in Bosnia.

The Roma have no such national booster. The community has had to rely on itself for hundreds of years. 'Less than one percent of the Roma community consists of highly educated people,' Zjelko Jovanović told me. 'How do we deploy these limited human resources? Politics is usually not something affordable for people who are starving, who are illiterate, who are under pressure from discrimination every day. But if our leaders can establish pressure from the street, that would create a political potential to be deployed once the political structure is ready to enter elections. Then, once you are in government, you can start to engage in policy and make a bigger impact.'

The resistance strategy

Béla Rácz grew up in a small village in Hungary with a mixed Roma and non-Roma population. In 2009, far-right-wing groups targeted his village. It was part of a wave of violence sweeping through the country. An organization called the Hungarian Guard was intervening to 'protect' the non-Roma population in the countryside.

Béla was part of a group of Roma who used their cars to block access to the village so that the Guard couldn't enter. 'You know who was calling them to our village?' Béla asked me as we sat in his office at the Open Society Foundation in Budapest. 'The local Catholic priest and one or two young Guards. But what's good in our village, if there is an emergency, the Roma will protect each other.'

The meeting between the Guard and the local Roma was anything but cordial. 'We said many bad things like, "If you come here, you will die!"' Béla continued. 'And of course they said the same things to us. So, it was a question of who was stronger. When the police came to us, we said we wouldn't move. The police went to the Guard and said, "It's not good if you go there. I'm sorry but we can't protect you." So they left and didn't come back.'

Much of the resistance organized by Roma resembles the nonviolent organizing African-Americans did during the civil rights movement. Several Roma groups have staged sit-ins. Also effective have been organized marches, like the one in 1993 in the Hungarian city of Eger, where a thousand Roma joined together with 2,000 non-Roma to protest against a series of skinhead attacks.

But there has been another tradition of resistance within the African-American community that hasn't involved turning the other cheek. Armed resistance by African-Americans didn't begin 'in the 1960s with angry "militant" and "radical" young Afro-Americans, but in the earliest years of the United States as one of the African people's responses to oppression,' writes historian Charles Cobb.[48] Roma too have considered this other tradition of resistance.

When the Hungarian Guard was just being formed, 'I was organizing a boxing league for kids,' Roma activist Aladár Horváth told me. 'The head of this league, a Roma boxer, said, "Tell those paramilitary people that twenty-eight of us will go there, and we'll have a fight, with bare hands. If we lose, they can form their Guard. But if we win, they should stop the organization." I thought about it, but we didn't do it. Now I think we should have come face to face with them. I don't think there's a way to practice non-violence against fascism.'

Nicolae Gheorghe understood the impulse. 'At the time when people were setting Roma houses on fire, there were some Roma who said that we should set Romanian houses on fire as well,' he told me. 'People were saying, "If they speak with fire, we respond with fire. Why do we have to be peaceful in the face of violence?"' The acute violence has subsided, but none of the root causes of Roma despair has been addressed. Nicolae added, sadly, 'I wonder if the frustrated, uneducated young guys at the grassroots will join together with radical intellectuals to create a cocktail that will explode.'

The cultural strategy

It is never easy, as a minority, to achieve success in the mainstream society and yet preserve one's culture at the same time. Roma activist Anton Karagiosov remembers sleeping on carpets made of cane and small twigs when he was growing up in Bulgaria. His neighborhood drew water from only two taps. Today, his grandchildren go to kindergarten, sleep in separate bedrooms, and don't speak much Roma at all.

'Little by little we sometimes forget typical Roma things,' Anton told me. 'But there are things that we cannot forget, such as our customs. We closely follow our Roma holidays, such as the New Year. There is also an important holiday for Roma in April. Then there is the Roma family culture, the respect of the children. There is the traditional dress, the traditional music.'

A lively debate takes place within Roma communities about customs that come into conflict with the mainstream, such as underage marriages. 'The issue of early marriage is also not politically correct to talk about,' István Forgács told me. 'They say, "Oh, but it's a cultural heritage to have a baby at fourteen!" It's simply not true. It's a culture of poverty. I have to tell you: having a baby at the age of fourteen is not a cultural tradition that I support.' Old-fashioned gender roles are also pervasive in the community. 'Women are the lowest in the family hierarchy,' Roma activist Ilona Zámbó told me. 'After they get married they are only allowed to do what their husband allows them. Women have to endure infidelity, physical and emotional abuse, humiliation. Violence against women is widespread. For me it was a great shock to learn of the oppression of Roma women.' A new generation of Roma are challenging these cultural practices from within the community.

The reality TV show *Big Brother* might seem an unlikely place to address cultural prejudices toward Roma. But in Croatia, the show's viewers chose a Roma as the winning participant. In Bulgaria, Maria Metodieva told me, 'We have a young Roma singer, an artist who's invited to take part in that program. She's been very active on mainstream issues, as active as any other participant. But at the same time there are these comments on the online forums and by the other participants on the show that she's Roma and therefore she's stupid. Or that she's not good enough to be on this *Big Brother* reality show. This is the common opinion of the average Bulgarian.' Similarly negative reactions attended a Serbian reality show in which a pair of celebrities went to live with a Roma family. On the other hand, the celebrities seemed to experience a genuine transformation of attitude as a result of their brief homestay. Even the program's narrator concluded that prejudice disappeared after two days: 'These people, the Roma, are our neighbors. They fight for their own spot under the sun, and, therefore, they deserve respect.'[49]

According to the 'talented tenth' model, success often comes at the price of collective identity. The best performers turn their back on their communities in order to gain acceptance from the wider world. They can't help raise up their communities because they effectively don't belong to them any more.

Many Roma, like Violeta, the successful journalist, don't have that choice. Their pigmentation marks them as Roma in a society that pays close attention to skin color. Violeta's brother, however, could follow a different path, which other prominent Roma have taken over the years. He doesn't have dark skin, and you wouldn't know he was Roma unless he told you. Like some light-skinned African-Americans over the years, he could 'pass.'

Once, when Violeta's picture appeared on the cover of a popular magazine, a classmate of her brother's brought the magazine to his attention and said, 'This woman is beautiful.' Her brother called her up to ask what he should do.

'I am proud of you,' her brother said. Then he added, 'But if I tell them that you are my sister, they will know about me.'

Some Roma have managed to obtain first-class seats on the journey to Europe. But most Roma, as Violeta told me, don't even know that the train exists, much less manage to get on board. Violeta doesn't view the journey as a one-way trip. Her goal is to make it without turning her back on the Roma community: 'Ultimately, Romani integration will only be a reality when we can confidently pursue our dreams and openly preserve our culture while living in both worlds.'[50]

8
The New Dissidents

Răzvan Ion is a successful entrepreneur and professor. He is also, as a gallery owner and the producer of the Bucharest Biennale, very much part of Romania's thriving contemporary art scene. He fits right in with the avant-garde set. A tattoo wraps around his bicep, his head is shaven, and above his neatly trimmed beard a mustache curls up at the ends in the style of Salvador Dali. Răzvan travels the international art circuit but maintains a comfortable academic appointment at home. He is very much at the center of things in Bucharest.

It's a far cry from the Răzvan Ion that I first met in 1993 when he was working with AIDS sufferers. Not that Răzvan wasn't unconventional in those days. But homosexuality was still a crime in Romania in the 1990s, and Răzvan was taking considerable risks by refusing to stay in the closet. Even though he was on the margins of Romanian society at the time, he managed to accomplish what an earlier generation of dissidents had also done: change the system against long odds.

In 1993, Răzvan was working with an organization distributing condoms and information about HIV/AIDS.

As if that weren't difficult enough in a homophobic society with a comparatively primitive healthcare system, he eventually decided to mount a legal challenge to the country's anti-homosexuality statutes. 'I tried to get people out of prison, people who were imprisoned for being gay or for exhibiting "homosexual behavior,"' he told me in 2013 as we sat in his gallery space above a bank in Bucharest. 'Many of the trials were almost with no proof. If one of those trials had taken place in any other country, and that law had existed in any other country, they wouldn't have been put on trial.'

When Romania joined the Council of Europe in 1993, one of the conditions was repeal of the anti-homosexuality law. Yet the Romanian government continued to make arrests. Milorad Mutusco, a former detective no less, spent over three months in prison in Timișoara for violating the law. 'It was awful,' Mutusco said. 'Every prisoner treated me like garbage.'[1] As journalist Barbara Demick reported at the time, 'the Timișoara police aggressively publicized the arrest. The weekly police newspaper carried not only the names and photographs of the two lovers, but also their home address.'[2] Accusations of homosexuality were used against political opponents. And daily life for gays and lesbians was a series of potential dangers. 'It was the police who made your life hard by regular raids,' one anonymous source recalled of that period. 'Then the homophobic guys who would beat you in the cruising areas.'[3]

Răzvan was not only out of the closet in 1993, he was the editor of *Gay 45*, the community's only magazine. He was cooperating with a number of international human rights organizations, including Helsinki Watch. In his campaign against the anti-homosexuality statute, he was determined to work publicly to normalize gay life.

He started with Timișoara, the city in Transylvania where the uprising against Ceaușescu began and where Milorad Mutusco had experienced the terrible prison conditions. Choosing the case of two men who'd been arrested and imprisoned under the anti-homosexuality statue, Răzvan opted for a novel legal approach. Romania had passed a new constitution in 1991 that officially transformed the country into a democratic republic. He decided to argue that the anti-homosexuality law violated the new constitution. Although one lawyer after another refused to take the case, he eventually located a young advocate who was game. 'She said immediately, "Yeah, I will take it. And let's go to constitutional court,"' he recalled. 'In six months, the law was suspended, and they were released.' Over the next few months, everybody was released.

It was not an entirely happy ending. 'One of the two guys in Timișoara, after he was released, he killed himself, and I'm sure it was because of the time he spent in prison,' Răzvan remembered. And, despite the ruling, the police continued to arrest gays and lesbians. Mariana Cetiner, imprisoned for three years for attempting to seduce another woman, became one of Amnesty International's prisoners of conscience in 1997.[4] The Romanian government decriminalized public manifestations of homosexuality only in

2000 and repealed the last discriminatory law in 2002. To force these changes, the European Union applied considerable pressure during the accession process. So did the United States, which sent an openly gay ambassador to Bucharest in 2000. But it was also the brave organizing of activists inside Romania that changed the country's laws.

The changes have extended beyond the letter of the law to alter the very DNA of Romanian society. In 2005, the first GayFest march took place in Bucharest. By 2016 the festival has expanded to a week of events culminating in a march that attracted a thousand participants.[5] An annual gay film festival now takes place in Cluj. Inevitably, since Romania remains a conservative country, there's been pushback. Intolerance toward the LGBT community remains strong, particularly in rural areas.[6] Same-sex marriage is still not legal. In 2016, spurred on by the Orthodox Church and a petition signed by 3 million people, the constitutional court cleared the way for a referendum to change the constitution from defining a marriage as between two 'spouses' to that of 'a man and a woman.'[7] Still, for a new generation of Romanians, homosexuality is a normal part of culture. In 2013, a Romanian reality show featured the country's first televised same-sex ceremony. 'Not only did Daniel and Mihai win the luxury honeymoon grand prize, the episode became the most watched TV production on that Thursday's evening prime time slot,' according to a blog report.[8]

In the two decades since we first met, Răzvan too has observed a huge change in the LGBT situation in Romania.

'But I don't believe that applies to the whole country: it's mostly for Bucharest and the big cities,' he reports. 'Crimes against homosexuals are zero at this moment – I don't remember any cases, at least none that is reported. I'm sure there are some problems. But the gay community is becoming less and less political and more and more directed toward entertainment, which I don't like much.'

The first wave of dissent in eastern Europe spread unevenly throughout the region. Although the Solidarity movement commanded the loyalties of a quarter of the population in Poland, only a few individuals stood up against the tyrannical government of Enver Hoxha in Albania and only a couple of anti-state rebellions – the miners' strike in the Jiu Valley in 1977 and the riot in Brașov in 1987 – challenged the Ceaușescu reign. Along the spectrum in between, small knots of people waged uphill struggles against determined state apparatuses, from Charter 77 in Czechoslovakia and the Danube Circle in Hungary to Ecoglasnost in Bulgaria and the Pankow Peace Circle in East Germany. In 1989, those groups all achieved their major goal of upending an unjust status quo.

In many cases, however, these victories didn't propel the dissidents into decision-making positions in the new states. In the most extreme situation, in East Germany, the dissidents gathered in New Forum and other small groups barely managed to get a toehold in the new democratic parliament, and, with a few exceptions, they disappeared from politics altogether after reunification. Professional politicians, in East Germany as elsewhere, came to the fore, because the new governments required technocrats, not movement organizers. In every country except East Germany and Czechoslovakia, former communist parties eventually returned to power when discontent with economic reforms boiled over – or, in the cases of Bulgaria and Romania, former communist officials maintained power after 1989 in the somewhat altered forms of the Bulgarian Socialist Party and the National Salvation Front. In Slovakia, many of the participants in the Velvet Revolution of 1989 returned to the streets to protest against Vladimir Mečiar, who was taking their country in an autocratic direction. In Serbia, the first wave of dissidents didn't achieve their goal until they ousted Slobodan Milošević in 2000.

After 1989, eastern Europe didn't automatically adopt the human rights standards of western Europe. Although accession to various European institutions – the Council of Europe, the European Union – put enormous pressure on the governments in aspiring member countries to adopt more liberal legal frameworks, many countries continued to discriminate against ethnic minorities, women, the LGBT community, whistleblowers, and the like. Răzvan Ion is a member of eastern Europe's second generation of progressive dissidents, the ones who have taken up the mantle of the 1989 generation in continuing to fight injustice.

The new dissidents won some of their early battles, such as the overturning of Romania's anti-homosexuality statutes.

Some of the struggles, like the plight of the Erased, went all the way to the European Court of Human Rights before achieving resolution. Elsewhere the struggle continues – against restrictive abortion regulations in Poland, against anti-Muslim actions in Bulgaria, against the segregation of Roma throughout the region. Anti-austerity and anti-corruption protests brought down the government in Bulgaria in 2013, forced the Romanian government to back away from a controversial executive order decriminalizing some forms of corruption in 2017, and have periodically mobilized the populace elsewhere in the region on an issue-by-issue basis.

The new dissidents face opponents that are at least as powerful as the communist regimes had been. The Catholic Church in Poland not only has institutional power but far greater legitimacy than the Communist Party ever had. In Hungary, the new dissidents wage campaigns against a ruling party with a parliamentary supermajority that allows it to change the constitution if the courts reject any of its legislation. In Serbia, the new dissidents have had to deal with death threats and ostracism for challenging prevailing norms of nationalism. With a backlash against liberalism gathering force, the new dissidents are not just trying to advance the human rights agenda but also preserve some of the key gains of the last twenty-five years. In so doing, they often square off against former dissidents like Volen Siderov of Ataka or Antoni Macierewicz, who are very much part of the backlash against liberalism.

The new progressive dissidents also face the difficult reality that eastern Europe remains a few steps behind western Europe in its economic and political development. To make the leap across the development gap, these new dissidents will play a critical role. They can mobilize new energy to overcome old problems. Their 'hard-nosed utopianism,' to use a phrase from Peter Berger's *Pyramids of Sacrifice*, can provide the transformative vision the region so desperately needs.[9] Conversely, their mobilization of the marginalized may lead to a deeper anti-liberal backlash against the politics of inclusion.

In 1988, the direction eastern Europe would take was not at all clear. The fall of the Berlin Wall became inevitable only in retrospect. In the current tug of war between liberals and illiberals, the future trajectory of the region is similarly opaque. But uncertainty is also a prerequisite for hope.

Krytyka Polityczna

Its corner location was unbeatable. But Brave New World Café faced steep competition on Warsaw's most fashionable thoroughfare: a pricey French bakery, a trendy sushi restaurant, and the famous Café Blikle, which began serving coffee and pastries well before World War I. Moreover, as even its passionate defenders would admit, the food at Brave New World, though relatively cheap, was not exactly destination dining.

The thousands of customers who flocked to the café after its opening in 2009 did so for a different reason: first-rate conversation and events. The fabulously successful café and cultural center was an intellectual magnet. And the brains behind Poland's equivalent of Les Deux Magots were neither hipster entrepreneurs nor savvy expats. Instead, the proprietors were unabashedly devoted to critical theory and left-wing politics, all wrapped in a mordant sense of humor. The café's dystopian name, itself a critique of Poland's postcommunist 'Eden,' was also a play on its location on New World Street.

Such a combination of caffeine, critique, and sly comedy would certainly attract crowds in the East Village or the Left Bank. But this was Poland, where the official left had at least two historical strikes against it: an association with communism before 1989 and an embrace of austerity capitalism in the go-go years afterward.

The proprietors of the café, a cadre of activist-intellectuals that call themselves Krytyka Polityczna (Political Critique), represent a new generation of dissidents in Poland. Krytyka is uncompromised by any connection to Stalinism or the country's postcommunist party. From the debut of its eponymous journal in 2002 to its collaboration on Poland's controversial offering in the 2011 Venice Biennale, Krytyka has somehow made the left sexy in Poland, also inspiring activists elsewhere in the region to take up its call.

By the early 2010s, the ground was well prepared for an independent left in eastern Europe. Voters revolted against successive waves of austerity measures by electing social democratic leadership in several countries, including the Czech Republic, Slovakia, Croatia, and Slovenia. In Bulgaria, students, environmentalists, and other civil society activists protested for more than a year against political and economic corruption until the government stepped down in July 2014. Eastern Europeans were becoming tired of establishment politics.

But the message of the new dissidents on the left has been coopted by right-wing populists who have challenged the austerity economics of the liberals and attempted to pin those policies on the left more generally. Moreover, critics in Poland are not sure Krytyka is what everyone has been waiting for. They argue that the movement missed its opportunity to translate its visibility into real political influence. The Brave New World Café closed in 2012 – thanks to a much-lamented decision of the municipal authorities – and some of the smaller Krytyka clubs around Poland have evaporated as well. And the young man whose name is so intertwined with the short history of Krytyka is no longer at the center of the organization's life.

Even intellectuals skeptical of the Great Man theory of history acknowledge the outsized role played by Krytyka's founder, Sławomir Sierakowski, whom friends and colleagues call Sławek. In the course of a decade, Sławek leapfrogged to prominence as an intellectual, activist, and public figure. He's thirty-something, still boyish with his short blond hair and glasses: a Polish Harry Potter who uses the language of critical theory for his spells.

And Sławek insists that the magic is still there. Krytyka, he argues, continues to go from strength to strength and has never been more vital. In 2012, for instance, the organization opened a high-profile Institute for Advanced Studies in its new office a couple of blocks away from the shuttered café. It continues to dominate the intellectual scene in Poland with a slew of publications and its organizing in and around Ukraine.

'The golden era is not dead,' Sławek told me when I interviewed him at Harvard University, where he had been awarded a fellowship, in 2013. 'The golden era is ahead.'

Before he came on the scene, the Polish left was dominated by the former Communist Party (SLD), which had reorganized itself around a core of technocratic reformers. 'They have resources,' explains journalist Jacek Żakowski. 'They have people. They have political stars like Aleksander Kwaśniewski and Leszek Miller. They are supported by public money, which is granted to parliamentary political parties. So they very easily prevail over any new initiatives. And, of course, they have experience.'

Poland's economic crisis in the early 1990s propelled the SLD to power. Particularly in its second tenure, under President Kwasniewski and Prime Minister Miller from 2001 to 2004, the SLD governed like U.S.-style conservatives. It supported austerity economics, US wars in Afghanistan and Iraq, and even a secret CIA interrogation site on Polish soil. It also guided Poland into the European Union, but only after securing the support of the Catholic Church in return for preserving the country's anti-abortion laws.

As the SLD monopolized the oxygen on the left side of the political spectrum, the independent left was what Sławek calls mere 'plankton,' a thin soup of 'three-member groups.' The re-established Polish Socialist Party (PPS) failed to rebrand socialism in a voter-friendly way. Left economist Ryszard Bugaj established a Labor Party that faded. Samoobrona capitalized on discontent in the countryside, but drifted rightward after a strong showing in the 2001 elections.

'If we had had more technical power – money, structures, people – we could have appealed to all the people who, year by year during the 1990s, were more disappointed by what was going on in Poland, who lost their health, their money, their livelihoods during the transition period,' says Zuzanna Dąbrowska, an organizer in the 1990s with the Democratic Revolution faction of PPS. 'But to find these people and unite them, you had to have much greater organizational power.'

Krytyka aimed to pull together precisely that organizational power.

When barely out of his teens, Sławek Sierakowski published a piece in Poland's most prominent liberal newspaper, *Gazeta Wyborcza*. 'It was a naïve article, a teenage article about how we were unhappy with what was going on in Poland,' he admits. 'It's nothing I would sign today.' Veteran oppositionist and sociologist Kinga Dunin, herself a *Gazeta* columnist, took the young Sławek to task in print. Out of this critique, the older woman and the younger man developed a close working relationship.

'Krytyka Polityczna, the leftishness, the idea that you have to combine the cultural left with the economic left and that neoliberalism is not the freshest cake in our national bakery – that came from the feminist analysis of Kinga,' American studies professor and Krytyka associate Agnieszka Graff says.

In 2002, Krytyka made its mark in intellectual circles through the traditional Polish tactic of a quarterly journal. But for their next trick, the duo of Sławek Sierakowski and Kinga Dunin, the yin and yang of the new Polish left, tried something a little different. Their call to arms, in the form of a 2003 open letter, catapulted Krytyka Polityczna not only to domestic fame but international acclaim. Their letter, which ultimately attracted the signatures of 250 top Polish intellectuals, weighed in on the most pressing issue of the day: membership of the European Union. It supported membership but urged that the EU move in a more progressive direction. After its publication in major European newspapers, Polish public opinion began to swing in favor of the letter's arguments.

'It was a very important lesson for us,' Sławek remembers. 'You can enter big politics with just a good idea, a pencil, and sheet of paper.'

As a result of its intellectual feats, Krytyka began to attract a generation of young activists who'd been born after the Solidarity period and only dimly remembered the transition period of the 1990s. There was a romance to Krytyka, an almost nineteenth-century fusion of politics and poetry that was so lacking in Poland's new market-driven life. With its combination of top-flight discussion and hard-nosed activism, Krytyka mobilized political romantics, budding academics, and the 'third sector' of NGO activists. The first two set off the intellectual fireworks; the latter built the organization.

'We are a very professional and very competent organization,' Sławek says with pride. 'A lot of people hate us because we are always winning. It's because of the women of the third sector.' Indeed, Krytyka is remarkable for the number of female staffers and for its engagement on gender issues. Yet the roles are not equal. 'I was hoping that Krytyka would give women intellectuals an opportunity to become public figures,' Agnieszka Graff laments. 'But I'm sad to see that this hasn't happened with the girls. They see themselves more as editors of other people's ideas.'

Krytyka has successfully launched new ventures at a rate of nearly one a year. It has established a foothold on the web with its Opinion Daily. Its publishing arm now puts out dozens of books a year, including translations of such titles as Thomas Frank's *What's the Matter with Kansas?* and the more abstruse works of Slavoj Žižek and Giorgio Agamben. It has established clubs across Poland, satellite ventures in Ukraine and Russia, and outposts in Berlin and London. Major figures like filmmaker Agnieszka Holland have burnished the organization's reputation by publishing with Krytyka and serving on its advisory board. On the activist front, Krytyka has organized to stop evictions, promote LGBT rights, and support protesting nurses.

Krytyka's success in some sense is tied to Poland's shortcomings. True, the Polish economy recovered enough from the near-collapse of the 1990s to produce talk of a 'green island' of growth in the midst of a continent in the red. But young people, the ones so interested in Krytyka's combination of economic and cultural left messages, have not benefitted from this growth. Unemployment has been very high among youth – averaging nearly 30 percent from 1997 to 2016 and rising to up to 44 percent in 2002, the year of Krytyka's birth.[10] Even those with jobs must deal with short-term 'trash contracts' that come with few if any benefits.

'People emigrate, to find jobs or, if they have bigger aspirations, to educate themselves,' Krytyka staffer Michał Sutowski says. 'Over 1.5 million people have emigrated from Poland' since EU accession in 2004, the largest number of people to emigrate during peacetime in modern Polish history.

Krytyka offered something new: a young leader who could rally his generation. 'The way these kids worked, sixteen hours a day without pay, it had to do with his charisma,' Agnieszka explains. 'Getting a word of praise from Sławek was worth collapse.'

'Without his determination,' adds sociologist and Krytyka associate Maciej Gdula, 'we would have many small initiatives, but we wouldn't have people coming together to act.' Without Sławek, in other words, the independent Polish left would remain little more than plankton. He brought star quality to the new dissidents, a flash of charisma. He even appeared as an actor in the film trilogy *And Europe Will Be Stunned*, playing a leader of a movement to bring Jews back to Poland. Directed by Israeli artist Yael Bartana, the films were Poland's official entry in the 2011 Venice Biennale and attracted large audiences at major museums around the world.[11]

Furthermore, changing the discourse in Poland is no small thing. 'It's no longer crazy to say you're a leftist here in Poland, or that you're against war, or that you don't consider nationalism to be a natural perspective, or that you are for taxes and against inequality,' Maciej Gdula argues. 'You can use class language overtly and not be considered someone from the past. We really did introduce critical language and left-wing perspectives into public debate.'

For some, however, Krytyka's reach exceeds its grasp. 'They started out with extraordinary success,' journalist Konstanty Gebert recalls. 'No one expected it was possible. Krytyka Polityczna clubs were mushrooming. Forget Warsaw – in Warsaw the left is trendy and chic. Clubs were appearing in the boondocks like Konin. A normal left-wing movement would have cherished those clubs. They would have sent good organizers there to support these clubs, nurture them, feed them, for years if need be. But no, Krytyka Polityczna was looking for a quick fix. It was interested in selling more copies of their journal *Krytyka*. And those clubs disappeared. It breaks my heart.'

For others, Krytyka has been very effective at marketing itself and creating a new left brand, but hasn't translated that brand into concrete political programs.[12] 'Instead of tackling authentic problems that are connected with the left – like poverty, homelessness, work issues – it dealt with substitute topics, things that the intelligentsia was concerned with,' former Green Party activist Zygmunt Fura told me. 'The program of a left party should arise out of real values, not marketing.' But Krytyka was very clear about not creating a political party, and that for some has been a major strike against it. 'They're nice guys,' Zuzanna Dąbrowska says. 'But I think they suffer from the same problem as the East Coast in the States. They are organized around their own discussions. Of course it's very important to discuss and to know what to think and to have a strong point of view. But if you don't do any more than that, it's a problem, for the left especially.'

Sławek dismisses talk of political parties. He is after something more transformative. 'I can't do that in party politics,' he says. 'It would just be stupid quarrels. You might say: you can be more honest, more substantial. But no, if I did that, I would lose! Put Václav Havel into an election today and he would lose.' And Krytyka is not just a talking shop, he insists. 'We've changed many things in Poland,' he points out. 'For instance, we changed the laws on narcotics. We had a very conservative law in Poland that automatically put people in prison if anything was found on them. It was the criminalization of the young generation. Then, when they were released from prison, they were real bandits. Now the law is different. Did any political party change this? No! It was a coalition of NGOs that changed it.'

Despite its accomplishments, Krytyka failed to prevent the rise of the populist right, which was also critiquing neoliberal austerity economics and promising such left-wing standards as a minimum-wage increase and a national employment program. A new left party, Razem, formed in May 2015 to challenge the rising right. However, it not only failed to get enough votes to breach the 5 percent threshold to send representatives to parliament but also drew enough votes away from the United Left coalition to prevent it from entering parliament as well.[13] After the elections in 2015, in which the resurgent right won both the presidency and a parliamentary majority, a new Committee for the Defense of Democracy (KOD) brought thousands of people onto the streets to protest against the government's illiberal policies.

As in the 1980s, the new dissidence is perhaps stronger in Poland than anywhere else. But other left formations have emerged to challenge Margaret Thatcher's famous dictum that 'there is no alternative' to market liberalism. Some liberals, under the influence of Occupy and other movements, have even moved to the left. Robert Braun, for instance, focused on human rights in the 1980s, when he helped found Hungary's Raoul Wallenberg Association. He ran for parliament in the 2014 elections – and ultimately lost – on a different platform: social justice. 'Twenty years ago, it was human rights and civil liberties that mattered. But now, it's social rights and social liberties,' he told me. 'The one percent that has made it into Europe, myself included, we're living the life of mainstream Europe – the same cars, the same lifestyle – but we are living that life on the shoulders of the ninety-nine percent.'

The politics of inequality has motivated NGO activists in the region to work with those living precarious lives: refugees, the homeless, the unemployed. A new generation of young intellectuals has formed groups like the Student Network in Hungary, CriticAtac in Romania, and New Left Perspectives in Bulgaria, all of which have sought to distinguish their worldview from the dominant liberal discourse. New left-leaning parties, such as LMP (Politics Can Be Different) in Hungary and the Initiative for Democratic Socialism in Slovenia, have promised a brand new type of politics, even if they've ultimately succumbed to all-too-familiar compromises and infighting.

Out of this mixture of efforts has emerged a New Left. 'We use this term to try to carve out space between the old left – what we call the hardline communist left, which is nostalgic about socialism in a conservative, nationalist way,' Bulgarian activist Georgi Medarov says, 'and Bulgaria's Social Democratic Party, which became quite neoliberal and quite conservative at the same time.'

The message of Krytyka Polityczna has inspired a New Left in eastern Europe because of its refreshing take on contemporary issues as well as its conscious evocation of an earlier, almost forgotten tradition. 'Only action produces togetherness,' Sławek Sierakowski says. 'If you and I cooperate to do something, in time it will produce enough trust so that we will risk something together.' It's a message with deep resonance in a country where millions once risked their lives many years ago to create a mass movement called Solidarity.

The feminization of dissent

Marina Grasse is a biologist who was deeply involved in the independent peace movement in East Germany in the 1980s. I met her in 1990 to talk about how one of the most remarkable and long-lived independent peace groups in the region, the Pankow Peace Circle, was adapting to the new circumstances in a democratic East Germany. At that time, she was also passionately interested in educational reform. In fact, on the evening the Berlin Wall fell in November 1989, she helped to organize a forum on the topic in East Berlin. She booked a large conference hall but realistically expected a modest turnout of ten to twenty people. She was shocked when the hall filled with a couple of thousand people. She was similarly surprised when that audience began to trickle out during the course of the evening – as news filtered in about what was happening at the border checkpoints with West Berlin.

Later, in 1990, Grasse joined the newly democratic East German government. During that partial year of living independently and democratically, the East German government was a grand coalition between the GDR branches of the Social Democratic Party and the Christian Democratic

Union. The coalition decided, as a result of pressure from NGOs, to create the position of state secretary responsible for equal opportunities for women and men. 'Some people in the Social Democratic faction knew me,' Marina told me in a 2013 interview in her apartment in Pankow, a neighborhood in Berlin. 'I didn't know what a state secretary was, and I didn't know what "equal opportunity" meant. But nevertheless they invited me.'

The position of state secretary for equal opportunity was controversial to begin with. The ministry was a demand of the Independent Women's Association (UFV), which some Germans dismissed as an organization of *emancen*, a pejorative word for feminists. 'Many people in the opposition said that legally, according to the East German constitution, women were equal to men,' Petra Wunderlich of the UFV told me in 1990. 'So what did women then want, they asked? The *emancen* wanted superiority was the answer. Nevertheless, the round table approved this not terribly radical resolution.'

This was the position that Marina was considering. She had four children at the time, two boys and two girls. She had a full-time job. Still, she decided to go to the Volkskammer to undergo the parliamentary vetting process for the position.

The MPs asked her, 'Now, what are you going to do?'

'What should I do?' she replied.

'You'll be the state secretary for equal opportunity.'

'But I don't know what that is!'

'It doesn't matter, we don't either!' they admitted. 'Now tell us your biography and some ideas about equal opportunity …'

She didn't know what to say. After some reflection, however, she managed, 'Okay, equal opportunity for women means that, since probably women are discriminated against, they think they need equal opportunity …'

It was not an easy conversation, and Marina had her doubts about taking on the new responsibility. But the question-and-answer session decided it for her.

'We have heard you are the mother of four children,' a man stood up to confront her. 'How do you think you can combine your private responsibilities as a mother with your responsibilities as state secretary?'

Marina was taken aback. She thought, 'What am I doing here? This is completely stupid!'

But then another MP stood up and said, 'That's a very interesting question because in this group there are many men who have two, three, four kids. And never, never, never, never has somebody asked them how they could combine their responsibilities.'

It was a revelatory moment for Marina. 'That's when I understood what it was about, and I agreed to do it,' she told me.

Soon she discovered, however, that equal opportunity was not on the new government's agenda. The East German parliament, tasked to oversee the transformation of East Germany into a democratic society, very quickly became focused on one issue above all else: reunification. And reunification, in turn, imposed a very abrupt term limit on all the new members of the East German government. Out of a job when the two Germanys came together, Marina decided to apply the principles of equal opportunity for women more broadly by establishing a regional network of women to exchange their experiences after the fall of communism.[14]

Those experiences included the achievements women secured under communism both nominally in the constitutions and also substantively. Out of necessity, eastern European women entered the workforce in large numbers after World War II. The countries had been devastated by war, and many able-bodied men had died as soldiers and forced laborers. Since communism also emphasized full employment, women in the region eventually participated in the labor market in rates higher than in any other developed part of the world. 'To ensure that women would seek out paid work, the wage structure was altered; wage setting was centralized and state-controlled, and the family wage was abolished,' according to a report by the UN agency UNIFEM. 'In the early years of this transformation, women were expected to do the same jobs as men, receive the same training and wages, and take on the same leadership responsibilities.'[15] In Germany, when the Wall fell, 90 percent of women in the East worked, compared to only 55 percent of women in the West.[16] Sexism by no means disappeared during the communist period, and the political structures remained heavily dominated by men. Still, largely as a result of their participation in the workforce, women saw a collective improvement in status.

The fall of communism meant a setback for women in some respects. In united Germany, for instance, women faced more restrictive abortion laws, less generous family leave policies, and fewer options for day care. And this in a country that was, by and large, quite progressive in terms of women's issues. It would take more than fifteen years before Angela Merkel, originally an East German dissident politician, reinstituted more generous family leave and day-care policies, bringing the practices of unified Germany more in line with what had once been the East German norm.[17]

In part, the setbacks for women in the region reflected the leadership of the civil movements that dislodged the regimes. Before 1989, the leaders of dissident movements were overwhelmingly male. In Poland, Solidarity had a few women activists such as the crane operator Anna Walentynowicz, whose firing in 1980 triggered the strike that launched the independent trade union movement, as well as underground organizers during martial law like Ewa Kulik.[18] A handful of women, like Jiřina Šiklová, signed Charter 77 in Czechoslovakia. Judit Vásárhelyi played a critical role in the Hungarian environmental movement. Dimitrina Petrova was an important force behind Ecoglasnost in Bulgaria. The Pankow Peace Circle, to which Marina Grasse belonged, was led by Ruth Misselwitz, a pastor, and attracted a number of key women activists.

More frequently women were active behind the scenes, where the male leadership often slighted their contributions. According to a legendary story among activists in Poland, a sign at the shipyard in Gdańsk, where Solidarity got its start in 1980, read: 'Women, do not disturb us. We are fighting for Poland.' Although nobody actually saw the sign, many people firmly believe that it existed. 'The sign is very important to Polish feminism,' activist and literary critic Agnieszka Graff told me. 'It puts in a nutshell the kind of arrogance but also the beauty of Polish patriarchal patriotism: "Don't disturb us, ladies, we are the strong and tragic men who are fighting for Poland and we want to give it to you with a rose."'

The break with the communist system in 1989 was for many women a bittersweet experience. Women had been at the forefront of the liberalization in Yugoslavia, which had the most successful women's movement in the region before the wars of the 1990s. The new nationalists targeted these women as part of their surge to power. In 1992, for instance, the *Globus* newspaper accused seven Croatian women of being witches. 'That is, they were accused of not being patriotic enough,' feminist and peace activist Svetlana Slapšak told me. '*Globus* published their names and photos and such data as who they were married to, whether they had Serbian husbands. This was so that everyone could harass them.' Women pushed back against the nationalists. Women in Black, which emerged first in Israel to resist the Palestinian occupation, spread throughout former Yugoslavia to protest against the war. 'There were no women from the Yugoslav women's movement at the beginning of the war or before the war who embraced those nationalist positions,' Svetlana continued. 'During the war, all of these women performed services for other women, like taking care of refugees and victims, helping people in other territories, and never losing contact through our network.'

Even where war didn't strengthen patriarchal institutions, women lost ground after 1989. 'We thought that with the abolition of communism would automatically come change and more freedoms, also for women,' long-time Polish feminist and peace activist Małgorzata Tarasiewicz points out. 'It was unimaginable that, instead of freedoms, restrictions for women's rights might be introduced! As women we were so marginalized – there was only one woman at the round table discussions. Today it would be unimaginable. We would demand a women's rights working group. But at the time of rapid change we were taken by surprise.' Małgorzata's own effort to head up the women's section in Solidarity was short-lived because of the union leadership's disdain for the enterprise.

In Poland, the Church continues to promote a traditional version of a woman as a *matka polka*, a 'mother of Poland' who stays at home, takes care of children, and doesn't participate in the public sphere. Many Polish women, and not just those who had jobs outside the home during the communist era, have refused to accept the traditional roles that Germans call *kinder, kuche, kirche* (children, kitchen, church). It's a persistent theme that has returned in force with the rise of right-wing populists throughout the region. In 2012, for instance, István Varga of Fidesz in Hungary publicly stated that the 'most important calling for women and ladies, especially for young ladies, is to give birth. It is obvious that if everybody gave birth to two, three or four children, a gift to the fatherland, everybody would be happy. After that task is over, every woman can fulfill herself and may work at different jobs.'[19]

In Poland, many women activists shifted their organizing away from the Solidarity model of a mass movement to issue-focused organizing such as preserving a pro-choice option. In spring 1990, as the Health Ministry began to impose new restrictions on abortion, such as requiring a woman to go through a series of consultations with doctors and psychologists, the Polish parliament discussed a draft resolution on 'the protection of unborn life' that would jail a woman for two years for 'killing' her fetus and put her doctor in prison for three years. A subsequent 'milder' version was introduced that September, which provided a prison term only for the doctor. The law provided for 'unconditional' protection of the fetus. The legislation sparked outrage among women, activist Jolanta Plakwicz told me at the time, doing 'for the women's movement what we couldn't do for ten years!' Parliament continued to debate different versions of the legislation, with different penalties, until finally passing a restrictive bill in early 1993.[20]

Wanda Nowicka is a member of the new generation of women activists. In the early 1990s, she established the organization Federation of Women and Family Planning. 'The antiabortion law was introduced after the transformation – as a result of the change and also by arguing that everything under communism was bad, including the abortion law,' she told me. 'Also the role of the Church was something that we noticed as a very negative phenomenon, and the position of the Church is constantly growing.' She added, 'Over the last few years, there's been the debate on in-vitro fertilization [IVF]. Eight years ago, IVF was not controversial. It was a normal medical procedure, and the Church had nothing to do with it. When the Church decided to engage with IVF, it became the most controversial issue. Although sixty-five percent of Poles support IVF, politicians are unable to pass the law due to the strong pressure of the Church.' In 2015, the new conservative government announced that it would end the state-run IVF program.[21]

'Supporting women's rights was asking for big trouble' because of the power of the Church, Małgorzata told me. 'It meant that you were not in the mainstream and you didn't have any chance of being in the political establishment. You were immediately excluded from any hope of having a political career. In the 1990s, if you wanted to be a mainstream politician, you had to accept traditional values.' Anna Popowicz, for instance, was appointed the first minister for women, family, and youth in 1991. She was actually quite conservative politically, but when she began to challenge the doctors' code of ethics as too dismissive of women's health concerns, the government fired her and left her position vacant.[22]

Women have not simply accepted their derogation. In 2000, responding to a police raid on a gynecology clinic, activists began organizing what they called 'Manifa,' a kind of feminist manifestation. 'We thought of ourselves as the new dissidents – this time resisting the power of the Church and conservative politicians,' Agnieszka Graff told me. 'The first Manifa included an interview with Matka Polka played by a very large feminist psychologist, who was in an apron, and I was a silly journalist in a purple wig. The idea is that she came to us to tell us that she was making pierogi in patriotic heaven and just couldn't stand it any more. Our first poster, in fact, was "I've had it!" – signed "Matka Polka." I remember getting phone calls from people who had had run into a tree when they saw the poster.'

In Poland today, women occupy quite a few positions of political and economic power, though it's not yet at the level of equality that Manifa activists demanded. The prime minister who took over in 2015, for instance, is a woman, and there are quite a few female mayors throughout the country. Another sign of the new power is the Congress of Women, which has met annually since 2009, not just in Warsaw, where 10,000 people gathered in June 2013, but also in various regional conferences. It defines itself as a social movement and makes such demands as gender parity in electoral lists. A number of prominent businesswomen – including Henryka Bochniarz, the head of Lewiatan, the Polish Confederation of Private Employers – have made sure that the Congress is well funded and prominently covered in the press.

'The Women's Congress is the mainstream wing of Polish feminism. I have a sort of willfully naïve enthusiasm for it,' Agnieszka says. 'But I've always been like that – I persuade myself to trust the mainstream's capacity to embrace change … It doesn't matter with whom you work: as long as you are helping women get their lives back.'

When the conservative PiS government again pushed for greater restrictions on abortion, the Congress of Women forcefully supported the huge demonstrations that thronged Warsaw and other major cities in autumn 2016.[23] 'A group of religious fanatics who hate women decided to move on to further Stop Abortion regulation,' a Congress statement read in part. 'We have to act, we have to protest – on our behalf, on behalf of all women, of our daughters and grand-daughters, on behalf of European civilization, where women's rights are a great trophy and should be sacred.'[24]

The green alternative

Every few years in eastern Europe, a new political movement emerges that challenges not only the status quo but the very assumptions of the political system. Sometimes the movement targets the party patronage system. Sometimes it represents a new kind of populism. Sometimes it elevates a set of issues that the media or the political elite has ignored.

In Hungary, environmentalists have long nurtured outside-the-box alternatives. During the last decade of communist rule, a grassroots movement against the Nagymaros-Gabčíkovo dam on the Danube river between Hungary and Slovakia played a key role in focusing opposition to the communist government. As in communist China in the 1990s, environmentalists in communist Hungary in the 1980s could complain about the status quo more openly than critics of the *nomenklatura* or advocates of an independent union.[25] Not that the environment wasn't an urgent concern in and of itself in Hungary. In the late 1980s, air pollution exceeded international standards for 40 percent of the population and was implicated in one in seventeen deaths.[26] Hungary had one of Europe's worst life expectancy rates, the Danube was unswimmable, and less than half the population lived with an adequate sewage system.[27] Despite the efforts of environmentalists to raise awareness of these problems, the first major action in Hungary after the fall of communism was in many respects anti-environmental: a taxi strike that shut down the capital city of Budapest because the first democratic government raised the price of gas to market levels.

Peace activist Pál Kochis was one of the founders of Hungary's first Green Party, which didn't attract enough electoral support to get into parliament in the 1990 elections. As a result, he and other original members were kicked out of the party. It was a story emblematic of the period. 'The intellectuals responsible for carrying out the transition movement were either kicked out of parties or out of politics,' he told me. 'The second line remained: the people who didn't dare to open their mouths, the cowards. Of course I understand their frustration since they were not there at the transition. But this is the reason why politics after the transition period became debilitated.'

'At the beginning of the 1990s, with the Danube movement behind us and the transition ahead of us, a lot of people thought that Hungary would have a green future with very strong green NGOs,' green activist Jávor Benedek told me. Gradually, as with women's issues, environmental concerns took a backseat to the other political and economic priorities of transition. 'By the middle of the decade, some disillusionment set in,' he continued. 'People realized that a lot of former green activists were not green any more because they'd become party politicians in parliament. Green NGOs couldn't achieve many things. Green parties were unsuccessful, partly because of personal fights inside the parties, partly because the existing mainstream parties attracted successful green politicians.'

The green movement managed to push through some important legislation on nature conservation, forestry, and hunting, and successfully promoted the presidential candidacy of environmentalist László Sólyom. Rather than heralding a new green era for Hungary, these achievements represented the high-water mark of environmental activism. Meanwhile, outside institutions that might have been expected to encourage Hungarian efforts to preserve the environment proved disappointing. Poland arranged debt-for-nature swaps to reduce its foreign indebtedness, but it turned out that Hungary, because it owed money to banks rather than states, could not avail itself of that option. The EU, which Hungary joined in 2004, established quotas for renewable resources. 'But one by one, they turn out to have unexpected side effects,' environmental activist Judit Vásárhelyi told me. 'Wind turbines turn out to be very expensive. Bioethanol destroys territory that could be used for food. When the EU gave support for biomass, they started to cut down the real Hungarian forests and turn the wood into energy.' It profoundly disillusioned Judit. 'We should at this moment be proud of this dowry and try to save it,' she continued. 'We shouldn't, like a bridegroom, go to the pub and drink it up! But many European institutions simply want economic development and growth, and they don't seem to care about exploiting these remaining ecological resources.'

This engagement with larger economic questions propelled green NGOs like Védegylet (Protect the Future) and Zöfi to expand their focus and bring a new excitement to green politics – among both seasoned activists and a new cadre of young people. It also emboldened some of the more politically minded to try again with a green party.

But in 2009, when activists pulled together a new initiative, Lehet Más a Politika (LMP), they didn't call it a Green Party. Instead, they wanted to transform the entire process of doing politics in the country. The name of the party said it all: Politics Can Be Different. It reflected a disgust with what politics had become in democratic Hungary, as well as a frustration with the narrowness of Green Party activism. It wasn't the antipolitics of Hungarian dissident György Konrád. Nor was it the 'politics as usual' of the new liberal technocrats that ruled Hungary in the 1990s. It was both an affirmation of the importance of politics – of party politics and not just NGO politics – and a rejection of the narrow, adversarial political climate that enveloped Hungary. It recalled the original energy of Germany's Green Party when, in 1980, it challenged stale left–right dichotomies and the liberal-conservative consensus on economic growth.

LMP's embrace of environmental sustainability and its attempt to alter the political status quo were both attractive to Katalin Ertsey, one of the first generation of Fidesz activists in the late 1980s. Unhappy when Fidesz veered in a conservative direction in the 1990s, she went into NGO work. When she heard about LMP, she quickly enlisted.

'Obviously we knew that a green party was needed sooner or later in Hungary, but we didn't see that it was possible to break up the monolithic system of Hungarian parties,' she told me. 'I still believe that LMP has brought the only new idea into politics for twenty years. This "politics can be different" suggests a whole new look at politics. I actually took that seriously.' Like Krytyka Polityczna, LMP was not interested in exhuming an older dissident tradition. It was 'not just about hugging trees,' Katalin told me. 'LMP has been a whole new way of looking at the world and development.'

Katalin entered parliament with LMP in 2010 and expected to work with all willing partners on the issues that LMP held dear, such as sustainable development, deliberative democracy, and anti-corruption campaigns. But working across the aisle, she quickly learned, was not going to be easy, even with Fidesz members she still knew from the old days. Politics had become as polarized in Hungary as it was throughout the region. She reached out, for instance, to a woman she appreciated for her work visiting people put in prison after the anti-government riots in 2006. 'Again, naïvely, I thought on women's issues that we could form a non-partisan caucus,' Katalin said. She soon discovered that party affiliation trumped policy preferences.

Eventually LMP, too, fell victim to the divisive effects of Hungarian politics. In advance of the elections of 2014, the opposition tried to pull together an anti-Fidesz coalition. Half of LMP thought it was possible to align with the Socialist Party, among others, to defeat the ruling party. The other half, reminded of the coalition that Hungarian liberals engineered with the Socialist Party between 1994 and 2008, preferred to remain independent. LMP split into two factions. The party that retained the name LMP managed to nose just above the 5 percent threshold to get five seats in parliament. A breakaway faction, Dialogue for Hungary/PM, joined the left-wing Unity Coalition, which achieved a little more than 25 percent of the vote and thirty-seven seats. Fidesz, meanwhile, won the elections by a comfortable margin.

Katalin decided to leave politics altogether. 'Politics will not be different until we face the root of the problem.

As a nation, we have never faced our past: the Holocaust, communism, the various national tragedies of the twentieth century. It's very clear in LMP's opening statement that we are not giving up on having a dialogue on that,' she concluded. 'This is one of the projects or ideas that very much excites me: to go back and look at our past through something like a truth-and-reconciliation committee.'

The new politics of self-determination

At the beginning of 1990, the country that looked most likely to dissolve into ethnic fratricide was not Yugoslavia. It was Romania.

More than a million ethnic Hungarians live in Romania – about 6 percent of the population. They are the children of Trianon, the 1920 treaty that reduced Hungary by two-thirds, with Transylvania and a large Hungarian population becoming part of Romania. As Ceaușescu moved in a more nationalist direction in his final years, the Hungarian community bore the brunt of his paranoia. Those tensions burst into the open in mid-December 1989 when the initial protests broke out in Timișoara around the resistance of an ethnic Hungarian pastor, László Tőkés.

Tensions between the ethnic Hungarian and Romanian communities didn't go away with the death of Ceaușescu. Throughout Transylvania in early 1990, Hungarians, Romanians, and Roma eyed each other warily. Would Hungarians take advantage of the uncertainty of the times to declare an independent republic or try to reattach territory to Hungary proper? Would pogroms by Hungarians and Romanians against Roma escalate into outright genocide? László Borbély, one of the founders of the Democratic Union of Hungarians in Romania, suspected that the Communist Party would 'promote interethnic conflict between the Hungarians and the Romanians as a diversion.' That was his explanation for the violence that broke out in March 1990 in Târgu Mureș, leaving five people dead and hundreds injured.

But none of these worst-case scenarios played out in Romania. One of the reasons for the lack of escalation was the Hungarian minority's embrace of what Polish intellectuals once called a 'self-limiting revolution.' Solidarity, in Poland, did not push for a maximalist agenda of regime change in the early 1980s because it knew that the Polish government – with the Soviet Union breathing down its neck – would use such demands as an excuse to eradicate the movement, if necessary by plunging the country into civil war. Eventually this self-limiting strategy would translate into a staged transformation of Polish politics and society in 1989.

Faced with rising nationalism in Romanian society, the Hungarian minority had a choice. It could pursue the more militant tactics of street demonstrations and confrontation. Or it could adopt a self-limiting strategy by channeling its anger and frustration into the political realm.

László Borbély favored the latter strategy. 'We could go out on the streets and not accept interethnic dialogue and the parliament and the local authorities and the democratic way of fighting for our rights,' he told me in an interview in his office at the Romanian parliament in May 2013. 'Or we could compete in the elections for parliament and win our rights that way. Fortunately, we chose the way of democracy and the way of dialogue. That's why the first six years were the most difficult because the Romanian society was not prepared to discuss this kind of question.'

Maria Koreck, a member of the ethnic Hungarian community who now lives in Târgu Mureș, agrees that the situation for ethnic Hungarians is better today than it was when I was in the country in the early 1990s. 'Ethnic issues are no longer a priority,' she told me in 2013, citing economic issues as more important. 'And being a minority is no longer felt to be a handicap. Generally minorities no longer feel like second-class citizens even though sometimes they are still put in situations where they feel that way.' But there is considerable disagreement among Hungarians about how to achieve further progress on civil rights. 'I'm from Timișoara, where we are not the majority, so we have one way of thinking,' Maria explains. 'But in Harghita and Covasna counties Hungarians are the majority, and they have another way of thinking. There are now fewer and fewer Hungarians in Romania. Those who are living as the majority have the view that there has to be a strong core where they live, and that will help the others, too. But others don't agree with this because they see that what is good for the majority is not applicable when you are in the minority

… And the thing is that more Hungarians are now living in areas where they are the minority.'[28]

This disagreement can be seen clearly in the debate over bilingualism. 'Of course, in Harghita county everyone speaks Hungarian publicly,' Koreck points out. 'The Democratic Alliance of Hungarians fought for and won the right that wherever the minority constitutes at least twenty percent of the population, then the language of that minority can be used publicly in court, at the mayor's office, or wherever. Everything has to be written bilingually, not like in Târgu Mureș where we are fighting to make the street signs fully bilingual. We don't think the law has been implemented fully but it's going in the right direction. Those from the majority think that this has to be done everywhere immediately, that it's a right and it's not negotiable.'

Despite these tensions, ethnic Hungarians have made considerable gains. When I met Kinga Kerekes in 1993, she was part of a student movement demanding Hungarian-language instruction at the Bolyai University in Cluj. Twenty years later, she teaches all of her economics classes in Hungarian. In the 1990s, she told me, 'everything in Cluj was painted in the colors of the Romanian flag – dustbins, benches, everything. Since 2010, there's a week of Hungarian cultural days in August. There have been three editions of it without any major problems.'

One of these festivals even held a showing of the rock opera *István, a király* (*King István*). 'It's a cult thing, something like the Hungarian *Hair*,' Kinga told me. 'In 1985 or 1986, it was composed and presented in Hungary with famous Hungarian rock musicians. It became very popular. But it was forbidden in Romania even to listen to it! You could be charged if you had a tape of that music. István was the first Hungarian king, and it's about his story. It's history, but it has a lot of connotations of freedom, of becoming a nation. It had a lot of meaning in the 1980s, perhaps even more meaning for Hungarians here than in Hungary.'

Kinga was surprised and delighted when the film was projected on a screen in the very middle of Cluj: 'If five years ago you told me that something like that would happen, I would have said you were wrong, that it would never be accepted by Romanians or by the authorities.'

The rise of the precariat

Whether in the opposition like Solidarity or as an official part of the communist power structure, labor unions were powerful and influential institutions in eastern Europe during the Cold War. After 1989, however, labor unions no longer commanded the same power or prestige. The privatization of state firms disenfranchised the core constituency of the unions, and their membership plummeted.

In Poland, the bond between Solidarity the union and the politicians elected on a Solidarity-linked platform posed a nearly insoluble dilemma: could one half of Solidarity go out on strike against the other half in power? The unionists and the politicians solved the dilemma by parting company, the union severing formal ties with the representatives it helped get elected. Soon enough former colleagues faced each other across picket lines. Given the enormous disruptions in the Polish economy in the early 1990s, strikes were not surprising. More surprising was how few there actually were. The number of strikes actually declined from 1989 to 1990, from 900 to 250 when the economic reforms began to bite, and it only nosed up a fraction to 305 in 1991.[29] The unions were often willing to give their former colleagues a pass, at least for the time being.

Poland quickly passed through its era of worker actions. In 1993, the country experienced a high of 7,443 strikes. By the next year, there were only 429.[30] As analyst David Ost argues, Solidarity struck off in a different direction, channeling its oppositional energies into social issues – banning abortion, rooting out former secret police informers – to mobilize its constituents.[31] The independent trade union once counted 60 percent of the workforce as members.[32] By 2013, trade union membership overall in Poland had dropped to only 10 percent, one of the lowest in Europe.[33] Solidarity had lost an opportunity to mobilize the disgruntled.

The Podkrepa trade union in Bulgaria faced the same dilemma when the opposition Union of Democratic Forces (UDF) formed a government in 1991. Podkrepa separated itself from the UDF and tended to its shrinking membership. The once official trade union, CITUB, witnessed an even more dramatic decline, from a membership of 2.5 million to a mere 300,000. It wasn't just the closure of factories. The days of a relatively stable workforce were gone. 'The companies dismiss people that have permanent contracts and hire people from these agencies at half-salaries,' Oleg Chulev of Podkrepa told me. 'The notorious EU directive on Flexibility and Security in the Labor Market is all about the growth of temporary agencies, part-time workers, distance workers, and so on. In Bulgaria, this means flexibility for workers – they must be very mobile, be willing to work flexible hours – and security is only for capital.'

It's the same problem in Poland, which has a name for this new kind of employment: *umowa śmieciowa* or 'junk contracts.' If you're young and lucky enough to have a job in Poland these days, it's likely to be short-term and come without benefits. 'Poland is an indisputable leader of the so-called junk contracts,' Solidarity activist Sławomir Rakowiecki told me. 'These contracts provide for two to three months of temporary employment with minimum salary, which literally means creating a new class of employees "under the table." Therefore people are permanently afraid to lose jobs where even their health and pension insurance is not covered.'

This new class of workers are part of what some analysts call the 'precariat.' As economist Guy Standing puts it, 'Every progressive political movement has been built on the anger, needs and aspirations of the emerging major class. Today that class is the precariat.'[34] Joining temporary workers in this precariat are unemployed youth, migrants, disenfranchised minorities, the homeless, the criminalized – anyone who lives a precarious and insecure existence. Unlike workers at a fixed workplace, they are not easily organized. Their relationship to employers is highly contingent if they have any jobs at all.

Bálint Misetics is an energetic young Hungarian with long black hair tied into a ponytail. He has been working with the homeless since he was a teenager, organizing charity concerts in subway stations around Christmas. As he grew older, he felt that such charity work wasn't enough, that 'what needed to be done was something much more political, that you need to appeal to justice and rights as opposed to humanitarian concerns or the goodwill of the rich,' Bálint told me. He began to organize sleep-outs in the subway stations to show that homelessness 'is not something that you can make invisible, which the authorities wanted to do.'

After spending some time studying at Bard College in the United States, Bálint began to change his mode of organizing: rather than working *for* the homeless, he began to think about working *with* the homeless. That was the origin of The City Is for All, a joint project of the homeless and the non-homeless. 'The first protest we had with The City Is for All was against a so-called socialist mayor in the eleventh district who campaigned with the slogan of "homeless-free zones,"' Bálint explained. 'We were outraged by that. But one and a half years later that slogan became government policy. And in that respect there is a very important difference. Now we are not talking about local initiatives or something happening outside the law or against the law. Now they have made the criminalization of homelessness the law.'

Bálint casts his web widely when considering the potential constituency his organization serves. 'If you think of homelessness in a very strict sense, there are about 30,000 people, around half of whom live in Budapest,' he said. 'If you think of homelessness according to a broader definition, then you'd end up with numbers like 800,000 or even up to three million.' The larger number, which represents 30 percent of the Hungarian population, covers all those that Bálint says 'live in substandard housing, whose housing is overcrowded, or who are indebted and in danger of losing their homes.'

The precariat is another way of describing those who have not profited from the transition. Rather than appeal to all those who feel insecure, however, populist politicians have been more likely to pit one part of the precariat against another: pensioners versus the homeless, for instance, or the unemployed against the Roma. Scapegoating, a powerful political tool, is an integral part of the nationalist agenda: the transitions, they argue, were unsuccessful because of the Roma, the lazy, the foreigner. The precariat as a whole has not found its political representative, though Standing goes so far as to suggest that it has become the contemporary equivalent of the proletariat: a class that possesses a singularly transformative potential.

The ranks of the precariat have swelled in the last few years with the arrival of millions of refugees streaming out of conflict zones within reach of Europe, such as Afghanistan and Syria. The refugee crisis in Europe, which has provided right-wing populists with yet another stick with which to cudgel the EU bureaucracy, is part of a global catastrophe. Nearly sixty million people are now classified as refugees, more than at any time since such records have been kept, according to the UN Refugee Agency.[35] Every day, 45,000 people slip into the post-apocalyptic world of refugeedom. Every month, the equivalent of a San Diego joins the surplus army of the dispossessed. Thousands have died trying to make the passage by land and by sea from the Middle East and North Africa to Europe – nearly five thousand died in the Mediterranean crossing in 2016 alone, a significant increase over the year before.[36] Of the 1.3 million asylum seekers in Europe in 2015, nearly 100,000 were unaccompanied children.[37]

For the most part, the refugees have not managed to make it to eastern Europe (unless you count Greece as part of the region). Those who have traveled up through the Balkans have no desire to stay there, preferring to settle in Germany and Scandinavia. And populist politicians have worked hard to oppose EU proposals to more evenly distribute the burden of hosting refugees.

Peter Kamara was comparatively lucky to have made the crossing before the latest wave of refugees and before Hungary effectively shut down its borders. Coming by boat from Sierra Leone, Peter was dropped off somewhere along the European coast, probably Croatia, though he is not altogether certain. He and his group walked for four days and four nights with no map and nothing to eat, fearful of the sound of dogs and unwilling to approach strangers. Finally arriving in Hungary, he ended up in a refugee camp at Bicske, not far from Budapest. He was able to count on the help of a number of individuals and organizations who made it possible for him to stay and work in the country. He also began to put together a series of remarkable initiatives, starting with the Migrants' Help Association of Hungary. With nothing but his powers of persuasion, he was able to cobble together a computer-training course that provided refugees with job skills and some small measure of security.

'For a small organization, it was hard to keep going,' Peter told me. 'People want to give money to a more known and recognized organization. But I gave it my heart. And we were as economical as possible. But you could see the satisfaction on the faces of the refugees when they learned something. You could see their happiness when they accomplished something.'

His next project was the One Seat Project with universities in Budapest, which provides one free space to a migrant or a refugee to do a degree program. 'Many refugees and migrants are qualified to go to university,' Peter told me. 'But they don't have the opportunity. When I was at the camp, many people I met already had degrees from their home countries. But a university degree from a Third World country is not a ticket.'

Peter is not exactly a dissident. But his efforts are ultimately just as subversive as what the 1989 generation did.

He is changing the very demography of Hungary, transforming a relatively homogeneous society into something considerably more multicultural.

Exporting dissent

After 1989, some of the dissidents of eastern Europe went back to their original jobs as journalists or engineers or teachers. Others threw themselves into politics, as Václav Havel somewhat reluctantly did. The most exclusive minority were those who became professional dissidents.

Democracy, after all, did not triumph everywhere after 1989, not even everywhere in eastern Europe. There were still some tyrants to topple. Some of the experienced alumni of 1989, using skills honed over the years of underground activism, helped their friends in Serbia overthrow Slobodan Milošević. Others looked farther afield to the former Soviet Union, where the Color Revolutions beckoned. Still others could be glimpsed behind the scenes of the Arab Spring.

Deyan Kiuranov is a professional regime changer, though he is too modest to adopt that moniker for himself. He was deeply involved as a dissident in Bulgaria in the 1980s. After working in Bulgarian civil society after 1989, he went to Serbia to help out the anti-Milošević forces. When Milošević eventually fell, he turned his attention to Belarus.

'After the fall of Milošević, the Balkans were not really that interesting to me any more,' Deyan told me in Sofia. 'Before, I had been working with the Serbs trying to topple him in a peaceful way. And after that did miraculously happen, I had nothing to do. I was just going through the motions.' The authoritarian control Alexander Lukashenko exerted over Belarus represented an interesting challenge. 'I'm a very lazy guy,' Deyan said. 'I don't want to invent new behaviors after I invented the one for Bulgaria. In Serbia I was repeating more or less what I did here. In Belarus as well. In a sense, I'm not really a relic from the 1980s and beginning of the 1990s. As long as I'm working on the same situations, I'm not a relic.'

Slovaks were on the receiving end of regime-change assistance when they were trying to oust Vladimir Mečiar in the 1990s. After getting rid of Mečiar, Slovak activists participated in the campaigns to democratize Serbia and Croatia.[38] Many Slovaks traveled around the world to help NGOs learn how to monitor the media and the electoral process. 'Many people from transitional countries came to Slovakia to learn from our experience, and our activists are often invited abroad, and in the last two years, I was invited to do a training in civic organizing in Arab countries,' activist and former foreign minister Pavol Demeš explained. 'I hate to use the term "exporting models," because it is total nonsense. You can share and, if you are sensitive to their situation, they might adopt your suggestions.'

Slovak political scientist Michal Šimečka believes that Slovak NGOs often oversold their efforts in order to continue to receive foundation support for their work in other countries. Not only did this exaggeration slight the contributions of opposition politicians in Slovakia during the anti-Mečiar campaign, it could lead to geopolitical problems, for instance in the post-Soviet space. 'The interpretation that these revolutions were somehow manufactured by NGOs, with Western donors, fed into the Russian perspective that this was all somehow orchestrated by Washington,' he told me. 'Which wasn't necessarily the case.'

Still, some of the transnational connections were exhilarating, and the learning process was two-way. Rasto Kuzel, who learned how to monitor the media during the democratization campaigns in Slovakia in the 1990s, brought his expertise to Burma. 'We spent ten days in Mae Sot, in a rented house, doing training barefooted to follow the traditions,' he told me. 'Eating with these people and spending hours in discussions resulted in feeling that it wasn't me who was trying to share some experiences with them in media monitoring, but it was me who learned a big lesson about many things from them.'

Polish journalist Konstanty Gebert also worked with Burmese. 'About three years ago I spoke to this Burmese illegal migrant in Chiang Mai in Thailand,' he told me. 'This woman was a poor, semi-literature peasant from a village somewhere in Burma who had crossed the minefields, found a job, and taught herself some English. At a training on human rights, I spent a long time talking to her, which was difficult since I didn't speak her language and her English was poor. Finally, she said, "Listen, lady come and tell us human right. I go home. I think. Human right? I have right!" Wow. This is the one thing you can't achieve with texts. This is what's happening. A lot of disenfranchised people are now taking seriously what we have been saying all along, that everyone has rights. As for "trust us, we'll take good care of you," their answer now is "fuck no, we'll take care of ourselves.'"

It was inevitable that some of the old dissidents would, like Deyan and Rasto, continue in their old ways but in new settings. They were subject to the same QWERTY effect as the region as a whole: once embarked on a particular path, it was quite difficult to jump to another one. The heady days of democracy promotion have passed even though such efforts are by no means passé. The Arab Spring has given way to an autumn of patriarchs. Ukraine has become, like Georgia and Moldova, a frozen conflict. And throughout eastern Europe, democracy is again under assault, not by rogue autocrats like Vladimir Mečiar but by establishment politicians and parties.

These illiberal leaders have reached out to a constituency that the new dissidents have largely ignored: members of the majority who had lost economic status. They weren't members of the precariat or, at least, they didn't think of themselves that way. They didn't self-define as feminists. Unions didn't appeal to them. They didn't have a minority identity connected to ethnicity or sexual preference to serve as a basis for solidarity. They weren't energized by a set of issues like the environment or human rights. They were mostly concerned about their own 'pocketbook.' And they were susceptible to nationalist appeals.

This was Eastern Europe B. Quite often, the organizing of the new dissidents simply solidified the sentiments of this conservative, white, patriotic majority who felt that their interests were slighted in favor of one minority or another. This was, in some sense, a replay of the confrontation of the Cold War period between cosmopolitan dissidents and the conformist majority. Then, too, the ruling parties appealed to nationalism and cunningly deployed a version of economic populism to portray the minority of intellectuals or striking workers as enemies of the state. The current crop of illiberal democrats is heir to the communist tradition in more ways than one.

Such patterns of thinking run deep in the region. Some people choose the Terminal One strategy of just leaving the old conflicts behind. But there are other ways of thinking outside the box.

9
The Next Generation

Marie Landsberg barely remembers November 1989. She was only six years old. 'I understood that there was some change,' she recalled twenty-four years later, 'and I asked my mother, "What is happening, is everything okay?" And she said, "Yes, we will get some help from the West."'

It was either the night the Berlin Wall fell or the following night when her family piled into their tiny East German Trabant and visited West Berlin. Marie remembers a fruit shop, owned by a Turkish woman, which dazzled her with all the new sights and smells. This one night is more vivid in her memory than all the preceding years in East Germany. By the time she was ready for primary school, her country had disappeared. A *wendekind* – a child of the transition – Marie was part of a new generation of Germans who grew up in a unified country.

'At school when we did history, we didn't really deal with the GDR past,' Marie told me as we sat across from each other in 2013 at one of Berlin's co-working spaces. The schoolbooks were very one-sided, she recounted, all written from the Western perspective. 'It was like the teachers didn't know how to touch this topic because it was still so close,' she said. 'The first one that tried to touch the East–West situation, the GDR, and West Germany was a very young teacher from West Germany who tried to deal with it in the lessons. But he was also a bit insecure because he didn't want to touch anyone's emotions.'

Too young for East German communism to have made much of a mark on her, Marie could shrug off the past like a set of outgrown clothes. Except, as it turned out, she couldn't. She felt different from young people who'd grown up in the former West Germany. Sometimes it was in the way that people treated her as someone from 'over there.' For instance, when she visited Scandinavia as a teenager, Norwegians wouldn't bat an eye if she mentioned that she was German. But if she said she'd been born in East Germany, suddenly she became 'exotic.' The Norwegians 'have another perspective on all of this Iron Curtain history, on the role of America and the Soviet Union,' she told me. 'For them, we were part of the communist part so we were the former enemies. I have never seen it this way. For me we were never communistic.'

Marie's experience was not unique. 'I did not talk about my past often, because I did not want to be treated like an exotic bird,' journalist Sabine Rennefanz wrote in the *Guardian* twenty years after reunification. 'When people at some point found out where I grew up the reaction was always the same. They shrieked: "Oh, you don't really look like you are from the east." They had expected a granny perm, washed-out jeans at half mast and a Saxonian accent, a kind of *Fawlty Towers* version of an east German.'[1]

Marie also found confirmation of her experience in an organization for young Germans from East and West called Third Generation East. The organization's founder, Adriana Lettrari – who was also born in the GDR and was ten years old when the Wall fell – was inspired to form Third Generation East when she watched the television coverage of the twentieth anniversary of 1989. 'She just realized that there were the same old men sitting there discussing the collapse of the Wall and the time after,' Marie related. 'It was always the same people discussing East and West: always the same old men. She got angry, and I think that's an experience a lot of people in our generation had – a point where they really get angry about the one-sided narrative. People from the opposition in East Germany are heard and so are people from the West, from the old Federal Republic, with their very special Western, Cold War perspective. We are just different, and she thought that our perspective is needed in these discussions.'

What made the *wendekind* of the former GDR different, but not exotic, was partly the culture passed down through the family. Partly it was the economic disparity that still existed between the two Germanys, even a quarter-century after reunification. And partly it was the sense of being a minority within reunified Germany and, like many minorities, second-class citizens.

After hearing Lettrari talk about Third Generation East, Marie joined the staff and organized discussions among young people all around East Germany. From these conversations, she learned that her generation was tired of the silence of their elders. They wanted an honest conversation about the process of reunification, about the uglier parts of the past like the Stasi, what might have been admirable about East Germany, and what could be done to translate the concerns of the next generation into concrete policy.

'If you want to change the mind of the majority and you're a minority, you have to be very loud and bang your hand on the table and say, "Hey, listen to us, we have something to tell you and you should deal with it!"' Marie told me. 'All minorities have to be very loud, like the Turkish minority. If they want the majority to listen to them, they can't wait. We have to ask for it very strongly and show a lot of self-consciousness.' The comparison with the Turkish minority was not accidental. Third Generation East has more recently expanded its audience beyond ethnic Germans on both sides of the former Wall to include the children of immigrants.[2]

To demonstrate how reunification has successfully knitted together the two populations, some Germans will point to the careers of former East Germans like Angela Merkel (the long-serving chancellor), Joachim Gauck (the president from 2012 to 2017), or Antje Traue (the actress in *Man of Steel*). But as Sabine Rennefanz points out, Angela Merkel notwithstanding, 'East Germans represent 20% of the population but under 5% of the elite in politics, business, science and media.'[3] Only one of the politicians in Merkel's current cabinet was born in the East,[4] East German CEOs are rare,[5] and West Germans continue to dominate the leadership of trade unions, the judiciary, and universities in the eastern Länder twenty-five years after reunification.[6] The dominance of West Germans in the East is partly a function of numbers. A brain drain emptied out the former GDR after the Wall fell, as one in six eastern Germans moved westward in search of jobs during the first fourteen years.[7]

The initial exodus of young people from newly democratic East Germany anticipated the flow of young people from eastern Europe more generally. Over two million Poles, the majority of them young people, have left the country since the country joined the EU in 2004.[8] Romania's population has dropped by 3 million people since 1989, and Balkan countries rank at the very bottom of the World Economic Forum's list of nations according to their capacity to retain talent.[9] The flight of young people has become so severe in Hungary that the government passed a law requiring university graduates who received education grants from the state to stay in the country after graduation (which only pushed more students to study abroad).[10] Freedom of movement within the EU, which East Germans enjoyed after reunification in 1990, produced the same predictable result elsewhere: young people followed the money.

But not all young people have left, and not all young people have stayed abroad. A new generation has decided to clean up the messes created by previous generations.

Yanina Taneva is one of the returnees. Studying abroad, she learned about NGO culture in the West. Now she heads up a Bulgarian initiative called the Idea Factory. 'We started it in 2006,' she told me in the organization's headquarters in a Sofia apartment. 'Everything that we were watching as children on television, all this inequality, made us so angry, but we were kids and couldn't do anything. But some of us studied in universities outside Bulgaria and then came back. What we saw was huge injustice, especially regarding the environment. This topic became so well known in Bulgaria because we started a few campaigns that turned out to be huge. And people recognized in environmental problems everything they didn't accept for so many years: corruption, injustice, inequality, poverty.'

It all began when, having recently returned to Bulgaria, Yanina received a letter from a young girl about a plan to build a big hotel in a beautiful park area. 'We were watching "investments" coming in, and they were building on the Black Sea coast, these Russian, Irish, and UK "investors," destroying a lot of places that everyone loves,' Yanina told me. 'Bulgarians have grown up camping because there isn't much else to do. This culture of camping is quite beloved. This girl was the first one to talk about stopping the hotel project. Many of us were thinking this but didn't know how to act. So, three or four of us formed the core of a group. I was coming from advertising and PR, so I used the skills I knew. Others came from web design so they designed the website.'

Yanina and her friends managed to create a new culture of activism. 'Until that moment, after socialism, "activist" was a very dirty word that you didn't want to be linked to,' she continued. 'We managed to make activism cool, particularly for young people. We had a twenty-four-hour party so that everyone could come, including mothers with children. We tried to reach everyone. At that time, there was no Facebook, so it was hard to do it so easily. We used our contacts with the media. We made a statement that was really clear. We were the first to say that we just weren't accepting these things.'

The younger generation has been a force for change in part because it refuses to accept the status quo as a given. Young people are motivated by what the literary theorist Viktor Shklovsky once called the 'energy of delusion.'[11] If we knew the true magnitude of a task beforehand, we wouldn't undertake it in the first place. Thus, the older we get, and the more experience of challenge and failure that we endure, the less likely we are to attempt the impossible. In a region that elected very young prime ministers in an effort to transcend the politics of the past – Stanislav Gross was thirty-four when he became Czech prime minister in 2004, Pandeli Majko only thirty when he became Albanian prime minister in 1998, and Milo Djukanović only twenty-nine when he became Montenegro's prime minister in 1991 – it's not surprising that young people would prove to be the pivotal change agents in the non-governmental sphere as well.

The next generation has been instrumental in implementing the third type of transformation in their countries after politics and economics. This third transformation involves how people think. Yanina has put together a 'Changemaker Academy' to build 'the capacity for change, helping people build whatever they want to build: an initiative, an NGO, a social enterprise, an informal group,' she said. 'We acquaint them with the theories, with experiential learning, with the people they need to know. We also put it all into the global context. People here think that Bulgaria is the worst place on earth to live. But I think there are a lot of social resources here.' Yanina and her colleagues are using culture, particularly the arts and the media, to build informal networks, strengthen solidarity, and ultimately change culture.

Michal Šimečka has gone off on a different path than either Yanina or Marie, and it has something to do with his lineage. His grandfather, Milan, was a famous dissident in Czechoslovakia who, before he died unexpectedly in 1990, served as a trusted advisor to Václav Havel. Michal's father Martin is a famous journalist and novelist, and his mother Marta is a key civil society activist in Bratislava. Michal went to London for a PhD and then to Brussels to serve as a foreign policy advisor to members of the European Parliament. He too represents a generation that is fully comfortable in a new European space that doesn't recognize the divisions between east and west.

'The main defining political struggle of my parents' generation was around values such as democracy and freedom against autocracy, against the state, but also against nationalism and other poisonous forces in politics,' Michal told me over cups of hot chocolate in downtown Bratislava when he was home on a family visit in 2013. 'Politics was defined by the struggle between these two very broad camps or set of ideas. I think this is an outdated paradigm. At some point we have to stop fighting for democracy and start looking at other aspects.'

For his grandfather's generation, the challenge was to transform communism. His parents were also involved in that struggle, but after 1989 they campaigned against Vladimir Mečiar's brand of authoritarian nationalism. Michal, however, operates at the European level. 'Today, there are new challenges and new problems that can't be conceptualized along this dimension of good democrats versus bad autocrats,' he said. 'Obviously the European crisis is such a problem. The entire concept of democracy requires some rethinking at the European level. The biggest challenge, institutionally, is to fashion a democracy at the EU level.'[12] Michal's words would prove prophetic when the British voted in June 2016 to leave the European Union in part because of perceptions that the EU was not sufficiently democratic.

The great unease among young people in Europe today can be measured in a variety of ways. The protests that have swept the continent over the last couple of years – the *indignados* in Spain, the Occupy demonstrations, the anti-austerity demonstrations in Greece, the *Nuit Debout*

(Up All Night) protests in France against a more neoliberal labor law – brought young people into the streets to voice their anger over their diminished economic prospects. According to a Gallup poll in 2013, an overwhelming number of young people around the continent believe that their lives will be worse off than those of their parents.[13]

In eastern Europe after 1989, most people thought that the transitions would last a few years, maybe a decade. Now they realize that catching up will take at least a generation, if not more. 'For me, this whole period of transition, well, they say "transition," but I don't see the end of it coming,' Maya Mircheva, a young Bulgarian woman, told me in 2012. 'It's been twenty years. It's the longest transition in history! I can see that young people are very disillusioned. They lack this spark. They don't feel that anything depends on them or that they can do anything to change the world.'

Maya Mircheva, Marie Landsberg, Yanina Taneva, and Michal Šimečka are part of this pivotal generation, with one foot in the past and one in the future. They function at very different levels and grapple with very different issues than did the architects of the 1989 transformations. They must operate within inherited structures. But they are extraordinarily lucky not to be trapped in the sterile political categories of their parents. In the words of one Polish poet, 'our generation won the lottery.'[14]

The new generation is not necessarily a liberal one. Many young people don't care about politics much at all. Fewer young people are voting in European Parliament elections:

only 28 percent in 2014, down from 33 percent in 2005.[15] At the same time, support has surged among young people for extremist politics on the right, with the neo-fascist Golden Dawn organizing in the public schools in Greece and Jobbik attracting considerable youth support in Hungary. A 2012 report on 'subterranean politics' in Europe argues that young people are focusing their dissatisfaction at political elites, which explains their affinity for populism.[16]

Liberalism, after all, became the received wisdom, the ideology of an older generation of political and economic leaders. Ultimately the failure of this ideology can be traced to its inability to appeal to the next generation.

Young republicans

Poland has never been a particularly liberal country. In other words, its political culture has not traditionally focused on the individual or individual rights. Consider the great confrontation of the 1980s: between the collectivist ideology of the Communist Party and the spirit of solidarity of the opposition. Both sides were animated by older republican virtues – a focus on the public good. It's telling that in those days communist-leaning intellectuals read the daily *Rzeczpospolita* while the opposition read the underground *Res Publica*, both titles deriving from the Latin for 'public thing.' Neither side embraced liberal-style economics or promoted liberal-style political institutions either. That would come later.

'The Polish tradition has no liberal traits. That was an intellectual import during the 1990s,' Jan Filip Staniłko told me over coffee in Warsaw's Old Town in 2013. 'The only heritage of original thinking in Poland, original in the sense that it has deeply rooted origins, is republicanism. It is rooted in the fifteenth and sixteenth centuries, and it lasted politically, in terms of institutions, until the end of first Polish Republic. But in Polish culture, it lasted much longer, until the end of the nineteenth century, and it was a fundamental part of the intelligentsia's state of mind. That means that every member of the intelligentsia, even if they were a peasant or worker in origin, was somehow republican in thinking, with the notion of the common good at center.'

Jan is the conservative version of Sławek Sierakowski, the founder of Krytyka Polityczna. Young, energetic, well versed in philosophy and political science, Jan has worked with several think tanks in Poland, including the Warsaw Institute for Economic Studies (WISE). He is very much the public intellectual. He was instrumental in organizing the Great Poland Project, a right-wing forum for ideas. He is equally comfortable talking about the big picture and burrowing down into specific policy proposals. And he is often scathing in his critique of the trajectory of Polish politics over the last two decades.

'There was no general shaping vision of how Poland was supposed to look after twenty years. Since 2007 we've had five hundred strategic documents in Poland. That means we've had no strategy,' he told me. 'For these twenty years, we used Western intellectual tools to transform ourselves. One part of the elite – the leftist parties – wanted to transform into something that is Western, European, pro-choice. And the right part of the elite wants to *rediscover*, which means to anchor us in some parts of our history and recreate a new spirit.'

Jan aims his critique at both the leadership and the political machine that enacts policy. He suggests that the challenges facing Poland require the kind of 'adaptive leadership' that public policy guru Ronald Heifetz has articulated for the business and non-profit world.[17] 'You have lots of reengineering in corporations because they must move fast,' Jan continued. 'The proper leader should help workers adapt to changes. We have in a similar way a huge transformation in Poland, but people still have not adapted to the effects of transformation. It's only been twenty years. How long did it take France to adapt to the French Revolution? A hundred years at least. We must as a society adapt to the effects of transformation and then adapt to the challenges of globalization at the same time. We don't need a leader who will punish everyone. We need a leader to help people to adapt, for instance to help them migrate within Poland rather than to another country.'

Jarosław Kaczyński, the leader of the Law and Justice Party (PiS), could be just such a leader, according to Jan. 'I know Kaczyński, and I like him,' he said. 'He's a very brilliant politician ... but he is somehow a quixotic person. He is also an old-fashioned conservative in a psychological sense.

He's afraid of having young, fast, innovative people in power. They like him, but he is afraid of them ... If he becomes prime minister, he will succeed if he nominates young, dynamic people and protects them.' Kaczyński, the supreme representative of the Solidarity generation, could only succeed with the help of the next generation, Jan believed. Indeed, when PiS did return to power in 2015, Kaczyński installed someone a generation younger – fifty-two-year-old Beata Szydło – as prime minister. She in turn chose a significant number of cabinet members her age or younger.

Because liberalism became the status quo in Poland in the 1990s, conservatives became the insurgents, the ones who want radical change in the 2000s. Michał Łuczewski is a sociologist who works closely with a Catholic think tank in Warsaw connected to the thinking of Polish pope John Paul II. 'I'm not conservative in the American meaning,' Michał told me in his office, which was a stone's throw from where I'd met with Krytyka Polityczna staff. 'And I'm not conservative in the sense that I want to conserve reality. I would say, in contrast, that my liberal friends here are actually conservative. *Gazeta Wyborcza*, for example, is the most conservative journal in Poland because they try to conserve what happened in Poland twenty-three years ago. They say: we brought you through the democratic breakthrough, and you now have the free market and democracy, so just shut up and listen to us. This is a conservative type of thinking. They are trying to pacify the masses. They are afraid of any kind of populism.'

Part of the rejection of liberalism, then, involves a generational distrust of the status quo. The liberalism that became orthodoxy in eastern Europe in the 1990s was initially a radical ideology that swept away institutions, challenged received values of family and community through its promotion of individualism, and even altered conceptions of the nation by facilitating membership in the supranational European Union. As the market took hold and democracy became established practice, and as Poland lost a fraction of its sovereignty through EU membership, some portion of the younger generation began to grow uncomfortable with what their parents had put in place. So had an earlier generation of young people rejected the communism of their elders and an even earlier generation of communist activists opposed the stuffy liberalism – or the more dangerous right-wing extremism – of the 1930s and 1940s.

In Hungary, a similar rejection of liberalism took place with the wide margin of victory of Fidesz in the 2010 elections. Journalist Paul Lendvai, a longtime observer of Hungarian society, has pointed out that the political parties that guided the country after 1989, the more liberal Alliance of Free Democrats and the more conservative Democratic Forum, were both thoroughly discredited by the economic programs they implemented and the corruption they tolerated (or in some cases encouraged). Young people, in particular, craved something new, Lendvai wrote in 2012: 'No fewer than three-quarters of young people believe in the possibility of a new system change with the renationalization of key companies and a reckoning with the guilty politicians who have so damaged the country.'[18]

Fidesz captured some of this constituency. But having won a parliamentary majority in 2010 by abandoning its original youthful base and appealing to an older, more traditionally conservative generation, it had become a party of stuffed shirts. Young people who wanted a more disruptive conservatism turned instead to the far-right Jobbik. 'As a journalist I witnessed how Jobbik first emerged on the street, occupying the street, and that's partly how they became cool,' journalist Szilvia Varró told me. 'They began to use social media. In the beginning of 2000s, they gradually became mainstream.' By mainstream, she meant that they used mainstream tactics to make their extremism socially acceptable. Jobbik's cultivation of an 'outlaw' image added considerably to its appeal. According to an April 2016 poll, Jobbik was the clear favorite of the young people surveyed: 53 percent of fifteen- to thirty-four-year-olds said they'd vote for Jobbik compared to only 17 percent for second-place Fidesz.[19] Young people in particular perceive the party as an alternative to the government, even though the platforms of Jobbik and Fidesz overlap considerably.[20]

Jobbik is by no means a republican organization as Jan Filip Staniłko would describe it. But it is comparably anti-liberal in its suspicion of capitalist elites, cosmopolitan influences that erode Hungarian culture, and the democratic politics that produced corrupt elites and dysfunctional institutions. By appealing to countryside values, it also reflects an urban–rural divide in Hungarian politics – *népi–urbánus* – that has prevailed since the nineteenth century.

In Slovakia, meanwhile, the conservatives are not in power. The ruling party, Smer, defines itself as social democratic. Yet it shares many of the same positions as PiS and Fidesz, particularly when it comes to economics. Slovak prime minister Robert Fico, who has dominated the country's politics since first taking office in 2006, has coopted the populist spirit that might have powered a conservative opposition. He has railed against immigrants, tilted the country away from the EU and toward Russia, and expressed considerable skepticism about 'wild capitalism.'

Eva Ohrablová is a young woman who has worked on a number of political campaigns for right-wing parties in Slovakia. The left and the right are distinguished not by issues, she argues, but by the fact that the former is 'united' and the latter is 'broken.'

'The problem is that nobody has a vision nowadays,' she explained to me over coffee at a café in Bratislava. 'With the leftists ruling now, the people on the right side think, "We can't do anything because they are in charge." Even though the politicians on the right side of the spectrum say something, nobody listens. They have no power, so people think that, "Why are you talking if you can't change anything?"' This cynicism has particularly affected young Slovaks, she added.

Young liberals

Liberalism took a beating in Poland in the twentieth century. It was overwhelmed by nationalism in the 1930s, by Nazi occupation in the 1940s, and by a succession of communist governments during the Cold War period. Finally, when the full political spectrum was restored to the country after 1989, liberalism became almost exclusively associated with its neoliberal variant. For most Poles, 'liberal' meant economic austerity and its accompanying hardships, which did little to rescue its reputation.

But a new generation of political actors in Poland has taken up the challenge of rescuing liberalism from these particular associations. *Kultura Liberalna* is a weekly magazine established in 2009. It has spawned a website as well as an intellectual circle that has attracted a younger set of academics and intellectuals who are committed to restoring liberalism to its fullest meaning.

'We're convinced that liberalism had been one of the victims of the "holy transformation,"' Karolina Wigura, a young woman who heads up the political section of Kultura Liberalna, explained to me in the organization's offices in Warsaw in 2013 when Civic Platform (PO) was still in power. 'Not in the meaning that this state is not liberal. It's of course liberal, and it has its flaws like every state. But the meaning of liberalism, which is never clear in any political culture, is rather fuzzy here.'

The mission of Kultura Liberalna is, in some sense, to bring clarity to what has been a very opaque discussion in Poland. 'Here, when you say "liberal," you think "economics" and "free market" and that's all,' Karolina continued. 'So, first we try to show that liberalism is a very rich tradition. When we think of liberalism, we think of it as complicated as Isaiah Berlin or Alexis de Tocqueville showed it to be. But on the other hand, we also think that our experience of this region is central to our understanding of European liberalism ... This means that a region that has been touched by totalitarian systems, which are very well described in Timothy Snyder's *Bloodlands* or Tony Judt's *Postwar*, has a special idea or feeling of liberalism that is constructed of skepticism toward any radical ideologies plus a belief in personal freedom and an empathy for social problems.'

This combination of skepticism and empathy is both a political and an intellectual approach. The atmosphere of Kultura Liberalna is one of questioning, not of rebellion. It is the latest incarnation of a political-intellectual lineage, and it tries to honor that lineage rather than reject it.

'We have always been challenged by our elders,' Karolina said with a smile. 'They have always asked, "Why don't you just rebel against us? Why are you so polite? What's wrong with you?" This is a generational thing. We don't oppose the former generation. Every milieu has its own approach. In Kultura Liberalna we try to understand more than to propose. Also, there is a strong conviction that if you just focus on your father you will never go forward. You just have to create your own things.'

For other young Poles, liberalism continues to be the vehicle their country can use to rejoin the mainstream of European thought.

'We must get our country from the periphery, where it's been since the sixteenth or seventeenth century, and back into the core,' Leszek Jażdżewski told me. Like Karolina Wigura, he is part of the younger generation of intellectuals who are trying to remake liberalism in their own image, in this case a European one. 'We're in the EU so we're in some sense in the core, but it may not last for ever. Because of our history there should be more Europhiles among Poles. We can't afford not to be engaged in Europe. The discussion of the future of Poland separate from the future of the whole continent is pointless.'

Above all, Leszek and his journal, *Liberte!*, are devoted to maintaining liberalism against its illiberal challenges – in Poland and in the region. Movements like Fidesz or PiS, he argued, 'seek support in democratic elections but want to dismantle the whole constitutional system of liberal democracy that was widely supported in this region in the 1990s, with the exception of Slovakia at certain moments. The support for political liberalism is declining almost everywhere. Here we are trying to call ourselves liberals without adding another adjective to it: social or conservative or neo.'

Leszek is not interested in simply replicating the liberal politics of the current crop of politicians. 'Most of the 1989 generation who were in their twenties when the change happened didn't really get engaged in politics,' he told me. 'Some of them were in the media. Most of them went into business, the most talented ones at least. A lot of my colleagues are not in politics but in NGOs, think tanks, and publications. A lot of young people are doing an amazing job in the NGO sector. The ones in politics, however, are shadows of their elder colleagues. They were carrying their suitcases, as we say. That's not the way to create real leaders. My generation, which is too young to take over any time soon, would be quite different from our decade-older colleagues. We, the children born during martial law, were the generation of the demographic peak. We are a generation of limited expectations.'

Young radicals

Liberalism isn't much of an option in Hungary. Fidesz embraced the concept and then discarded it. The liberal party, Alliance of Liberal Democrats, withered away. Young people who find the status quo unacceptable and Jobbik's challenge of it even worse have gravitated farther leftward.

The Student Network in Hungary, for instance, has been one of the most vocal and visible opponents of the Fidesz government. In Hungarian, the network has a memorable name: HaHa (Hallgatói Hálózat). Formed a year after Viktor Orbán and Fidesz regained power in 2010, HaHa has focused on the government's education reforms, opposing proposed cuts in state support and requirements to remain and work in Hungary after graduation. They've engaged in various forms of resistance, including street demonstrations and an occupation strike at one of the top universities.

Student activists have not restricted their actions to education reform. HaHa also conducted a flash mob occupation of the Ministry of Human Resources to protest against the government's opaque bureaucratic approach.[21] Many members participated in an occupation of Fidesz headquarters in 2013. And students have been a critical part of the homeless advocacy group Bálint Misetics formed.

HaHa 'has grown much bigger than we could have imagined two years ago,' Csaba Jelinek, a student activist who worked with the group, told me in 2013. 'Those who formed the group were ideologically oriented at the beginning. Then the Network started to become more practical and attracted younger students. These younger students were more practice-oriented. They made it very big this year, when we older ones left the movement. We were on the front page of the conservative *Magyar Nemzet* newspaper every day last January. We were accused of being financed by Soros and the Jews and the Americans.'

Romania is perhaps the last place to expect an independent left to take root. Unlike in Poland or Hungary or Yugoslavia, a critical socialist movement didn't emerge in response to the orthodox communists in power. And the social democrats that crawled from the wreckage of the 1989 revolution – first as part of the National Salvation Front and then in their own Social Democratic Party – embraced a politically and economically conservative platform. They signal left, as the Romanian joke goes, but turn right.

Liberalism, meanwhile, had a limited appeal. 'Liberalism never really took root after 1989,' political theorist Florin Poenaru told me. 'It was a tiny minority of people, some of whom have become more open to left ideas and more critical of these conservatives. Liberals never really had a response to 1989 and didn't build a genuine counterforce to this conservatism.'

Ágnes Gagyi was one of those young people who gravitated to the left. Born into the Hungarian minority in Romania, she was 'raised in an atmosphere of "socialism with a human face,"' she told me. She wasn't political as a teenager. At university in Cluj, she cared only about theories like deconstructionism. 'Then I started to realize that these theories didn't help me understand the world I was living in,' she continued. 'But I also couldn't find a political environment that felt relevant. In those days, as a member of the Hungarian minority, you had to choose which side of the ethnic divide you wanted to work on, and I didn't feel that that was the way the world was structured.'

Only when she began to study the anti-globalization movement did her political education begin: 'When I was twenty, I began to meet these activists that were traveling around in eastern Europe, people who came from the left activist environment in the West … Then, as luck would have it, a Norwegian NGO called Patrir that was connected to Johan Galtung bought a house and began some activities in Cluj. They brought along a fantastic library from Chomsky to David Harvey. I read that through. But I still had the problem that I didn't have anyone to talk to about it. With my friends, if I started to talk about these things, they just laughed at me.'

Eventually she found a home with a coalescing New Left. A group of young intellectuals – academics, journalists, writers – launched CriticAtac in Romania to discuss 'banks, the health system, trade unions, state institutions and services, elections, public policies, the Church, urbanism and any other topics of major public interest' and to do so 'without academicism, snobbery or preciousness,' according to one of the coordinators, journalist and writer Costi Rogozanu. The group's irreverence is evident in its own self-description: 'Our ideology is leftist, but we are not a sect and we don't go around patting each other on our backs for the brilliant and concerted line of our ideas.'[22]

At a café in the park across from the massive parliament building in Bucharest, Costi told me about his own political trajectory. 'I had a liberal approach,' he said of his school years. 'Liberalism was the mark of progress. Every young guy wanted to be this way. We would talk all day long about rights. This was the only way back then in the mid-1990s.' He finished university and became a journalist. As he began to encounter a wide range of social problems, he moved to the left. 'So many things that happened in the 1990s I couldn't explain with the liberal approach,' he told me.

The 1990s were not a particularly happy time for most Romanians. The country suffered a large drop in GDP, and unemployment rose sharply into the double digits. 'The liberal story was of moving forward with free market and privatization,' Costi explained. 'But these things were catastrophes for sixty percent of the people. There was also a lack of transparency about what happened with these processes. This was enraging for young guys like me and my friends. We conducted some anti-mainstream strikes when we were at the college in Bucharest. All our professors were liberal. They all said that we had to suffer in order to get to the free market in a good, neoliberal way.'

Yet CriticAtac has failed to capitalize on all the dissatisfaction in the country. 'We cannot have manifestations because we don't have power of any kind,' Costi lamented. 'We're just writers. We have some good people on the academic side, but they are not very powerful. We don't have important jobs or big support from parties … We want to create something new, so this will take some more time.' When mass demonstrations broke out in Romania in early 2017, they didn't address the larger economic agenda of CriticAtac but instead focused almost entirely on the corrupt practices of the ruling party, one of the successors to the National Salvation Front that guided the country through the transition in 1990.

The radicalism on the right, meanwhile, has proved equally appealing, if not more so, to the young generation in the region. It's not just Jobbik in Hungary and Ataka in

Bulgaria that have made inroads with youth. In Poland, Janusz Korwin-Mikke has attracted a considerable following among young people with his libertarian and Euroskeptical views. 'They find appealing his radicalism and political incorrectness as well as his being against the mainstream,' Michał Sutowski told me. 'This is a legacy of post-communism. Most of the critique of capitalism after 1989 was right-wing. It criticized not capitalism itself but the post-communist version of it. The problem was not capital but the "red capitalists" who inherited or stole wealth to make their careers in the late 1980s.'

In Croatia, the younger generation is more nationalist-oriented than even their parents. Human rights activist Tin Gazivoda told me about 2010 data that showed how high school students who grew up in the 1990s 'have more intolerant positions than their parents. It's not a surprise: They grew up in a war environment and with textbooks shaped by that context.'

The next generation in eastern Europe has not gotten behind a single ideology. But whatever group young people join, they've largely rejected the orthodox liberalism handed down by those who constructed the post-1989 order. The republicans and extremists have challenged this neoliberalism from the right; the radicals have launched their critiques from the left. Even liberals, like those around Kultura Liberalna, have been busy trying to distinguish their version of liberalism from what has become so discredited in the public sphere.

What does unite the new generation, however, is a belief that their experiences and viewpoints are distinct from those of the older generation and their voices must be heard. Moreover, whatever they might think about European integration, they have grown up with all the benefits (and responsibilities) of EU membership. And, like Yanina, many of them are returning to their countries in the hope of making a difference. As with all up-and-coming generations, they must decide whether to reform the existing order or create new worlds on the foundations, ruined or otherwise, of the old.

10
Creating New Worlds

It was a prison during the Austro-Hungarian Empire. Then it served as a barracks for the Yugoslav National Army. By the end of the 1980s, the half-dozen buildings sat empty on over 12,000 square meters of prime real estate in Ljubljana, the tidy, compact, and colorful capital of Slovenia. The abandoned complex was called Metelkova, after a nearby street, and the anarchists had their eye on it. The problem was, the city intended to demolish the site and turn it over to developers. Slovenian anti-war activist Marko Hren was part of the band of anarchists who occupied Metelkova beginning in 1993. They demanded that the city turn the property over to them as the previous communist regime had promised.

In 2012, I met with Marko at a café located at one corner of the Metelkova complex. Short, blond, and boyish despite his years, he bears a passing resemblance to the actor Steve Zahn. He was acutely conscious of the importance of Metelkova, and of his role in it.

'We are at the present cultural center on Metelkova Street, which used to be the Yugoslav Army headquarters but has been turned into an open agora through a grassroots action,' Marko told me. 'It's a living monument to the Slovenian Spring. The project was led by hundreds of groups and individuals that were active in the 1980s locally in Slovenia. It's a result of a project that began before the war and which symbolically speaks to that period of time. I was an initiator and a head of the project here.'

During the Slovenian Spring that began in 1987, a nonviolent movement campaigned for a democratic, independent country. At the time, the demands seemed outlandish: federal Yugoslavia would never permit such a thing. But two years later, in the same month that the Berlin Wall fell, the Slovenian government introduced a multiparty system that set into motion the changes that would culminate in independence. It was this government of reform communists that promised Metelkova to a rainbow coalition of civil society organizations. By 1992, however, a more market-oriented government took over that had no intention of honoring that agreement. The land held too much commercial value. On 9 September 1993, the city sent over the demolition crew.[1]

Marko and his fellow squatters moved in to protest against the decision. They occupied the half-dozen buildings and erected walls to keep out the bulldozers. Artists flocked to the site and covered the compound with art. Musicians showed up to play concerts.[2] The city retaliated by cutting off the supply of electricity and water. The occupation lasted for days, then weeks, then months.

'It was really difficult to survive at Metelkova at the beginning,' squat supporter Jelka Zorn told me. 'I slept over a couple times. Maybe if I didn't have a place to live, probably I would have stayed there. But it was not so easy. No electricity, no water. You had to figure out your own way to shower, to cook. We had to sit in meetings with candles. At the beginning it was fun, but after a while it was annoying.'

'The conversion of the Metelkova barracks was very difficult,' Marko confessed. 'We faced lobbyists from the city and from the construction lobby. We were in the squat for years without electricity – from 1993 to 1995 – and it was a very tough time. On one hand there was the apocalypse in the Balkans and our feeling that we had failed, that genocide was our failure, Europe's failure. And on the other hand there was the squat and lots of drug addicts because the only methadone center was on the street here. We were located in a center of urban pathology.'

But the squatters persisted. By 1996, the site again had electricity and running water. It was sponsoring more than a thousand events a year, including a women's festival and a punk gathering known throughout the world. The city succeeded in knocking down one of the Metelkova buildings in 1997, but the squatters, now well organized, held on.

Ultimately, the two sides came to an agreement worthy of King Solomon. The property was divided in half, with the city administering one part and civil society the other. Both halves, however, were decidedly public. On the city side, the authorities built a new contemporary art museum and offices for the Ministry of Culture, with a large, open square stretching between the buildings. When I visited on a sunny autumn day in 2012, the square was very nearly empty and, despite an excellent collection, so was the museum.

On the civil society side, meanwhile, Metelkova looked like something out of a Terry Gilliam movie. Outlandish sculptures sprouted from the ground and the walls of buildings. Colorful murals and graffiti decorated nearly every surface. Several buildings housed music clubs. The largest building was devoted to NGOs, including the Peace Institute, which led the legal effort on behalf of the Erased. The actual prison had been rehabbed and rechristened the youth hostel Celica, each of the two dozen cells redesigned by an architect and an interior decorator according to a different theme: an updated jail cell, a devotional space featuring niches from the six major world religions, the 'Russian cell' with a huge fresco, the room that doubled as an art gallery.

'Nowadays cultural, educational, social and other activities are taking place there, but no one lives there any more,' reports Jelka. 'Unfortunately for the younger generation, it is just a place of fun and excessive drinking. Therefore one part inside Metelkova is called the Square without Historical Memory – *Trg brez zgodovinskega spomina* – because many people have obviously not grasped the conceptual and historical meaning of the place.'

Marko also has a mixed assessment of the project. 'Our ambition was to revitalize the urban structures. And now here in Metelkova, we've got the biggest NGO cluster in Europe, the biggest urban infrastructure for NGOs and artists in Europe,' he told me. On the other hand, he was disappointed with what he calls the 'lazy, comfort-zone elite' that emerged from the squatter community. 'I did not understand the problem of caste divisions until after I cut my teeth with the constituency at Metelkova,' he continued. 'Why are they so lazy? Why don't they want to create enterprises to survive? How come we can't make cooperatives and earn money for our survival and for self-sustainability? These were the questions that I posed to myself, and the answer to them is: "Because they don't need to." They go home to eat out of the refrigerators of their parents and then come back to party.'

Both halves of Metelkova, the city-run museum area and the anarchic NGO and music club area, have become an established part of the city. 'One half is nice and clean, with yellow façades, and a big open space in the middle, but it's dead,' anthropologist and activist Sara Pistotnik told me over beers at the best place in Ljubljana for the grilled meatballs known as ćevapčići. 'The other half, the autonomous half, is changing all the time, and so many things are happening there.'

But even this autonomous half of Metelkova has become too conventional for a younger generation of activists, including Sara. Since March 2006, she and others have occupied Rog, a second site less than half a mile away. Rog was an abandoned bicycle factory, and the city had plans for it as well. 'It was closed at the beginning of the transition and had sat empty for fifteen years,' Sara told me. 'Nobody bothered with it. Then various groups came together and decided to open Rog. We only planned to use it temporarily until the municipality decided what to do with it.'

Like Metelkova, Rog attracted activists and artists. But it also aspired to create a new kind of social arrangement. 'The main structure here is the Rog Assembly,' Sara continued. 'We are non-hierarchical. We are also trying to work on a new concept of the commons that goes beyond public and private.' Toward that end, Sara and others have transformed the factory into a lively space. The venue that hosts concerts is called, evocatively, the Hall of Sighs. Readings and theater performances take place in the Blue Corner while visual art can be seen in the Endless Gallery. The facility boasts two indoor skateboard parks and even a trapeze for circus workshops.[3] In a side building, the Social Center tackles pressing political issues, such as the rights of foreign workers led by a new IWW, the Invisible Workers of the World. 'Rog and Metelkova are also in the middle of the city for a purpose,' Sara observes. 'They would be on the periphery if they wanted just to make a commune of self-contained people.'

As with Metelkova, the city of Ljubljana has wanted to cut a deal with Rog according to its own vision of a public–private partnership. In 2008, it decided to build a new complex that consisted of two skyscrapers with shops and high-end apartments, an underground parking garage, and a contemporary art center. 'It's not what we wanted – something for the common good,' Sara said. 'Only a small percentage of the center will be public, and the rest would be private. You see, this factory is from the beginning of last century. The city can't tear it down because of historic preservation. They can't tear it down, but they also don't want strange people living inside.'

Sara was worried about the site's future. 'Rog is more precarious because of Metelkova, because it's only five hundred meters away,' she explained. 'One reason to tear down Rog is that Metelkova exists, and a city like Ljubljana doesn't need another squat as big as this. On the other hand, because Metelkova is more established in the city and has its own history, it's also positive for Rog, because of all the positive effects of Metelkova on the city itself.'

The global financial crisis in 2008 saved Rog. The city wanted to go ahead with its public–private venture, but private investors were no longer so enthusiastic. 'The crisis hit Slovenia quite hard, especially in the construction sector,' Sara noted. 'It's hard to get anyone to invest in such a risky plan. Until they get a private investor, we're quite safe.' For a few years at least. In summer 2016, its finances more secure, the city moved once again to demolish Rog, and the activists prepared to counter the bulldozers. After mobilizing local activists and international support, Rog was just able to keep the developers at bay.

Metelkova and Rog are two of a diminishing number of social experiments that emerged after 1989. Throughout eastern Europe, even before the collapse of the Berlin Wall, young people and anarchists and critical intellectuals set up alternative communities that functioned like autonomous worlds, what Slovak social scientists used to call 'islands of positive deviation.'[4] Former dissident Ladislav Snopko fondly remembers a group of seven huts in the north of Slovakia, by the Polish border in a region called Brizgalky, where dissidents would meet up on weekends. 'These places in nature used to serve as basic communication stimuli for Czech and Slovak people with similar thinking,' he told me. In Slovenia, the OHO group of artists retreated from the mainstream to construct their own back-to-nature intentional community.[5] In Hungary as well, the Eastern-bloc equivalent of hippies formed communes in the 1970s,[6] while novelists and poets who refused to follow the dictates of the government created their own 'republic of writers.' Poles set up 'flying universities' during the 1970s, underground classrooms that provided alternative education and were patterned on a similar experiment from the nineteenth century.

In East Berlin, Marxist critics of the socialist state in the late 1960s created a commune based on the famous Kommune I of West Berlin, but it didn't last long.[7] Later, dissidents Gerd and Ulrike Poppe joined together with a group of friends to establish an independent kindergarten in the early 1980s that existed for three years before the authorities destroyed it. As the Wall came down, these islands of positive deviation spread throughout the city. The House for Democracy once housed most of the East German civil society groups in 1990. It not only still exists but is at least three times larger in its new location. In Prenzlauer Berg, an innovative space called Adventure Playground, which started in April 1990, is still around, its wild area featuring an open fire, a forge, and a sand pit where children build (and destroy) their own structures.

Alternative spaces continue to thrive in former Yugoslavia. The Subversive Festival in Croatia has become such a fixture of cultural life that the mainstream media devotes considerable space to its coverage. The *Feral Tribune*, a satirical weekly that started in Split in 1993 and skewered the nationalist pretensions of Croatia's ruling HDZ party, folded in 2008, but many of the writers continue to contribute to a Serbian-language newspaper published in Zagreb. In Belgrade, meanwhile, the Center for Cultural Decontamination, established in 1994, still provokes public fascination and outrage, for instance when it sponsored a photo exhibit, *Ecce Homo*, in 2013 that featured Jesus in various LGBT tableaux.

Tying together all these disparate postcommunist movements is a search for solidarity – the revival of mutual support networks sundered by the market economy's emphasis on the individual. The days of such mass movements as Solidarity are, at least for the moment, over. But activists and artists continue to imagine new worlds: in the squats of Ljubljana, the political organizing of radical NGOs, and the cheeky output of contemporary artists throughout the region. This isn't dissent, exactly, since it's not just about critiquing the existing order. It's about building something entirely new.

Eastern Europe has long been a locale for dystopias on the ground and utopias of the spirit. Many in the region were initially drawn to communism because of its promise of a new world – and a 'new man' – that transcended the horrors of World War II. That same utopian spirit, taken down a notch or two, inspired various reform efforts, most notably the Czech effort to create 'socialism with a human face' that animated the Prague Spring of 1968. The collapse of communism in 1989 appeared to signal the end of such utopian aspirations in favor of pragmatic reality. 'As communism helped to wipe out alternative socialisms, the dystopia of real existing socialism helped destroy the appeal of utopia itself,' writes sociologist Michael Kennedy. 'Real existing socialism created only the eutopia of "normality."'[8] Borrowing an insight by biologist Patrick Geddes, Kennedy understands 'eutopia' as the perfection of an existing place as opposed to the 'utopia' of an imaginary place.

But even normality can acquire a utopian dimension. The promissory notes of 'capitalism' and 'democracy' and 'Europe' all conjured up paradisiacal visions, before the populations of the region encountered their real existing forms. For writer Svetlana Boym, utopianism survived in the form of 'Central Europe,' which represented for some a 'third way,' the hoped-for alternative to both capitalism and communism that had a minor surge of popularity after 1989.[9] Even as capitalism and democracy began to set into institutional forms in the 1990s, the 'third way' lives on in eastern Europe as it does elsewhere in the world – in the form of new forms of democracy, new syntheses of environmentalism and economics, and new types of intentional communities. This is no naïve commitment to a rigid ideology. Rather, it's a continued search for Peter Berger's 'hard-headed utopianism.'

Squat paradise

In November 1989, it was exhilarating to be a young person in East Berlin. Not only did the physical wall fall on 9 November, so too did the many invisible walls that so oppressed East German non-conformists. 'If you were not a part of this big group of equals – if you were homosexual, if you looked different or had a different political opinion – then life was not nice in the GDR,' labor activist Renate Hürtgen told me, citing the Stasi's repression of such 'social misfits.' All those who had been largely hidden from sight – punk rockers, dissidents, transvestites – stepped out of the closet on 10 November into a newly liberated public realm. To support their non-conformist lifestyle, they just needed a cheap place to stay.

In the months before the Wall fell, thousands of East Germans had already taken advantage of the changes in neighboring countries to flee – decamping to Prague or traveling through Hungary to Austria. Even more streamed across when the border first opened to West Germany. They left behind their jobs, their Trabants, and, perhaps most importantly, their apartments. Those who stayed behind, especially young people, could suddenly pick and choose among a huge number of empty places to occupy. Entire sections of the city, such as Prenzlauer Berg, had become squat paradises. Many young West Germans went east to hang out in this new terra incognita. I, too, was fascinated. In March 1990, I went to one of the squat cafés in Prenzlauer Berg, where I listened to the Talking Heads, ate Indian food supplied by local Hare Krishnas, and had heated political arguments in the smoky space. The original pop-ups, these cafés moved from place to place every few days or weeks.

It was not only East Berlin. 'Leipzig was really famous for those houses that were left alone and falling apart with everything intact – water, electricity, gas,' recalls Marcel Rotter, who lived for eighteen months in one of the Leipzig houses. 'We got furniture from the open apartments of people who had gone to the West. There were whole blocks that had been condemned, but nothing had been done to them and they were still in livable condition.'

As a young man, Dirk Moldt became involved in the opposition movement in East Germany, particularly the Church from Below group that operated independently of the official Protestant Church structures. At one point, the Church was one of only three ways to escape the GDR, as musician Wolf Biermann put it (the other two being suicide and trying to get across the Berlin Wall).[10] Dirk helped pioneer a fourth way: the squat. Because of limited dorm space in East Berlin, students had begun to create a squat culture even before the Wall came down. In a café in Friedrichshain, which had once been a primary squat neighborhood in East Berlin, Dirk told me about how the movement blossomed in those early days after the Wall fell.

'We had a feeling of elation,' Dirk told me. 'Every day you encountered boundaries. There was the Wall. But there were also invisible boundaries. And there were a lot of functionaries and police. There were also normal citizens who always said: "It has always been like that and it is good like that and what you do is wrong and so on."' He found it exhilarating when people outside the tiny opposition movement finally understood that their 'idyllic world' was falling apart.

For several years after the Wall fell, the eastern part of Berlin was in constant flux: new laws, new opportunities, a new openness. The housing sector was particularly subject to change because, unlike in the West, many buildings had no owners and were managed by the state. The district administrations actually invited people to occupy the empty apartments. '"Those who want to live here, should come,"' Dirk remembered them saying. 'This was because so many flats were empty.' Friedrichshain was a gentrified, middle-class neighborhood when I met Dirk for coffee there in 2013. But in the 1980s, he told me, 'it was a proletarian environment. Many flats here were in very bad condition. They had stoves, but only very few had radiators. There were few bathrooms. Toilets were outside the flat on the stairway. And a lot of flats were empty.'

The squatters moved in and upgraded the properties – not simply according to individual tastes but to serve the collective interests of the group of people living in the building. Dirk and his friends also told their friends on the other side of the now-dismantled Wall to come over and help occupy all the empty properties. To describe this kind of squatting, the Germans used the word *instandbesetzen*, a combination of renovating and occupying. The squatters not only transformed the landscape – they began to change the culture, at least on the neighborhood level. At one point in 1990, squatters had commandeered 130 houses in East Berlin.[11]

'On Mainzer Straße, there were eleven buildings squatted,' Dirk remembered. 'On the street there were several different groups. One house, for instance, had transvestites. The boys walked around with very hot female clothes. It looked like in a movie. They were wearing make-up and blond little curls and short skirts, it looked really crazy. Other houses were really militant where they were always wearing black clothes and hooded jackets. All the houses were draped with flags and banners. Every evening, people would sit in front of their houses eating, chatting, and drinking.'

But the squats occupied only one side of the street. 'On the other side of the street, normal people were living,' he continued. 'The problem was that they had to get up early to go to work. Most of them didn't dare tell the squatters to please be quiet. If they called the police, the police said: "We are not stupid, we are not going in there." A street where the police doesn't go? No state can tolerate this.'

And not all the squatters had the best of intentions. 'Every avant-garde has its *Hängefraktion*, a group of losers who are just hanging around,' Dirk pointed out. 'Sometimes they're the ones on top, sometimes the others.'

Not long after the two Germanies reunited in 1990, the police eventually evicted the Mainzer Straße squatters in a terrifying street fight that put seventy policemen in hospital and 417 squatters in jail.[12] It wasn't only the neighbors or the state that took exception to the squatters. So did the neo-Nazis, who experienced a rapid resurgence in the midst of a general uptick in intolerance. One night in 1992, one of Dirk's closest friends and a fellow squatter, Silvio Meier, was heading to a party with a small entourage when they encountered some neo-Nazi teenagers wearing patches that proclaimed 'I am proud to be a German.'[13] Meier and the others confronted the teenagers. In response, the neo-Nazis took out their butterfly knives. They killed Meier and seriously wounded two others. 'The young Nazis were given juvenile sentences, since they weren't adults,' Dirk said. 'First the police and then also the politicians said: "This is like a brawl in a pub. It has nothing to do with politics."'

The killing was the end of an era, and the years following were hard for Dirk. 'It was like a darkness to me,' he said. 'Not just because of the GDR but also because of the many changes. And there was no evening when you could go out on the streets without being afraid.'

In 1989, Dirk Moldt and his fellow squatters believed in a third way, a combination of socialism and anarchism. They looked at reunification with great skepticism. They felt closer to people in Prague and Budapest than to their fellow Germans in Bonn. Even the West German squatters seemed to belong to an entirely different culture. After the political party that promised fast-track reunification won the East German elections in March 1990, Dirk thought the process would take several years, that something unique about the GDR could be preserved. That didn't happen. So, Dirk set off on a different trajectory. He raised a family. He went to university and eventually relinquished many of his old ideas. One thing, however, remains from that time. He still lives in the apartment in which he squatted so many years ago. Reflecting the middle-class transformation of the neighborhood, he now owns the place.

Berlin is once again the capital of Germany. Large swathes of what was once East Berlin have been torn down to make room for sleek modern buildings. A reconstructed version of the old imperial City Palace will replace the 1970s-era Palace of the Republic. The interconnected courtyards of the art nouveau masterpiece, Hackesche Höfe, have been spectacularly upgraded and now serve as the anchor of a new center of nightlife. An exhibition hall for East Berlin's 'City of Tomorrow' – a 1957 effort by world-renowned architects to construct a hypermodern quarter in the Hansaviertel, a once stylish section of the city destroyed in World War II – has become perhaps the world's most stylish Burger King. Prenzlauer Berg, where I had visited a squat café in 1990, has become the Brooklyn of Berlin, and the neighborhood's version of hipsters worry about an invasion of 'Swabians,' shorthand for the uptight moneyed class from the German heartland.

The neighborhoods of the former East Berlin have succumbed to the lure of gentrification. One complex that held out longer than most was a once chic, turn-of-the-century department store on Oranienburger Straße. Soon after the Wall came down, squatters moved into the vast, crumbling structure, which they dubbed Tacheles, from the Yiddish word for 'straight talk.' The building had quite a lineage. After its debut as one of the first shopping arcades in the city in 1908, it became a showroom for an electric company, a party headquarters and prison for the Nazis, and a communist trade union building. Shortly after Tacheles formed in 1990, I visited the squat and marveled at its cafés and movie theater and artist studios. There seemed to be unlimited room to create an alternative society.

Two decades later, when I returned to Berlin and Oranienburger Straße, squat culture was nearly dead. In 2012, HSH Nordbank – the owner of the Tacheles site – finally evicted the remaining artists. According to a news report, 'before police arrived, two black-clad artists played a funeral march but bailiffs were able to clear the building without resistance.'[14] It was a quiet end for what had been a bold and loud experiment. In early 2013, I could only take photographs of the boarded-up space. Although the creative chaos of Tacheles had departed the shell of its building, the soul of the enterprise lives on in a 3-D version available on the Web.[15]

Artopia

Mladen Miljanović grew up during the wars that split apart Yugoslavia. He lived in the area of Bosnia that became Republika Srpska, the predominantly Serbian section of the country. His home was near one military base, his school near a second. More than once he got a lift home from school by military helicopter.

'Guns became a normal thing for me,' Mladen told me. 'Going to school, passing behind the big artillery guns, that was very normal for me. Sometimes me and my friends watched with binoculars how houses just disappeared. It was awful to look at that: fascinating, but awful.'

Later, after the war had been over for several years, Mladen became even more familiar with guns. He served his compulsory nine months in the army at the Reserve Officer School in the Vrbas military barracks in Banja Luka, the capital of Republika Srpska. He rose to the rank of sergeant and, in his last few months, even trained a cohort of thirty soldiers.

He could have stayed on in the army and risen even higher. Instead, he opted for something completely different. He decided to go to art school. He didn't have to go very far. By a trick of fate, the military barracks where he once served had become Banja Luka's new art academy.

For his senior project, Mladen decided to spend nine months, as long as he spent in the military, doing an extended art performance that he called 'I Serve Art.' Every day of this alternative service, on the same terrain as his military training, he produced new paintings, photos, and performance pieces. It was his rebirth as an artist.

'When I returned to the base to study as an artist, I was able to be free, to speak about everything, which is completely, diametrically opposite to being in the military,' Mladen recounts.[16] 'Everything that's bad can become very good. This area had the function that it had, and now it has changed that function diametrically. Instead of a military orientation, it has assumed a humanistic, intellectual orientation.'[17]

Each day of the nine-month project, Mladen set about 'decontaminating' the space by photographing himself at attention, body rigid military-style, in different parts of the former barracks.[18] Here once stood a sentry, the photos say, and now here stands an artist, establishing the location's new identity and marking the artist's territory. In one of the more memorable works he created during this art service, Mladen shouldered his army rifle and shot at a series of targets. But instead of aiming for the kill zones, he used the bullets to outline the figure, thus bringing it to life. It was a perfect swords-into-plowshares metaphor for his personal transformation and, ideally, the transformation of his country.

During the communist era, disaffected artists created alternative spaces where different rules and conventions applied. Sometimes, 'art' was simply a safer designation for something the authorities would have otherwise forbidden. In the last decade of communism, Polish art students in

Wrocław's Orange Alternative enacted elaborate 'street theater' in the city's downtown that mocked communist iconography and incorporated befuddled police in the performances. One particularly popular happening 'celebrated' the seventieth anniversary of the Bolshevik Revolution with a reenactment of the storming of the Winter Palace, which deliberately put the Polish police into the roles of anti-revolutionary actors.[19] It was all done in the spirit of what Orange Alternative called 'socialist surrealism.'[20]

In more restrictive Czechoslovakia, Jiří Kovanda had less freedom of maneuver, so his art took on even more deceptive camouflage. He would stand in the middle of Prague's Wenceslas Square and engage in various 'acts,' such as obstructing the flow of traffic on the sidewalk or enlisting two friends to document his attempt to meet a female stranger.[21] 'When he was doing his performances in the 1970s and 1980s, even for some of his friends it was a joke. Even the guy documenting his performances wasn't sure what was going on, whether it was an art action or not,' curator Tomáš Pospyszl told me. Other artists, such as Václav Ambrěz or Vladimír Havlík in Moravia, would organize parties for their friends. 'Sometimes it was difficult to distinguish whether it was a party or a happening or a performance,' Tomáš added. 'Or maybe it was a strategy to endure the bad times and find a way to express creativity and build a small niche where one could live under the conditions we had.'

Then there was the utopia of the dance floor. Even in restrictive Bulgaria, rock and roll offered young people an escape and even some coded messages of hope. 'There was no way to get on stage and say that all this is bullshit, that this system is nothing – unless you wanted to commit suicide!' Konstantin Markov of the popular rock group Tangra told me. His group started out doing Deep Purple and other hard rock. 'But then, we started singing in Bulgarian and we had a very strong message. It wasn't completely clear at the beginning, but if you read the text several times and if you thought about it, then you could figure out what we wanted to say. And that was our biggest reward.'

Konstantin and his musician friends looked to the West for inspiration, at one point shifting practically overnight from heavy metal to New Wave. But the country right next door exerted as great an influence. In certain neighborhoods in Sofia, young people could watch Yugoslav television. 'Yugoslavia was from some points of view even better than in the West,' Konstantin continued. 'It was a huge scene there: very talented musicians and very good bands. But they were free. Rock 'n' roll equals freedom.'

In Yugoslavia, punk groups like Električni Orgazam and Prljavo Kazalište drew admirers from across Europe, while young Yugoslavs traveled from republic to republic to follow their favorite bands. Even more so than in Bulgaria, rock music was where young people in particular could voice political and cultural discontent. 'Punk rock music was a form of contestation,' explains sociologist and politician Pavel Gantar. 'In the late 1970s, rock music substituted for the absence of political and social criticism.'

One of the great bands of the era, the Slovenian industrial music group Laibach, constantly baited the authorities by juxtaposing symbols of socialist realism and national socialism in their concerts and musical iconography (and, many years later, would do the same in a concert in, of all places, North Korea).[22]

This multiethnic musical community, like Yugoslavia itself, fragmented in the 1990s. Some musicians, caught up in the nationalist fervor of the times, played propaganda songs for their respective governments. Others gravitated toward anti-war music. Today, thanks to technology, you can still listen to all the old, pre-war music on Internet radio stations devoted to what's called 'YU-Rock.' In his book *The Seventh Republic*, journalist Ante Perković provides a history of the Yugoslav rock scene in the 1990s and 2000s. The last chapter, called 'Ona se budi?' ('Is she waking up?'), is about its revival. 'The Yugoslav rock scene has out-survived all state institutions of Yugoslavia and become transformed into a globalized rock scene,' musician and journalist Rüdiger Rossig told me.

Artists continue to challenge the status quo, whether it's liberal injustices or nationalist pieties. Andreja Kulunčić, who studied art in both Croatia and Hungary, does work that often focuses on those who have become invisible or who have lost the power to command the attention of the majority. She has worked with migrants, the jobless, pregnant teenagers, prisoners, stigmatized minorities: the precariat. She has used her position as an artist as a kind of bullhorn: to grab the attention of passers-by. One of her projects, for instance, used advertising posters to draw attention to the plight of workers at a state-owned store in Croatia that the government wanted to privatize. It was the early days of the transition to the market, and Kuluncic realized that billboards and bus shelter ads could administer a 'shock of the new' to attract interest in those made 'redundant' by the 'transition.'

In Dunaújváros, a small industrial city south of Budapest, Andreja did a project called 'A Republic of One's Own' that enabled residents to envision a new future for their town. 'The local politicians thought I belonged to some political party and that I wanted to do something political,' she told me. 'Three days before the opening of the project, when we had everything ready, they said that they would have to close the gallery if the project went forward. So I said, "No, it's not worth closing the gallery because of one project." The gallery showed it as a documentation, but in a kind of hidden way.' Closing down a space to prevent people from imagining the future of their city – it was a throwback to what Andreja called 'formal-socialist behavior.' It was also a testament to the enduring power of utopian thinking.

Of course, many artists are decidedly anti-utopian in their perspective. One of the most famous artists to emerge from the region is David Černý, who made his name as an art student in Prague by painting a Soviet tank. For years he had walked by the tank mounted on a pedestal in Kinsky

Square and fumed. The tank commemorated the Soviet liberation of Czechoslovakia in 1945, and indeed the square was once known as the Square of Soviet Tank Crews. But the tank also reminded the citizens of Prague of the Soviet troops that entered the city in 1968 to put down the Prague Spring. So, one night in the spring of 1991, David painted the tank pink. The Russian embassy filed a complaint. The Czechoslovak army repainted the tank green. And a group of Czech parliamentarians, in solidarity with the artist, repainted the tank pink again. The tank was finally removed. It's reportedly sitting in a military history museum outside Prague – still pink.

Today, David's sculptures pop up all around Prague. Outside the Kafka museum, there's a fountain sculpture of two men urinating into a pool. The pool is shaped like the Czech Republic. If you send a text to a number posted on the site, the men will inscribe your message on the map of the country. 'There's a Czech idiom about "peeing over somebody," which I guess translated into English would be to "get one over on somebody." That's what the peeing men mean. It's the way our country behaves,' David told *The Los Angeles Times*.[23] David told me that he considered this just a 'nice sculpture' that's not controversial at all. But then again, like his figures of the two men, he likes to 'take the piss,' as they say in Britain.

David's most infamous sculpture is Entropa, commissioned by the Czech Republic to mark its presidency of the Council of the European Union in 2009. It was supposed to be a collective effort of twenty-seven artists from each of the member states. David fabricated the whole thing himself, along with several assistants, making up bios for all the 'contributing artists.' The different sections of the huge 8-ton sculpture depict imaginary coats of arms for each of the EU member states.[24] They are not, to say the least, flattering. Bulgaria is represented by squat toilets. Germany's emblem is the intersection of Autobahn highways that resembles a swastika. For Italy, a number of football players are masturbating on the pitch. The United Kingdom is depicted by a missing piece, a particularly prescient representation given the future Brexit vote.

'Unexpectedly the Polish part was actually exhibited in the main hall of the Warsaw National Museum,' David told me. 'The Polish section looked like a bunch of priests raising a gay flag in the middle of a potato field. It looked like the raising of the flag at Iwo Jima. They somehow understood it. I expected protests from Britain. I expected it would be too much for the Italians, but nothing happened. Germany did protest. Merkel, if I remember correctly, sent a fax with "Okay, but why?"'

The transitions in 1989 began with Europe as utopia. Twenty years later, Europe had been reduced to *Entropa*, an anti-utopia box. If Europe is to survive, however, it has to be able to laugh at itself, for it's better for history to repeat as farce then again as tragedy.

Utopia boxes

In the middle of Sofia is a large space where the mausoleum of Georgi Dimitrov once stood. Dimitrov was one of the more revered communist figures in the Soviet bloc. After the famous Reichstag fire of 1933, he stood up to the Nazis by defending himself against charges that he was responsible for the blaze. Acquitted, he was sent to the Soviet Union and later served as the first communist leader of Bulgaria. He died in 1949. In 1990, the removal of Dimitrov's preserved body, followed by its cremation and burial, was a symbolic rejection of the old regime. The mausoleum itself was taken down in 1999, though a majority of Bulgarians opposed the demolition.[25] It took the authorities four attempts and lots of dynamite to bring down the solid marble structure. Other than a small tent occupied by a religious hermit, the space was empty for over a decade.

In 2011, the architect Sylvia Aytova – with the help of the Ideas Factory – put up a wooden pavilion called the Utopia Box. It was an ingenious construction: a box that could be turned into a stage, a place for workshops, an exhibition space. Here the citizens of Sofia could imagine a new, fluid public reality. The creators of the box provided the pavilion as a gift to the municipality. The city, which had in fact co-sponsored the structure, simply tore it down not long after it was constructed. It was as if nothing could substitute for the failed promise of communism.

New ideas sometimes take a little while to take hold. But fortunately the new ideas keep coming off the assembly line of the Ideas Factory, which has been translating the energy and creativity of Bulgaria's next generation since 2006. One of the projects is the Beglika Festival, an annual gathering at a lake in the Rhodope Mountains where 'we try to build a Balkan identity through culture and music,' Yanina Taneva told me. Another is 'invisible theater,' which turns everyday life into a performance. 'You have a bunch of people who are actors but no one knows because they look normal,' Yanina said. 'They go on the street, into the subway. For instance, a beautiful blonde lady kisses an African-American really passionately, different situations like that that challenge people.' And then there was the art installation of an environment of real bushes, artificial light, and a fake rainbow. 'It was a very surreal but very "natural" environment where you can think about what "natural" means and why everyone is so keen to be natural,' Yanina said.

The Ideas Factory is, in some ways, a Utopia Box unto itself: flexible, innovative, and responsive to the needs of the public. 'Smaller organizations have the advantage of being flexible,' Yanina told me. 'Established organizations can't change easily. Our strategy is to stay small and maintain contact with lots of associated people. We just need to stay flexible. Change is the only thing that is happening for sure in the world.'

Other NGOs in the region function like 'utopia boxes' in their efforts to break from the QWERTY effect. In

Poland, for example, Stocznia attempts to recreate the spirit of solidarity in Poland that animated Solidarity. 'I'm very much into something at the moment called the "script of cooperation,"' Stocznia creator Kuba Wygnański told me. During the communist period, 'your car broke down every winter, so you had to rely on other people. There were so many needs because we were not self-sufficient. I'm not trying to turn back the clock of history and say that that was a better time. But now we live in the worst possible time because we believe that we are self-sufficient and even mentioning that you need help from other people is kind of embarrassing.'

In Romania, meanwhile, architect Mariana Celac and her colleagues – three architects and three sculptors – set out to create their own version of 'utopia boxes' that people could actually inhabit. 'We went to a remote place where there was no electricity, no nothing,' she told me. 'We started an experiment in building with only local materials and very simple tools – and very quickly. We started with this idea after there had been a big flood on the Danube, and we had seen how the adobe houses had melted away in a few hours because they were poorly built.'

The area was a site near the Danube delta where archeologists had been excavating Greek, Roman, and Byzantine settlements. For three or four years running, Mariana and her colleagues constructed a building in two or three weeks from bottom to top. 'The materials were stone,' she continued. 'We got the stones by hand. And adobe. We were helped by the Gypsy community in the nearby village. We also used the local wood. Because it's a very arid area, the trees were small. They also grow wheat for the horses, so we used thatch.'

The buildings were experimental, designed to house the archeologists and their assistants. But it was also designed as a demonstration project. 'The idea was to make sure that people know what they have to do to build good, safe houses,' Mariana told me. 'If the flood comes, people are waiting for the authority to come and to rebuild the village, but a number of factors intervene. So we are working right now on a number of rules that are simple and understandable for building houses in rural areas by people themselves.'

The rallying cry after 1989 was 'no experiments.' The people of the region were suspicious of utopian visions, which they knew often led to dystopian realities. They wanted the tried and true. They wanted what worked.

But under the banner of pragmatism, the people of eastern Europe embarked on a series of unprecedented experiments in the 1990s: large-scale privatization, the opening of secret police archives, a dramatic expansion of the European Union. In place of the construction of *Homo sovieticus* – the 'new man' imagined by communism – they participated in the construction of *Homo capital-democraticus,* the 'new man' of the modern age. Many were sacrificed on the altar of this idea: the Erased, the precariat, those struggling to make ends meet in the countryside.

Meanwhile, those who lived at a slight angle to mainstream society – artists, activists, squatters – were imagining other worlds. When the region turns away from the regressive visions of the region's populists, these other worlds can serve as a source of future alternatives.

Conclusion: The Future of Illiberalism

When I met civil society activist Sonja Licht in Belgrade in 1990, she was very clear about the threat that nationalism posed to Yugoslavia. At a time when eastern European countries were celebrating their first democratic elections and anticipating their welcome party into the European community, Sonja sounded like a perverse Delphic Oracle in predicting that 'something like the dissolution of Yugoslavia will not happen without a civil war and make things much worse in this part of the world.'

When we'd sat down together for the interview that September the unravelling had already begun, though the outside world was not paying attention. The League of Communists of Yugoslavia had dissolved itself after a fractious final meeting the previous January. A national, pro-independence party had won the first democratic elections in Croatia, and some ethnic Serbs there had begun talking about their own secessionist movement. Slovenia, too, had declared its sovereignty, as had Bosnia, while Serbia was busy hijacking the federation for its own purposes. Still, in September 1990, there hadn't been any violence, so I was taken aback by Sonja's dire forecast.[1] Over the next months and years, it was terrifying to watch her prediction come true.

Twenty-two years later, I met up again with Sonja in Belgrade – now the capital of Serbia after the dissolution of Yugoslavia – and she was equally pessimistic. This time, though, she was anxious about the entire continent. The EU in the 2010s, she felt, was following the same trajectory of failed federalism as Yugoslavia had in the 1990s. 'As I was worried about the future of my own country in 1989, I am extremely worried about Europe,' she told me in 2012. 'I survived somehow the dissolution of my own country, but I don't think I can survive the dissolution of the EU. It would be too much even for such a stubborn, already aging person like myself. The falling apart of Europe as a project would be a major catastrophe for the whole world, not only for Europe.' Bidding farewell to Sonja, I was reminded of a title of a Yugoslav film from the 1970s: *Goodbye until the Next War*.[2]

Before 2016, the European Union seemed solid enough. In 2013, with the accession of Croatia, it had expanded to twenty-eight members. Even with only modest growth – of less than 1 percent since the financial crisis of 2008/09 – the combined economic power of the EU ($19.1 trillion) remained ahead of that of the United States ($17.9 trillion) and just behind that of China ($19.5 trillion) in 2015.[3] The European project still met former British foreign secretary Ernest Bevin's description of being able 'to take a ticket at Victoria Station and go anywhere I damn well please.'

Then, on 23 June 2016, the citizens of the United Kingdom chose by referendum to leave the EU in a close vote of 52 percent to 48 percent. It didn't matter that the morning after, once they learned the truth about the benefits of membership (and the penalties for early withdrawal), many Britons had second thoughts about their votes to leave. It didn't matter that the exit option, or Brexit, would be a long process of negotiations that might require the UK to accept measures unpopular with voters – such as free movement of people – in order to maintain privileged access to the EU market. By this slender margin, the referendum challenged the irreversibility of European integration.

It's sobering to remember that, at one time, Yugoslavia too seemed solid. It was the country that, in the aftermath of World War I, southern Slavs enthusiastically carved out of the dead empires of the nineteenth century. It was reinvented after the peoples of Yugoslavia suffered more than one million deaths – or nearly 11 percent of the population – in World War II.[4] For a multiethnic country whose major ethnic groups had waged a terrible civil war during the larger conflict with the Nazis, the slogan of 'brotherhood and unity' promoted by communist leader Tito offered a forward-looking ideology that, at least temporarily, papered over the anger and desire for revenge that dominated the immediate post-war period. With that philosophy, Yugoslav communists attempted to construct a federal system that would accommodate the interests of the primary ethnic groups and also reduce the economic disparities between the richer and poorer regions of the country.

'Brotherhood and unity' kept Yugoslavia bound together for almost half a century. Ironically, the country began to fall apart just as Europe coined its own mirror slogan – unity in diversity – as a means of keeping all of *its* many ethnic groups together in a common house. The centrifugal tensions within Yugoslavia and the European Union bear some resemblance. In Yugoslavia, the transfer of resources from the richer republics of Slovenia and Croatia to the less well-off southern regions created resentment and perceptions that Serbia was skimming off more than its fair share of the administrative costs of maintaining the system. Similarly, Germans complain about supporting the profligate 'Mediterranean' lifestyles of the Greeks even as the southern tier accuses the banking sector of the northern tier of undue profits. Right-wing nationalist parties like the National Front in France and the Alternative für Deutschland in Germany employ the same racism-tinged rhetoric and emphasis on sovereignty as the Croatian Democratic Union promoted in the early 1990s, while democratically elected leaders such as Viktor Orbán in Hungary show as little regard for the rule of law as Franjo Tuđman once did in Croatia.

The European Union has without question been a remarkable achievement of modern statecraft. It turned a continent that seemed destined to wallow in 'ancestral hatreds' into one of the most harmonious regions on the planet. But as with the portmanteau states of the Soviet

Union, Yugoslavia, and Czechoslovakia, the complex federal project of the EU has proved fragile in the absence of a strong external threat like the one that the Cold War provided. The Schengen system of free movement is under attack; the Euro currency is in crisis; there is little enthusiasm for expanding the EU or deepening the relationships among the members; the economic deals that the EU has made with regions like Wales and Catalonia, bypassing central governments, have paradoxically weakened rather than strengthened federalism.[5]

Another economic shock comparable to the financial crisis of 2008/09 or a coordinated political challenge could tip the system over the edge. The victory of Donald Trump in the US presidential election in 2016 may put wind in the sails of nationalist movements in the region that want to follow the UK out of the EU. For many former Yugoslavs, it's déjà vu all over again.

'It is nationalism that tore Yugoslavia apart, and it will be nationalism, albeit masked in economic terms, that may rip apart the Eurozone and the enlarged EU,' poet and cultural critic Aleš Debeljak told me in an interview in August 2013 in Vienna. Slovenia was a creditor within the former Yugoslavia. But when Slovenia's economy took a nosedive during the financial crisis, it found itself in the position of debtor within the European Union, and the rhetoric shifted. Aleš continued, 'Now we say, "Wait a moment, what about European solidarity? What about renegotiating the debt? What about the tremendous profits that creditors get from debtor countries? Shouldn't we rethink solidarity?"' Such second thoughts, like the ones that assailed Brexit supporters, usually come along too late to have much impact.

Daniel Bučan isn't one for second thoughts. He never had much faith in Yugoslavia. He was an early supporter of Croatian independence and was working in the Tuđman government when I met him in 1990. Twenty-two years later, he'd retired from the diplomatic corps. Even though he'd been posted to Strasbourg to serve at the Council of Europe, he'd lost whatever faith he'd once had in the European project as well.

'I don't believe anymore in the European Union,' Daniel Bučan told me. 'As soon as the EU tries to become a political union, it will end in a bad way. You cannot make a state out of Europe. Look at Yugoslavia, look at the Soviet Union, look at Czechoslovakia. Such multilingual, multicultural, multi-religious, multinational constructs are always kept together by force. When I say by force, I don't necessarily mean by tyranny, but by any kind of power. The Soviet Union, Yugoslavia, and Czechoslovakia were kept together by the force of the Communist Party and communist dictatorship. The EU is kept together by the power of Germany and France.'

Yugoslavia is indeed the worst-case scenario for the EU. But the current situation of former Yugoslavia offers some slender hope. Like a brain recovering from trauma, the post-Yugoslav countries are beginning to make new connections. It's not Yugonostalgia. Rather, it's cooperation born of pragmatism. Politician Vojko Volk had become the Slovenian ambassador to Croatia when I saw him again after twenty-two years. He told me of a program he called 'reconnecting the Balkans.' 'There is no success in the Balkans without reconnecting, reconnecting everything except politics,' he said. 'We should reconnect everything in former Yugoslavia: energy, roads, railways, sports, culture, economy, market.' It's one thing for a Slovenian to speak of such reconnections, but cooperation has even been rekindled between Serbia and Croatia. 'Serbian pop singers are singing all over Croatia,' historian Ivo Goldstein told me in 2012. 'According to polls on Facebook, the most Facebook friends of Croats are Bosnians, Serbs, and Slovenes … The cultural connections are not as intensive as they were before the war in the 1990s, but something is going on. Nobody speaks about Serbian tourists coming to Croatia as a problem.' This kind of cooperation doesn't make headlines. In the newspaper business, as the adage goes, if it bleeds, it leads. 'Serbs and Croats Now Get Along' might merit a short article in a US media outlet, but it's not going to be a ten-part series in *USA Today*.

Eurocrats in Brussels similarly emphasize the common interests of the member states. They talk in glowing terms of unity in diversity. But the EU needs more than pretty rhetoric and good intentions to stay glued together. If it doesn't come up with a better recipe for dealing with economic inequality, political extremism, and social intolerance, its opponents will soon have the power to hit the rewind button on European integration. The collapse of the European project, a culmination of the rising illiberalism in the region, would be a tragedy not only for Europe but for all those who hope to overcome the dangerous rivalries of the past and provide shelter from the murderous conflicts of the present.

Stepping back and leaping forward

The first half of this book chronicled all the steps backward eastern Europe has taken over the last twenty-five years. Large sections of the population – what I've called Eastern Europe B – have not experienced the benefits of transition. They view privatization as theft, economic growth as unequal, and membership in the European Union as just another oppressive federalism. Market reforms have created highly stratified societies marked by corruption and very low levels of social trust. A widening urban–rural split has isolated liberal intellectuals – and, by extension, liberalism – from the mainstream of society. The application of lustration has often been politically motivated and undermined commitment to the rule of law. With their messages of nationalist renewal and ethnic scapegoating, right-wing extremist parties have capitalized on widespread dissatisfaction with economic globalization, political elites, and the cultural vanguard. In these messages can be glimpsed a replay of the forces that tore apart Yugoslavia and that could, in a different key, unravel the European Union.

The second half of the book offered a somewhat more optimistic reading of the last twenty-five years. The transitions provided tremendous opportunities for individuals and even communities to reinvent themselves. Even among the most marginalized communities, a new generation of leaders has emerged to challenge injustice and abuse of power. Young people in particular are trying to break out of the path dependence established by their elders. Artists and activists are imagining new worlds that offer startling alternatives to the status quo. The energy and dynamism of these efforts could indeed propel the region forward to close the economic, political, and cultural gap that has continued to divide the two parts of Europe.

Rather than black-and-white representations, the picture that emerges from these two narratives resembles the well-known symbol of Taoism in which a spot of yin resides in the apostrophe of yang, and vice versa. Thus, the younger generation is just as likely to support authoritarian alternatives as democratic ones. On the other hand, some illiberal populists have sought to temper the worst excesses of what they call 'wild capitalism' with policies that spread the wealth more evenly. I have quoted at length from the nearly three hundred interviews I conducted in the region in 2012/13 in order to convey the richness of the experiences and the complexity of the challenges in eastern Europe – and to remind readers that actual people, not just impersonal forces, have determined the trajectory of the region. I talked to some prophets, like Sonja Licht. But no one could tell me whether the steps backward that eastern Europe has taken will lead to further stumbles or whether the region will muster the energy to overcome its divisions and leap forward to arrive at a more equitable and prosperous landing point.

For the last twenty-five years, the primary mechanism for such a catapult forward has been membership in the European Union, both the promise that has motivated necessary reforms and the reality that has released important resources for development. But membership in the EU, like privatization before it, is an 'only once' phenomenon. As economic historian Robert Gordon points out, the rapid economic development that took place in the United States largely in the twentieth century can be attributed to singular changes such as the shift away from agriculture and the revolution in communications: 'The economic revolution of 1870 to 1970 was unique in human history, unrepeatable because so many of its achievements could happen only once.'[6] Emerging from the communist era, eastern Europe has had a couple of shots to make up for lost ground. More chances may not be forthcoming.

If eastern Europe remains on the margins of Europe, in a perpetually unstable zone hard up against the former Soviet Union, its 'loser' status may well institutionalize illiberal populism, perpetuating clientelistic states and intolerant cultures. It's not hard to see how such an eastern Europe could contribute to the dissolution of the EU, as Sonja Licht feared. But of course, such a deterministic view of the region, circa 1987 or even 1988, could not have anticipated the transformations of 1989. Indeed, when West German researchers asked their fellow citizens in 1985 how long they thought the Berlin Wall would remain intact, the average response was thirty-four years.[7] The locomotive of history never follows its expected itinerary for long. The monorail of the past is always branching into multiple tracks in the present.

This final chapter will follow four of these possible tracks into the future of Europe. The current negotiations on Serbia's membership of the EU – and the status of Kosovo – will be a test case of the power of nationalism versus the benefits of integration. The large influx of people fleeing conflicts in the Middle East is challenging the EU's bureaucratic and political capacity to respond, but it is also spurring a conversation about what unity in diversity really means for Europe. Economic globalization continues to sharpen the divide between Europe A and Europe B: will the EU mitigate this economic trend or accelerate it? Finally, the post-World War II period has been marked by a liberal-conservative consensus on governance. The rise of illiberal politicians threatens to reorder European politics. Will liberals regather their forces, or will an entirely different political ideology challenge the new populists?

Serbia on the edge

In April 2013, Serbia and Kosovo signed a landmark normalization treaty. The deal, in what might seem a paradoxical quid pro quo, gave Kosovo authority over the Serbian pocket in the north and provided greater autonomy to an estimated 150,000 Serbs living in that region. Despite protests from some Serbs in that area as well as their supporters in Serbia, the parliament in Belgrade approved the agreement. Then in Kosovo, which had declared its independence five years earlier, the parliament also voted in favor of the arrangement, with equally vehement protestors in the streets outside denouncing the deal.

Serbia and Kosovo have exchanged liaison offices and continue working out the various details regarding borders and trade. But Serbia has still not recognized Kosovo. Nor did Serbia automatically join the European Union as a result of the compromise. Moreover, violence still sporadically erupts between the two sides as well as between the government and the opposition on the ethnic Albanian side. Economic stagnation and an unemployment rate of around 40 percent have prompted 10 percent of the population to leave Kosovo.[8]

But the 2013 agreement marked the necessary first step toward eventual reconciliation. Kosovo received a bump up in status, with Egypt shortly thereafter becoming the 100th country to recognize its independence.[9] And Serbia began negotiations over EU accession in January 2014. In December 2015, Belgrade opened its first two chapters of the accession process – on financial control and on normalization of relations with Kosovo.[10]

'Of course Serbia, to become a member of the EU, will have to recognize Kosovo one day,' Ivan Vejvoda, vice-president for programs at the German Marshall Fund, told me in 2012. 'But if I had to make a guess it would be at the doorstep of Europe. That would mean everyone holding hands at the same time and making the jump together. I don't think that anyone on the Serbian side has any illusion about that. But no one will ever say that. That's how politics works … This is a European issue involving essentially European historical identity. It's a cultural issue, a linguistic issue. So please bear with Serbia as it moves through this process. Don't try to force it through, especially after the promise and commitment to resolve the issue peacefully.'

For Ivan, the soft power of the EU is gradually having an impact in the region. 'Maybe this is the only region where it works, but the magnet is still very strong,' he said. But, he stressed, the Kosovo issue is not the priority for most Serbs. 'Opinion polls show that Kosovo is somewhere between the sixth or seventh issue in the hierarchy of importance after jobs, obviously, and everything that relates to standard of living and the future of the family,' he pointed out. Serbia's economic problems include an unemployment rate hovering between 15 and 20 percent.[11]

Supporters of European integration believe that the accession process can be the leverage reformers on the inside need to transform the Serbian state and strengthen the rule of law. 'The European integration process for Serbia is, in a sense, a state-building process,' Srdjan Majstorović, the deputy director of the EU Integration Office in Belgrade, explained to me in 2012, 'not in the sense of building a

Serbian state, which has existed for centuries, but in the sense of creating modern democratic institutions based on the rule of law that can sustain serious political pressure and threat within a democratic institutional setting. For that, we need to continue the EU integration process, because it is the most important transformative power tool in this region, and not only in Serbia.'[12] Despite the length of the accession process, the entrance requirements that the EU has demanded, and the less appealing prospects for EU members in the aftermath of the financial crisis, support in Serbian society for the EU path remains around 50 percent. More importantly, Srdjan pointed out, the pro-EU faction in the Serbian parliament has now reached over 90 percent. In the April 2016 parliamentary elections, the pro-EU Progressive Party won 50 percent of the votes, giving it a mandate to pursue the reforms required for membership. Perhaps as important, Serbs are war-weary. According to an early 2017 poll by the Belgrade Center for Security Policy, 73 percent of respondents said that they wouldn't go to war to keep Kosovo.[13]

Central to Serbia's bid to join the EU has been the political conversion of president Alexandar Vučić and former president Tomislav Nikolić of the ruling party, along with prime minister Ivica Dačić of the Socialist Party. All three had worked in the Milošević regime. All three executed an about-face, cooperated with the tribunal in The Hague, and threw their support behind the EU accession process. It was part of a generational shift among the younger politicians of the 1990s generation.

What is striking about the political situation in Serbia, however, is the failure of the next generation to follow suit. Although a majority of Serbs still favor EU membership – by 55 percent, according to a July 2016 poll – a slim majority of those under twenty-nine years old prefer siding with Russia.[14] That's a 10 percent increase in the last four years.[15] Moreover, in the aforementioned poll by the Belgrade Center for Security Policy, those most willing to go to war were aged eighteen to twenty-nine. The rise of nationalism among young people in Serbia can be seen in Dveri Srpske (Serbian Doors), which began in 1999 as a right-wing Christian youth organization and now espouses its opposition to LGBT rights and Kosovo independence from its clutch of seven seats in the Serbian parliament. Thus the preference for illiberal alternatives so apparent in the support of two-thirds of young people for right-wing parties in Poland's 2015 parliamentary elections[16] reaches even into EU candidate countries, where citizens haven't yet had a chance to become jaded about the privileges of membership. It suggests that the window for Serbia to join the EU might have a demographic time limit.

Meanwhile, the enthusiasm in the rest of Europe for expanding the borders of the EU has encountered 'enlargement fatigue.' In 2013, 80 percent of Germans opposed further expansion.[17] And there is a very clear pecking order of which countries should go first if the door opens. According to a 2008 Eurobarometer poll, more than 70 percent of EU citizens would welcome Norway and Switzerland with open arms (not that either country has made overtures to Brussels of late). A little more than half favored membership for Croatia (which would gain admittance five years later). Only 38 percent were willing to accept Serbia.[18]

The question is not so much whether Serbia will manage to slip through the door and into the EU. It probably will. However, will the EU lock the door after Serbia?

If the European Union manages to survive the current onslaught of Euroskepticism on the right and the left, it may well move in the direction of Fortress Europe to protect itself from the surge of refugees and the chaos along the Russian periphery. Turkey has moved in an increasingly autocratic direction, and despite talk of reopening accession talks, several EU members refuse to contemplate the incorporation of so many more Muslims. Ukraine has become yet another frozen conflict like those in Georgia and Moldova. Bosnia, Albania, and Kosovo are all too politically fragile and economically challenged at the moment to go through the rigors of the vetting process. Greece continues to block Macedonia's bid. Only Montenegro (and Iceland) have much of a chance of joining the club in the near future.

The EU doesn't have to grow in order to survive. But the Fortress Europe that populists like Viktor Orbán and Marine Le Pen prefer, along with its stripped-down regulatory and judicial functions, will stagnate and ultimately slip into irrelevance, so much so that it might as well have disintegrated.

During the waning days of the Cold War, Mikhail Gorbachev revived the earlier French idea of a common

European home stretching from the Atlantic to the Urals. George H. W. Bush also found this notion appealing, reformulating it as 'Europe whole and free.' But first the expansion of NATO eastward and then the rise of the iron-fist leader Vladimir Putin removed Russia from those hopeful visions. The subsequent mobilization of illiberal democrats throughout Europe, but particularly among the eastern members, threatens to shrink the vision even further. A house divided will not long stand.

The culture of Europe

The subtitle of Benjamin Disraeli's novel *Sybil*, about Britain of the mid-nineteenth century, refers to the 'two nations' of rich and poor.[19] The gap between these two halves of society was a central preoccupation of social reformers during the Industrial Revolution. This divide between rich and poor in Europe has not gone away, despite the efforts of the welfare state. Indeed, in recent years, the divide has only grown wider.

Traveling by train from London to Berlin, however, I was struck by a different divide that has opened up in Europe – between the mobile and the stationary. These 'two nations,' like the one that so engaged Disraeli, have had an equally profound impact on the politics of the moment.

In the mobile version of Europe, you can commute by train from London to Brussels in two hours – faster than the trip by Amtrak from New York to Washington, DC – through the Chunnel umbilicus that connects the UK to Europe. For those in a greater hurry, cheap airline tickets bring people rapidly from Dublin to Athens and Lisbon to Gdańsk.

The tribe of the mobile is not restricted to the leisure class or the elite. The opening of the borders within the European Union facilitated an extraordinary labor migration as Poles moved westward, Britons moved south, Spaniards moved north, and the adventurous sought jobs eastward in Prague and Bucharest and Sofia. The definition of guest workers has expanded enormously, as have the overall numbers, and bureaucrats now prefer the term 'mobile workers.' Nor is it just the young who are on the move. 'Retirement migration' has created the European version of snowbirds. Some are on the move to escape racist violence or political intolerance. Others have been trafficked against their will.

This mobility within Europe, on top of the waves of immigrants and asylum-seekers coming from outside the continent, has destroyed any vestige of the ethnically homogeneous European state. The end of empire, and the flow of people from former colonies to the imperial metropoles, had already made England and the Netherlands and France into multiethnic environments. But now even Scandinavia and Ireland are being remade by the new otherlanders. Europe has now become not just a continent of regions but a continent of neighborhoods: the French quarter of South Kensington in London, the Turkish milieu of Kreuzberg in Berlin, the Vietnamese community in Warsaw's Praga section. Thanks to immigration and low birth rates, Europe has been changing from below for some time. Multiculturalism is not a choice in a school curriculum – it is a demographic fact.

But not everyone is on the move. The other half of Europe has stayed put. It has remained in the same place, the same village, even the same house for generations. This Europe speaks of centuries of family involvement in municipal affairs or tending the same vineyards or defending the country against invaders. This part of Europe has no intention of pulling up roots and moving to some strange land. The younger generation might peel off and join mobile Europe. But still, someone stays behind to tend the family hearth. According to 2005 data, only 22 percent of Europeans have moved outside their region or country – compared to 32 percent of Americans who moved outside the state where they were born.[20] That means that a large majority of Europeans stay close to home. 'It is clear that for many Europeans,' writes Tara Zahra in her study of mobility in Europe and the dangers that face migrants, 'true freedom includes the freedom to stay home.'[21]

You could attribute this divide to liberals versus conservatives. But what makes these debates so heated is not so much the ideological division but the deep cultural gulf. Half of Europe clings to what it believes are native traditions tied to land, language, and lifestyle. The other half has embraced a completely different Europe that is not defined by national identity or, at least, one national identity. There is hybrid Europe, and then there is the Europe that imagines itself to be a rack of indivisible nation-state billiard balls that can kiss or collide but not merge.

Novelist Milan Kundera once defined Europe as 'maximum diversity in minimum space.'[22] The new populists prefer minimum diversity in maximum space. The far right – and its many quiet supporters among mainstream conservative parties – wants the impossible: the ethnic homogeneity of a bygone (and imaginary) era. Immigrants threaten this minimum diversity in two different ways: through their physical presence and their stubborn retention of some degree of cultural difference expressed in their clothing, food, accent, or religion. The challenge has been around for decades, the only difference now being one of magnitude. In 1991, Europe was overwhelmed by 500,000 applications for asylum, prompting a headline in the *New York Times*: 'Europeans look for ways to bar door to immigrants.'[23] In 2015, by comparison, the EU dealt with 1.3 million asylum applications.[24]

The European Community was an effort to erase the traumas of the first and second world wars. The future Europe Union, if it is to survive its current economic challenges, will similarly attempt to erase the traumas of the Cold War and the conflicts that immediately sprang up in its wake. In so doing, the EU must also grapple with a more fundamental tension between a traditional past and a multicultural future that the Cold War diverted attention from for several decades.

Europe is not just a geographic designation or a bureaucratic organization. Europe is aspirational – not just for the many millions trying to move there but also for those who are already there. On a tram in Sofia, I once saw a sticker on the window with a Bulgarian flag and an EU flag. 'Please be Europeans. Don't litter and don't destroy the vehicle,' the caption read. 'This really tells you something about Europe and us not being part of Europe,' a young Bulgarian told me. 'Europeans are civilized, the ones who behave. And we are still barbarians. This is how Bulgarians think of Europe.' Bulgarians, since they occupy the lowest economic position in the EU, still see Europe as a goal rather than a given.

'If we want an EU, we need to create European people,' historian Marin Lessenski told me. 'This has to be engineered somehow, and NGOs, trans-border NGOs engaged in much more cooperation, will be important in this.' The tension between these new European people with a transnational sensibility and the more settled parts of the EU with their more traditional sense of place will either continue to drive forward a dynamic Europe or lead, fatally, to its collapse.

A division like this is ripe for the exploiting. In a 2013 speech, Vladimir Putin chastised the Euro-Atlantic countries for 'rejecting their roots, including the Christian values that constitute the basis of Western civilization. They are denying moral principles and all traditional identities: national, cultural, religious and even sexual.' In this way, Putin has been angling to lead the populist movements throughout Europe on the basis of conservative values: Christianity, the family, the nation.[25] It's the same trio of values that formed the bedrock of Donald Trump's support in the United States. In a way, it also informs those well-known dichotomies 'jihad' and 'McWorld' (political scientist Benjamin Barber) and the 'Lexus and the olive tree' (journalist Thomas Friedman).[26] The world is waiting to see whether Europe can find a way to turn a potentially explosive divide between the mobile and the fixed into a benign and even creative tension.

The impact of globalization

The Cold War was an era of economic alternatives. The United States offered its version of freewheeling capitalism, while the Soviet Union peddled its brand of centralized planning. In the middle, continental Europe offered the compromise of a social market: capitalism with a touch of planning and an abiding concern for the welfare of all members of society (even several eastern European governments flirted with versions of market socialism during the Cold War). Cooperation, not competition, was the byword of the European alternative. Americans could have their dog-eat-dog, frontier capitalism. Europeans would instead stress greater coordination between labor and management, and the European Community (the precursor to the EU) would put genuine effort into bringing its new members up to the economic and political level of its core countries.

Then, at a point in the early 1980s when the Soviet economic model had ceased to exert any influence at all globally, along came TINA.

At the time, British prime minister Margaret Thatcher and American president Ronald Reagan were ramping up their campaigns to shrink government, while what later became known as economic globalization – knocking down trade walls and opening up new opportunities for the financial sector – began to be felt everywhere. Thatcher summed up this brave new world with her TINA acronym. 'There is no alternative' to globalized market democracy, she declared.

Not surprisingly, in the post-Cold War era, European integration began to prioritize the removal of barriers to the flow of capital. At the same time, the expansion of Europe no longer came with an implied guarantee of eventual equality. The deals that Ireland (1973) and Portugal (1986) had received on accession had become like the Marshall Plan, an artifact of another era. In the 1990s, the sheer number of potential new members knocking on Europe's door put a strain on the EU's coffers, particularly since the economic performance of countries like Romania and Bulgaria was so far below the European average. But even if the EU had been overflowing with funds, it might not have mattered, since the new 'neoliberal' spirit of capitalism now animated its headquarters in Brussels, where the order of the day had become: cut government, unleash the market.

At the heart of Europe, as well as of this new orthodoxy, lies Germany, the exemplar of fiscal rectitude. Yet in the 1990s, that newly reunified nation engaged in enormous deficit spending, even if packaged under a different name, to bring the former East Germany up to the level of the rest of the country. It did not, however, care to apply some version of this 'reunification exception' to other former members of the Soviet bloc. Acting as the effective central bank for the European Union, Germany instead demanded balanced budgets and austerity from all newcomers (and some old-timers as well) as the only effective answer to debt and fears of a future depression.

The rest of the old Warsaw Pact has had access to some EU funds for infrastructure development, but nothing on the order of the East German deal. As such, they remain in a kind of economic halfway house. What those countries experienced after 1989 – one course of 'shock therapy' after another – became the medicine of choice for all EU members at risk of default following the financial crisis of 2008/09 and then the sovereign debt crisis of 2009. Forget deficit spending to enable countries to grow their way out of economic crisis. Forget substantial debt renegotiation. The unemployment rate in Greece and Spain continues to hover around 20 percent, with youth unemployment near 50 percent, and all the EU members subjected to heavy doses of austerity have witnessed a steep rise in the number of people living below the poverty line.[27] The best that the European Central Bank can offer is'quantitative easing' – a monetary sleight-of-hand to pump money into the Eurozone – and that is too little, too late. Inequality has increased dramatically in Europe, as it has throughout the world.[28] According to the OECD, inequality within European countries has grown substantially since the 1980s, while a 2016

Economist analysis demonstrates that the gap between rich and poor countries within the Eurozone has also widened over the last decade.[29]

The major principle of European integration has been reversed. Instead of eastern and central Europe catching up to the rest of the EU, pockets of the 'west' have begun to fall behind the 'east.' The GDP per capita of Greece, for example, has slipped below that of Slovenia and, when measured in terms of purchasing power, even Slovakia. This economic trend has prompted criticisms from both the right and the left that the EU is engaged in 'neo-colonialism.' 'Greece is a colonized state,' Slovenian philosopher Tomaž Mastnak told me. 'These political moves are incomprehensible within any democratic political framework. A half-informal body somewhere appoints the governments without elections. This is not a democratic deficit. This is the end of democracy.' Daniel Bučan shared the same sentiment about Croatia, but from the other side of the political spectrum: 'How we are going to reach the same level with western Europe, in terms of economy, production and everything? It's impossible if we are going to become a new kind of colony.'

Economic globalization, which at some level could be seen as a larger expression of European integration, undermined the principles of equity that the EU's founders built into their project. During the 1980s, the liberalization of trade became detached from the obligation to care for the most vulnerable sectors of the population. In 1992, the European Community made the decision to start on the path toward a single currency, which debuted ten years later in physical form. All of the countries that adopted the euro – the nineteen out of twenty-eight EU members that thus belong to the Eurozone – yoked themselves to an economic philosophy as well. The nations using the euro could no longer adjust their interest rates, the value of their currencies, or the size of their budget deficits to spur economic growth. They'd ceded that power to the EU – or, rather, to Germany, the largest creditor. As a result, after the financial crises that swept through Europe at the end of the 2000s, 'The single currency has created a situation of low or no growth and high unemployment, spurring popular anger and disaffection,' writes financial journalist John Lanchester.[30] Certainly the euro was enriching German bankers, as well as financiers, high-wage workers, and comfortable bureaucrats all over Europe. But the logical endpoint of this process was the collapse of European integration – and the liberal project it represents – because it benefits a smaller and smaller group of people. After coming to this same conclusion, economist Joseph Stiglitz laments that the 'European project is too important to be sacrificed on the cross of the euro.'[31] And yet, as political scientist Claus Offe points out, the euro 'is a mistake the undoing of which would be an even greater mistake.'[32] Ensuring that the Eurozone system benefits those who have not prospered under intensified globalization – through a full employment strategy as Stiglitz recommends – is critical to the survival of a united Europe.[33]

In 2013, István Horváth, a sociologist from Cluj, told me that he'd ceased being a liberal since I'd last talked to him in the early 1990s. Instead, he'd become something of a leftist. 'I was a naïve person who believed that political integration into Europe would create wealth and more democracy,' he told me. 'I thought the market was the solution to many things. Now I realize that the market is not necessarily a solution to anything. It can also be a source of problems. I was expecting that a much more globalized and internationalized way of thinking would bring more democracy and stability. Now I see that globalization means a lack of control by states over resources and wealth.'

In a measure of the true impact of economic globalization on eastern Europe, István's comments would not have been out of place coming from Tamás Hegedűs or even Volen Siderov. The economic changes of the last several decades have scrambled the political spectrum.

The new political order

The history of political parties can be rather boring. Not much has changed since the French Revolution, which introduced the terms 'left' and 'right' to reflect where people sat in the National Assembly. The early twentieth century saw the rise of communist parties on the far left. Later, fascist parties began to emerge on the far right. Aside from these challenges from the margins, most European countries have produced some version of a conservative (Christian Democrat, Tory) party and a liberal (Labor, Social Democratic) party, which have alternated in power, sometimes even ruling in coalition.

The one major innovation of the last fifty years has been the Green Party. Starting in Australia but achieving greatest prominence in Germany, green parties have been both conservative (in terms of preserving the environment) and radical (in challenging economic orthodoxy). There are green parties in ninety countries around the world. They have participated in several European governments. But they have not fully transformed politics. The traditional liberal and conservative parties have simply made a little room on the political spectrum for their green colleagues.

Now, however, this stable political order seems on the verge of collapse. Throughout Europe, and indeed all over the world, people in democratic societies have grown disgusted with politics as usual. The success of Viktor Orbán in Hungary and Jarosław Kaczyński in Poland has emboldened populist politicians like Marine Le Pen in France, Nigel Farage in the UK, and Norbert Hofer in Austria. On the outskirts of Europe, Vladimir Putin in Russia and Recep Tayyip Erdoğan in Turkey rose to power through elections only to challenge the very institutions that facilitated their rise and legitimated their rule. The victories of Donald Trump in the United States, Rodrigo Duterte in the Philippines, and Daniel Ortega in Nicaragua suggest that the appeal is international in scope.

These leaders call themselves different things: left, right, socialist, nationalist. They also all function within democracies. But they all share one thing in common. They are 'illiberal.' They are not very interested in civil liberties. They will manipulate the rule of law to 'get things done.' They tend to appeal to religious or national identity rather than political ideology to move their followers. They also generally favor greater state intervention in the economy, even if it's only to enrich their own followers. In short, they defy the usual political categories.

These illiberal populists have benefited electorally from three overlapping backlashes.

The first is cultural. Movements for civil liberties have been remarkably successful over the last forty years. Women, ethnic and religious minorities, and the LGBTQ community have secured important gains at a legal and cultural level. It is remarkable, for instance, how quickly same-sex marriage has become legal in more than twenty countries when no country recognized it before 2001. Resistance has always existed to these movements to expand the realm of civil liberties. But this backlash increasingly has a political face. Parties have arisen to challenge multiculturalism and immigration in Europe, movements throughout Africa and Asia support majority demands over minority concerns, and Trump has engineered a takeover of the Republican Party with his appeals to primarily white men of a certain age and educational background. In the United States, Europe, and Russia, racism (or 'white nationalism') lurks just beneath many of the attacks on multiculturalism.

The second backlash is economic. The globalization of the economy has created a class of enormously wealthy individuals (in the financial, technology, and communications sectors). But globalization has left behind huge numbers of low-wage workers and those who have watched their jobs relocate to other countries. Illiberal populists have directed all that anger on the part of people left behind by the world economy at a series of targets: bankers who make billions, corporations that are constantly looking for even lower-wage workers, immigrants who 'take away our jobs,' and sometimes ethnic minorities who function as convenient scapegoats. The targets, in other words, include both the very powerful and the very weak. Right-wing populists, as political scientist Jan-Werner Müller points out, 'typically claim to discern a symbiotic relationship between an elite that does not truly belong and marginal groups that are also distinct from the people.'[34]

The third backlash, and perhaps the most consequential, is political. It's not just that people living in democracies are disgusted with their leaders and the parties they represent. Rather, as political scientists Roberto Stefan Foa and Yascha Mounk write in the *Journal of Democracy*, 'they have also become more cynical about the value of democracy as a political system, less hopeful that anything they do might influence public policy, and more willing to express support for authoritarian alternatives.'[35] Foa and Mounk are using twenty years of data collected from surveys of citizens in western Europe and North America – the democracies with the greatest longevity. And they have found that support for illiberal alternatives is greater among the younger generation than the older one.

These three backlashes – cultural, economic, political – are also anti-internationalist. After all, international institutions have become associated with the promotion of civil liberties and human rights, the greater globalization of the economy, and the constraint of the sovereignty of nations (for instance, through the European Union or the UN's 'responsibility to protect' doctrine).

It's not yet clear what political system will emerge from this illiberal assault on democracy. Perhaps the existing system will absorb the populist challenges much as it did the environmental critiques of the greens. It may usher in a new era of polarization and volatility in which different populist formations contend for power. Or perhaps a new politics of internationalism will emerge, strengthened by these challenges to globalization, European federalism, and cultural universalism.

Looking ahead

This final chapter has explored a set of divides: between those inside and outside the EU, between the cosmopolitan and the national, between those who have benefited from economic globalization and those who haven't, and between political elites and the citizenries who rage against them. A country can accommodate one or two such divisions. But when such unbridgeable conflicts start to accumulate and intensify, as they have over the last twenty years, the existing system becomes increasingly untenable.

In 1944, the Hungarian-American political economist Karl Polanyi discussed how the passions of the time had swept away the pillars of the nineteenth-century system. Gone was the balance of power and the gold standard. Under attack were the laissez-faire economy and the liberal state. A 'great transformation' was underway, though it was difficult to imagine, in the midst of World War II, what new order would be born. Tested by extremists, the liberal phoenix eventually rose from the ashes of its previous incarnation and presided over the Cold War era, at least in the West. It survived largely by borrowing the practice of greater state intervention in the economy – through the New Deal and the emerging European Community – from its illiberal challengers.

The pillars of the twentieth century are now similarly under attack. Gone is the balance of power of the Cold War. The laissez-faire market of economic globalization is being challenged from left, right, and center. The liberal political consensus and the rights paradigm seem similarly exhausted. Additionally, the very international community – understood regionally in the form of the European Union or globally in the form of the International Monetary Fund – has been stretched to the breaking point.

As in 1944, it is difficult to see what will replace what had once seemed such a durable status quo. Like the activists at Metelkova, we are squatting in the ruins of the old, holding on to a vision of what could be as wars and economic turmoil swirl around us. We could be evicted at any moment, our temporary home bulldozed. Or perhaps we can hold out long enough to reimagine our surroundings.

The illiberal populists described in the first part of this book want to pull their countries back to an imagined past. The progressive visionaries described in the second part of this book want to pull their countries forward into an imagined future. For the time being, both of these paradises are deferred, and we must reckon with the morbid symptoms – and the hopeful signs – that proliferate in the interregnum between the collapse of the old and the birth of the new.

I returned to Eastern Europe to conduct my interviews in 2012 and 2013 – before the return to power of PiS in Poland, before the Brexit vote in the UK, before the election of Donald Trump in the United States. Illiberal sentiment has only gotten stronger, and it's not yet clear whether it has peaked. Eastern Europe was, in many ways, the canary in the coalmine, as people there engaged in some of the earliest criticisms of liberalism, voicing their dissatisfaction with economic reforms that produced growth but not widespread prosperity, democratic systems that promised participation but not satisfactory representation, and involvement in the larger world that brought trade-offs that prompted many to turn from the global to the warm embrace of the parochial.

'This still very much alive neoliberal model is the third-worst thing that has happened since the beginning of the last century,' Sonja Licht told me in Belgrade in 2012. 'We had of course the huge tragedy of Stalinism. Then we had the huge tragedy of fascism. And I'm afraid that this third thing, this neoconservative, neoliberal imposed model, will be the third huge tragedy. It has brought out such egoism in each society, in people, in states.'

The Aztecs sacrificed themselves on their pyramids, first a long line of individuals and then the society as a whole, and all that's left are the pyramids themselves. Sonja Licht watched the sacrifice of Yugoslavia and worries about the sacrifice of the European Union. She confirmed that she remains both an optimist and an activist. 'The two things don't go together, pessimism and activism,' she reminded me.

But as I prepared to leave her office in 2012 after our first conversation in nearly twenty years, she looked up at me and said, apropos her past fears about Yugoslavia and her current anxieties about the EU, 'I hope that you and I don't meet in twenty years and talk about how we are worried about the planet in the same way.'

It was said not with a note of defeat but in the voice of someone prepared once again to stand up and leap into action.

Notes

Introduction

1 Merlene Davis, 'Immigrant couple helping with Lexington's literacy,' *Lexington Herald Leader*, 6 August 2011; www.kentucky.com/news/local/community/article44119464.html.
2 Although the fertility rate rebounded back to 1.5 per cent by 2013, the overall population continued to drop. See, e.g., www.google.com/publicdata/explore?ds=d5bncppjof8f9_&met_y=sp_dyn_tfrt_in&idim=country:BGR:ROM:HRV&hl=en&dl=en.
3 Nicole Crowder, 'The steep decline of Bulgaria's population in its post-Soviet era,' *Washington Post*, 10 November 2014; www.washingtonpost.com/news/in-sight/wp/2014/11/10/the-steep-decline-of-bulgarias-population-in-the-post-soviet-era/?utm_term=.547c8a440c81.
4 Andrei Shleifer and Daniel Treisman, 'Normal countries,' *Foreign Affairs*, November/December 2014.
5 Marcin Piatkowski, 'Poland's new golden age,' Policy Research Working Paper, World Bank, 1 October 2013; documents.worldbank.org/curated/en/2013/10/18347962/polands-new-golden-age-shifting-europes-periphery-center.
6 Quoted in Nick Thorpe, *'89: The Unfinished Revolution* (London: Reportage Press, 2009), pp. 191–2.
7 John Feffer, *Shock Waves: Eastern Europe after the Revolutions* (Boston, MA: South End Press, 1992).
8 A full list is available here: www.johnfeffer.com/full-interview-list/.
9 Tony Judt, *Postwar* (New York: Penguin, 2006).
10 Anna Manchin, 'Greeks still most pessimistic globally,' Gallup, 18 July 2013; www.gallup.com/poll/163556/greeks-pessimistic-globally.aspx.
11 'Gallup study: Bulgaria citizens most pessimistic in world,' Novinite, 25 May 2009; www.novinite.com/view_news.php?id=103934.
12 Ivan Krastev, 'Optimistic theory about the pessimism of the transition,' Centre for Liberal Strategies, 16 December 2003; www.cls-sofia.org/en/papers/optimistic-theory-about-the-pessimism-of-the-transition-40.html.
13 Hanna Kozlowska, 'The Czech government wants to change the constitution to let its citizens use guns against terrorists,' Quartz, 4 January

2017; qz.com/877905/the-czech-interior-ministry-wants-to-change-the-constitution-to-let-its-citizens-use-guns-against-terrorists/.

14 Jerzy Szacki, *Liberalism after Communism* (Budapest: CEU Press, 1995), pp. 10, 146.

15 In *The Great Transformation* (London: Victor Gollancz, 1945), Karl Polyani shows how the American welfare state, the Stalinist version of communism, and the fascist economic program were all responses to the same global economic crisis.

16 The phrase is Shakespeare's, but it was applied to the region by journalist Timothy Garton Ash in *The Uses of Adversity* (New York: Random House, 1989).

17 Joseph Rothschild, *Return to Diversity* (New York: Oxford University Press, 2007).

18 Paul Hockenos, *Berlin Calling* (New York: New Press, 2017), pp. 187–8.

19 Timothy Garton Ash, 'Revolution: the springtime of two nations,' *New York Review of Books*, 15 June 1989.

20 Paul Lendvai, *Hungary: Between Democracy and Authoritarianism* (Budapest: Central European University Press, 2012), p. 68.

21 Vlad Odobescu, 'Nicolae Ceausescu's legacy reconsidered amid nostalgia for communism in Romania,' *Washington Times*, 18 April 2016; www.washingtontimes.com/news/2016/apr/18/nicolae-ceausescus-legacy-reconsidered-amid-nostal/.

22 Craig Smith, 'Populism rises in polarized central Europe,' *New York Times*, 30 October 2006; www.nytimes.com/2006/10/30/world/europe/30iht-hungary.3329849.html?_r=0.

23 Michael Shafir, 'Romania's road to "normalcy,"' *Journal of Democracy*, 8(2) (April 1997), p. 155.

24 Martin Bútora, 'Slovakia's foreign policy: legacies and new horizons,' in Olga Gyarfasova and Grigorij Mesežnikov (eds), *Visegrad Elections 2010: Domestic Impact and European Consequences* (Bratislava: Institute for Public Affairs, 2011), p. 215.

25 Ivan Krastev, 'The strange death of the liberal consensus,' *Journal of Democracy*, 18(4) (October 2007), p. 56. Also see Jacques Rupnik, 'Populism in eastern Europe,' *Eurozine*, 10 September 2007.

26 Janine Wedel, *Collision and Collusion* (New York: St Martin's Press, 1998), p. 22.

27 Zsolt Darvas, '10 Years EU enlargement anniversary: waltzing past Vienna,' Bruegel, 1 May 2014; bruegel.org/2014/05/10-years-eu-enlargement-anniversary-waltzing-past-vienna/.

28 The genealogy of this William Gibson quote is somewhat complicated. See, for instance, the website Quote Investigator: quoteinvestigator.com/2012/01/24/future-has-arrived/.

29 The 1991 figures can be found here: data.worldbank.org/indicator/NY.GDP.PCAP.CD?page=4.

30 The 2015 figures for GDP per capita, which reflect purchasing power parity, can be found here: en.wikipedia.org/wiki/List_of_sovereign_states_in_Europe_by_GDP_(PPP)_per_capita. The gaps in the respective nominal figures, which reflect the literal exchange rates, are much larger: en.wikipedia.org/wiki/List_of_sovereign_states_in_Europe_by_GDP_(nominal)_per_capita.

31 See, e.g., Peter Coy, 'Afghanistan has cost the US more than the Marshall Plan,' Bloomberg, 31 July 2014; www.bloomberg.com/news/articles/2014-07-31/afghanistan-has-cost-the-u-dot-s-dot-more-than-the-marshall-plan.

32 Nick Dearden, 'Greece and Spain helped postwar Germany recover. Spot the difference,' *Guardian*, 27 February 2013; www.theguardian.com/commentisfree/2013/feb/27/greece-spain-helped-germany-recover.

33 Barry Newman, 'Disappearing act,' *Wall Street Journal*, 23 February 1994. For instance, as Newman reports, 'Brussels awarded 546 contracts worth $286 million in 1991; Polish consultants got half a percent of that.'

34 'One estimate pegs grant aid from the West in the 1990s, in relation to its GNP, as just one-fiftieth of what the United States had committed to Europe in the 1940s and 1950s,' writes Padraic Kenney in *The Burdens of Freedom* (London: Zed Books, 2006), p. 19.

35 Ibid., p. 18.

36 'The study of Eastern Europe as a region in political science faces a tripartite crisis,' write Michael Bernhard and Krzysztof Jasiewicz. 'First, the very concept of Eastern Europe has lost coherence, and many in academia and outside see this field as obsolete – a mere residuum of the Cold War. Second, the support for research on Eastern Europe and the training of specialists, which was more substantial though never abundant in past decades, is drying up. Third, political science, and in particular the subfield of comparative politics, has moved away from an area-centered approach and is driven by both theoretical and methodological concerns in which the specificities of area are less important.' Michael Bernhard and Krzysztof Jasiewicz, 'Whither Eastern Europe? Changing approaches and perspectives on the region in political science,' *East European Politics and Societies and Cultures*, 29(2) (May 2015), p. 311.

37 Dubravka Ugrešić, *Thank You for Not Reading* (McLean, IL: Dalkey Archive Press, 2003), p. 25.

38 George Konrad and Iván Szelényi, *The Intellectuals on the Road to Class Power* (New York: Harcourt Brace Jovanovich, 1979), p. 82.

39 Lawrence Goodwyn, *Breaking the Barrier* (New York: Oxford University Press, 1991), p. 342.

40 Lonnie Johnson, *Central Europe: Enemies, Neighbors, Friends* (2nd edn) (New York: Oxford University Press, 2002), p. 33.

41 Valentina Dimitrova-Grajzl writes, for instance, 'I posit that the Ottoman legacy enabled the establishment of highly restrictive socialist regimes (referred to as 'Patrimonial' Socialism), with low bureaucratic quality, lasting prevalence of corruption, which in turn instilled less trust in government and more reliance on closed personal networks (e.g. trust in the family) in Ottoman successor states. The Habsburg legacy, on the other hand, with its exposure to markets and property rights, led to a resistance to the adoption of socialism, more openness to the West and the establishment of less restrictive socialist regimes.' Valentina Dimitrova-Grajzl, 'Trust, path dependence and historical legacy: the second decade after transition,' in Nicolas Hayoz, Leszek Jesień, and Daniela Koleva (eds), *20 Years after the Collapse of Communism* (Bern: Peter Lang, 2011), p. 145.

42 Quoted in Marcus Tanner, *Croatia: A Nation Forged in War* (New Haven, CT: Yale University Press, 2010), pp. 127–8.

43 Milan Kundera, 'The tragedy of central Europe,' *New York Review of Books*, 26 April 1984.

44 Quoted in Alina Polyakova, *The Dark Side of Integration* (Stuttgart: Ibidem Verlag, 2015), p. 36.

45 Václav Havel, *To the Castle and Back* (New York: Knopf, 2007), p. 22.

1 Pyramids of Sacrifice

1 Matevž Krivic, 'Post scriptum,' in Jasminka Dedić, Vlasta Jalušič, and Jelka Zorn (eds), *The Erased: Organized Innocence and the Politics of Exclusion* (Ljubljana: Mirovni Institut, 2003), p. 158.

2 Ibid., p. 159.

3 The case of the Erased was not completely hidden during these years. For instance, the first case went to the Slovenian Constitutional Court in 1994, and the court ruled that the erasure was unconstitutional in 1999. See, e.g., Vlasta Jalušič and Jasminka Dedić, '(The) Erasure – mass human rights violation and denial of responsibility: the case of independent Slovenia,' *Human Rights Review*, 9(1) (2008), p. 97.

4 'Almost EUR 20m in compensation granted to Erased so far,' *Slovenia Times*, 4 June 2015; www.sloveniatimes.com/almost-eur-20m-in-compensation-granted-to-erased-so-far.

5 'War for Slovenia 1991,' Republic of Slovenia website; www.slovenija2001.gov.si/10years/path/war/.

6 Alenka Kuhelj, 'Rise of xenophobic nationalism in Europe: a case of Slovenia,' *Communist and Post-Communist Studies*, 44(4) (December 2011). Similar protections were not accorded the Serbian minority.

7 The death toll included between six and seven million people who died during the famine in Ukraine in 1932/33.

8 Frank Dikötter, *Mao's Great Famine; The Story of China's Most Devastating Catastrophe* (New York: Walker and Co., 2010), p. 320.

9 Ibid., p. xii.

10 Manuel Aguilar-Moreno, *Handbook to Life in the Aztec World* (New York: Facts on File, 2006), p. 174.

11 Peter Berger, *Pyramids of Sacrifice* (New York: Anchor Books, 1976), p. 8.

12 Ibid., p. xiii.

13 On this process in China, see, for instance, Ho-fung Hung, *The China Boom* (New York: Columbia University Press, 2015), pp. 44–7.

14 In the 1970s, South Korean universities came to be known as 'monuments of cow skeletons,' for farmers would do anything to send their children to the cities for education, even to the point of selling their cows and their land and taking out loans. Cho Young-rae, *A Single Spark: The Biography of Chun Tae-Il* (Seoul: Dolbegae Publishers, 2004), p. 69.

15 'GDP in eastern Europe, 1980-1989,' *World Facts* (Washington, DC: World Bank, 1992); chnm.gmu.edu/1989/items/show/667.

16 In 1988, Yugoslavia first prepared to make a bid for European Community membership. See Aleksandar Zigic, 'Queuing up for EC membership?' *Christian Science Monitor*, 29 August 1988, and Stephen Sestanovich, 'Yugoslavia's struggle to remake itself,' *Christian Science Monitor*, 25 October 1988. In February 1990, Yugoslavia applied for associate status. See Richard Caplan, *Europe and the Recognition of New States in Yugoslavia* (Cambridge: Cambridge University Press, 2005), p. 183.

17 Robert Kaplan, *Balkan Ghosts* (New York: St Martin's Press, 1993), p. xxi.

18 Mark Mazower, *The Balkans* (New York: Modern Library, 2000) p. 147.

19 See, for example, Timothy Snyder, *Bloodlands* (New York: Basic Books, 2010).

20 For the inflation rate, see Craig Forman, 'East bloc lesson,' *Wall Street Journal*, 20 February 1990; for the unemployment rate, see Mark Baskin and Paula Pickering, 'Yugoslavia,' in Sharon Wolchik and Jane Curry (eds), *Central and East European Politics: From Communism to Democracy* (Lanham, MD: Rowman and Littlefield, 2008), p. 285.

21 Chip Gagnon, 'Yugoslavia in 1989 and after,' *Nationalities Papers*, 38(1) (January 2010).

22 At the November 1989 Paris Summit, the European Community offered associate agreements to eastern European countries on the basis of four political conditions including free and fair elections to be held in 1990. See Richard Caplan, op. cit., pp. 181–2.

23 Paul Hockenos, *Homeland Calling* (Ithaca, NY: Cornell University Press, 2003).

24 'European Community imposes economic sanctions on Yugoslavia,' UPI, 8 November 1991; www.upi.com/Archives/1991/11/08/European-Community-imposes-economic-sanctions-on-Yugoslavia/2962689576400/.

25 Quoted in Sonja Biserko, *Yugoslavia's Implosion* (Oslo: Norwegian Helsinki Committee, 2012), p. 86.

26 'Presidents apologize over Croatian war,' BBC, 10 September 2003; news.bbc.co.uk/2/hi/europe/3095774.stm.

27 World Bank, 'Bosnia and Herzegovina: from reconstruction to European integration,' 4 December 2009, p. 2; documents.worldbank.org/curated/en/118171468007530787/pdf/519530BRI0ida110Box345548B01PUBLIC1.pdf; calculation based on 2009 dollar-Euro exchange rate.

28 The death toll from the Kosovo conflict remains controversial, with figures as low as 2,100 based on exhumations and as high as 11,000 based on eyewitness reports. See Ian Williams, 'The Kosovo numbers game,' Institute for War and Peace Reporting, 16 November 2005; iwpr.net/global-voices/kosovo-numbers-game.

29 Tony Karon, 'Who'll pick up the tab for Kosovo?' *Time*, 22 June 1999; content.time.com/time/arts/article/0,8599,27123,00.html.

30 Tina Rosenberg, *The Haunted Land* (New York: Random House, 1995), p. 161.

31 Lech Wałęsa, *The Struggle and The Triumph* (New York: Arcade, 1992), p. 31.

32 Quoted in David Ost, *The Defeat of Solidarity* (Ithaca, NY: Cornell University Press, 2005), p. 37.

33 Lawrence Weschler, 'Shock,' *New Yorker*, 10 December 1990, pp. 122–3.

34 Juliusz Gardawski, 'The dynamics of unemployment from 1990 to 2002,' Eurofound, 28 October 2002; www.eurofound.europa.eu/observatories/eurwork/articles/the-dynamics-of-unemployment-from-1990-to-2002.

35 Solidarity membership fell to 5 percent of the workforce and that of the All-Poland Alliance of Trade Unions (OPZZ) to 4 percent. See Jane Hardy, 'Poland,' in Donnacha Ó Beacháin, Vera Sheridan and Sabina Stan (eds), *Life in Post-Communist Eastern Europe after EU Membership* (New York: Routledge, 2012), p. 13.

36 Liam Ebril, *Poland: The Path to a Market Economy* (Washington, DC: International Monetary Fund, 15 September 1994), p. 85.

37 Jane Curry, 'Poland,' in Wolchik and Curry, op. cit., pp. 183–4.

38 Jeffrey Sachs and David Lipton, 'Poland's economic reform,' *Foreign Affairs*, Summer 1990, p. 60; www.foreignaffairs.com/articles/poland/1990-06-01/polands-economic-reform.

39 The 1986 figure comes from Janine Wedel, *Collision and Collusion* (New York: St Martin's Press, 1998), p. 68. The 1991 figure comes from Andrew

Dawson, 'Poland,' in Patrick Heenan and Monique Lamontagne (eds), *The Central and Eastern Europe Handbook* (London: Fitzroy Dearborn Publishers, 1999), p. 7.

40 Mary Battiata, 'Factory's downfall symbolizes problems of Polish reforms,' *Washington Post*, 5 August 1991.

41 John Feffer, 'Poland after Solidarity,' *Peace and Democracy News*, Winter 1992/93.

42 Adam Michnik, *In Search of Lost Meaning* (Berkeley: University of California Press, 2011), p. 5.

43 Dena Ringold, 'Social policy in postcommunist Europe: legacies and transition,' in Linda Cook, Mitchell Orenstein, and Marilyn Rueschemeyer (eds), *Left Parties and Social Policy in Postcommunist Europe* (Boulder, CO: Westview Press, 1999), p. 20.

44 David P. Conradt and Eric Langenbacher, *The German Polity* (Lanham, MD: Rowman and Littlefield, 2013), p. 40.

45 Padraic Kenney, *The Burdens of Freedom* (London: Zed Books, 2006), p. 28.

46 Cited in Michael Kennedy, *Cultural Formations of Post-Communism* (Minneapolis: University of Minnesota Press, 2002), p. 109.

47 Anthony Robinson and Virginia Marsh, 'Hungarian reforms bit into cherished high living,' *Financial Times*, 24 November 1995.

48 'In certain respects, the rise in unemployment during the 1990s can be seen as a healthy development, a sign of the rationalization of production and employment.' Sharon Fisher, 'Recreating the market,' in Wolchik and Curry, op. cit., p. 71.

49 Joseph Schumpeter, *Capitalism, Socialism, and Democracy* (London: Allen & Unwin, 1954), p. 83.

50 Katherine Verdery, 'Faith, hope, and Caritas in the land of the pyramids,' *Comparative Studies in Society and History*, 37(4) (October 1995), p. 635.

51 Ibid., p. 627.

52 Tony Barber, 'Romanians storm city as scam ruins millions,' *Independent*, 15 January 1994; www.independent.co.uk/news/world/romanians-storm-city-as-scam-ruins-millions-1407128.html.

53 Fred Abrahams, *Modern Albania* (New York: New York University Press, 2015).

54 Bernard Rorke, 'Segregation in Hungary: the long road to infringement,' European Roma Rights Centre blog, 30 May 2016; www.errc.org/blog/segregation-in-hungary-the-long-road-to-infringement/106.

55 Barbara Demick, 'Anti-Gypsy pogroms rampant in Romania,' *Philadelphia Inquirer*, 29 November 1993.

56 In Hungary, for instance, local politicians in particular openly engage in 'abusive language, slander, and terms of mockery' when discussing Roma. János Zolnay, 'Abusive language and discriminatory measures in Hungarian

local policy,' in Michael Stewart (ed.), *The Gypsy 'Menace'* (London: Hurst and Co., 2012).

57 'Roma in central and eastern Europe,' GESIS Leibniz Institute for the Social Sciences, February 2009; www.gesis.org/fileadmin/upload/dienstleistung/fachinformationen/series_ssee_01/Roma_in_Central_and_Eastern_Europe.pdf.

58 Dragan Todorović, Lela Milošević and Dragoljub Đorđević, 'Social distance of Romas of southeastern and southwestern Serbia towards members of other nations and national minorities,' www.komunikacija.org.rs/komunikacija/knjige/index_html/knjiga04/29TodorovicD_MilosevicL_DjordjevicDB_eng.pdf.

59 Roma were relocated to the former Sudetenland after the country kicked out Germans from that territory in 1945.

60 Human Rights Watch, 'Roma in the Czech Republic foreigners in their own land,' 1 June 1996; www.refworld.org/docid/3ae6a7ea0.html.

61 European Roma Rights Centre, 'Czech Republic amends anti-Romani law,' 5 September 1999; www.errc.org/article/czech-republic-amends-anti-romani-law/980.

2 The Journey to Utopia

1 'Political Parties Act,' Republic of Bulgaria National Assembly, 10 April 1990; unpan1.un.org/intradoc/groups/public/documents/UNTC/UNPAN016314.pdf.

2 Umut Korkut, *Liberalization Challenges in Hungary: Elitism, Progressivism, and Populism* (New York: Palgrave Macmillan, 2012), p. 114.

3 'The overwhelming response of the intelligentsia to the idea of a renewal of socialism in the GDR raised hopes that later turned out to be yet another incidence of self-deception,' writes Feiwel Kupferberg in *The Rise and Fall of the German Democratic Republic* (Piscataway, NJ: Transaction Publishers, 2002), p. 94.

4 Cited in Samuel Moyn, *The Last Utopia* (Cambridge, MA: Harvard University Press, 2010), p. 120.

5 The feline image, according to economist Jeffrey Sachs, comes from Bolivian planning minister Gonzalo Sanchez de Lozada, who said in 1986: 'If you are going to chop of a cat's tail, do it in one strike, not bit by bit.' Jeffrey Sachs and David Lipton, 'Poland's economic reform,' *Foreign Affairs*, Summer 1990, p. 56.

6 Francis Fukuyama, *The End of History and the Last Man* (New York: Free Press, 2006).

7 Ibid., p. 46.

8 Ralf Dahrendorf, *Reflections on the Revolution in Europe* (New Brunswick, NJ: Transaction Publishers, 2014), p. 42.

9 The term 'transition,' writes sociologist Michael Kennedy, 'focuses one's sensibility on forward movement rather than explicitly engaging the system from which nations sought to escape. It is a term very well suited, therefore, to those whose expertise is oriented toward the future, such as those in economic modeling or business plans, even though the broader and even more futuristic term emerging markets might eventually overwhelm transition's competitive conceptual advantage.' Michael Kennedy, *Cultural Formations of Post-Communism* (Minneapolis: University of Minnesota Press, 2002), p. 5.

10 Larry Wolff, *Inventing Eastern Europe* (Stanford, CA: Stanford University Press, 1994), p. 4.

11 See, e.g., Christian Giordano, 'Mythologies of postsocialism,' in Nicolas Hayoz, Leszek Jesień, and Daniela Koleva (eds), *20 Years after the Collapse of Communism* (Bern: Peter Lang, 2011), pp. 283–4.

12 Petru Clej, 'Daring to question the Romanian revolution,' BBC News, 21 December 2009; news.bbc.co.uk/2/hi/europe/8417046.stm.

13 For a useful account of transitologists and their critics, see Charles King, *Extreme Politics* (New York: Oxford University Press, 2010), p. 88ff.

14 Graeme Gill, *Democracy and Post-Communism* (New York: Routledge, 2002), p. 194.

15 See, e.g., Japhy Wilson, *The Strange Case of Dr Shock and Mr. Aid* (London: Verso, 2014).

16 Lawrence Weschler, 'A grand experiment,' *New Yorker*, 13 November 1989; www.newyorker.com/magazine/1989/11/13/a-grand-experiment.

17 Leszek Balcerowicz largely agreed, at least in a 1991 interview he gave to the *Warsaw Voice*: 'A doctrinaire liberal would probably oppose expanding state social welfare institutions. But I personally think such institutions should exist, as long as their performance is reasonable, and their costs don't undermine the whole economic program.' 'The risk option,' *Warsaw Voice*, 3 March 1991.

18 'There were and still are many question marks [about] how the economy will respond,' Polish economist Stefan Kawalec said at the time. 'In this, Sachs had no knowledge at all because he was not familiar with Communist economies. He tried to treat this economy the same as Latin American ones.' Quoted in Janine Wedel, *Collision and Collusion* (New York: St Martin's Press, 1998), p. 57.

19 See, for example, Venelin I. Ganev, 'The spell of Marx and Jeffrey Sachs: social theory and post-communist politics,' *East European Politics and Societies and Cultures*, 29(1) (May 2015), p. 447.

20 In a similar way, the social market program of Ludwig Erhard in post-war Germany resembled that of Albert Speer in the Nazi era. See, e.g., Tony Judt, *Postwar* (New York: Penguin, 2006), p. 355.

21 Tadeusz Kowalik, *From Solidarity to Sellout* (New York: Monthly Review Press, 2011), p. 166.

22 Balcerowicz was indeed more of an adherent of minimal government typical of the thinking of Friedrich Hayek. For instance, he favored both a flat tax and faster privatization. See, e.g., Leszek Balcerowicz, 'Poland,' in Anders Åslund and Simeon Djankov (eds), *The Great Rebirth: Lessons from the Victory of Capitalism over Communism* (Washington, DC: Peterson Institute for International Economics, 2014).

23 Grzegorz W. Kolodko, 'Polish hyperinflation and stabilization 1989–1990,' *Economic Journal on Eastern Europe and the Soviet Union*, 1 (1991); https://www.researchgate.net/publication/226032041_Polish_hyperinflation_and_stabilization_1989-1990.

24 'Transition did not cause financial hardship, but it was unleashed by financial collapse. All formerly socialist countries except Czechoslovakia were in severe financial crises when they entered transition,' writes Anders Åslund. *How Capitalism Was Built* (Cambridge University Press, Kindle edn, 2013), p. 117.

25 Quoted in Tadeusz Kowalik, *From Solidarity to Sellout*, op. cit., p. 11. Other politicians – such as Aleksander Małachowski, the speaker of the Sejm, the lower house of parliament – felt bamboozled. 'We were somewhat like sheep led for slaughter and easily gave into the promises of the politicians, who had the decisive voice in the practical implementation of harmful schemes,' Małachowski recalled. 'Balcerowicz and his mentor Jeffrey Sachs plainly tricked us, parliamentarians without experience.' Ibid., p. 132.

26 Ibid., p. 136.

27 The larger figure of 500,000 comes from Virginie Wojtkowski, 'Are half a million people homeless in Poland?' Cafe Babel, 1 March 2012; www.cafebabel.co.uk/society/article/are-half-a-million-people-homeless-in-poland.html; also: Maciej Dębski, 'Homelessness in Poland,' *European Journal of Homelessness*, 5(1) (August 2011); www.feantsaresearch.org/IMG/pdf/ejh_2011_5.1_article-5.pdf.

28 'Fertility rate,' Google Public Data; www.google.com/publicdata/explore?ds=d5bncppjof8f9_&met_y=sp_dyn_tfrt_in&idim=country:POL:DEU:RUS&hl=en&dl=en.

29 Lorraine Waller, 'Is the fertility of Polish women higher in the UK than in Poland?' Openpop.org, 19 March 2014; www.openpop.org/?p=761.

30 World Bank, GINI Index; data.worldbank.org/indicator/SI.POV.GINI?end=2012&locations=PL&start=1985&view=chart&year_high_desc=false.

31 Jane Hardy, 'Poland,' in Donnacha Ó Beacháin, Vera Sheridan, and Sabina Stan, *Life in Post-Communist Eastern Europe after EU Membership* (New York: Routledge, 2012), p. 23.

32 Sachs and Lipton, op. cit., p. 53.

33 Robert Hutchings, *American Diplomacy and the End of the Cold War* (Washington, DC: Wilson Institute, 1997), p. 232.
34 Sachs and Lipton, op. cit., p. 64.
35 Ilian Mihov, 'The economic transition in Bulgaria, 1989–1999,' in Mario Blejer and Marko Škreb, *Transition: The First Decade* (Cambridge, MA: MIT Press, 2001), p. 407.
36 Janine Wedel, *Collision and Collusion* (New York: St Martin's Press, 1998), p. 28.
37 Maria Ivanova, 'Why there was no "Marshall Plan" for eastern Europe and why this still matters,' *Journal of Contemporary European Studies*, 15(3) (December 2007).
38 On the new round of borrowing, see Viachaslau Yarashevich, 'External debt of post-communist countries,' *Communist and Post-Communist Studies*, 46 (2013).
39 Anders Åslund, *How Capitalism Was Built* (Cambridge University Press, Kindle edn, 2013), p. 10.
40 See, e.g., Tony Judt, *Postwar* (New York: Penguin, 2006), p. 98.
41 Ho-fung Hung, *The China Boom* (New York: Columbia University Press, 2015), p. 49.
42 Ibid., pp. 60, 68.
43 Anna Husarska, 'Interview with Adam Michnik,' *The New Leader*, 3-17 April 1989.
44 Umut Korkut, 'More reform, less action,' *Problems of Post-Communism*, 57(1) (2010). pp. 17–27.
45 *Making Transition Work for Everyone: Poverty and Inequality in Europe and Central Asia* (Washington, DC: World Bank, 2000), p. 127.
46 Quoted in Anna Porter, *The Ghosts of Europe* (New York: St Martin's Press Press, 2010), p. 59.
47 Václav Havel, 'The power of the powerless,' in Václav Havel et al., *The Power of the Powerless* (New York: Routledge, 1985), p. 119.
48 Steven Szonberg, *The Fall* (Amsterdam: Harwood Academic Publishers, 2001), p. 395.
49 Andrew Schwartz, *The Politics of Greed* (Lanham, MD: Rowman and Littlefield, 2006), p. 119.
50 David Binder, 'Bulgarian strategy is made in U.S.,' *New York Times*, 9 October 1990; www.nytimes.com/1990/10/09/business/bulgarian-strategy-is-made-in-us.html.
51 Andrada Fiscutean, 'How these communist-era Apple II clones helped shape central Europe's IT sector,' ZDNet, 12 February 2016; www.zdnet.com/article/how-these-communist-era-apple-ii-clones-helped-shape-central-europes-it-sector/.
52 Tim Judah, 'Bulgarian avenger infects West's computers,' *Sunday Times*, 16 December 1990.

53 *Slovenia: From Yugoslavia to the European Union* (Washington, DC: World Bank, 2004), p. xxiii.

54 'Privatisation of state-owned enterprises in Czech Republic,' European Commission, International Cooperation and Development, 18 July 2013; ec.europa.eu/europeaid/privatisation-state-owned-enterprises-czech-republic_en; Jan Hanousek and Eugene Kroch, 'The two waves of voucher privatization in the Czech Republic: a model of learning in sequential bidding,' CERGE-EI Working Paper Series no. 84, 1 June 1995, p. 3.

55 Interview with Wolfgang Ullmann, East Berlin, March 1990. Stuart Speiser (ed.), *Mainstreet Capitalism* (New York: New Horizons Press, 1988).

56 Hanousek and Kroch, op. cit.

57 'Another U.S. whistleblower behind bars? Investor jailed after exposing corrupt Azerbaijani oil deal,' Democracy Now, 15 October 2013; www.democracynow.org/2013/10/15/another_us_whistleblower_behind_bars_investor.

58 Ian Willoughby, 'Why do most Czechs regard early 90s voucher privatisation as unfair?' Radio Praha, 6 January 2005; www.radio.cz/en/section/curraffrs/why-do-most-czechs-regard-early-90s-voucher-privatisation-as-unfair.

59 Andrew Weiss and Georgiy Nikitin, 'Performance of Czech companies by ownership structure,' Working Paper, Boston University; www.bu.edu/econ/files/2012/11/dp85.pdf, p. 8.

60 Craig Whitney, 'East Germans occupying mine they seek to save,' *New York Times*, 21 July 1993; www.nytimes.com/1993/07/21/world/east-germans-occupying-mine-they-seek-to-save.html.

61 See, e.g., this travelogue: www.itcwebdesigns.com/tour_germany/erlebnisbergwerk01.htm.

62 K. H. Domdey, 'Privatisation in the New Bundesländer,' in Thomas Lange and J. R. Shackleton (eds), *The Political Economy of German Unification* (New York: Berghahn, 1998), p. 45.

63 Ibid., p. 52.

64 Actually, there were originally twelve sugar companies in Hungary in 1989 – Hegedűs is probably referring to a time after some consolidation had taken place. Only one of these companies remains. See Anna Burger, 'The situation of Hungarian agriculture,' Paper presented at International Scientific Conference, 27–29 May 2009, Vilnius; ageconsearch.umn.edu/bitstream/90651/2/THE%20SITUATION%20OF%20HUNGARIAN%20AGRICULTURE.pdf.

65 Ost, op. cit., p. 154.

66 Agnieszka Paczynska, 'Confronting change: labor, state, and privatization,' *Review of International Political Economy*, 14(2) (May 2007), p. 346.

67 Gareth Dale, *The East German Revolution of 1989* (Manchester: Manchester University Press, 2006), p. 181.

68 Frank Heiland, 'Trends in East–West German migration from 1989 to 2002,' *Demographic Research*, 7, 17 September 2004, p. 178; www.demographic-research.org/volumes/vol11/7/11-7.pdf.

69 Johannes Gernandt and Friedhelm Pfeiffer, 'Wage convergence and inequality after unification: (East) Germany in transition,' SOEPpapers 107, Deutsches Institut für Wirtschaftsforschung, June 2008, p. 5; www.diw.de/documents/publikationen/73/diw_01.c.85462.de/diw_sp0107.pdf.

70 Rüdiger Dornbusch and Holger Wolf, 'Economic transition in Eastern Germany,' Brookings Papers on Economic Activity, January 1992; www.brookings.edu/~/media/Projects/BPEA/1992-1/1992a_bpea_dornbusch_wolf_alexander.PDF.

71 Heiland, op. cit., p. 176.

72 Francine S. Kiefer, 'Costs of German reunification slow Europe's economic engine,' *Christian Science Monitor*, 21 April 1992; www.csmonitor.com/1992/0421/21011.html.

73 'Interview with former German finance minister,' Der Spiegel Online, 12 September 2011; www.spiegel.de/international/europe/interview-with-former-german-finance-minister-germans-will-have-to-pay-a-785704-3.html.

74 'Easterners are not the only ones who say that what followed the end of Communism has been a raw deal for many of the ordinary people who suffered under it,' wrote Craig Whitney in the *New York Times*. '"The biggest scandal of reunification is that by and large it's not the east but the west that got richer because of it," said Karl Otto Pohl, a financier in Frankfurt.' Craig Whitney, 'East Germans occupying mine they seek to save,' *New York Times*, 21 July 1993; www.nytimes.com/1993/07/21/world/east-germans-occupying-mine-they-seek-to-save.html.

75 Claudia Bracholdt, 'Why the former East Germany is lagging 24 years after the Berlin Wall came down,' Quartz, 7 March 2013; qz.com/60481/why-the-former-east-germany-is-lagging-24-years-after-the-berlin-wall-came-down/.

76 'Germany's reunification 25 years on,' *Economist*, 2 October 2015; www.economist.com/blogs/graphicdetail/2015/10/daily-chart-comparing-eastern-and-western-germany.

77 Jiri Pehe, 'Europeans skeptical about their future,' RFE/RL, 8 March 1995; www.rferl.org/a/1140890.html.

78 Ralph S. Clem and Marek Jan Chodakiewicz, 'Poland divided: spatial differences in the June 2003 EU accession referendum,' Jean Monnet/Robert Schuman Paper Series, 4(1) (January 2004), p. 4; aei.pitt.edu/8115/1/poland%20divided.pdf.

79 Andrew Nagorski, 'Backlash in the East,' *Newsweek*, 12 May 2002; www.newsweek.com/backlash-east-145257.

80 *EU Funds in Central and Eastern Europe, Progress Report 2007–2013* (Amsterdam: KPMG, 2016), p. 10; assets.kpmg.com/content/dam/kpmg/pdf/2016/06/EU-Funds-in-Central-and-Eastern-Europe.pdf.

81 Ibid., p. 12.

82 Matthew Holhouse, 'Czech Republic "will follow Britain out of EU,"' *Telegraph*, 23 February 2016; www.telegraph.co.uk/news/worldnews/europe/czechrepublic/12170994/Czechs-will-follow-Britain-out-of-EU.html.

83 *Intensifying Euroscepticism in East Central Europe: A Study by the Republikon Institute*, 2013; www.esee.fnst.org/Reports-News/1213c27180i1p/index.html.

84 Bruce Stokes, 'Euroskepticism beyond Brexit,' Pew Research Center, 7 June 2016; www.pewglobal.org/2016/06/07/euroskepticism-beyond-brexit/; according to an August 2015 Eurobarometer survey, a majority of citizens in the Czech Republic (63 percent), Slovenia (61 percent), Hungary (51 percent), and Slovakia (51 percetn) – and a plurality of citizens in Croatia (46 versus 44 percent), and Poland (39 versus 37 percent) – distrust the EU. European Commission, 'Standard Eurobarometer 84,' Autumn 2015, p. 109; ec.europa.eu/COMMFrontOffice/publicopinion/index.cfm/ResultDoc/download/DocumentKy/72444.

85 Marja Novak, 'Reluctant Slovenia faces fire sale of state assets,' Reuters, 31 May 2013; www.reuters.com/article/us-slovenia-privatisation-idUSBRE94U05H20130531; by 2015, the Slovenian government had privatized only four of fifteen properties on a list presented to the EU. In 2016, the government continued to hold about half of the economy. See 'Slovenia should pursue privatisation – European Commission's Dombrovskis,' Reuters, 5 June 2015; www.reuters.com/article/slovenia-privatisation-idUSL5N0YR2BD20150605; and Marja Novak, 'New Slovenian finance minister sees no need for faster privatization,' Reuters, 30 September 2016; www.reuters.com/article/us-slovenia-minister-idUSKCN1201WL.

86 Anna Manchin, 'EU leadership approval at record low in Spain, Greece,' Gallup, 8 January 2014; www.gallup.com/poll/166757/leadership-approval-record-low-spain-greece.aspx.

87 Jan Sonnenschein and Sofia Kluch, 'EU leadership regains approval across Europe,' Gallup, 2 March 2015; www.gallup.com/poll/181772/leadership-regains-approval-across-europe.aspx.

88 Tara John, 'Is Czexit next?' *Time*, 1 July 2016; time.com/4391005/czexit-milos-zeman-referendum-nato-eu-czech/.

89 Some EU members have called for fellow members to be penalized economically for refusing to take in more refugees. Nick Squires, 'Italy

calls for EU funding to be cut to eastern European countries that refuse to accept refugees,' *Telegraph*, 12 October 2016; www.telegraph.co.uk/news/2016/10/12/italy-calls-for-eu-funding-to-be-cut-to-eastern-european-countri/.

90 Niamh Michail, 'Multinational firms sell poorer quality (but more expensive) food to eastern Europeans,' FoodNavigator.com, 26 May 2016; www.foodnavigator.com/Policy/Multinational-firms-sell-poorer-quality-but-more-expensive-food-to-Eastern-Europeans.

91 László Pordány, 'The eastern European scene,' *Journal of American History*, 93(2) (2006), p. 446.

92 IDEA, 'Voter turnout data for Czech Republic,' www.idea.int/vt/countryview.cfm?id=60.

93 IPU, 'Bulgaria: elections held in 1990,' www.ipu.org/parline-e/reports/arc/2045_90.htm.

94 IDEA, 'Voter turnout data for Croatia,' www.idea.int/vt/countryview.cfm?id=98.

95 IDEA, 'Voter turnout data for Romania,' www.idea.int/vt/countryview.cfm?CountryCode=RO.

96 'The pulse of Europe,' *Times Mirror*, 1991; www.pewglobal.org/files/2014/01/Pulse-of-Europe-Full-Report.pdf, p. 5.

97 Andreas Illmer, 'The vote that set the course for German reunification,' DW, 18 March 2010; www.dw.com/en/the-vote-that-set-the-course-for-german-reunification/a-5364284.

98 'This draft that was made in the end with the support of important Western constitutional experts did not differ fundamentally from the Grundgesetz,' Gerd Poppe remembers. 'But it included some interesting amendments. It had a greater focus on human rights. There were stronger possibilities for holding referendums to support initiatives coming from the people.' Interview with Gerd Poppe, Berlin, 6 February 2013; www.johnfeffer.com/creating-a-parallel-society/.

99 Milan Šimečka, *The Restoration of Order* (London: Verso, 1984), p. 17.

100 György Konrád, *Antipolitics* (New York: Harcourt, 1984).

101 Graeme Gill, *Democracy and Post-Communism* (New York: Routledge, 2002), pp. 121–2.

102 Richard Wike, 'Hungary dissatisfied with democracy, but not its ideals,' Pew Research Center, 7 April 2010; www.pewglobal.org/2010/04/07/hungary-dissatisfied-with-democracy-but-not-its-ideals/.

103 Václav Klaus, 'Czechoslovakia and the Czech Republic: the spirit and main contours of the postcommunist transformation,' in Åslund and Djankov, op. cit., p. 58.

104 On the Physiocrats, see Albert O. Hirschman, *The Passions and the Interests* (Princeton, NJ: Princeton University Press, 2013), p. 98. On the Leninist

tradition, Ken Jowitt, 'The Leninist legacy,' in Vladimir Tismăneanu (ed.), *The Revolutions of 1989* (New York: Routledge, 1999), pp. 222–3.

105 Jacques Rupnik, 'From democracy fatigue to populist backlash,' *Journal of Democracy*, 18(4) (2007), p. 121. See also Åslund: 'The slower reforms were, the greater was the danger that rent-seeking interests would become entrenched and block democratization and the combat of corruption, of which they were the main beneficiaries.' Åslund Anders, *How Capitalism Was Built* (Cambridge University Press, Kindle edn, 2013), p. 6.

106 *Warsaw Voice*, 23 September 1990.

107 Claus Offe, *Varieties of Transition: The East European and East German Experience* (Cambridge, MA: MIT Press, 1996), p. 41.

108 Quoted in John Lewis Gaddis, *Strategies of Containment* (New York: Oxford University Press, 1982), p. 3.

109 Quoted in Christian Joppke, *East German Dissidents and the Revolution of 1989* (New York: New York University Press, 1995), p. 34.

110 Quoted in Vladimir Tismăneanu, 'Rethinking 1989,' in Vladimír Tismăneanu and Bogdan Iacob (eds), *The End and the Beginning: The Revolutions of 1989 and the Resurgence of History* (Budapest: Central European University Press, 2012), p. 23.

3 The Revenge of the Provinces

1 The administrative area of Niš has a somewhat larger population closer to 260,000.

2 Rory Archer, 'Assessing turbofolk controversies: popular music between the nation and the Balkans,' Koninklijke Brill NV, Leiden, 2012; www.suedosteuropa.uni-graz.at/sites/default/files/publications/SEEU_036_02_Archer-1_published%5B1%5D.pdf.

3 Brad Cohen, 'Where folk songs meet Serbian criminals,' BBC, 27 October 2013; www.bbc.com/travel/story/20131017-where-folk-songs-meet-serbian-criminals.

4 Slobodan Kostić, 'Happy return to 1989,' *Politika*, 24 July 2007 (translation BBC).

5 Statistical Office of the Republic of Serbia, 'Population projections of the Republic of Serbia 2011–2041,' 2014; pod2.stat.gov.rs/ObjavljenePublikacije/Popis2011/Projekcije%20stanovnistva%202011-2041.pdf, pp. 13, 74.

6 Violette Rey and Marin Bachvarov, 'Rural settlements in transition – agricultural and countryside crisis in central-eastern Europe,' *GeoJournal*, 44(4) (1998). p. 347.

7 Nicole Crowder, 'The steep decline of Bulgaria's population in its post-Soviet era,' *Washington Post*, 10 November 2014; www.washingtonpost.

com/news/in-sight/wp/2014/11/10/the-steep-decline-of-bulgarias-population-in-the-post-soviet-era/?utm_term=.547c8a440c81.

8 Vladimir Drgona and David Turnock, 'Policies for rural eastern Europe,' *GeoJournal*, 50 (2000).

9 Oliver Goldsmith, 'The deserted village,' www.poetryfoundation.org/poems-and-poets/poems/detail/44292.

10 Balazs Szelenyi, *The Failure of the Central European Bourgeoisie* (New York: Springer, 2006), p. 39.

11 Teresa Rakowska-Harmstone, *Communism in Eastern Europe* (Bloomington: Indiana University Press, 1984), p. 164.

12 Mark Engler and Paul Engler, *This Is an Uprising* (New York: Nation Books, 2016), p. 67.

13 Steven Erlanger, 'Striking Serbian coal miners preserve solidarity,' *New York Times*, 4 October 2000; http://www.nytimes.com/2000/10/04/world/striking-serbian-coal-miners-maintain-solidarity.html.

14 Janine di Giovanni, *Madness Visible* (New York: Knopf, 2003), p. 168.

15 A number of scholars support Mladen's contention about the relationship between decentralization and conflict. 'Decentralized systems of government are less likely to experience intercommunal conflict and antiregime rebellion than centralized systems of government,' writes Dawn Brancati; 'Decentralization: fueling the fire or dampening the flames of ethnic conflict and secessionism?' *International Organization*, 60(3) (Summer 2006), p. 681.

16 The National Alliance for Local and Economic Development.

17 Gorm Jacobsen, 'Poland: twenty years with market economy,' *International Business and Economic Research Journal*, 9(11) (November 2010); www.cluteinstitute.com/ojs/index.php/IBER/article/viewFile/35/33.

18 Emily Cintora, *Democratic Governance in Eastern Europe* (Bratislava: UNDP, 2009); www.hks.harvard.edu/fs/pnorris/DPI403%20Fall09/Emily%20Cintora%20Report%20Democratic_Governance_in_Eastern_Europe.pdf.

19 Norbert Maliszewski, 'Welcome to European Union B,' *Politico*, 9 June 2016; www.politico.eu/article/welcome-to-european-union-b/; John Feffer, 'Donald Trump and America B,' TomDispatch, 26 June 2016; www.tomdispatch.com/blog/176157/.

20 'Warsaw world's 35th most expensive city,' Export.by, 9 April 2008; export.by/en/?act=news&mode=view&page=10&id=3385.

21 'This is what happened to France in the 1950s,' Konstanty Gebert added, 'which very nearly broke the neck of the French economy then.' Interview with Konstanty Gebert, Warsaw, April 1990; www.johnfeffer.com/solidarity-after-solidarity/.

22 Gerd Schwarz, 'Social impact of the transition,' in Charalambos Christofides et al. (eds), *Poland: The Path to a Market Economy* (Washington, DC: International Monetary Fund, 1994), p. 85.

23 Janusz Igras (ed.), *25 Years of Polish Agriculture* (Warsaw: High Profile Strategic Advisors, 2014).

24 Państwowa Komisja Wyborcza, 'Wybory do Sejmu i Senatu Rzeczypospolitej Polskiej,' 2015; parlament2015.pkw.gov.pl/.

25 Annie Proulx, *That Old Ace in the Hole* (New York: HarperCollins, 2002).

26 Alan Mathews, 'The distribution of CAP payments by member state,' CAPreform.eu, 20 October 2013; capreform.eu/the-distribution-of-cap-payments-by-member-state/.

27 Steven Erlanger, 'Not even a prosperous Slovakia is immune to doubts about the E.U.,' *New York Times*, 17 December 2016; www.nytimes.com/2016/12/17/world/europe/slovakia-european-union-populists-migrants.html?_r=0; see also Alena Kluknavská and Josef Smolík, 'We hate them all? Issue adaptation of extreme right parties in Slovakia 1993–2016,' *Communist and Post-Communist Studies*, 49 (2016). They make the argument that Kotleba's party started out focusing more on local issues but opportunistically shifted emphasis to anti-minority, anti-foreigner, and anti-establishment rhetoric to be more politically successful.

28 The exception was Scotland, which uniformly wanted to stay within the EU. Gregor Aisch, Adam Pearce, and Karl Russell, 'How Britain voted in the E.U. referendum,' *New York Times*, 24 June 2016; www.nytimes.com/interactive/2016/06/24/world/europe/how-britain-voted-brexit-referendum.html.

29 'Understanding the EU Common Agricultural Policy,' Stratfor, 8 April 2014.

30 'Hungary: rural population, percent,' TheGlobalEconomy.com; www.theglobaleconomy.com/Hungary/rural_population_percent/.

31 'Hungary: GDP share of agriculture,' TheGlobalEconomy.com; www.theglobaleconomy.com/Hungary/Share_of_agriculture/.

32 Johan F. M. Swinnen, Kristine Van Herck, and Liesbet Vranken, 'Shifting patterns of agricultural production and productivity in the former Soviet Union and central and eastern Europe,' in *The Shifting Patterns of Agricultural Production and Productivity Worldwide* (Ames: The Midwest Agribusiness Trade Research and Information Center, Iowa State University, 2010); www.card.iastate.edu/books/shifting_patterns/pdfs/chapter10.pdf.

33 Ibid.

34 Kristóf Szombati, 'Why Hungarian voters are turning away from Fidesz and towards Jobbik,' Heinrich Boll Stiftung, 2 June 2015; www.boell.

de/en/2015/06/02/why-hungarian-voters-are-turning-away-fidesz-and-towards-jobbik.

35 European Commission, 'Facts and figures on organic agriculture in the European Union,' October 2013, p. 11.

36 Lonnie Johnson, *Central Europe: Enemies, Neighbors, Friends* (2nd edn) (New York: Oxford, 2002), p. 300.

37 Vladimir Tismăneanu, *The Great Shock at the End of a Short Century: Ion Iliescu in Dialogue with Vladimir Tismăneanu* (New York: Columbia University Press, 2004), p. 234.

38 Ulrich Koester and Karen Brooks, *Agriculture and German Reunification* (Washington, DC: World Bank, March 1997); www-wds.worldbank.org/external/default/WDSContentServer/IW3P/IB/2000/02/24/000009265_3971031092448/Rendered/PDF/multi_page.pdf.

39 Axel Wolz, Michael Kopsidis, and Klaus Reinsberg, *The Transformation of Agricultural Production Cooperatives in East Germany and Their Future* (Halle: Leibniz Institute of Agricultural Development in Central and Eastern Europe, 2008); icare.am/seminar2008/download/axel.pdf.

40 Ibid.

41 John Feffer, 'Grapes, not golf,' ZNet, 30 July 2004; www.johnfeffer.com/going-organic/.

42 Interview with Boris Fras, Ankaran, 5 August 2013; www.johnfeffer.com/going-organic/.

43 According to 2011 figures, about 7 percent of Slovenian agriculture was organic, low compared to the 13 percent of Czech agriculture but high in comparison to the 2 percent of Hungarian agriculture. European Commission, 'Facts and figures on organic agriculture in the European Union,' October 2013, p. 11.

44 Ivan Berend, *Central and Eastern Europe, 1944–1993* (Cambridge: Cambridge University Press, 1999), p. 344.

45 Frank Cibulka, 'The Czech Republic,' in Donnacha Ó Beacháin, Vera Sheridan, and Sabina Stan, *Life in Post-Communist Eastern Europe after EU Membership* (New York: Routledge, 2012), p. 43.

46 Geoffrey Pridham, *Designing Democracy* (New York: Palgrave Macmillan, 2005), p. 201.

47 'Polish farmers protest land sales to foreigners,' Radio Poland, 26 February 2014; www.thenews.pl/1/12/Artykul/163435,Polish-farmers-protest-land-sales-to-foreigners.

48 Clive Leviev-Sawyer, 'Bulgaria's protests, inspections against cheap vegetable imports continue,' Independent Balkan News Agency, 7 April 2013; www.balkaneu.com/bulgarias-protests-inspections-cheap-vegetable-imports-continue/.

4 The Faces of Illiberalism

1 'US ambassador condemns Jobbik MP's call for "Hungarian Ku Klux Klan,"' Politics.hu, 23 March 2011; www.politics.hu/20110323/us-ambassador-condemns-jobbik-mps-call-for-hungarian-ku-klux-klan/.

2 Ruth Ellen Gruber, 'Hungarian lawmaker claims Jews implicated in blood libel,' JTA, 5 April 2012; www.jta.org/2012/04/05/news-opinion/world/hungarian-lawmaker-claims-jews-implicated-in-blood-libel.

3 James Kirchick, 'Meet Europe's new fascists,' *Tablet*, 12 April 2012; www.tabletmag.com/jewish-news-and-politics/96716/meet-europes-new-fascists.

4 Quoted in 'Hungarian Guard,' Athena Institute, www.athenainstitute.eu/en/map/olvas/30.

5 European Roma Rights Centre, 'Attacks against Roma in Hungary: January 2008–September 2012,' 1 October 2012; www.errc.org/cms/upload/file/attacks-list-in-hungary.pdf.

6 Comparable figures would be 19 percent in Italy, 18 percent in Sweden, and 17 percent in the UK. European Commission, 'Discrimination in the European Union: perceptions, experiences and attitudes,' Special Eurobarometer 296, July 2008; ec.europa.eu/public_opinion/archives/ebs/ebs_296_en.pdf.

7 Sasa Woodruff, 'Increased hostility against Jews And Roma in Hungary,' NPR, 9 March 2014; www.npr.org/sections/codeswitch/2014/03/09/287342069/increased-hostility-against-jews-and-roma-in-hungary; Anikó Bernát, Attila Juhász, Péter Krekó, and Csaba Molnár, 'The roots of radicalism and anti-Roma attitudes on the far right,' 5 March 2013; www.tarki.hu/en/news/2013/items/20130305_bernat_juhasz_kreko_molnar.pdf.

8 Anti-Defamation League, 'Attitudes toward Jews in ten European countries,' March 2012; archive.adl.org/anti_semitism/adl_anti-semitism_presentation_february_2012.pdf.

9 Gergo Medve-Bálint, 'Towards a new one-party system?' in Olga Gyárfášová and Grigorij Mesežnikov (eds), *Visegrad Elections 2010: Domestic Impact and European Consequences* (Bratislava: Institute for Public Affairs, 2011), p. 46.

10 Eva Balogh, 'Fidesz versus Jobbik: not much difference,' Hungarian Spectrum, 24 May 2015; hungarianspectrum.org/2015/05/24/fidesz-versus-jobbik-not-much-difference/.

11 Marton Dunal, 'Hungary's Jobbik ditches far-right past to challenge Orban in 2018,' Reuters, 11 January 2017; www.reuters.com/article/us-hungary-jobbik-idUSKBN14V1PW; see also Eva Balogh, 'Gábor Vona and the transformation of Jobbik,' Hungarian Spectrum, 17 January 2017; hungarianspectrum.org/2017/01/17/gabor-vona-and-the-transformation-

of-jobbik/. Some argue that the shift occurred earlier, before the 2014 parliamentary elections; see Dae Soon Kim, 'The rise of European right radicalism: the case of Jobbik,' *Communist and Post-Communist Studies*, 49 (2016), p. 354.

12 Jamie Bartlett et al., *Populism in Europe: Hungary* (London: Demos, 2012), p. 26.

13 Archie Brown, *The Rise and Fall of Communism* (New York: HarperCollins, 2009), p. 215.

14 See, for example, Adam Michnik, *Ion Ratiu Democracy Lecture* (Woodrow Wilson International Center for Scholars, 2009), pp. 11–13.

15 Miklós Haraszti, 'Animal Farm scenarios,' in Henry Carey (ed.), *National Reconciliation in Eastern Europe* (New York: Columbia University Press, 2003), p. 199.

16 Quoted in Vladimir Tismăneanu, *Fantasies of Salvation* (Princeton, NJ: Princeton University Press, 1998), p. 83.

17 'The research also showed that a disproportionately high percentage of the offenders' parents were in some way related to the state apparatus – as bureaucrat, party apparatchik, Stasi, or military personnel,' writes journalist Paul Hockenos. 'The teenagers most inclined to criminal acts with right-wing motives were those who had been most thoroughly imbued with the values of the state.' Paul Hockenos, *Free to Hate* (New York: Routledge, 1993), p. 76.

18 Molly Laster and Sabrina Ramet, 'Xenophobia and rightwing extremism,' in Patricia Smith (ed.), *After the Wall: Eastern Germany since 1989* (Boulder, CO: Westview Press, 1998), p. 77; Mike Dennis and Norman Laporte, *The Stasi: Myth and Reality* (New York: Routledge, 2003), p. 171.

19 Quentin Peel, 'The faces of neo-Nazism,' *Financial Times*, 23 November 2012; www.ft.com/cms/s/2/dfda3010-3438-11e2-9ae7-00144feabdc0.html.

20 Stefan Auer, *Liberal Nationalism in Central Europe* (New York: Routledge, 2004).

21 Henry Kamm, 'At fork in road, Czechoslovaks fret,' *New York Times*, 9 October 1992; www.nytimes.com/1992/10/09/world/at-fork-in-road-czechoslovaks-fret.html; Stephen Engelberg, 'Czechoslovakia breaks in two, to wide regret,' *New York Times*, 1 January 1993; www.nytimes.com/1993/01/01/world/czechoslovakia-breaks-in-two-to-wide-regret.html?pagewanted=all&src=pm.

22 'In the magazine *Respekt*, in 1992, there was a title after the elections,' Martin Šimečka told me. '"Alone to the West or together to the Balkans." "Together to the Balkans" meant together with the Slovaks.' Interview with Martin Šimečka, Bratislava, 10 February 2013; www.johnfeffer.com/the-end-of-claustrophobia/.

23 Tina Rosenberg, *The Haunted Land* (New York: Random House, 1995), p. 76.

24 Karen Henderson, *Slovakia: The Escape from Invisibility* (New York: Routledge, 2002), p. 77.

25 Daniel Borsky, 'Mečiar calls for ethnic minorities to be swapped between Slovakia, Hungary,' *Slovak Spectator*, 25 September 1997; spectator.sme.sk/c/20014489/Mečiar-calls-for-ethnic-minorities-to-be-swapped-between-slovakia-hungary.html.

26 'The lustration law went into effect in November 1991 and the fate of the Federation was sealed seven months later,' writes Roman David. 'It also begs the question as to what Mečiar's motive was: was it because he feared that the lustration law would deprive him of the eligibility to become prime minister or because it would prevent him from blackmailing his political opponents?' See Roman David, *Lustration and Transitional Justice* (Philadelphia: University of Pennsylvania Press, 2011), p. 138.

27 Roman David, 'Lustration laws in action: the motives and evaluation of lustration policy in the Czech Republic and Poland (1989–2001),' *Law & Social Inquiry*, 28(2) (Spring, 2003), p. 416.

28 Anna Porter, *The Ghosts of Europe* (New York: St Martin's Press, 2010), p. 171.

29 Michael J. Kopanic Jr, 'Stealing the East Slovak steelworks,' *Central Europe Review*, 2(1) (10 January 2000); www.ce-review.org/00/1/kopanic1_steel.html.

30 See, e.g., the chapter on Slovakia in Valerie Bunce and Sharon Wolchik, *Defeating Authoritarian Leaders in Postcommunist Countries* (Cambridge: Cambridge University Press, 2011).

31 Milada Anna Vachudova, 'Democratization in postcommunist Europe,' in Valerie Bunce, Michael McFaul, and Kathryn Stoner-Weiss (eds), *Democracy and Authoritarianism in the Postcommunist World* (Cambridge: Cambridge University Press, 2010), p. 83; see also Karen Henderson, 'Slovakia and the democratic criteria for EU accession,' in Karen Henderson (ed.), *Back to Europe* (London: UCL Press, 1999).

32 Rob Cameron, 'Marian Kotleba and the rise of Slovakia's extreme right,' BBC News, 6 March 2016; www.bbc.com/news/world-europe-35739551.

33 'Fico: EU's migration policy is "ritual suicide",' EuroActiv, 26 January 2016; www.euractiv.com/section/central-europe/news/fico-eu-s-migration-policy-is-ritual-suicide/.

34 'Slovakia's PM calls journalists "dirty anti-Slovak prostitutes,"' *Guardian*, 23 November 2016; www.theguardian.com/world/2016/nov/23/slovakias-pm-calls-journalists-dirty-anti-slovak-prostitutes.

35 Anna Porter, *The Ghosts of Europe* (New York: St Martin's Press, 2010), p. 185.

36 'Fico: "privatizations were our biggest mistake,"' *FriedlNews*, 21 January 2013; www.friedlnews.com/article/fico-privatizations-were-our-biggest-mistake. In one particularly egregious case of corruption, his Ministry of Environment sold emission quotas at below-market prices to a mysterious firm called the Interblue Group, which turned out to be managed by officials of the same ministry, who then sold the quotas at market rates and pocketed the difference. Martin Bútora, Grigorij Mesežnikov, and Miroslav Kollar (eds), *Slovakia 2010* (Bratislava: Institute for Public Affairs, 2010), pp. 36–7.

37 Albert O. Hirschman, *Exit, Voice, Loyalty* (Cambridge, MA: Harvard University Press, 1970).

38 Jan-Werner Müller, *What Is Populism?* (Philadelphia: University of Pennsylvania Press, 2016, Kindle edn), Kindle Locations 62–63.

39 Ibid., Kindle Location 663.

40 Ibid., Kindle Locations 345–346.

41 Paul Taggart, 'Rethinking populism in contemporary Europe,' Policy Network, 5 December 2012; www.policy-network.net/pno_detail.aspx?ID=4298&title=Rethinking-populism-in-contemporary-Europe.

42 David Ost, *The Defeat of Solidarity* (Ithaca, NY: Cornell University Press, 2005), p. 109.

43 Ibid, p. 95.

44 Judy Batt, *East Central Europe from Reform to Transformation* (New York: Council on Foreign Relations Press, 1991), p. 53.

45 Chantal Mouffe, 'Radical democracy or liberal democracy,' *Socialist Review*, 20(2) (1990), p. 12–13.

46 Ania Krok-Paszkowska, 'Samoobrona: the Polish self defense movement,' in Detlef Pollack, Jorg Jacobs, Olaf Muller, and Gert Pickel (eds), *Political Culture in Post-Communist Europe* (Burlington, VT: Ashgate, 2003), p. 115.

47 Quoted in John Pickles and Adrian Smith (eds), *Theorizing Transition: The Political Economy of Post-Communist Transformations* (New York: Routledge, 1998), p. 261.

48 Ania Krok-Paszkowska, op. cit., p. 125.

49 Boris Gurov and Emilia Zankina, 'Populism and the construction of political charisma,' *Problems of Post-Communism*, 60(1) (2013), pp. 8–9.

50 Vera Stojarova, *The Far Right in the Balkans* (Manchester: Manchester University Press, 2013); Stephen Castle, 'Law and order, Bulgarian style,' *New York Times*, 20 July 2011; www.nytimes.com/2011/07/20/world/europe/20bulgaria.html.

51 Anna Kristeva, 'Bulgarian populism,' 25 December 2013; annakrasteva.wordpress.com/2013/12/25/bulgarian-populism/.

52 Markéta Hulpachová, 'Party seeks to restore monarchy,' *Prague Post*, 19 December 2007.

53 Siobhan Doucette, 'Antoni Macierewicz: from revolutionary to government minister,' *Notes from Poland*, 4 January 2016; notesfrompoland.com/2016/01/04/antoni-macierewicz-from-revolutionary-to-government-minister/.

54 Donald Snyder, 'As church attendance drops, Europe's most Catholic Country seeks modern Pope,' NBC News, 5 March 2013; worldnews.nbcnews.com/_news/2013/03/05/17184588-as-church-attendance-drops-europes-most-catholic-country-seeks-modern-pope?lite.

55 Antoon de Baets, *Responsible History* (New York: Berghahn, 2008), p. 63.

56 Wikileaks, 'New deputy defmins: Macierewicz stirs up controversy, while Winid gets to work,' 26 August 2006; wikileaks.org/plusd/cables/06WARSAW1798_a.html.

57 Wiktor Szary, 'Polish refocus on Smolensk crash could hurt relations with Russia,' *Business Insider*, 26 November 2015; www.businessinsider.com/r-polish-refocus-on-smolensk-crash-could-hurt-relations-with-russia-2015-11.

58 Vanessa Gera, 'Jewish group protests appointment of Polish defense minister,' AP, 13 November 2015; bigstory.ap.org/article/792124d0a8ab4e2bba76b29b834b7f01/jewish-group-protests-appointment-polish-defense-minister.

59 Tomasz Piatek, 'When NATO's man in Poland ran anti-Semitic paper,' *The Forward*, 27 July 2016; forward.com/news/world/345781/when-natos-man-in-poland-ran-anti-semitic-paper/.

60 Numerous efforts to reinterview Macierewicz in 2013 were rebuffed.

61 David Ost, 'Regime change in Poland, carried out from within,' *The Nation*, 8 January 2016; www.thenation.com/article/regime-change-in-poland-carried-out-from-within/.

62 David Jackson, 'Poll: 20% believe Barack Obama was born outside U.S.,' *USA Today*, 14 September 2015; www.usatoday.com/story/theoval/2015/09/14/barack-obama-cnnorc-poll-hawaii-muslim/72246866/; Ivan Krastev, 'The plane crash conspiracy theory that explains Poland,' *Foreign Policy*, 21 December 2015; foreignpolicy.com/2015/12/21/when-law-and-justice-wears-a-tinfoil-hat-poland-russia-smolensk-kaczynski/.

63 Quoted in Jan-Werner Müller, 'The problem with Poland,' *New York Review of Books*, 11 February 2016; www.nybooks.com/daily/2016/02/11/kaczynski-eu-problem-with-poland/.

64 Jarosław Adamowski, 'Polish defense minister says raid on NATO center agreed with Slovakia,' Defense News, 18 December 2015; www.defensenews.com/story/defense/international/europe/2015/12/18/new-polish-authorities-raid-nato-spy-center-fire-staff/77558342/.

65 Annabelle Chapman, 'Why did Poland raid a NATO-linked training

center?' *Daily Beast*, 19 December 2015; www.thedailybeast.com/articles/2015/12/19/why-did-poland-raid-a-nato-linked-training-center.html.

66 BBC, 'Black Monday: Polish women strike against abortion ban,' 3 October 2016; www.bbc.com/news/world-europe-37540139.

67 Christian Davies, 'Poland is "on road to autocracy", says Constitutional Court president,' *Guardian*, 18 December 2016; www.theguardian.com/world/2016/dec/18/poland-is-on-road-to-autocracy-says-high-court-president.

68 Jan-Werner Müller, 'The problem with Poland,' *New York Review of Books*, 11 February 2016; www.nybooks.com/daily/2016/02/11/kaczynski-eu-problem-with-poland/.

69 Vanessa Gera, 'Polish govt rejects renewed pressure from EU on rights,' *Washington Post*, 21 December 2016; www.washingtonpost.com/world/europe/polands-political-standoff-set-to-continue-through-holidays/2016/12/21/bccccac6-c776-11e6-acda-59924caa2450_story.html?utm_term=.c4c0591b6340.

70 'Polish opposition warns refugees could spread infectious diseases,' Reuters, 15 October 2015; af.reuters.com/article/commoditiesNews/idAFL8N12D39020151015.

71 Zosia Wasik and Henry Foy, 'Poland favours Christian refugees from Syria,' *Financial Times*, 21 August 2015; www.ft.com/content/6cdfdd30-472a-11e5-b3b2-1672f710807b.

72 Neil Buckley and Henry Foy, 'Poland's new government finds a model in Orban's Hungary,' *Financial Times*, 6 January 2016; www.ft.com/intl/cms/s/0/0a3c7d44-b48e-11e5-8358-9a82b43f6b2f.html#axzz4B6zIDjDD.

73 Ronald Bunn and William Andrews (eds), *Politics and Civil Liberties in Europe: Four Case Studies* (Princeton, NJ: Van Nostrand, 1967), p. 40.

74 Nikolaj Nielsen, 'Hungary's media crackdown slips off EU radar,' EUObserver, 17 January 2012; euobserver.com/justice/114899.

75 John Feffer, 'Stop the presses,' Foreign Policy in Focus, 12 October 2016; fpif.org/stop-the-presses/.

76 In a February 2017 poll, Fidesz and its Christian Democratic Party coalition partner continued to attract about one third of popular support, with no other party even close. 'Right-wing ruling parties retain lead in Hungary, fresh polls show,' *Hungary Today*, 9 February 2017; hungarytoday.hu/news/right-wing-ruling-parties-retain-lead-hungary-fresh-polls-show-17384.

77 Paul Lendvai, op. cit., p. 117.

78 Keno Verseck, '"Creeping cult": Hungary rehabilitates far-right figures,' Spiegel Online International, 6 June 2012; www.spiegel.de/international/europe/right-wing-extremists-cultivate-horthy-cult-in-hungary-a-836526.html.

79 Eric Westervelt, 'Homelessness becomes a crime in Hungary,' NPR, 6 April 2012; www.npr.org/2012/04/06/149526299/homelessness-becomes-a-crime-in-hungary; Margit Feher and Gordon Fairclough, 'Hungary lawmakers rebuff EU, US,' *Wall Street Journal*, 12 March 2013; www.wsj.com/articles/SB10001424127887323826704578353791817426424#articleTabs%3Darticle.

80 Keno Verseck, 'Hungary's racism problem,' Spiegel Online International, 11 January 2013; www.spiegel.de/international/europe/hungarian-journalist-says-roma-should-not-be-allowed-to-exist-a-876887.html.

81 Valérie Gauriat, 'Hungary's far right plays with fire,' *Euronews*, 26 April 2013; www.euronews.com/2013/04/26/hungary-s-far-right-plays-with-fire/.

82 Matthew Kaminski, '"All the terrorists are migrants,"' *Politico*, 23 November 2015; www.politico.eu/article/viktor-orban-interview-terrorists-migrants-eu-russia-putin-borders-schengen/.

83 Umut Korkut, 'Hungary,' in Donnacha Ó Beacháin, Vera Sheridan, and Sabina Stan (eds), *Life in Post-Communist Eastern Europe after EU Membership* (New York: Routledge, 2012), p. 86.

84 Lajos Bokros, 'Regression: reform reversal in Hungary after a promising start,' in Anders Åslund and Simeon Djankov (eds), *The Great Rebirth: Lessons from the Victory of Capitalism over Communism* (Washington, DC: Peterson Institute for International Economics, 2014), p. 40.

85 Csaba Toth, 'Full text of Viktor Orbán's speech at Băile Tuşnad (Tusnádfürdő) of 26 July 2014,' *Budapest Beacon*, 29 July 2014; budapestbeacon.com/public-policy/full-text-of-viktor-orbans-speech-at-baile-tusnad-tusnadfurdo-of-26-july-2014/10592.

86 Umut Korkut, 'More reform, less action dilemmas of economic Europeanization in Hungary,' *Problems of Post-Communism*, 57(1) (2010); www.academia.edu/527728/More_Reform_Less_Action_Dilemmas_of_Economic_Europeanization_in_Hungary.

87 Anna Porter, op. cit., p. 246.

88 Belin Tonchev, *Young Poets of a New Bulgaria: An Anthology* (Forest Books, 1991).

89 Kristen Ghodsee, 'Left wing, right wing, everything,' *Problems of Post-Communism*, May/June 2008, p. 36.

90 Iskra Baeva and Evgenia Kalinova, 'Bulgarian Turks during the transition period,' in Stefanos Katsikas (ed.), *Bulgaria and Europe: Shifting Identities* (New York: Anthem, 2011), p. 65.

91 Dia Anagnostou, 'Nationalist legacies and European trajectories: post-communist liberalization and Turkish minority politics in Bulgaria,' *Southeast European and Black Sea Studies*, 5(1) (2005), p. 104.

92 Bernd Rechel, 'The "Bulgarian ethnic model": reality or ideology?' *Europe-Asia Studies*, 59(7) (November 2007).

93 *A Guide to Ottoman Bulgaria* (Sofia: Vagabond Media, 2012), p. 9.

94 'Discrimination in the EU in 2015,' Special Eurobarometer 437, p. 36; ec.europa.eu/COMMFrontOffice/PublicOpinion/index.cfm/Survey/getSurveyDetail/instruments/SPECIAL/surveyKy/2077.

95 Viktória Serdült, 'Hungarian MEP György Schöpflin suggests putting pig heads on border fence,' *Budapest Beacon*, 22 August 2016; budapestbeacon.com/news-in-brief/fidesz-mep-gyorgy-schopflin-suggests-putting-pig-heads-on-border-fence/37986.

96 Bruce Bawer, *While Europe Slept* (New York: Anchor, 2007); Christopher Caldwell, *Reflections on the Revolution in Europe* (New York: Anchor, 2010); Bat Ye'or, *Eurabia* (Madison, NJ: Fairleigh Dickinson University Press, 2005).

97 I have changed his name for the purposes of this account.

98 John Feffer, *Shock Waves* (Boston, MA: South End Press, 1992), p. 219.

99 Chris Rogers, 'What became of Romania's neglected orphans?' BBC, 22 December 2009; news.bbc.co.uk/2/hi/8425001.stm.

100 Gil Eyal, Ivan Szelenyi, and Eleanor Townsley, *Making Capitalism without Capitalists* (New York: Verso, 1998), p. 115.

101 Cited in Ion Iliescu and Vladimir Tismăneanu, *The Great Shock at the End of a Short Century* (New York: Columbia University Press, 2004), p. 410.

102 This was the eighth demand of the Timișoara Proclamation put together in March by participants in the Timișoara uprising of the previous December.

103 Adrian Bridge, 'Angry mayor shows his colours,' *Independent*, 22 September 1994; www.independent.co.uk/news/world/europe/angry-mayor-shows-his-colours-gheorghe-funar-who-is-a-serious-patriot-insists-there-are-no-1450599.html.

104 Michael Shafir, 'Romania's Road to "Normalcy,"' op. cit., p. 147.

105 Peter Gross and Vladimir Tismăneanu, 'The end of postcommunism in Romania,' *Journal of Democracy*, 16(2) (April 2005), p. 148.

106 'European Parliament member denies Holocaust on Romanian TV,' Coordination Forum for Countering Antiemitism, 25 October 2012; antisemitism.org.il/article/75456/european-parliament-member-denies-holocaust-romanian-tv.

107 Wikipedia, '100 greatest Romanians'; en.wikipedia.org/wiki/100_Greatest_Romanians.

5 Unexploded Ordnance

1 Rosemary Kavan, *Love and Freedom* (New York: Hill and Wang, 1985), p. 50.

2 Ibid., p. 75.

3 Tina Rosenberg, *The Haunted Land* (New York: Random House, 1995), p. 12.

4 Rosemary Kavan, op. cit., p. 200.

5 Ibid., p. 232.
6 Franz Kafka, *The Trial* (New York: Modern Library, 1964), p. 3.
7 Lawrence Weschler, 'The Velvet Purge: the trials of Jan Kavan,' *New Yorker*, 19 October 1992.
8 John Feffer, 'A moral foreign policy,' in *Shock Waves: Eastern Europe after the Revolutions* (Boston, MA: South End Press, 1992).
9 Rosemary Kavan, op. cit., p. 29.
10 Weschler, 'The Velvet Purge,' op. cit., p. 67.
11 Klaus Wiegrefe, 'Ostpolitik: how East Germany tried to undermine Willy Brandt,' *Der Spiegel*, 8 July 2010; www.spiegel.de/international/germany/ostpolitik-how-east-germany-tried-to-undermine-willy-brandt-a-705118.html.
12 Quoted in Rosenberg, op. cit., p. 112.
13 That number declined to 32 percent when the law was extended in 2000. Roman David, 'Lustration laws in action: the motives and evaluation of lustration policy in the Czech Republic and Poland,' *Law and Social Inquiry*, 28(2) (Spring 2003), pp. 394, 414.
14 Weschler, 'The Velvet Purge,' op. cit., p. 68.
15 Ibid., p. 93.
16 Lawrence Weschler compares the case of Jan Kavan to that of Alfred Dreyfus, which polarized France at the turn of the nineteenth century. See Lawrence Weschler, 'From Kafka to Dreyfus,' *New Yorker*, 2 November 1992.
17 Weschler, 'The Velvet Purge,' op. cit., p. 90.
18 Jan Kavan was only one of the people falsely accused in the Czech lustration saga. There was also Zdena Salivarová-Škvorecká, whose life paralleled Jan Kavan's in many ways. In 1969, she moved to Canada with her husband, the acclaimed novelist Josef Škvorecki, to escape the Soviet invasion of her country. In Toronto, they set up a publishing house that issued hundreds of books by dissidents. She, too, was accused of being an informer. 'It took years for Zdena to clear her name,' writes Anna Porter. 'She sued the Ministry of the Interior and won, but she believed that her name hadn't been truly cleared. Once it was on that list, it would be muddied forever.' Anna Porter, *The Ghosts of Europe* (New York: St Martin's Press, 2010), p. 134.
19 'Kavindication,' *New Yorker*, 12 February 1996.
20 Rob Cameron, 'Former ministry official sent to prison over journalist murder plot,' *Inside Central Europe*, 1 July 2007; incentraleurope.radio.cz/ice/article/42490. In 2007, Jan Kavan would court controversy again when he 'admitted' that the government, though not he, had taken bribes from the British company BAE to facilitate the purchase of Gripen jet fighters. CTK News Agency, 'Former Czech foreign minister says corruption "known secret" in Gripens case,' 27 February 2007; translated by the BBC.

21 Milan Šimečka, *The Restoration of Order: The Normalization of Czechoslovakia* (New York: Verso, 1984), p. 42.

22 Ibid., p. 65.

23 Ibid., p. 102.

24 Elaine Feinstein, *Anna of All Russias* (New York: Knopf, 2007).

25 As Tina Rosenberg writes, 'In this department, each official had to have ten agents; in another one, perhaps fifteen. Or a certain eight-man unit had to recruit five new agents a year in a particularly field, for example the Youth Union.' Rosenberg, op. cit., p. 53.

26 Roman David, *Lustration and Transitional Justice* (Philadelphia: University of Pennsylvania, 2011), p. 144.

27 Tony Judt, *Postwar: A History of Europe since 1945* (New York: Penguin, 2006), p. 46.

28 In Slovakia, as journalist Juraj Alner reports, 'We would go into a factory and say, "we are People Against Violence and we are lustrating this factory. You must leave." Nobody knows how many people lost their jobs in this way. There were no legal trials. This became a process of everyone liquidating everyone else.' Rosenberg, op. cit., p. 115.

29 Quoted in Roman David, op. cit., p. 132.

30 Lavinia Stan, 'Vigilante justice and unoffficial truth projects,' in Lavinia Stan and Nadya Nedelsky, *Post-Communist Transitional Justice* (Cambridge: Cambridge University Press, 2015), p. 281.

31 Moira Lynch and Bridget Marchesi, 'The adoption and impact of transitional justice,' in Lavinia Stan and Nadya Nedelsky, op. cit., p. 106.

32 Vladimir Tismăneanu, *Fantasies of Salvation* (Princeton, NJ: Princeton University Press, 1998), p. 15.

33 *Kapitalism: Our Secret Recipe*, a film by Alexandru Solomon, 2011; icarusfilms.com/new2011/kapt.html.

34 Eva Balogh, 'Will communist-era internal security files finally be open in Hungary?' Hungarian Spectrum, 12 March 2017; hungarianspectrum.org/2017/03/12/will-communist-era-internal-security-files-finally-be-open-in-hungary/.

35 'Tymiński in Peru,' *New York Times*, 2 December 1990; www.nytimes.com/1990/12/02/world/evolution-in-europe-tyminski-in-peru-spiritual-awareness-then-cable-tv.html.

36 Stephen Engelberg, 'A rough campaign closes in Poland,' *New York Times*, 24 November 1990; www.nytimes.com/1990/11/24/world/a-rough-campaign-closes-in-poland.html.

37 *Gazeta International*, 6 December 1990.

38 Stephen Engelberg, 'A Polish emigre's odyssey to politics,' *New York Times*, 9 December 1990; www.nytimes.com/1990/12/09/world/a-polish-emigre-s-odyssey-to-politics.html.

39 Mary Battiata, 'Walesa's rival threatens disclosures,' *Washington Post*, 2 December 1990; www.washingtonpost.com/archive/politics/1990/12/02/walesas-rival-threatens-disclosures/8395e6ec-e819-46db-b920-78241c8fc1a2/.

40 Piotr Pacewicz, 'The last battle,' *Gazeta International*, 6 December 1990. p. 1.

41 Louisa Vinton, 'Poland's Party "X" prepares "Plan X,"' OMRI, 17 August 1993; www.friends-partners.org/friends/news/omri/1993/08/930817.html.

42 In a Facebook chat conducted in 2017, for instance, I learned from Tymiński that PiS, like all previous Polish administrations, was busy building an 'empire of Khazars' that is enslaving 100 million Poles and Ukrainians. Facebook communication with Stanisław Tymiński, 19 March 2017.

43 'Lech Wałęsa libel trial starts in Poland over spy claim,' BBC, 24 November 2009; news.bbc.co.uk/2/hi/europe/8377385.stm.

44 Monika Nalepa, *Skeletons in the Closet: Transitional Justice in Post-Communist Europe* (Cambridge: Cambridge University Press, 2010), pp. 231–2.

45 Bernard Osser, 'Poland's Lech Wałęsa was communist spy: secret police file,' AFP, 18 February 2016; www.yahoo.com/news/lech-Wałęsa-communist-agent-polish-institute-103218124.html?ref=gs.

46 Alex Duval Smith, 'Lech Wałęsa: I was not an agent of the Polish security services,' *Guardian*, 10 March 2016; www.theguardian.com/world/2016/mar/10/lech-waesa-not-agent-spy-polish-security-services-interview.

47 Bernard Osser, op. cit.

48 Alex Storozynski, *The Peasant Prince* (New York: St Martin's Press, 2009), pp. 188–97.

49 Quoted in Lech Wałęsa, *The Struggle and the Triumph* (New York: Arcade, 1992), p. 220.

50 Anna Porter, op. cit., p. 106.

51 Adam Michnik, *In Search of Lost Meaning* (Berkeley: University of California Press, 2011), p. 142.

52 Quoted in Vladimir Tismăneanu, *Fantasies of Salvation* (Princeton, NJ: Princeton University Press, 1998), p. 117. The quote echoes the frequent comment that anti-Semitism has survived in Poland without Jews.

53 Monika Nalepa, op. cit., p. 14.

54 See, e.g., Marci Shore, *Taste of Ashes* (New York: Broadway Books, 2014), pp. 312–13.

55 Michael Kennedy, *Cultural Formations of Post-Communism* (Minneapolis: University of Minnesota Press, 2002), p. 283.

56 Ibid., p. 285.

57 Adam Michnik, *In Search of Lost Meaning*, op. cit., p. 9.

58 Ibid., p. 14.

59 Maria Todorova, 'Introduction,' in Maria Todorova, Augusta Dimou, and Stephan Troebst (eds), *Remembering Communism* (Budapest: Central European University Press, 2014), p. 17.

60 The figure for 'trust in others' for eastern Europeans is 23.3 percent compared to 43.2 percent of western Europeans. Alina Polyakova, *The Dark Side of European Integration* (Stuttgart: Ibidem Verlag, 2015), p. 62.

61 Esteban Ortiz-Ospina and Max Roser, 'Trust,' Our World in Data; ourworldindata.org/trust.

62 'A legal battle between two Polish entrepreneurs,' *Financial Times*, www.ft.com/content/ec97d70c-2aff-11df-93d8-00144feabdc0#axzz3Pa4Vik2W.

63 In one of the most famous cases, the state charged computer entrepreneur Roman Kluska, the millionaire founder of Optimus, with tax fraud. The charges were ultimately dismissed, but the case nearly destroyed Optimus. See, e.g., Gerald Easter, *Capital, Coercion, and Postcommunist States* (Ithaca, NY: Cornell University Press, 2012), pp. 157ff.

64 '9 Miesięcy za Kratami. Bez Winy, Bez Dowodów, Bez Powodu,' Fact24, 18 April 2013; www.fakt.pl/wydarzenia/polityka/prokurator-skazal-biznesmena-na-9-miesiecy-biznesmen-lech-jeziorny-w-jednej-chwili/ver1xjp.

65 'Wyrok w Głośnej Sprawie Polmozbytu. Jeziorny, Rey i Nicia Skazani,' *Newsweek*, 11 November 2013; www.newsweek.pl/polska/wyrok-w-glosnej-sprawie-polmozbytu-jeziorny-rey-i-nicia-skazani-na-newsweek-pl,artykuly,275348,1.html; 'Bohaterowie Polskiego Filmu Skazani. Mają Oddać Spółce Pieniądze,' Fact24, 1 March 2016; www.fakt.pl/wydarzenia/polska/pawel-rey-i-lech-jeziorny-skazani-za-polmozbyt/h1p50hw.

66 'Who is who: assaulted Bulgarian ethnic Turkish leader Ahmed Dogan,' Novinite, 19 January 2013; www.novinite.com/articles/147005/Who+Is+Who%3A+Assaulted+Bulgarian+Ethnic+Turkish+Leader+Ahmed+Dogan.

67 Dia Anagnostou, 'Nationalist legacies and European trajectories: post-communist liberalization and Turkish minority politics in Bulgaria,' *Southeast European and Black Sea Studies*, 5(1) (2005).

68 Iskra Baeva and Evgenia Kalinova, 'Bulgarian Turks during the transition period,' in Stefanos Katsikas (ed.), *Bulgaria and Europe: Shifting Identities* (New York: Anthem, 2011), p. 67.

69 Toma Bikov, *The State Security File of Ahmed Dogan* (Sofia: Millennium, 2009); minaloto.org/index.php?option=com_content&view=article&id=330%3Athe-state-security-file-of-ahmed-dogan&catid=30%3Aarchives-and-documents&Itemid=45&lang=en.

70 A Bulgarian court acquitted Dogan of corruption charges. At issue, however, was not whether he pocketed the money but whether he had betrayed the public trust. 'Bulgaria ethnic Turks long-time leader behind

FBI scandal – Borisov,' Novinite, 20 June 2013; www.novinite.com/articles/151402/.

71 Kamen Kraev, 'Bulgaria's Turkish minority party: what went wrong?' *Vox Orientalis*, 25 January 2016; www.voxorientalis.com/bulgarias-turkish-minority-party-what-went-wrong/.

72 Georgi Lozanov, 'Freedom of the press or for the rabble?' *Vagabond*, 1 April 2007; www.vagabond.bg/politics/item/1196-freedom-of-the-press-or-for-the-rabble.html.

73 Simeon Djankov, 'Bulgaria: the greatest vacillations,' in Anders Åslund and Simeon Djankov (eds), *The Great Rebirth: Lessons from the Victory of Capitalism over Communism* (Washington, DC: Peterson Institute for International Economics, 2014), p. 145.

74 Michael Meyer, *The Year that Changed the World* (New York: Scribner, 2009), p. 25.

75 Anna Funder, *Stasiland* (London: Granta, 2003), p. 191.

76 Tina Rosenberg, op. cit., p. 291.

77 Laura Goehler, 'The Stasi files: Germany's 600-million-piece puzzle,' CNN, 7 November 2014; www.cnn.com/2014/11/07/world/europe/stasi-files-east-germany-secret-police/.

78 Tina Rosenberg, op. cit., p. 304.

79 Anna Funder, op. cit., pp. 62–4.

80 Christian Joppke, *East German Dissidents and the Revolution of 1989* (New York: New York University Press, 1995)), pp. 152–3.

81 By 1989, according to one estimate, the West German government had paid close to three billion Deutschmarks 'for releasing 34,000 prisoners, reuniting 2,000 children with their parents, and "regulating" 250,000 cases of family reunification.' Tony Judt, *Postwar* (New York: Penguin, 2006), p. 97.

82 Donna West Brett, *Photography and Place: Seeing and Not Seeing Germany after 1945* (New York: Routledge, 2015), p. 137.

83 Laura Goehler, op. cit.

84 Vladimir Tismăneanu, *Fantasies of Salvation*, op. cit., p. 137.

85 The Stasi did act on some of the information she provided. For instance, she revealed the escape plans of several acquaintances who were then subsequently jailed. Henryk Broder, 'Die nützlichen Idioten,' *Der Spiegel*, 25 September 1995; www.spiegel.de/spiegel/print/d-9221729.html.

86 Christian Joppke, *East German Dissidents and the Revolution of 1989* (New York: New York University Press, 1995)), p. 112.

87 *Holocaust*, http://www.museum.tv/eotv/holocaust.htm.

88 Elizabeth Braw, 'Tinker, tailor, pastor, spy,' *Newsweek*, 12 March 2014; www.newsweek.com/2014/03/21/tinker-tailor-pastor-spy-247989.html.

89 Irina Popescu, 'President wants Holocaust museum in Romania,' *Romania Insider*, 9 March 2016; www.romania-insider.com/president-wants-holocaust-museum-in-romania/. A few months later, the Romanian government announced that it would open a Holocaust museum in 2018 in Bucharest. Agence France Press, 'Romania opens first state-run Holocaust museum,' 10 October 2016; www.israelnationalnews.com/News/News.aspx/218858.

90 Andreea Nicolae, Elena Vijulie, and Dan Alexe, 'Lustration comes to Romania – but will the law be applied?' *EU Observer*, 1 June 2010; euobserver.com/news/30175.

91 Holger Dix and Corina Rebegea, 'The short history of the Romanian lustration law,' Konrad-Adenauer-Stiftung, 21 July 2010; www.kas.de/wf/doc/kas_20185-1522-2-30.pdf?100802134740. Also: 'No lustration for former communists,' VoxEurop, 29 March 2012; www.voxeurop.eu/en/content/news-brief/1712351-no-lustration-former-communists.

92 'Eight former Romanian officials sentenced for Timisoara killings,' *New York Times*, 9 December 1991; www.nytimes.com/1991/12/10/world/eight-former-romanian-officials-sentenced-for-timisoara-killings.html.

93 'Romania jails communist-era prison chief in landmark case,' BBC, 24 July 2015; www.bbc.com/news/world-europe-33649800.

94 'Romanian labour camp chief Ficior jailed for Periprava crimes,' BBC, 30 March 2016; www.bbc.com/news/world-europe-35926275.

95 In the first five years after 1989, only four countries in the region passed lustration laws. In the next five years, two more had done so. And between 2001 and 2005, an astonishing eight more had passed such laws. Monika Nalepa, op. cit., p. 99.

96 James Mark, *The Unfinished Revolution: Making Sense of the Communist Past in Central and Eastern Europe* (New Haven, CT: Yale University Press, 2010), p. 29.

97 Michael Žantovský, *Havel: A Life* (New York: Grove, 2014). See also Peter Green, 'Crime explosion sours Prague's brave new world,' *Sunday Times*, 13 May 1990.

98 Václav Havel, *To the Castle and Back* (New York: Knopf, 2007), p. 95.

99 Christopher Daase et al. (eds), *Apology and Reconciliation in International Relations* (New York: Routledge, 2015). Some descendants of the Sudeten Germans used the apology as the basis for claims for the restitution of confiscated property, which caused an uproar in certain sectors of Czech society. Only in 2016 did the Sudeten German association delete the article on property claims from its statutes. 'Sudeten Germans expelled from Czechoslovakia drop claim to territory,' i24 News, 29 February 2016; www.i24news.tv/en/news/international/europe/104564-160229-sudeten-germans-expelled-from-czech-republic-drop-claim-to-territory.

100 Moira Lynch and Bridget Marchesi, 'The adoption and impact of transitional justice,' in Lavinia Stan and Nadya Nedelsky, *Post-Communist Transitional Justice* (Cambridge: Cambridge Univerrsity Press, 2015), p. 102.

101 United Nations International Tribunal for the Former Yugoslavia, 'ICTY remembers: the Srebrenica genocide, 1995–2015'; www.icty.org/specials/srebrenica20/?q=srebrenica20/.

102 Human Rights Watch, 'ICTY/Bosnia: Karadzic convicted for Srebrenica genocide,' 24 March 2016; www.hrw.org/news/2016/03/24/icty/bosnia-karadzic-convicted-srebrenica-genocide.

103 'Dutch state liable for 300 Srebrenica massacre deaths,' *Guardian*, 16 July 2014; www.theguardian.com/world/2014/jul/16/dutch-liable-srebrenica-massacre-deaths.

104 Janine di Giovanni, *Madness Visible* (New York: Knopf, 2003), p. 207.

105 Misha Glenny, *McMafia* (New York: Vintage, 2008), p. 6.

106 Ibid., p. 12.

107 It was a fitting ending for someone who may well have arranged the assassination of former Bulgarian prime minister Andrei Lukhanov in 1996. 'Tycoon Iliya Pavlov "masterminded Bulgaria's ex-PM murder,"' Novinite, 2 October 2006; www.novinite.com/articles/70480/Tycoon+Iliya+Pavlov+%22Masterminded+Bulgaria's+Ex-PM+Murder%22. No one has ever been charged with Pavlov's murder.

108 Risk Monitor: riskmonitor.bg/en.

109 Initially, petty corruption was rare. 'At the barber's there would be a sign saying, "Don't insult us by offering a tip,"' writes Milan Šimečka. op. cit., p. 128.

110 Not everyone agrees that corruption was widespread. 'Corruption is relatively limited' in central Europe, writes Anders Åslund; *How Capitalism Was Built* (Cambridge University Press, Kindle edn, 2013), p. 3.

111 Quoted in Steven Szonberg, *The Fall* (Amsterdam: Harwood Academic Publishers, 2001), p. 121.

112 William Miller, Åse Grødeland, and Tatyana Koshechkina, *A Culture of Corruption* (Budapest: CEU Press, 2001), p. 64.

113 Rick Fawn and Jiří Hochman, *Historical Dictionary of the Czech State* (Lanham, MD: Rowman and Littlefield, 2010) p. 133.

114 K.S., 'Vaclav Klaus's controversial amnesty,' *The Economist*, 17 January 2013; www.economist.com/blogs/easternapproaches/2013/01/czech-politics.

115 Leslie Holmes, 'Corruption, weak states and economic rationalism in central and eastern Europe,' Paper presented at the Princeton University–Central European University Joint Conference on Corruption, Budapest, 29 October–9 November 1999, p. 6; 9iacc.org/papers/day1/ws2/dnld/d1ws2_lholmes.pdf.

116 Elizabeth Dunn, *Privatizing Poland: Baby Food, Big Business, and the Remaking of Labor* (Ithaca, NY: Cornell University Press, 2004), p. 31.

117 Quoted in Gabriel Kuris, 'How a resurgent Anti-Graft Bureau helped Croatia turn a corner on corruption,' in Yahong Zhang and Cecilia Lavena (eds), *Government Anti-Corruption Strategies* (New York: CRC Press, 2015), p. 169.

118 Liliana Popescu-Bîrlan, 'Privatisation and corruption in Romania,' *Crime, Law & Social Change*, 21 (1994), pp. 375–6.

119 Michael Hein, 'The fight against government corruption in Romania: irreversible results or Sisyphean challenge?' *Europe-Asia Studies*, 67(5) (2015), p. 748.

120 Jon Henley, 'Romania set to go to polls as anti-graft party eyes kingmaker role,' *Guardian*, 9 December 2016; www.theguardian.com/world/2016/dec/09/romania-election-anti-graft-party-usr-psd.

121 Misha Glenny, op. cit., pp. 42–3.

122 Jonathan Owen, 'Corrupt European countries costing EU nearly £800bn a year, says study,' *Independent*, 22 March 2016; www.independent.co.uk/news/world/europe/corrupt-european-countries-costing-eu-nearly-800bn-a-year-says-study-a6944436.html.

123 Transparency International, 'Corruption Perceptions Index 2016'; www.transparency.org/news/feature/corruption_perceptions_index_2016.

124 Anders Åslund, *How Capitalism Was Built*, op. cit.

6 Reinvention of Self

1 Janet Malcolm, 'The window-washer,' *New Yorker*, 19 November 1990; www.newyorker.com/magazine/1990/11/19/the-window-washer.

2 Frederick Harhoff, 'Original private letter Judge Frederik Harhoff,' 14 June 2013; www.vaseljenska.com/english/orginal-private-letter-judge-frederik-harhoff/.

3 As a result of the letter, Harhoff was disqualified from presiding over the case against Vojislav Šešelj of the Serbian Radical Party. UN International Criminal Tribunal for the Former Yugoslavia, 'Judge Harhoff disqualified from Šešelj case,' 29 August 2013; www.icty.org/sid/11357.

4 Václav Havel, *To the Castle and Back* (New York: Knopf, 2007), p. 70.

5 The occupation authorities faced a similar problem in Germany after World War II. See Tony Judt, *Postwar: A History of Europe since 1945* (New York: Penguin, 2006), p. 56.

6 Vladimir Tismăneanu, *Fantasies of Salvation* (Princeton, NJ: Princeton University Press, 1998), pp. 57–8.

7 Victor Sebestyen, *1946: The Making of the Modern World* (New York: Knopf, 2015), p. 40.

8 Tony Judt, *When the Facts Change* (New York: Penguin Random House, 2016).

9 Benjamin Novak, 'Zoltán Illés on the "decadence, destruction and erosion" of Hungary,' *Budapest Beacon*, 9 April 2015; budapestbeacon.com/public-policy/-illes-on-the-decadence-destruction-and-erosion-of-hungary/21576.

10 'Hungarian ex-official slams government's environmental policy,' *Népszabadság*, 19 January 2015, translated by the BBC. In October 2016, *Népszabadság* closed, despite being the country's largest-circulation newspaper.

11 Lawrence Marzouk, 'Spain, Hague targets in Kosovo ad campaign,' *BalkanInsight*, 4 November 2009; http://www.balkaninsight.com/en/article/spain-hague-targets-in-kosovo-ad-campaign. Ironically, some years earlier the same firm had tried to help Slobodan Milošević improve the image of Serbia in the West, a campaign that failed miserably. Josip Glaurdic, *The Hour of Europe* (New Haven, CT: Yale University Press, 2011), p. 235.

12 Katarina Subasic, 'Balkan youngsters emigrate en masse for better prospects,' AFP, 23 December 2016; sports.yahoo.com/news/balkan-youngsters-emigrate-en-masse-better-prospects-062328437.html.

13 Zala Volčič, 'Branding Slovenia,' in Nadia Kaneva (ed.), *Branding Post-Communist Nations* (New York: Routledge, 2012), pp. 151–4.

14 'Nobody is nostalgic for the Stalinist era but many old people are nostalgic for their youth,' the Czech novelist Ivan Klima told an interviewer. 'They missed the security of Communist times when they knew they would get a pension they could live off, prices were stable and they couldn't lose their flats or their jobs.' Quoted in Maria Todorova, 'Introduction: From utopia to propaganda and back,' in Maria Todorova and Zsusza Gille (eds), *Post-Communist Nostalgia* (New York: Berghahn, 2010), p. 7.

15 Svetlana Boym, *The Future of Nostalgia* (New York: Basic Books, 2001), p. xv.

16 Dubravka Ugrešić, *The Ministry of Pain* (New York: HarperCollins, 2005), Ebook, location 848 of 3774.

17 'The GDR's traditional German fare beat anything like it in West Berln, not a city known for its culinary specialities,' journalist Paul Hockenos writes of his visits to East Berlin in the 1980s. Paul Hockenos, *Berlin Calling* (New York: New Press, 2017), p. 119.

18 Rainer Gries, 'Hurrah, I'm still alive!' in Sibelan Forrester, Magdalena Zaborowska, and Elena Gapova (eds), *Over the Wall/After the Fall* (Bloomington: Indiana University Press, 2004), p. 185.

7 The Talented Tenth

1 Violeta Draganova, 'The challenge of finding a place in two worlds,' *Open Society News*, Summer/Fall 2005, p. 17.

2 Isabel Fonseca, *Bury Me Standing* (New York: Vintage, 1996), p. 113.

3 Ransom Riggs, 'Strange geographies: the first ghetto,' *Mental Floss*, 23 May 2010; mentalfloss.com/article/24757/strange-geographies-first-ghetto.

4 The official Roma population of Stolipinovo is 20,000, but estimates run as high as 80,000.

5 Renate Lackner-Gass, '"Stolipinovo," Bulgaria European case study,' EVN; www.evn.at/CMSPages/GetFile.aspx?guid=05c8c6b0-8d8f-439d-a6be-5376511fe513.

6 New York City's population density is 10,400 people per square kilometer; en.wikipedia.org/wiki/List_of_United_States_cities_by_population_density.

7 W. E. B. DuBois, 'The Talented Tenth,' in *The Negro Problem* (New York: James Pott, 1903).

8 Zeljko Jovanović in Will Guy (ed.), *From Victimhood to Citizenship* (Budapest: Pakiv European Roma Fund, 2013), p. 199.

9 W. E. B. DuBois, 'The Talented Tenth memorial address,' in Henry Louis Gates and Cornel West, *The Future of the Race* (New York: Vintage, 1997).

10 'The problem of the twentieth century is the problem of the color-line – the relation of the darker to the lighter races of men in Asia and Africa, in America and the islands of the sea,' declared W. E. B. Dubois in *The Souls of Black Folk* (New York: New American Library, 1982), p. 54.

11 European Commission, 'EU and Roma,' ec.europa.eu/justice/discrimination/roma/index_en.htm.

12 European Union Agency for Fundamental Rights, 'Data in focus report: the Roma,' 2009; fra.europa.eu/sites/default/files/fra_uploads/413-EU-MIDIS_ROMA_EN.pdf.

13 Two other Roma groups journeyed from Armenia to the Middle East and to the Caucasus. See Viorel Achim, *The Roma in Romanian History* (Budapest: CEU Press, 2004), p. 12.

14 Ibid., p. 29.

15 Zoltan Barany, *The East European Gypsies: Regime Change, Marginality, and Ethnopolitics* (Cambridge: Cambridge University Press, 2002), p. 87.

16 'Genocide of European Roma (Gypsies), 1939–1945,' *Holocaust Encyclopedia*, www.ushmm.org/wlc/en/article.php?ModuleId=10005219.

17 Adam Gopnik, 'The people who pass,' *New Yorker*, 13 January 2014; www.newyorker.com/reporting/2014/01/13/140113fa_fact_gopnik.

18 See, e.g., Margareta Matache, 'Word, image and thought: creating the Romani Other,' *Huffington Post*, 3 October 2016; www.huffingtonpost.com/entry/57f29d40e4b095bd896a156a?timestamp=1475519595732.

19 See, for example, Seyward Darby, 'Big fat disgrace,' *New Republic*, 31 May 2011; newrepublic.com/article/89173/my-big-fat-gypsy-wedding-tlc-traveller-roma.

20 Sudeep Reddy, 'World's extreme poverty cut in half since 1990,' *Wall Street Journal*, 29 February 2012; blogs.wsj.com/economics/2012/02/29/worlds-extreme-poverty-cut-in-half-since-1990/.

21 World Bank, PovcalNet, iresearch.worldbank.org/PovcalNet/index.htm?2.

22 European Union Agency for Fundamental Rights, 'Second European Union Minorities and Discrimination Survey (EU-MIDIS II) Roma – selected findings,' November 2016, p. 14; fra.europa.eu/en/publication/2016/eumidis-ii-roma-selected-findings.

23 Mose Apelblat, 'Roma integration far away despite EU funding,' *Brussels Times*, 18 December 2014; www.brusselstimes.com/opinion/1774/roma-integration-far-away-despite-eu-funding.

24 Zeljko Jovanović, 'Why Europe's "Roma Decade" didn't lead to inclusion,' Open Society Foundations, 21 September 2015; www.opensocietyfoundations.org/voices/why-europe-s-roma-decade-didn-t-lead-inclusion. The 'decade countries' were: Bulgaria, Croatia, the Czech Republic, Hungary, Macedonia, Montenegro, Romania, Serbia, Slovakia and Spain. Slovenia, the United States, Norway and Moldova also had observer status.

25 Keno Verseck, 'Right-wing terror: Hungary silent over Roma killing spree,' Spiegel Online International, 23 July 2013; www.spiegel.de/international/europe/trial-in-hungary-little-outrage-over-far-right-murders-of-6-roma-a-912709.html.

26 François-Xavier Bagnoud Center for Health and Human Rights, *Accelerating Patterns of Anti-Roma Violence in Hungary* (Boston, MA: Harvard University, 2014); cdn2.sph.harvard.edu/wp-content/uploads/sites/5/2014/02/FXB-Hungary-Report_Released-February-4-2014.pdf.

27 Kvetoslava Matlovičová, René Matlovič, Alexander Mušinka, and Anna Židová, 'The Roma population in Slovakia,' in J. Penczes and Z. Radics (eds), *Roma Population on the Peripheries of the Visegrad Countries* (Debrecen, 2012); www.unipo.sk/public/media/16282/The_Roma_population_in_Slovakia_Matlovicova_(2012)_Basic_Characteristics_of_the_Roma_Population_with_Emphasis_on_the_Spatial_Aspects_of_its_Differentiation.pdf.

28 'Slovak republic: situation of Roma, including employment, housing, education, health care and political participation,' Immigration and Refugee Board of Canada, 11 July 2012; www.refworld.org/cgi-bin/texis/vtx/rwmain?page=country&category=&publisher=IRBC&type=&coi=SVK&rid=4562d8b62&docid=503601022&skip=0.

29 China Mieville, *The City and the City* (New York: Del Rey, 2010).

30 Andrew Higgins, 'For Slovak Roma, echoes of U.S,' *International Herald Tribune*, 11 May 2013.

31 Kate Connolly, 'Czech Gypsies begin test case for pupils classed as retarded,' *Guardian*, 19 April 2000.

32 'D.H. and others v the Czech Republic,' European Roma Rights Centre, 5 February 2015; www.errc.org/article/dh-and-others-v-the-czech-republic/3559. For a similar court case involving Hungarian Roma, see Kerime Sule Akoglu, 'Removing arbitrary handicaps: protecting the Article 2 right to education in Horváth and Kiss v. Hungary,' *Boston College International & Comparative Law Review*, 37(3) (2014).

33 Barbara Matejčić, 'Fits and starts,' *Transitions Online*, 27 March 2013; www.tol.org/client/article/23685-fits-and-starts.html.

34 John Tagliabue, 'Bulgaria opens school doors for Gypsy children,' *New York Times*, 12 June 2001.

35 Andrew Richard Ryder, Iulius Rostas, and Marius Taba, '"Nothing about us without us': the role of inclusive community development in school desegregation for Roma communities,' *Race Ethnicity and Education*, 17(4) (2014), pp. 527–8.

36 John Feffer, *Out of the Margins: A Report on a Roma/African American Exchange* (Philadelphia: American Friends Service Committee, January 1996), p. 13.

37 Iulius Rostas, 'The establishment of "elite" schools for Roma is not an alternative to school desegregation,' 1 June 2012; irostas.wordpress.com/2012/06/01/the-establishment-of-elite-schools-for-roma-is-not-an-alternative-to-school-desegregation/.

38 Will Guy (ed.), *From Victimhood to Citizenship* (Budapest: Pakiv European Roma Fund, 2013).

39 'Nicolae Gheorghe, campaigner for the rights of Roma, died on August 8th, aged 66,' *The Economist*, 17 August 2013; www.economist.com/news/obituary/21583590-nicolae-gheorghe-campaigner-rights-roma-died-august-8th-aged-66-nicolae.

40 Nicolae Gheorghe in Will Guy, op. cit., p. 78.

41 Melvin van Peebles, '"Exhale" strikes chord with African American audiences: studios are inept, not racist,' *Los Angeles Times*, 8 January 1996; articles.latimes.com/1996-01-08/entertainment/ca-22240_1_african-american.

42 David Rieff, 'Multiculturalism's silent partner,' *Harper's*, August 1993; harpers.org/archive/1993/08/multiculturalisms-silent-partner/.

43 Nicolae Gheorghe in Will Guy, op. cit., p. 60.

44 Martin Kovats in Will Guy, op. cit., p. 126.

45 www.euroroma-bg.org/myindex.html.

46 'Bulgaria: Euroroma party official allegedly led "loansharking migrant smugglers,"' *Organized Crime and Corruption Organizing Report*, 16 May 2016; www.occrp.org/en/daily/5236-bulgaria-euroroma-party-official-allegedly-led-loansharking-migrant-smugglers.

47 See, e.g, Elena Marušiakova and Veselin Popov, 'The Bulgarian Gypsies – searching their place in the society,' *Balkanologie*, 4(2) (December 2000); balkanologie.revues.org/323?lang=en.

48 Charles Cobb, 'This nonviolent stuff'll get you killed,' *Washington Post*, 28 July 2014; www.washingtonpost.com/news/volokh-conspiracy/wp/2014/07/28/this-nonviolent-stuffll-get-you-killed/?utm_term=.be9f9dd3b9fb.

49 Uffie Anderson, 'Reality check,' *Transitions Online*, 3 July 2012; www.tol.org/client/article/23239-serbia-roma-tv-discrimination.html.

50 Violeta Draganova, 'The challenge of finding a place …' op. cit.

8 The New Dissidents

1 Quoted in Barbara Demick, 'It's still a crime to be gay in Romania,' *Philadelphia Inquirer*, 30 December 1993; articles.philly.com/1993-12-30/living/25944026_1_nicolae-ceausescu-romanians-homosexuals.

2 Ibid.

3 Talon Windwalker, 'The Life of gay people in Romania,' 27 August 2014; 1dad1kid.com/gay-people-in-romania/.

4 'Romania: Mariana Cetiner: prisoner of conscience,' Amnesty International, 17 December 1997; www.amnesty.org/en/documents/eur39/030/1997/en/.

5 'Bucharest Gay Pride rally draws crowds,' AFP, 25 June 2016; www.yahoo.com/news/bucharest-gay-pride-rally-draws-crowds-202135296.html.

6 Moraru Adela, 'Social perception of homosexuality in Romania,' *Procedia Social and Behavioral Sciences*, 5 (2010).

7 'Romania moves closer to ruling out possibility of legalizing same-sex marriage,' Reuters, 20 July 2016; www.reuters.com/article/us-romania-gaymarriage-idUSKCN1002KW.

8 Kyler Geoffroy, 'Romanian gay couple's wedding ceremony becomes country's first televised same-sex marriage,' *Towleroad*, 15 September 2013; www.towleroad.com/2013/09/romanian-gay-couples-wedding-ceremony-becomes-countrys-first-televised-same-sex-marriage/.

9 Peter Berger, *Pyramids of Sacrifice* (New York: Anchor Books, 1976), p. 8.

10 Trading Economics, 'Poland youth unemployment rate,' www.tradingeconomics.com/poland/youth-unemployment-rate (accessed 8 September 2016).

11 Roberta Smith, 'Yael Bartana: And Europe Will Be Stunned,' *New York Times*, 18 April 2013; www.nytimes.com/2013/04/19/arts/design/yael-bartana-and-europe-will-be-stunned.html.

12 'Krytyka is creating a Pop Left,' says Wojciech Przybylski. 'My interpretation is not so favorable for them even though I admire them for many of the things they do. But they are quite liberal (market oriented) in

the way they do things. They create a kind of corporation, with branding and marketing – which is not a bad thing since that's how things work. And they use the left brand or the New Left brand because there has been a huge demand for it.' Interview with Wojciech Przybylski, Warsaw, 7 August 2013; www.johnfeffer.com/polands-politics-of-dissatisfaction/.

13 See, e.g., Adam Przybyl, 'The promise of prosperity,' *The Nation*, 7 March 2017; www.thenation.com/article/the-promise-of-prosperity-poland-law-and-justice/.

14 The organization was OWEN, which stood for the East–West European Women's Network.

15 'Women and employment in central and eastern Europe and the Western Commonwealth of Independent States,' UNIFEM, 2006; www.unwomen.org/~/media/Headquarters/Media/Publications/UNIFEM/StoryBehindTheNumberseng.pdf.

16 Katrin Bennhold, '20 years after fall of wall, women of former East Germany thrive,' *New York Times*, 5 October 2010; www.nytimes.com/2010/10/06/world/europe/06iht-letter.html.

17 Friederike Heine, 'Germany promises daycare for all,' Spiegel Online, 1 August 2013; www.spiegel.de/international/germany/law-goes-into-effect-requiring-child-care-for-most-german-children-a-914320.html.

18 Shana Penn, *Solidarity's Secret* (Ann Arbor: University of Michigan Press, 2005). Interview with Ewa Kulik, Warsaw, 8 August 2013; www.johnfeffer.com/solidarity-underground/.

19 Eva Balogh, 'Fidesz macho in parliament,' Hungarian Spectrum, 11 September 2012; hungarianspectrum.wordpress.com/2012/09/11/fidesz-macho-in-parliament-womens-calling-is-to-produce-babies/.

20 For some of this history see, e.g., Małgorzata Fuszara, 'Abortion and the formation of the public sphere in Poland,' in Nanette Funk and Magda Mueller, *Gender Politics and Post-Communism* (New York: Routledge, 1993).

21 Jarosław Adamowski, 'Poland's new conservative government to scrap IVF programme,' *BMJ*, 7 December 2015; www.bmj.com/content/351/bmj.h6640.

22 Peggy Watson, 'The rise of masculinism,' in Monica Threlfall (ed.), *Mapping the Women's Movement* (London: Verso, 1996), pp. 219–20.

23 Andrew Roth, '"Her story is my story": how a harsh abortion ban has reignited feminism in Poland,' *Washington Post*, 18 November 2016; www.washingtonpost.com/world/an-anti-abortion-bill-revives-polands-feminist-movement/2016/11/17/4d2afca4-a04a-11e6-8864-6f892cad0865_story.html.

24 The Congress of Women, 'Statement of the Congress of Women on protests against Stop Abortion Project,' 4 October 2016; www.

kongreskobiet.pl/en-EN/news/show/statement_of_the_congress_of_women_on_protests_against_stop_abortion_project.

25 John Feffer, 'Goulash ecology,' in *Shock Waves* (Boston, MA: South End, 1992).

26 Susan Lacetti, 'In eastern Europe, pollution's choking quality of life,' *Atlanta Journal and Constitution*, 21 July 1991.

27 Google Public Data: Life Expectancy; www.google.com/publicdata/explore?ds=d5bncppjof8f9_&met_y=sp_dyn_le00_in&idim=country:HUN:CZE:SVK&hl=en&dl=en#!ctype=l&strail=false&bcs=d&nselm=h&met_y=sp_dyn_le00_in&scale_y=lin&ind_y=false&rdim=region&idim=country:HUN:BGR:ROM&ifdim=region&hl=en_US&dl=en&ind=false; *Eastern European Countries Mineral Industry Handbook*, vol. 1 (Washington, DC: International Business Publications, 2015), p. 67.

28 Ethnic Hungarians have an absolute majority in two counties – Harghita (85 percent) and Covasna (73 percent) – in the very heart of the country. Together with parts of Mures county, this region is known as Székely Land. This area maintained a high degree of autonomy – and cultural traditions distinct from those of other Hungarians – for 600 years from medieval times through the Austro-Hungarian Empire. Outside this area, the ethnic Hungarian concentration drops considerably. They represent significant minorities in other parts of Transylvania – Mureș, Satu Mare, Bihor, Sălaj, Cluj. But then the numbers drop even more. A tiny fraction of the population in Bucharest, less than 1 percent, is ethnic Hungarian. Ethnic map of Hungary, Wikipedia; en.wikipedia.org/wiki/File:MAGHIARI_2011_JUD.png.

29 Wlodek Aniol, Timothy Byrnes, and Elena Iankova, 'Poland: returning to Europe,' in Peter Katzenstein (ed.), *Mitteleuropa: Between Europe and Germany* (Providence, RI: Berghahn Books, 1997), p. 51.

30 Ibid., p. 52.

31 David Ost, *The Defeat of Solidarity* (Ithaca, NY: Cornell University Press, 2005).

32 Juliusz Gardawski, 'Declining trade union density examined,' EurWORK, 20 August 2002; www.eurofound.europa.eu/eiro/2002/08/feature/pl0208105f.htm.

33 Radio Poland, 'Trade union membership falls to all-time low in Poland,' 16 May 2013; www.thenews.pl/1/9/Artykul/135797,Trade-union-membership-falls-to-alltime-low-in-Poland.

34 Guy Standing, 'The precariat: the new dangerous class,' Policy Network, 24 May 2011; www.policy-network.net/pno_detail.aspx?ID=4004&title=+The+Precariat+%E2%80%93+The+new+dangerous+class.

35 UNHCR, 'World at war,' 2014; www.unhcr.org/556725e69.html#_ga=1.163569852.1284003813.1435094443.

36 Missing Migrants Project, 'Mediterranean Sea'; missingmigrants.iom.int/mediterranean.

37 Lauren Collins, 'The children's odyssey,' *New Yorker*, 27 February 2017, p. 54.

38 Valerie Bunce and Sharon Wolchik, 'Defining and domesticating the electoral model,' in Valerie Bunce, Michael McFaul, and Kathryn Stoner-Weiss, op. cit., p. 153.

9 The Next Generation

1 Sabine Rennefanz, 'East Germans are still different,' *Guardian*, 30 September 2010; www.theguardian.com/commentisfree/2010/sep/30/east-germany-angela-merkel.

2 'Woman of Europe Award 2016: Ariana Lettrari,' 12 November 2015; www.netzwerk-ebd.de/mitteilungen/woman-of-europe-2016-award-goes-to-adriana-lettrari/.

3 Rennefanz, op. cit.

4 Johanna Wanka, a founding member of New Forum and the only cabinet member originally from the GDR, is the minister of education and research.

5 Marcel Fürstenau, 'East Germans still marginalized, despite Merkel and Gauck,' DW, 23 March 2012; www.dw.com/en/east-germans-still-marginalized-despite-merkel-and-gauck/a-15828206.

6 Stefan Locke, 'Volk von Hier, Elite von Drüben,' *Frankfurter Allgemeine*, 30 May 2016; www.faz.net/aktuell/politik/inland/ost-und-west-volk-von-hier-elite-von-drueben-14254333.html.

7 Iaian Rogers, 'Brain drain cripples ex-communist Germany,' Reuters, 4 November 2003; www.timesofmalta.com/articles/view/20031104/business/brain-drain-cripples-ex-communist-east-germany.137368.

8 Adam Easton, 'Exodus of youth ages Poland's population,' *Financial Times*, 27 November 2014; www.ft.com/cms/s/0/41b93930-52c7-11e4-9221-00144feab7de.html#axzz4GZxmngUn.

9 Serbia ranks 137 out of 138, Bosnia 134, Romania 133, Croatia 132, Hungary 130, and Bulgaria 125. Both Macedonia, 115, and Montenegro, 101, fared slightly better. Klaus Schwab (ed.), *The Global Competitiveness Report 2016–2017* (Geneva: World Economic Reform, 2016).

10 Lucy Ash, 'Hungarian Government 'Traps' Graduates to Stop Brain Drain,' BBC, August 16, 2012; http://www.bbc.com/news/world-europe-19213488; Benjamin Novak, 'Hungary's Brain Drain,' *Budapest Beacon*, November 17, 2015;http://budapestbeacon.com/public-policy/hungarys-brain-drain-young-and-highly-educated-leaving-in-droves/29309

11 Viktor Shklovsky, *Energy of Delusion: A Book on Plot* (McLean, IL: Dalkey Archive Press, 2007).

12 Michal subsequently returned to his country – to join a think tank focused on European security issues.
13 Gallup, 'Outlook for the future of Europe's younger generation,' May 2013; www.scribd.com/document/141856647/Gallup-Debating-Europe-Poll-Europeans-expect-a-Bleak-Future-for-their-Young.
14 Quoted in Marci Shore, *The Taste of Ashes* (New York: Crown, 2013), p. 339.
15 Allan Pall, 'Why don't young people vote?' *EU Observer*, 7 November 2014; euobserver.com/opinion/126431.
16 Mary Kaldor and Sabine Selchow, 'The "bubbling up" of subterranean politics in Europe,' London School of Economics and Political Science, June 2012; www.gcsknowledgebase.org/europe/wp-content/themes/SubPol2/SubterraneanPolitics.pdf.
17 Ronald Heifetz, *The Practice of Adaptive Leadership* (Cambridge, MA: Harvard Business Review Press, 2009).
18 Paul Lendvai, *Hungary: Between Democracy and Authoritarianism* (Budapest: Central European University Press, 2012), p. 164.
19 The Millennial Dialogue, 'Hungary,' FEPS Activity Report, April 2016; www.millennialdialogue.com/media/1280/feps-millennial-dialogue-hungary.pdf.
20 Ádám Lestyánszky, 'Understanding Jobbik's appeal to Hungarian youth,' *Budapest Beacon*, 24 March 2015; budapestbeacon.com/politics/understanding-jobbiks-appeal-to-hungarian-youth/21143.
21 Nationalism Studies Network, 'Flash mob at the Hungarian Ministry of Human Resources,' 31 May 2013; nationalismstudiesnetwork.wordpress.com/2013/05/31/we-have-shut-down-the-ministry-of-human/.
22 CriticAtac website: www.criticatac.ro/despre-noi/.

10 Creating New Worlds

1 '100 years of Metelkova,' web.archive.org/web/20050122024652/http://www.ljudmila.org/retina/metelkova-katalo/100.html.
2 Robert Evans, '5 things you learn professionally squatting in a warehouse,' *Cracked*, 6 November 2015; www.cracked.com/personal-experiences-2010-5-things-you-learn-professionally-squatting-in-warehouse.html.
3 'Tovarna Rog,' www.culture.si/en/Tovarna_Rog.
4 Martin Bútora, 'Who's the deviant here?' Central European Forum Salon, 20 March 2013; salon.eu.sk/en/archiv/9851.
5 Beti Žerovc, 'OHO interviews,' *ArtMargins*, 16 October 2011; www.artmargins.com/index.php/5-interviews/648-the-oho-files.
6 'After a short period, I also moved into a commune, which was quite fashionable in intellectual circles at the time,' Anna Csongor told me. 'We

did a lot of extra learning – reading books and discussing books. That's a leftist sort of activity: living together and talking a lot.' Interview with Anna Csongor, Budapest, 7 May 2013; www.johnfeffer.com/funding-roma-autonomy/.

7 Paul Hockenos, *Berlin Calling* (New York: New Press, 2017), pp. 131–2.

8 Michael Kennedy, *Envisioning Eastern Europe* (Ann Arbor: University of Michigan Press, 1995), p. 154.

9 Svetlana Boym, *The Future of Nostalgia* (New York: Basic Books, 2001), p. 228.

10 Christian Joppke, *East German Dissidents and the Revolution of 1989* (New York: New York University Press, 1995), p. 86.

11 Paul Hockenos, *Berlin Calling*, op. cit., p. 217.

12 Ibid., p. 255.

13 Stephen Kinzer, '3 Turks killed; Germans blame a neo-Nazi plot,' *New York Times*, 24 November 1992; www.nytimes.com/1992/11/24/world/3-turks-killed-germans-blame-a-neo-nazi-plot.html.

14 'Authorities shut Berlin's iconic Tacheles arts squat,' BBC News, 4 September 2012; bbc.co.uk/news/world-europe-19473806.

15 'The Berlin Arthouse Kunsthaus Tacheles in 3D,' art-center-tacheles-berlin.berlinin3d.com/2012/09/tacheles-3d-online-art-gallery-has-now.html.

16 Marisa Mazria Katz, 'Intervening in the future: a conversation with Mladen Miljanović,' *Creative Time Reports*, 10 September 2015; creativetimereports.org/2015/09/10/intervening-in-the-future-mladen-miljanovic/.

17 'ESI interview with Mladen Miljanović 2007,' YouTube, 23 August 2015; www.youtube.com/watch?v=raX7NHRu1qM.

18 Mladen Miljanović, 'I Serve Art,' www.mladenmiljanovic.com/I-SERVE-ART.

19 Wojciech Marchlewski, 'The eve of the Great October Revolution: chronicle of a happening in Wroclaw,' *Performing Arts Journal*, 38 (May 1991).

20 Mirosław Pęczak, 'The Orange ones, the street, and the background,' *Performing Arts Journal*, 38 (May 1991).

21 'Kiss and tell,' Frieze.com, 2 March 2008; frieze.com/article/kiss-and-tell.

22 Kory Grow, 'Cannabis and "The Sound of Music": what Laibach learned in North Korea,' *Rolling Stone*, 25 August 2015; www.rollingstone.com/culture/news/cannabis-and-the-sound-of-music-what-laibach-learned-in-north-korea-20150825.

23 Jeffrey Fleishman, 'Czech artist is a dissident for a new era in Europe,' *Los Angeles Times*, 23 August 2004; articles.latimes.com/2004/aug/23/world/fg-prankster23.

24 'Entropa: the great EU art hoax,' *Guardian*, 14 January 2009; www.theguardian.com/artanddesign/gallery/2009/jan/14/entropa-eu-art-hoax.

25 'Europe communist bastion finally crumbles,' BBC News, 27 August 1999; news.bbc.co.uk/2/hi/europe/431854.stm.

Conclusion

1 Sonja was not the only one to make this prediction in 1990. 'I believe that the only way of dismantling Yugoslavia without creating any kind of new links or forms of common living would be if there is a war in some parts, maybe Kosovo-Serbia, maybe Croatia,' Slovenian political scientist Mitja Žagar told me that summer. 'But I think the most dangerous spot is Bosnia-Herzegovina.' Interview with Mitja Žagar, Ljubljana, September 1990; www.johnfeffer.com/could-the-yugoslav-wars-have-been-avoided/.

2 Dubravka Ugresic, *Thank You for Not Reading* (McLean, IL: Dalkey Archive, 2003), p. 177.

3 World Bank, 'Gross domestic product 2015, PPP,' 11 October 2016; databank.worldbank.org/data/download/GDP_PPP.pdf.

4 Mark Biondich, 'Croatia,' in Robert Frucht (ed.), *Eastern Europe: An Introduction to the People, Lands, and Culture*, vol. 1 (Santa Barbara, CA: ABC-CLIO, 2005), p. 463.

5 Tony Judt, *Postwar* (New York: Penguin, 2006), p. 531.

6 Robert Gordon, *The Rise and Fall of American Growth* (Princeton, NJ: Princeton University Press, 2016), p. 1.

7 Michael Meyer, *The Year that Changed the World* (New York: Scribner, 2009), p. 24.

8 Bahri Cano, 'Spiral of violence fuels Kosovo crisis,' *Deutsche Welle*, 16 February 2016; www.dw.com/en/spiral-of-violence-fuels-kosovo-crisis/a-19052311.

9 As of March 2017, the count stands at 115.

10 By March 2017, Serbia had opened eight of thirty-five chapters. 'Serbia opens two more chapters in EU accession talks,' B92, 27 February 2017; www.b92.net/eng/news/politics.php?yyyy=2017&mm=02&dd=27&nav_id=100617.

11 'Serbia unemployment rate,' 2008–16; www.tradingeconomics.com/serbia/unemployment-rate.

12 Ultimately, Serbia will face the challenging obstacles of dealing more effectively with corruption, the independence of the judiciary, and freedom of expression. The EU suffered considerable criticism for not demanding higher standards during the accession process for Bulgaria and Romania in particular. Serbia, as a result, will be held to more stringent criteria.

13 '73 percent of citizens opposed to war over Kosovo – survey,' B92; www.b92.net/eng/politics.php?yyyy=2017&mm=02&dd=100490.

14 Milivoje Pantovic, 'Study shows young Serbs turning against EU,' *Balkan Insight*, 28 July 2016; www.balkaninsight.com/en/article/serbia-s-youth-is-

getting-more-eu-sceptic-07-28-2016; by December, public support for EU accession had dropped to 47 percent, but such oscillations have been common over the last few years. Smiljana Vukojicic, 'Serbian confidence in accession process declining,' Euraktiv, 9 March 2017; www.euractiv.com/section/enlargement/news/serbian-confidence-in-accession-process-declining/.

15 'Serbia's youth turning increasingly anti-EU,' B92, 29 October 2012; www.b92.net/eng/news/politics.php?yyyy=2012&mm=10&dd=29&nav_id=82891.

16 'Polish youth versus Razem: the young Poles swinging right,' CafeBabel, 9 February 2016; www.cafebabel.co.uk/politics/article/polish-youth-versus-razem-the-young-poles-swinging-right.html.

17 '80% of Germans against EU enlargement, poll shows,' B92, 27 February 2013; www.b92.net/eng/news/world.php?yyyy=2013&mm=02&dd=27&nav_id=84902.

18 Lenard Cohen and John Lampe, *Embracing Democracy in the Western Balkans* (Baltimore, MD: Johns Hopkins University Press, 2011), p. 455.

19 Benjamin Disraeli, *Sybil, or the Two Nations* (New York: Penguin, 1980).

20 European Foundation for the Improvement of Living and Working Conditions, 'Mobility in Europe,' 2006; www.eurofound.europa.eu/sites/default/files/ef_files/pubdocs/2006/59/en/1/ef0659en.pdf. Although there have been no comparable comparisons made since this study, the findings of two studies suggest that the European percentages, which fell during the financial crisis of the late 2000s, have returned to roughly where they were in the mid-2000s. See Eurobarometer, 'Geographical and labour market mobility,' European Commission, June 2010; ec.europa.eu/public_opinion/archives/ebs/ebs_337_en.pdf; Sara Riso, Johan Ernest Olivier Secher, and Tine Andersen, 'Labour mobility in the EU: recent trends and policies' (Luxembourg: Publications Office of the European Union, 2014); www.eurofound.europa.eu/sites/default/files/ef_publication/field_ef_document/ef1456en_1.pdf.

21 Tara Zahra, *The Great Departure* (New York: Norton, 2016), p. 290.

22 Milan Kundera, 'Die Weltliteratur,' *New Yorker*, 8 January 2007; www.newyorker.com/magazine/2007/01/08/die-weltliteratur.

23 Craig R. Whitney, 'Europeans look for ways to bar door to immigrants,' *New York Times*, 29 December 1991.

24 Phillip Connor, 'Number of refugees to Europe surges to record 1.3 million in 2015,' Pew Research Center, 2 August 2016; www.pewglobal.org/2016/08/02/number-of-refugees-to-europe-surges-to-record-1-3-million-in-2015/.

25 Mitchell Orenstein, 'Geopolitics of a divided Europe,' *East European Politics and Societies and Cultures*, 29(2) (May 2015), p. 533.

26 Benjamin Barber, *Jihad versus McWorld* (New York: Ballantine Books, 1996); Thomas Friedman, *Lexus and the Olive Tree* (New York: Picador, 2012).

27 Lucy Rodgers and Nassos Stylianou, 'How bad are things for the people of Greece?' BBC, 16 July 2015; www.bbc.com/news/world-europe-33507802.

28 'In the 1990s, between 10 and 15 percent of the richest people controlled 80 to 90 percent of the wealth,' Slovenian political scientist Mitja Žagar told me. 'Now we have a situation with these derivatives that 1.5 percent of the population actually controls between 80 and 97 percent of the world. Even slave-owning societies weren't so unequal. That's not to say that on average people are worse off. But if I were to compare it with fifteen years ago, in Europe or the United States, particularly what used to be called the middle class is economizing as their costs have gone up and their incomes at best have been stagnant if not decreasing.' Interview with Mitja Žagar, Vrsar, 3 August 2013; www.johnfeffer.com/could-the-yugoslav-wars-have-been-avoided/.

29 Kaja Bonesmo Fredriksen, 'Income inequality in the European Union,' OECD Economics Department Working Papers no. 952, 16 April 2012; www.oecd-ilibrary.org/docserver/download/5k9bdt47q5zt-en.pdf?expires=1480547937&id=id&accname=guest&checksum=8CFB1DC907F666633FB1DA6FC346A975; 'The gap between poor and rich regions in Europe is widening,' *The Economist*, 29 October 2016; www.economist.com/news/europe/21709336-austerity-partly-blame-gap-between-poor-and-rich-regions-europe-widening.

30 John Lanchester, 'The failure of the euro,' *New Yorker*, 24 October 2016; www.newyorker.com/magazine/2016/10/24/the-failure-of-the-euro.

31 Joseph Stiglitz, *The Euro* (New York: Norton, 2016), p. 326.

32 Claus Offe, *Europe Entrapped* (Polity, Kindle edn, 2015), p. 54.

33 Stiglitz, op. cit., p. 240.

34 Jan-Werner Müller, *What Is Populism?* (Philadelphia: University of Pennsylvania Press, 2016, Kindle edn), Kindle Location 344.

35 R. S. Foa and Y. Mounk, 'The danger of deconsolidation: the democratic disconnect,' *Journal of Democracy*, 27(3) (July 2016).

Index

About the author

John Feffer is a freelance journalist and director of the Foreign Policy In Focus programme at the Institute for Policy Studies. His journalism has spanned eastern and central Europe, the Middle East, and East Asia. His previous books include *Shock Waves: Eastern Europe after the Revolutions* (1992), *Crusade 2.0: The West's Resurgent War on Islam* (2012) and the novel *Splinterlands* (2016).

ZED

Zed is a platform for marginalised voices across the globe.

It is the world's largest publishing collective and a world leading example of alternative, non-hierarchical business practice.

It has no CEO, no MD and no bosses and is owned and managed by its workers who are all on equal pay.

It makes its content available in as many languages as possible.

It publishes content critical of oppressive power structures and regimes.

It publishes content that changes its readers' thinking.

It publishes content that other publishers won't and that the establishment finds threatening.

It has been subject to repeated acts of censorship by states and corporations.

It fights all forms of censorship.

It is financially and ideologically independent of any party, corporation, state or individual.

Its books are shared all over the world.

www.zedbooks.net
@ZedBooks